THE
72ND
ART DIRECTORS
ANNUAL
AND
7TH
INTERNATIONAL
EXHIBITION

THE
72ND
ART DIRECTORS
ANNUAL
AND
7TH
INTERNATIONAL
EXHIBITION

PRESIDENT, ADC PUBLICATIONS, INC.

Anistatia R. Miller

EDITOR-IN-CHIEF

ART DIRECTION & DESIGN

Sara Giovanitti

LAYOUT DESIGN

Ryuichi Minakawa

PAINTINGS JACKET/PART TITLE PAGE

Seymour Chwast

PHOTOGRAPHY

Peter Bittner

Revon T.C. Wuorman

COPYEDITING/PRODUCTION

Jared M. Brown

ADC EXECUTIVE DIRECTOR

Rhoda Marshall

ADC EXHIBITION EDITOR

Carol LaPlante

Published in 1993 by
RotoVision SA
Route de Suisse 9, CH-1295 MIES/VD,
SWITZERLAND
for
The Art Directors Club, Inc.
250 Park Avenue South, New York NY
10003 USA

ISSN: 0735-2026
RotoVision SA ISBN: 2-88046-193-6
Watson-Guptill ISBN: 0-8230-6301-1

Distributed to the trade in the United States
and Canada by
Watson-Guptill Publications
1515 Broadway, New York NY 10036 USA

International Distribution by
RotoVision SA
Route de Suisse 9, CH-1295 MIES/VD,
SWITZERLAND

Printed in Singapore

TABLE OF CONTENTS

HALL OF FAME

1972
M.F. Agha
Lester Beall
Alexy Brodovitch
René Clark
A.M. Cassandre
Robert Gage
William Golden
Paul Rand

1973
Charles Coiner
Paul Smith
Jack Tinker

1974
Will Burtin
Leo Lionni

1975
Gordon Aymar
Herbert Bayer
Cipe Pineles Burtin
Heyworth Campbell
Alexander Liberman
L. Moholy-Nagy

1976
E. McKnight Kauffer
Herbert Matter

1977
Saul Bass
Herb Lubalin
Bradbury Thompson

1978
Thomas M. Cleland
Lou Dorfsman
Allen Hurlbert
George Lois

1979
W.A. Dwiggins
George Giusti
Milton Glaser
Helmut Krone
Willem Sandberg
Ladislav Sutnar
Jan Tschichold

1980
Gene Federico
Otto Storch
Henry Wolf

1981
Lucian Bernhard
Ivan Chermayeff
Gyorgy Kepes
George Krikorian
William Taubin

1982
Richard Avedon
Amil Gargano
Jerome Snyder
Massimo Vignelli

1983
Aaron Burns
Seymour Chwast
Steve Frankfurt

1984
Charles Eames
Wallace Elton
Sam Scali
Louis Silverstein

1985
Art Kane
Len Sirowitz
Charles Tudor

1986
Walt Disney
Roy Grace
Alvin Lustig
Arthur Paul

1987
Willy Fleckhaus
Shigeo Fukuda
Steve Horn
Tony Palladino

1988
Ben Shahn
Bert Steinhauser
Mike Tesch

1989
Rudolph de Harak
Raymond Lowey

1990
Lee Clow
Reba Sochis
Frank Zachary

1991
Bea Feitler
Bob Gill
Bob Giraldi
Richard Hess

1992
Eiko Ishioka
Rick Levine
Onofrio Paccione
Gordon Parks

1993
Leo Burnett
Yusaku Kamekura
Robert Wilvers
Howard Zieff

SPECIAL AWARDS

1983
Bill Bernbach

1987
Leon Friend

1988
Silas Rhodes

1989
Herschel Levit

1990
Robert Weaver

1991
Jim Henson

AS SELECTION COMMITTEE CHAIRMAN for the Art Director Club Hall of Fame I found making a selection, for a true tradition of excellence to be difficult. This year's committee consisted of Lou Dorfsman, Kurt Haiman, Onofrio Paccione, George Lois, Bob Cato, Paul Davis, Gene Marcellino, and William Buckley. We finally found a gentleman in Japan—Yusaku Kamekura—and three in the U.S.—Howard Zieff, Bob Wilvers, and Leo Burnett.

TONY PALLADINO

CHAIRMAN, 1993 HALL OF FAME SELECTION COMMITTEE

HOWARD ZIEFF is the advertising legend whose comic eye and flawless direction put Benson & Hedges 100s and Alka Seltzer on the map. He is also the Hollywood film director whose boundless energy, attention to detail, and acute sense of timing contribute immeasurably to the success of films like *Private Benjamin* and *My Girl*.

Zieff grew up in Los Angeles and at eighteen enlisted in the Navy. He was stationed in San Diego as a staff artist for the *Navy News*. Then the call came for a staff photographer so Zieff went through the Navy's

ALKA SELTZER'S MAMA MIA SPICY MEATBALL

photographic and motion picture program. Once Zieff finished with his military tour, he enrolled in the Los Angeles-based Art Center School. He worked as a newsreel photographer and local television director in Los Angeles for a while, but decided that advertising was the medium he really wanted to break into.

HOWARD ZIEFF

The relocated Zieff became one of Madison Avenue's best-known photographers, riding the crest of a highly-energetic creative revolution in advertising. He contributed images of reality and humor to the business of selling products and became a master of the art of persuasion through laughter. He made his name for his still photographic work on posters for *New York Daily News* and Levy's. Doyle Dane and Bernbach assigned him to the Revlon, Polaroid and Volkswagen accounts. His unique illustrative format: situational humor cast with real people was also used on campaigns for Kellogg's Corn Flakes, Lipton Soup, and the new Sony line of miniature portable TVs.

Zieff was one of the first still photographers on Madison Avenue to move into television commercials. The realities of urban life and indigestion took the form of a series of rapid-fire situational tummy close-ups in "No Matter What Shape You're In" for Alka Seltzer. The frustrations of commercial production for both director and actor were portrayed at their ironic best in Alka Seltzer's "Mama Mia Spicy Meatball." (This spot is still regarded as an industry art form and the best-remembered television commercial of all time according to a Broadcast Museum poll.)

Benson & Hedges introduced its new 100mm length cigarettes with ironic Zieff humor. The biggest disadvantage of smoking Benson & Hedges 100s seemed to be getting used to keeping distance between you and everyone or everything else. In a quick rash of real-life scenarios one quickly realized that you could get your cigarette crushed while talking on the telephone or entering an elevator; they wouldn't fit in conventional cigarette cases; and could be a

THE DISADVANTAGES
OF BENSON & HEDGES 100MM CIGARETTES

fire-hazard at crowded cocktail parties or while reading the morning paper.

Zieff worked his charms for two major airlines. In one Braniff Airlines spot, the announcer is packaged "en crate" and flies via baggage class to prove that Braniff takes better care of your luggage when traveling overseas. When TWA wanted to stress their commitment to service, they also called on Zieff to show how dedicated to the challenge—and to the incentive of a million dollars in bonuses—their employees were to giving their passengers the best in conscientious attention.

American Motors also fell under the Zieff spell introducing the sportiness of the Javelin on regular city streets; the racecar-like handling of the AMX at the racetrack; and the classiness of the Ambassador in a spot entitled "Homecoming." A young Robert DeNiro is cast as the Lower East Side boy who makes good and comes home to show how well he's done uptown by taking his mother for a drive in his new Ambassador.

Zieff's work for Volkswagen's print campaigns earlier in his career for highly successful, but when they paired up again on

television, the combination was magical:

Taking a page from a Hollywood classic, the townspeople storm down to the castle of Dr. Frankenstein. But the dear doctor and his six monster/assistants make their getaway bag-and-baggage in a Volkswagen bus.

MACAULAY CULKIN IN SCENES FROM MY GIRL

Hollywood's portrayal of John Steinbeck's *Of Mice and Men* provided the base elements for Volkswagen's introduction of the Automatic Stick-Shift Beetle.

Pre-Nixon Sino-American relations were the basis of the yet another VW spot: a Volkswagen Camper Wagon is refused entry at a Red Chinese border outpost because it can handle larger loads than any of their economically priced vehicles.

Zieff brought the virtue of pragmatic values home again in another well-remembered VW spot. In *Funeral*, we see a procession cruising down the freeway on their way to paying their last respects to an obviously self-made millionaire. The voiceover provides us with the background on the series of characters and their cars via the reading of the deceased's will. The large, luxury car owners with their wasteful, spendthift habits lose out to the inheritor of the vast estate: the practical, common man nephew Harold who is driving a VW Bug.

When *Time* magazine named Zieff the "Master of Mini Ha-Ha," Hollywood took special notice. In 1972, after several offers, he accepted MGM's invitation to film the comedy *Slither* for his directorial debut. He cast James Caan, Sally Kellerman and Peter Boyle into a script that included extravagantly detailed comic vignettes of a classic chase spoof.

Slither became the first of string of comedies with the Zieff imprint: *Hearts of the West* with Jeff Bridges and Andy Griffith humorously depicts urban-rural relocation; *House Calls* is a satirical look at modern mores and the medical profession starring Glenda Jackson, Art Carney and Walter Matthau; and *The Main Event* is a farce about the fight game with Barbra Streisand and Ryan O'Neal.

He then directed *Private Benjamin*, which earned Goldie Hawn an Academy Award nomination for her portrayal of a Jewish American Princess who winds up in the Army. It also drew an Oscar nomination for Eileen Brennan for her hilarious performance as a tough drill sergeant.

Private Benjamin chronicles how the shallow life of a pampered, directionless Beverly Hills debutante-turned-wedding-night-widow changes when she impulsively

PRIVATE BENJAMIN

enlists into the Army (only to change her mind once she arrives at boot camp) and grows into a woman of initiative and self-confidence.

Zieff summed up his approach to film directing as follows: "Directing is a constant conversation between the actor and the director. In comedy, you are recruiting somebody who already has the talent and the facility of delivery. All you, as a director, have to know is what you want and how to express it—and let the actors give you the gifts of embroidery."

After the incredible success of *Private Benjamin*, he continued to hone his philosophy on more features. In *Unfaithfully Yours*, Zieff orchestrated the talents of Dudley

Moore and Nastassja Kinski in the story of a rich, famous symphony conductor who is struck with a bolt of possessiveness over his beautiful Italian wife. Imagine Films Entertainment produced *The Dream Team*, an off the wall comedy starring Michael Keaton, Christopher Lloyd, Peter Boyle, and Stephen Furst as four mental patients on the loose in Manhattan.

An admirer of Capra, Zieff was drawn to the script of *My Girl* because the humor was grounded totally on human relationships and character. This film stars Macaulay Culkin, Jamie Lee Curtis, and Dan Akroyd.

Throughout his career in both advertising and filmmaking, Howard Zieff has shown us that relentless hard work and a perfectionistic eye combined with a detective's nose for finding humor in reality creates the form of infectious humor and universal accessibility that is the true mark of great comedy.

ROBERT WILVERS

BOB WILVERS says he has won the "required amount of awards over the years." He's received Clios for Carling Black Label, Toni Innocent Color, Hush Puppies, Vespa Motorscooters, Salada Tea, Alka Seltzer, and the Gillette campaigns. He's been awarded Art Directors Club Gold Medals for Gillette Techmatic, Salada Tea, and Gillette Blades ads. Wilvers has also won a number of Andys and New York International TV and Film Festival awards.

Wilvers started his advertising career at the age of sixteen working on displays at a downtown Milwaukee, Wisconsin department store. A little over a year after he started there, the store's advertising manager asked him to become an advertising layout man. Wilvers accepted because it meant more money even though he had no idea at all what advertising was all about. It meant that he could afford the materials he needed to pursue his true aspiration—painting.

Working nights on his art paid off. He won the top prize for watercolor at the University of Wisconsin Salon, had two shows at the Open Studio gallery in Milwaukee. He then began shipping his work to shows around the country: the Chicago Art Institute, the Pennsylvania Academy of Fine Arts, the Butler Institute of Fine Arts, the Corcoran Gallery in Washington D.C., and the American Watercolor Society located in New York.

Manhattan seemed a logical next step in his career. And despite a certain amount of trepidation voiced by his new bride, the couple moved to New York where he landed a job at Macy's Department Store. He stayed there for the next five years where he felt he truly paid his dues.

He still painted every night after dinner and managed to get a one man show at the Kaymar Gallery and won an Emily

VESPA
MOTORSCOOTERS'
A MOTORCYCLE
IT AIN'T

Lowe Foundation prize. He was even freelancing *Fortune* and *Herald Tribune* magazine covers and illustrating his wife's magazine articles. Despite this, his interest in painting started to wane because he'd discovered the magic of film and TV advertising—that was a medium he felt held a real future.

Wilvers got his break into Madison Avenue advertising thanks to Steve Kambanis who had worked with him at Macy's who introduced him to Joe La Rosa. From there he made a brief stop at Benton & Bowles where he met Elaine Gargano. She was so impressed with Wilvers talent that she mentioned him to her husband Amil who was with Carl Ally. That was the beginning of the creative team of Ed McCabe and Bob Wilvers.

Wilvers and McCabe did one memorable spot in which little old lady bikers clad in leathers roar up to the diner on 1000cc Harley for their Salada Tea. The team also created the strikingly minimalist elements of motoscooter visual and strong headlines like "A Motorcycle It Ain't," "If You Want an Economy Car, You Don't Want a Car," and "Maybe Your Second Car Shouldn't Be a Car" for the Vespa motor scooter print campaign. Wilvers still feels these are still amongst the best projects he created with McCabe.

At Jack Tinker and Partners he was teamed up with Gene Case, newly arrived from Doyle Dane Bernbach. For Gillette they reminded housewives everywhere that Gillette Razor Blades were an important facet of keeping their husbands happy and looking good despite the early morning vision of the grungy, pajama-clad spouse in front of the bathroom mirror they all knew so well.

When Mary Wells, Dick Rich, and Stu Greene left Tinker in 1966, Bob Wilvers and Gene Case were made partners in the agency and took over the creative responsibility of accounts like Heublein, Shulton products, Carnation Slender, Toni Innocent Color (which Wilvers worked on with Rene Guion), Alka Seltzer Plus, the Gillette Techmatic Band.

Wilvers teamed up with Bob Schulman on the Coca Cola account. The result was a spot that took the viewer back to World War II as the announcer introduces the audience to a young pilot who is flying his thirtieth mission in 1944 with his lucky bottle of Coke dangling on a string above him in the cockpit. The announcer returns the audience to 1967 where that same bottle of Coke is now nestled amongst other fond memorabilia in a chest of drawers back home. "You Don't Drink an Old Friend," the announcer reminds us.

For Bonniers' Instant Frames, Wilvers visualized an ample woman wearing a black and white floral print shift, costume jewelry, red patent mod shoes and all

holding up a framed black and white photo of her husband in front of her face.

Wilvers fashioned a mouthwatering *Gourmet* magazine-style poster entitled "Italy" for one Alka Seltzer campaign that featured a cornucopia of luscious, spicy foods like peppers, onions and sausages.

After Jack Tinker and Partners closed in 1969, Wilvers rejoined Ed McCabe at Scali, McCabe and Sloves. Their combined talents were assigned to the Volvo campaign. Volvo's ability to handle American road wear was featured in "Things Are Tough All Over." Wilvers exemplified six

COCA COLA'S YOU DON'T DRINK AN OLD FRIEND

ALKA SELTZER'S PLOP, PLOP, FIZZ, FIZZ

typical problems encountered by American drivers nationwide: bumps, hills, holes, bad roads, weather, and curves. The car's solid construction was emphasized with the use of a ground-level perspective shot of a lost hub cap in "Do You Arrive with Less Than You Started With?" The reliability of the new Volvo imports was illustrated using a classic Manhattan sight of abandoned cars under a bridgeway with a dramatic skyline view as background in "The Roads of America Are Strewn with Broken Promises."

Wilvers dropped out of the business shortly after this, gave up painting entirely, and started directing spots himself. This career change lasted about a year and a half before he decided to work for Wells, Rich and Greene.

He worked with Paul Marguilies on the "Plop, Plop, Fizz, Fizz Oh What a Relief It Is" campaign for Alka Seltzer utilizing scenes from the sixties popculture that surrounded them. One spot featured a nightclub scene with a girl-group à la the Supremes singing the joys of relief from indigestion while a customer sips down a glass of the bubbly product.

Wilvers also worked on a number of other memorable campaigns at Wells, Rich and Greene: Citibank's "The Citi Never Sleeps"; Ford Motor Company's "There's

Ford in America's Future"; the testimonial campaign series for Alka Seltzer Plus; and Chase Manhattan Bank's "The Chase Is on for Chase." He also worked with Peter Murphy on the award-winning Hush Puppies TV campaign; with Charlie Moss and Stan Dragoti on Hertz's "America's Wheels" campaign; and with Mark Chappell on introducing a new Proctor & Gamble coffee.

For one PanAm "You Can't Beat the Experience" spot he employed the shared father-and-son experiences of PanAm's first class transoceanic service to Manila. The father reminisces about the comfort and luxury his first flight onboard the China Clipper airship. Then, the scene cuts to

BONNIER'S INSTANT FRAMES

present-day as he shares his son's first-flight experience in the first-class comfort of PanAm's 747 fleet.

The last writer Wilvers worked with at the agency was Charlie Carlson. Together they created the first year campaign for MCI at the agency, depicting MCI representatives' conscientious sales and excellent service in a communications world lacking in quality-oriented values.

Wilvers lives in Connecticut these days and still does some consulting work for Wells. But mainly he writes. There are a number of unpublished novels stacked in his cupboard which he is feverishly trying to add to every day.

THE DEPRESSION had a firm grip on Chicago in 1935. But this didn't deter Leo Burnett from mortgaging his home and borrowing on his life insurance in a $25,000 gamble despite the fact he had a wife and children to feed. And when he put a bowl of red delicious apples out on the reception desk to greet visitors to his eight man office the odds had it on the street that he wouldn't last out the year. Three clients came and stayed for more than a decade because they believed in Leo Burnett's goal: to create advertising "that talked turkey to the majority of Americans."

SANTA FE RAILROAD

Years later, David Ogilvy commented on Leo Burnett's statement : "I wonder if he realized that his kind of advertising could also talk turkey to the majority of people in every other country?"

Born in St. Johns, Michigan, Leo Burnett showed early interest in art, designing and illustrating posters for his high school football team and for his university's opera and theatre productions. After graduation from the University of

LEO BURNETT

Michigan he found himself working as a full-time journalist for the Peoria Journal. He had already gained a lot of experience as editor of a number of campus newspapers and magazines. After covering corrupt municipal politics and murder trials without a byline for $18 a week, Burnett was finally rewarded in 1915 with both a byline and a new biweekly column on railroads which ran for three months: "Right of Way, a Column About Railroads and Those Who Run Them. "

But he realized that the railroad was not America's future: it was the automobile. His own paper's auto column had grown to a full section, and an old classmate of his had gotten a job as house organ editor for the Packard Motor Company. Enlisting the aid of his favorite English professor Dr. Fred Newton Scott, Burnett landed a job starting a House organ for the Cadillac

Motor Company located in Detroit. This was after a skeptical first interview and the test assignment of writing a "bromide" about the importance of cleanliness in selling automobiles, and waiting two months for a reply and a final interview.

Cadillac was where Burnett got his first taste of the advertising world. There he met Theodore F. MacManus, the creator of Cadillac's million plus print ad "The Penalty of Leadership." As a part of his editorial duties, he covered publicity for Cadillac at the New York and Chicago auto shows. Burnett's publicity and contact work earned him the position of advertising head for the company within a couple of years. While he was in Detroit, he met and married his wife of over fifty years Naomi, who stood by his side from that point on. (She even helped him practice semifour while on their honeymoon before

KELLOGG'S CORN FLAKES

he left for active service.)

A year after World War I, Leo Burnett became the advertising manager for the newly formed LaFayette Motor Company located in Indianapolis. The car was designed to compete with the Cadillac and Rolls Royce in luxury and price. (Leo and Naomi, however were driving a Ford sedan with a self-starter. They did manage to test drive an experimental LaFayette which caught fire the second day they had it out.)

Leo's first project for the company was to find an ad agency to handle this elite market. After gleaning through the *Saturday Evening Post* for the best campaigns he could find, he picked the Chicago-based Erwin, Wasey and Company.

Burnett went to Chicago one Saturday morning to call on them. "I discovered that, even in those days, some offices were closed on Saturdays—at least this one was."

Sitting in an unlit reception room, he hailed a mailroom clerk to ask if Mr. Erwin was in. Neither Erwin or Wasey were in on Saturdays.

Only one person was available to speak to him: the copy chief Art Kudner who was sitting in front of his typewriter in his shirtsleeves. He was writing a Goodyear tire ad in his tiny office. Burnett asked him if the agency would be interested in handling the LaFayette Motor business. Of course, Kudner's answer was affirmative. So, Burnett told them it was theirs: a transaction

THE MEAT INSTITUTE

that took all of five informal, unannounced minutes.

The ad campaign was simple: familiar road sights executed as line drawings with a quick run of clean copy. They only ran 200 lines deep in the newspapers, but even the dealers remarked how effective they were.

Unfortunately, the $7000 price tag per car was a little steep for the 1920s buying market and only 700 cars were sold. The company decided to reduce expenses by moving to the smaller town of Kenosha, Wisconsin. Prices for labor and material prices were soaring nationwide, and belts

were tightening on luxury spending. The car had come on the market right in the midst of a serious recession and couldn't survive after sales plummeted in 1924.

Burnett had purchased $2000 worth of LaFayette stock when he joined the company—paying partly in cash and partly in a bank loan. When LaFayette failed, he had to pay off the bank loan, despite the fact he was without a job, had a new baby son and a wife to support.

He joined the Indianapolis agency Homer McKee, where he wrote and laid out his own ads. His accounts were the Marmon, Stutz, and Peerless automobiles.

In 1930, things started top go bad with these accounts. So Burnett contacted Art Kudner and ended up taking a standing offer: working at Erwin, Wasey in Chicago for the next five years.

The Burnett agency landed one of its biggest early clients in 1942 when Leo cold-called the the Santa Fe Railroad after hearing that they were reviewing the account amongst thirty-four contenders: Burnett was the thirty-fifth. He sent his best writer Jack O'Kieffe on the Super Chief to Los Angeles that night with the instruction to write his entire experience and telegraph it to Chicago—ASAP. The longest telegram ever to be wired to to the city arrived shortly thereafter. Thirty-nine hours after his initial meeting with the railroad executive, Burnett and Dick Heath arrived armed with a leather-bound presentation case stamped with the Santa Fe insignia, containing 5000 words about the romance of trains and the Southwestern landscape. They won the account.

The American Meat Institute, and The Minnesota Valley Canning Co. (now called the Green Giant Co.) also took a chance, and Burnett's investment grew. The Burnett logo—a hand reaching for the stars —reflects the founder's philosophy of supporting the creation of superior advertising and the cultivation of lasting relationships.

It's not often in the advertising business that one man's dream, spurred on by deeply seated determination and relentless hardwork creates client-agency matches maintained for decades, but Leo Burnett cultivated some very solid bonds that are still going strong: Green Giant (1935), Philip Morris Co. (1954), Pillsbury (1944), Kellogg's (1949), Proctor & Gamble (1952), Commonwealth Edison (1954), Maytag

(1955), Allstate (1957), Heinz Pet Products (1958), Starkist (1958), First Brands (1961), United Airlines (1965), General Motors Oldsmobile (1967), and Keebler Co. (1968) are just a few. Brand identity characters developed under the watchful eye of Burnett include: the Jolly Green Giant, Pillsbury Dough Boy, Tony the Tiger, the Marlboro Man, Charlie the Tuna, and the Keebler Elves. And slogans like "You're in Good Hands with Allstate" and "When You're Out of Schlitz You're Out of Beer" have brought America's buying public running for more.

When Philip Morris came to Burnett with the Marlboro business in 1954, the cigarette had the smallest market share in its category. A complete repositioning of the product and implementation of a strong advertising strategy changed the tide. In the sixties, Burnett introduced "Marlboro Country" using the musical score from the film *The Magnificent Seven*. The popularity of this campaign led to the rise of Marlboro to the number one slot in market share by the end of the decade.

The concept remains the base creative

strategy for the product to this day. But with the implementation of Burnett's marketing strategy on the account, a new non-traditional medium was developed for the products that maintained strong imaging continuity throughout. The Marlboro Adventure Team was a year-long promotion that included producing print ads, point-of-sale materials, and a catalogue full of Marlboro gear: clothing and other cowboy and autoracing paraphernalia like belt buckles and lighters emblazoned with the Marlboro logo.

The fifty-five full-service offices of Leo Burnett are located in 49 countries with combined billings last year of $4 billion. International billings of $2.2 billion in 1992 placed Burnett in the forefront of worldwide agencies: nearly quadrupling their business in this sector in the last seven years alone with additional clients like McDonald's, Hallmark Cards, Miller Brewing Company, Samsonite, and H.J. Heinz.

And, not surprisingly, a bowl of red delicious apples still sits on the reception desk in every Burnett office around the world.

YUSAKU KAMEKURA

FEW DESIGNERS achieve more than a half century of professional longevity—let alone continue in that time to find new solutions and challenges in their work. But the President of the Japan Graphic Designers Association, Inc. (JAGDA) Yusaku Kamekura has accomplished this and more in his lifetime.

Kamekura was born on April 6, 1915 in Japan's Niigata Prefecture. He studied at a particularly unique design school for that time: the Bauhaus-oriented Institute of New Architecture and Industrial Arts built by Ranahichiro Kawakita.

Immediately after graduation he went to work for Nippon Kobo, publishers of *Nippon* magazine and the Thai publication *Kaupapu*. In 1960 Kamekura became the publishing house's managing director. During his early years he also designed posters for Daido Worsted Mills and Nikon, and an identity program for Nippon Kagaku, K.K. In 1956 Japan Advertising Art Club Exhibition awarded him the Membership Prize for his *Peacefully Use Atomic Energy* poster which included the collage work of his friend the Ikebana artist Sofu Tashigahara.

Despite the post-war western influences of modernism on design in Japan, Kamekura has managed to find a synthesis between the rational, logical and functional design systems of the west and the classical grace of traditional Japanese design. Most known for his use of uncluttered, solid shapes in an elementally sparse plane, one can also find unexpected lyricism behind these solid forms.

His stark elemental utilization of light and dark forms dramatize an otherwise simple image of a light bulb in his 1968 poster for the Yamagiwa International Competition for Lighting Fixtures Exhibition. A similar scheme was used in the design of a poster for a Kyoko Edo Piano Recital in which two butterfly silhouettes are juxtaposed in a Rorhschach pattern.

In contrast a 1984 poster employs an overall texture and kanji characters in soft pastels interwoven into its fabric to promote the Morisawa type foundry. Another 1984 poster entitled *Tradition et Nouvelles Techniques: 12 Graphistes Japonais* utilizes multicolored pastel ellipses vibrating with springing motion against a deep black background.

Kamekura's utilization of a distinctly traditional sensitivity has brought a unique style to his work that reaches far beyond the admitted western influences of Cassandre, Herbert Bayer and the Bauhausian design school. A pair of 1993 posters entitled "I'm Here" incorporate Kamekura's distinct, colorfully minimalist approach with the obvious adaptation of an Oskar Schlemmer piece appearing as the central figure. Throughout his career, Kamekura's analyses of his observations of both the occidental and oriental has subsequently strongly influenced design in Japan today.

Kamekura has never become enslaved by corporate executive policy. Rather he will only work for a company if he is convinced that the work is something that he can conceptually and ethically agree with and work on directly with the executives.

"No matter how much money I am offered, I will not do work that I am not convinced is right. This means that I refuse to do any work for political parties or religious groups because I find that I usually cannot agree with their ideals and purposes...I simply cannot get an inspiration to do work that does not seem worthwhile and of interest to me," he stated in an article in *Graphic*

Design magazine. "My work is only valid if I am involved in creating the image for the entire company in terms of logos and poster designs and so forth, and I don't like to leave even a single poster design in an ambivalent stage of development."

This type of commitment was part of his working strategy when he became a freelance designer in 1962 and is best exemplified in one of his most famous design programs. Kamekura has always been a sports enthusiast—specifically fast sports like motorboats and skiing. He admits that he forgets everything he knows about design

during ski season. His trademark poster for the 18th Olympics—consisting of the Olympic five-ring symbol, Tokyo 1964, and the red sun of the Japanese flag—was selected for its simplicity, strength and freshness from an artist roster that included Kohel Suguira, Kazumasa Nagai and Ikko Tanaka. It was Kamekura's poster series with its dramatically-angled photographic images of swimmers and runners that lent the publicity campaign its active punch. He also won gold and silver awards from the Tokyo Art Directors Club, Mainichi Industrial Design, and Japan Advertising Art Club.

Aside from his work on the 18th Olympic Games, a number of other projects are considered by many to be his masterworks. His poster design for the Japan EXPO '70 was recognized by the Tokyo ADC, the Warsaw International Poster Biennale and Milan International Travel Poster Exhibition. Another distinctive piece is his Hiroshima Appeals poster, illustrated by Akira Yokoyama which won First Prize at the Lahti Poster Biennale.

He received a grand prize from the Ministry of Education in 1961. He has received numerous awards including a 1980 Purple

1964 OLYMPICS POSTER

THE HIROSHIMA APPEALS POSTER

Ribbon Medal; 1985 Third Class Order of the Sacred Treasure; 1991 Person of Cultural Merits; Gold, Silver, Art and Special Awards from the Warsaw International Poster Biennales from 1960 through 1992; awards from the Brno International Graphic Design Biennales; and the Osaka 6th International Design Award in 1993.

Since 1989, Kamekura has been the editor, cover designer, and organizer of *Creation* Magazine, a series of publications limited to twenty issues which focus on international graphic design, art, and illustration work by a variety of artists.

A POSTER FOR THE JAPAN LIGHTING EXHIBITION

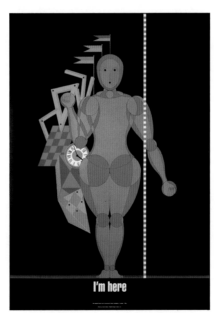

THE HIROSHIMA APPEALS POSTER

NATIONAL MEDALISTS

CHAIRPERSON: Advertising

Gary Goldsmith
GOLDSMITH/JEFFREY, INC.

CO-CHAIRPERSONS

Bob Barrie
FALLON MCELLIGOTT

Allan Beaver
CONSULTANT

Tracy Wong
LIVINGSTON & CO.

JUDGES

Nick Cohen
MAD DOGS & ENGLISHMEN

Dean Hacohen
GOLDSMITH/JEFFREY, INC.

Mark Hughes
LORD, DENTSU &
PARTNERS

Harry Jacobs
THE MARTIN AGENCY, INC.

David Jenkins
DDB NEEDHAM
WORLDWIDE, INC.

Bill Miller
FALLON MCELLIGOTT

Ty Montague
CHIAT/DAY/MOJO, INC.

Noam Munro
GOLDSMITH/JEFFREY, INC.

Bill Oberlander
KIRSCHENBAUM & BOND

Todd Seisser
AMMIRATI & PURIS, INC.

Steve Stone
GOODBY, BERLIN
& SILVERSTEIN

Leslie Sweet
FREELANCE

Marty Weiss
WEISS, WHITTEN,
CARROLL & STAGLIANO

**CHAIRPERSON: Editorial
& Graphic Design,
Photography & Illustration**

Seymour Chwast
THE PUSHPIN GROUP, INC.

CO-CHAIRPERSONS

Stephen Doyle
DRENTTEL DOYLE
PARTNERS

Sheila Levrant
de Bretteville
THE SHEILA STUDIO

Paula Scher
PENTAGRAM DESIGN

Michael Vanderbyl
VANDERBYL DESIGN

JUDGES

Walter Bernard
W.B.M.G., INC.

Steven Brower
CAROL PUBLISHING GROUP

Bob Cato
BOB CATO DESIGN

Henrietta Condak
CONDAK DESIGN

Paul Davis
PAUL DAVIS STUDIO

Louise Fili
LOUISE FILI, LTD.

Carl Fischer
KEN & CARL FISCHER
PHOTOGRAPHY

Dan Friedman
DAN FRIEDMAN DESIGN

Steff Geissbuhler
CHERMAYEFF
& GEISMAR, INC.

Sara Giovanitti
GIOVANITTI
DESIGN GROUP

Nancy Kent
THE NEW YORK TIMES

Scott Menchin
ART DIRECTOR/
ILLUSTRATOR

Tony Palladino
DESIGNER/ART DIRECTOR

Martin Solomon
PDR ROYAL, INC.

Richard Wilde
SCHOOL OF VISUAL ARTS

Fred Woodward
ROLLING STONE MAGAZINE

WHEN I look at the published lists of juries for many of the ever-growing number of award shows, one thing is obvious: everyone has a different set of criteria for selecting judges.

There's the "advertising luminary" school of selection. This is based on the theory that if you get the biggest, most well-known names in the industry, regardless of what they've done or haven't done in the last fifteen years, people will be impressed—and gladly enter. Then there's the big agency power broker theory. This theory is based on the assumption that if you place judges from large agencies—regardless of talent—on the panel, you'll at least get the entries from their agencies. There's also the "Johnny-one-shot" school of thought. These panels consist of people so current, new, fresh, and hip, that no one has heard of them. If they've produced one campaign of value, that's a lot.

I chose the judges for the 72nd Annual Art Directors show on a much less complicated set of criteria. If I had to pick someone to do a campaign within the next week, who would it be? Who has consistently produced great work over the last several years? Who has a reputation for integrity, taste and honesty? Who has personally done the quality work that should be included in the show?

Happily, I was able to get the people I wanted. And for four days, and a couple of nights they stopped doing ads and generously gave their time to come judge some. By the time they left, they had whittled down over 13,000 entries to 1275 finalists and medalists.

In my opinion, it is a show that is representational of the best work currently being done in our field. As you flip through the following pages, I hope you'll agree.

GARY GOLDSMITH

CHAIRMAN, ADVERTISING JUDGING COMMITTEE

WHILE the Art Director's Club has an international reputation, its strength lies in its position as a center for all creative communication. The membership of this umbrella organization is comprised of art directors, designers, illustrators, and photographers in every aspect of our profession. In order to reflect this the national exhibit had two chairmen.

Gary Goldsmith selected a jury with specific expertise in advertising while I was in charge of editorial and graphic design, photography, and illustration. My judges, all of whose work I highly respect, accepted with great enthusiasm the task of evaluating thousands of entries. They came out of a long weekend with a show of which we can be proud.

The other innovation was the initiation of a "Best of Show" award, designated by the chairmen from gold medal winners in each of the two major categories. The results found in this book, will show that proper attention has been paid to the best.

SEYMOUR CHWAST

CHAIRMAN, GRAPHIC DESIGN JUDGING COMMITTEE

ADVERTISING

Best of Show/Gold/Television

ART DIRECTOR/DIRECTOR
Chris Hooper

COPYWRITER/DIRECTOR
Scott Vincent

PRODUCER
David Verhoef

AGENCY
Chiat/Day/Mojo

CLIENT
TV Guide

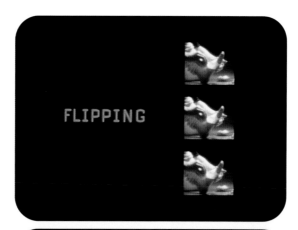

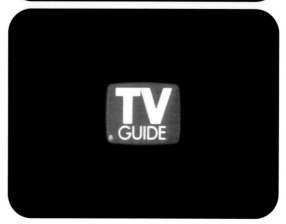

VO: Hey. Hey! It's me again. Your TV. Look, I got thirty seconds before a commercial comes on, so I'll make this quick. You gotta stop flipping around with the remote. I can't take it. Listen. Read *TV Guide*. It's got everything you need, so you won't miss the shows you want to see. Here's this week's issue. It shouldn't be too hard to find. So go get it. 'Cause if you're not gonna work with me, I'll just amuse myself. Ooh, excellent shot. Why, thank you. Oh, and uh...Don't watch TV in the dark. Every channel. Don't watch TV in the dark.

Gold/Television
ART DIRECTOR/DIRECTOR
Chris Hooper
COPYWRITER/DIRECTOR
Scott Vincent
PRODUCER
David Verhoef
AGENCY
Chiat/Day/Mojo
CLIENT
TV Guide

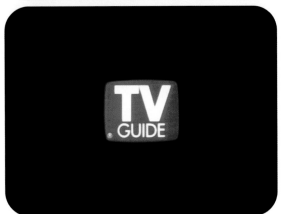

VO: Hey, it's me again. Your TV. You know, the new fall
shows are coming. Now you can find out which ones you're
gonna like using this simple equation. Hmmm... Or you
can pick up *TV Guide*. 'Cause the Fall Preview issue has
the scoop on all the new shows. So you'll definitely find
something you like. And we have a better time together.
ANNOUNCER: You know, I don't wanna scare you,
but one minor miscalculation, and you could end up
watching something like this. I wouldn't risk it.
Don't watch TV in the dark.

Gold/Television

ART DIRECTOR
Kirk Souder

COPYWRITER
Court Crandall

PRODUCER
Randy Zook

DIRECTOR
Kinka Usher

AGENCY
Stein Robaire Helm

CLIENT
IKEA

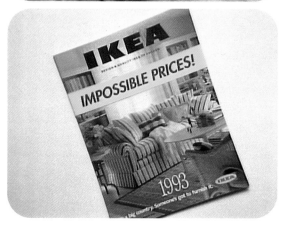

MAN: You need some new furniture.
VO: The 1993 IKEA catalog is here. And not a moment too soon.

Silver/Television

ART DIRECTOR
David Angelo

COPYWRITER
Paul Spencer

PRODUCER
Eric Herrmann

DIRECTOR
John Lloyd

AGENCY
DDB Needham Worldwide

CLIENT
New York State Lottery

Silver/Television

ART DIRECTOR
Chuck Finkle

COPYWRITER
Dean Hacohen

PRODUCER
Patricia Quaglino

DIRECTOR
Henry Sandbank

AGENCY
Goldsmith/Jeffrey

CLIENT
NYNEX Business-to-Business Directory

SFX: Birds. Outside noises.
MAN: Does it come with cable?
AGENT: Ah, well...
VO: New York Lotto. Hey, you never know.

SFX: Seagulls cawing. Bomb dropping whistle.
   Splat. Window being rubbed clean.
VO: The NYNEX Business-to-Business Directory.
   Where one business finds another.

Silver/Television

ART DIRECTOR/DIRECTOR
Chris Hooper

COPYWRITER/DIRECTOR
Scott Vincent

PRODUCER
David Verhoef

AGENCY
Chiat/Day/Mojo

CLIENT
TV Guide

Silver/Television

ART DIRECTOR
Brian Nadurak

COPYWRITERS
Thomas Hripko, Brian Nadurak

PRODUCER
Harvey Lewis

AGENCY
The Richards Group

CLIENT
Motel 6

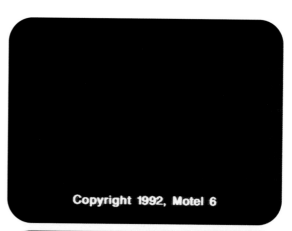

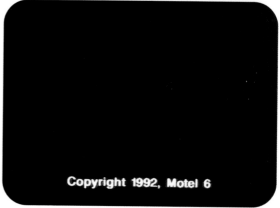

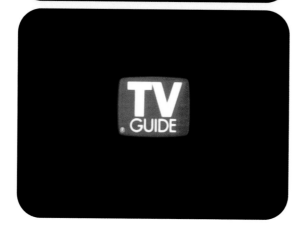

VO: Hey. Hey! We've never been formally introduced, but it's me, your TV. Look, we've had some great times together.
ASTRONAUT: Roger, Houston.
SFX: "I Love Lucy" theme.
RUDOLPH: Ready, Santa.
AL MICHAELS VO: Do you believe in miracles?
VO: But now you just flip the remote. Which is very irritating. You know, there's a better way to watch TV. Just pick up *TV Guide*. It's got all the stuff you need to find the shows you want to watch. So go get it. 'Cause if you're not going to cooperate, I'll pick something for you.
POLKA TIME VO: It's polka time.

TOM: Hi. Tom Bodett for Motel 6 with some insight for the traveler. This is what one of our rooms look like when you're sleeping. And you know, it looks just like those big fancy hotels. Only difference is ours only cost you around twenty-five bucks. More in some places, less in others, but always the lowest prices of any national chain for a clean, comfortable room. Makes you sleepy just looking at it. I'm Tom Bodett for Motel 6 and we'll leave the light on for you.

Distinctive Merit/Television

ART DIRECTOR
David Angelo

COPYWRITER
Paul Spencer

PRODUCER
Eric Herrmann

DIRECTOR
John Lloyd

AGENCY
DDB Needham Worldwide

CLIENT
New York State Lottery

Distinctive Merit/Television

ART DIRECTOR
David Angelo

COPYWRITER
Paul Spencer

PRODUCER
Eric Herrmann

DIRECTOR
Brent Thomas

AGENCY
DDB Needham Worldwide

CLIENT
New York State Lottery

SFX: Music throughout.

J.P.: In short gentlemen, our capitalization plan has paid handsome dividends. Johnson here will fill you in on the details.

JOHNSON: Thank you, J.P. Let me begin by saying...
(*door slams*)

MAN: We've been acquired.

J.P.: By whom? The Omega Corporation?

MAN: No, Chuck...from the mail room.

CHUCK: Hi boys, Ms. Whittiker.

VO: New York Lotto. Hey, you never know.

CHUCK: Coffee, Johnson.

SFX: Opera music. Music stops.

WOMAN: Thank you.

SFX: Music continues.

VO: New York Lotto. Hey, you never know.

Distinctive Merit/Television

ART DIRECTOR
David Angelo

COPYWRITER
Paul Spencer

PRODUCER
Eric Herrmann

DIRECTOR
Brent Thomas

AGENCY
DDB Needham Worldwide

CLIENT
New York State Lottery

Distinctive Merit/Television

ART DIRECTOR/DIRECTOR
Jeremy Postaer

COPYWRITER/DIRECTOR
Steve Simpson

PRODUCER
Ben Latimer

AGENCY
Goodby, Berlin & Silverstein

CLIENT
Chevys Restaurants

MAN: Faster...Faster. Faster!!!!
VO: New York Lotto. Hey, you never know.

Distinctive Merit/Television

ART DIRECTORS/COPYWRITERS
John Butler, Mike Shine

PRODUCER
Shelly Predovich

DIRECTOR
Barry Sonnenfeld

AGENCY
Goodby, Berlin & Silverstein

CLIENT
Isuzu

Distinctive Merit/Television

ART DIRECTOR
Chuck Finkle

COPYWRITER
Dean Hacohen

PRODUCER
Patricia Quaglino

DIRECTOR
Henry Sandbank

AGENCY
Goldsmith/Jeffrey

CLIENT
NYNEX Business-to-Business Directory

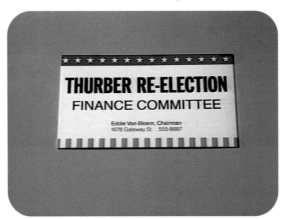

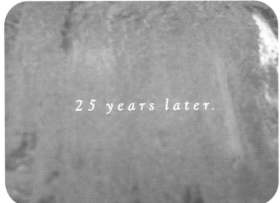

SFX: 1960s style music throughout.
VO: They say our personality traits are formed at an early age.
SFX: Music changes to speedy rock.
VO: Presenting the 3.1 liter, V6 Rodeo from Isuzu. After all, growing up does have its rewards.

SFX: Police sirens approaching. Paper shredding.
VO: The NYNEX Business-to-Business Directory. Where one business finds another.

Distinctive Merit/Television

ART DIRECTOR
Chuck Finkle

COPYWRITER
Dean Hacohen

PRODUCER
Patricia Quaglino

DIRECTOR
Henry Sandbank

AGENCY
Goldsmith/Jeffrey

CLIENT
NYNEX Business-to-Business Directory

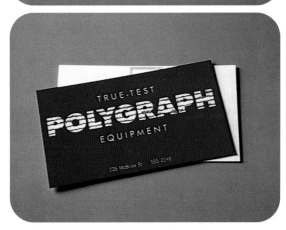

MAN: A little background? Sure. I graduated Ivy League at fifteen. Got my MBA at sixteen. Headed up two Fortune 500 companies at seventeen...I was worth two billion by the age of eighteen...
VO: The NYNEX Business-to-Business Directory. Where one business finds another.

Distinctive Merit/Television

ART DIRECTOR
Michael Fazende

COPYWRITER
Mike Lescarbeau

PRODUCER
Judy Brink

DIRECTOR
Roger Woodburn/Park Village Productions

AGENCY
Fallon McElligott

CLIENT
The Lee Co.

SFX: Male tenor sings Italian aria.
SFX: ZZZZZIP!
SFX: Male voice replaced by soprano.
VO: Need a little more room in your jeans? Try Relaxed-Fit Jeans from Lee.

Gold/Campaign/Television

ART DIRECTOR/DIRECTOR
Chris Hooper

COPYWRITER
Scott Vincent

PRODUCER/DIRETCOR
David Verhoef

AGENCY
Chiat/Day/Mojo

CLIENT
TV Guide

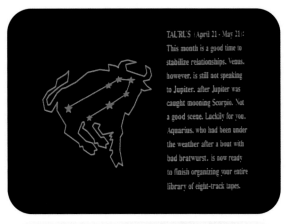

VO: Hi. It's me again, the TV. Look. If we're going to spend quality time together...I think we need to open up a little. So. I'm a Taurus. Turn-offs are dust, power surges, and people who flip the remote. Favorite reading? *TV Guide.* Because *TV Guide* has the best stories about...me. So you're tuned in and we have a better time together. Now, tell me about you. Oh, out of time. Here's the new issue so you know what to look for. Cool cover, huh? Oh, and uh, don't watch TV in the dark.

Silver/Campaign/Television

ART DIRECTOR
Ian Potter

COPYWRITERS
Eric Grunbaum, Steve Rabosky

PRODUCER
Jennifer Golub

DIRECTOR
Brent Thomas

AGENCY
Chiat/Day/Mojo

CLIENT
Eveready Batteries

Silver/Campaign/Television

ART DIRECTOR
David Angelo

COPYWRITER
Paul Spencer

PRODUCER
Eric Herrmann

DIRECTOR
John Lloyd

AGENCY
DDB Needham Worldwide

CLIENT
New York State Lottery

VO: If atomic particles had been square instead of round, it probably wouldn't have happened. If it had been a wet cell instead of a dry cell, it's doubtful. And if the positive terminal had been negative, who knows. There might never have been a battery called Energizer.
Or the Engerizer bunny. But luckily, everything happened just right.

SFX: Music throughout.
J.P.: In short gentlemen, our capitalization plan has paid handsome dividends. Johnson here will fill you in on the details.
JOHNSON: Thank you, J.P. Let me begin by saying... (*door slams*)
MAN: We've been acquired.
J.P.: By whom? The Omega Corporation?
MAN: No, Chuck...from the mail room.
CHUCK: Hi boys, Ms. Whittiker.
VO: New York Lotto. Hey you never know.
CHUCK: Coffee, Johnson.

Silver/Campaign/Television

ART DIRECTORS
Donna Weinheim, Kevin Donovan,
Bruce Hurwit, Cliff Freeman
COPYWRITERS
Cliff Freeman, Donna Weinheim,
Rick LeMoine, Don Austen
AGENCY
Cliff Freeman & Partners
CLIENT
Little Caesars

Distinctive Merit/Campaign/Television

ART DIRECTOR
Steve Stone
COPYWRITER
Bob Kerstetter
PRODUCER
Debbie King
DIRECTOR
Michae Karbelnikoff
AGENCY
Goodby, Berlin & Silverstein
CLIENT
Norwegian Cruise Line

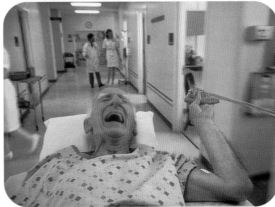

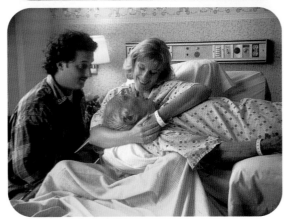

SFX: Squeak of the wheels of the gurney. Echoey voice of nurse fades in.
NURSE: Now let's get those tonsils out.
NURSE #1: Is it too brassy?
NURSE #2: I like that color.
SFX: Stretching sound begins. Dramatic sound of the doors being opened. Loud swinging sound of the door.
MAN: Woo-Hooo-Hooo!
NURSE: Here's your baby.
MAN: Wooo-Hooo!
VO: Little Caesars Cheeser! Cheeser! Two pizzas with extra cheese, ...up to three toppings and free Crazy Bread for $8.98.
LITTLE CAESAR: Cheeser! Cheeser!

Script for all three spots.

SFX: instrumental version of "I'm Getting Sentimental Over You" under throughout.

Gold/Television

ART DIRECTORS/COPYWRITERS
Peter Cohen, Leslie Sweet

DIRECTOR
Laura Belsey

CINEMATOGRAPHERS
Tami Reiker, Leighton Edmundson

AGENCY
Streetsmart Advertising

CLIENT
Coalition for the Homeless

**IT'S UP TO YOU
NEW YORK, NEW YORK.**

CURTIS: (*singing*) Start spreading the news, I'm leaving today,
  I want to be a part of it...
JOHN: (*singing*) New York, New York.
AMEEN: (*singing*) I want to wake up in a city that
  doesn't sleep.
JIM: (*singing*) And find I'm king of the hill,
JESSE: (*singing*) Top of the heap.
JULIUS: (*singing*) These little town blues, are meltin' away,
TERESA: (*singing*) I'll make a brand new start of it, in old
  New York.
BOB: (*singing*) If I can make it there, I'll make it anywhere...

Gold/Television

ART DIRECTOR/DIRECTOR
Ted Demme

COPYWRITER
Denis Leary

CREATIVE DIRECTORS
Judy McGrath, Abby Terkuhl

PRODUCER
Christina Norman

STUDIO
MTV Network

CLIENT
MTV Network

LEARY: One word, drugs. I grew up in the 70s, we did a lot of drugs and listened to a lot of bad music and wore a lot of stupid clothing like bell bottoms and platform shoes.
So you want some advice? Here it is...these are your pants. These are your pants on drugs, okay? Five words folks: K.C. and the Sunshine band. Cocaine. There's good idea. I want to do a drug that makes my penis small, makes my heart explode, makes my nose bleed, and sucks all my money out of the bank. Can I do that? Can I sit in a room and sweat for seven hours? I wanna make this face all night...I want to talk to complete idiots about nothing for hours on end with no penis and a nosebleed. Is that possible? Where can I sign up for that? And when it comes to crack, I got a little piece of advice for you folks...Never, do a drug named after a part of your ass, okay? I think you hear me knockin' and I think I'm coming in. I'm already in! I'm wandering around the house, and you know what? I found your bell bottoms. Ha, Ha, Ha!

ADVERTISING

Gold/Television

ART DIRECTOR/DIRECTOR
Ted Demme

COPYWRITER
Dennis Leary

CREATIVE DIRECTORS
Judy McGrath, Abby Terkuhl

PRODUCER
Christina Norman

STUDIO
MTV Network

CLIENT
MTV Network

LEARY: One word folks, racism. One more word, Earth.
If anybody on this planet gets mail from outerspace,
that's going to be the mailing address, okay? He's white,
he's red, he's yellow, he's black. I don't like him 'cause he's
different from me. Hey folks, you know something?
My hate is not based on color or creed, it's based on
performance, okay? I have a cousin, a white Irish cousin
that looks just like me. Ya know something, he's an idiot!!
He's lazy, he's ignorant, he's a huge pus-filled boil on
the ass of society. I'm a spic, I'm a mick, I'm a wop,
I'm a Jew. And where do you all live? New York.
Great folks, get in the pot, okay? Get in the great big giant
melting pot, because we're making soup. American soup.
I got two words for ya, David Duke. Two more words,
nose job, okay? Yeah, I think you hear me knockin' David
and I think I'm coming in, and I'm bringing a black guy,
a Jewish guy, and a whole South Vietnamese family with
me and we're all going to sit down and watch "Do the
Right Thing" until we get it right this time, okay?
And guess who's making the popcorn...

ADVERTISING

Gold/Public Service Television

ART DIRECTORS/COPYWRITERS
Peter Cohen, Leslie Sweet

DIRECTOR
Laura Belsey

CINEMATOGRAPHERS
Tami Reiker, Leighton Edmundson

AGENCY
Streetsmart Advertising

CLIENT
Coalition for the Homeless

**IT'S UP TO YOU
NEW YORK, NEW YORK.**

CURTIS: (*singing*) Start spreading the news, I'm leaving today,
I want to be a part of it...
JOHN:(*singing*) New York, New York.
AMEEN: (*singing*) I want to wake up in a city that
doesn't sleep.
JIM: (*singing*) And find I'm king of the hill,
JESSE: (*singing*) Top of the heap.
JULIUS: (*singing*) These little town blues, are meltin' away,
TERESA: (*singing*) I'll make a brand new start of it, in old
New York.
BOB: (*singing*) If I can make it there, I'll make it anywhere...

Silver/Public Service Television

ART DIRECTOR
Sally Wagner

COPYWRITER
Christopher Wilson

PRODUCER
Mary Fran Werner

DIRECTOR
Chuck Statler

AGENCY
Martin/Williams

CLIENT
American Humane Association

Distinctive Merit/Public Service Television

ART DIRECTOR
Craig Hadorn

COPYWRITER
Dory Toft

PRODUCER
Shelley Winfrey

DIRECTOR
NASA

AGENCY
Livingston & Company

CLIENT
Museum of Flight

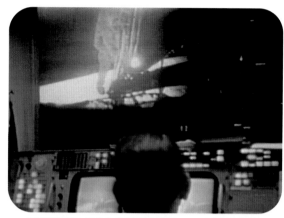

ALL VISUAL SUPERS: Who says you can't teach an old dog new tricks? Adopt an older dog. They're cool. American Humane Association.

ARMSTRONG: Okay, Houston. I'm on the porch.
HOUSTON: Roger, Neil. Okay, Neil, we can see you coming down the ladder now.
ARMSTRONG: I'm gonna step off the limb now. That's one small step for man. One block west of I-5.
HOUSTON: Roger, Neil. Is there free parking out there?
ARMSTRONG: Uh, that's affirmative, Houston.

ADVERTISING

Gold/Low-budget Television

ART DIRECTORS/COPYWRITERS
Peter Cohen, Leslie Sweet

DIRECTOR
Laura Belsey

CINEMATOGRAPHERS
Tami Reiker, Leighton Edmundson

AGENCY
Streetsmart Advertising

CLIENT
Coalition for the Homeless

IT'S UP TO YOU
NEW YORK, NEW YORK.

CURTIS: (*singing*) Start spreading the news, I'm leaving today,
   I want to be a part of it...
JOHN: (*singing*) New York, New York.
AMEEN: (*singing*) I want to wake up in a city that
   doesn't sleep.
JIM: (*singing*) And find I'm king of the hill,
JESSE: (*singing*) Top of the heap.
JULIUS: (*singing*) These little town blues, are meltin' away,
TERESA: (*singing*) I'll make a brand new start of it, in old
   New York.
BOB: (*singing*) If I can make it there, I'll make it anywhere...

Distinctive Merit/Low-budget Television
ART DIRECTOR
Brian Nadurak
COPYWRITERS
Thomas Hripko, Brian Madurak
PRODUCER
Harvey Lewis
AGENCY
The Richards Group
CLIENT
Motel 6

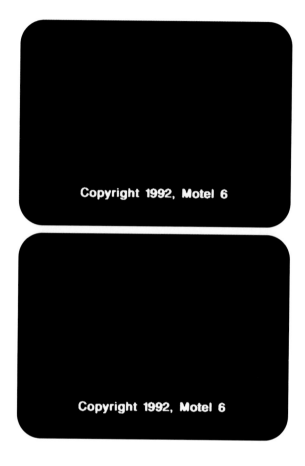

For reservations call
505-891-6161

TOM: Hi. Tom Bodett for Motel 6 with some insight for the traveler. This is what one of our rooms look like when you're sleeping. And you know, it looks just like those big fancy hotels. Only difference is ours only cost you around twenty-five bucks. More in some places, less in others, but always the lowest prices of any national chain for a clean, comfortable room. Makes you sleepy just looking at it. I'm Tom Bodett for Motel 6 and we'll leave the light on for you.

Silver/Promotional Video

ART DIRECTOR/COPYWRITER/DIRECTOR
Jerry Pope

PRODUCER
Greg Pope

STUDIO
Dublin Productions

CLIENT
Jerry Pope, DP/Director

Silver/Art Direction

ART DIRECTOR/COPYWRITER
Mark Hughes

PRODUCER
Elise Baruch

DIRECTOR
Gary Johns

AGENCY
Lord, Dentsu & Partners/New York

CLIENT
TDK Electronics Corp.

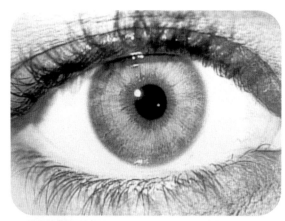

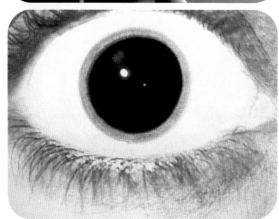

PENITENT: (*whisper, whisper*) Bless me father, I have sinned.
   It's been about...fourteen years since my last confession.
PRIEST: Go on, my son.
PENITENT: Well father, I've had impure thoughts.
PRIEST: Two Hail Marys.
PENITENT: And I...I touched myself.
PRIEST: Three Hail Marys.
PENITENT: A lot.
PRIEST: Four Hail Marys?
PENITENT: And also Father, I...I direct TV commercials.
PRIEST: Ouch!
PENITENT: Uh, Father?...Father?

SFX: Background sounds. Heavy breathing and heartbeat.

Distinctive Merit/Consumer Newspaper
ART DIRECTOR
Peggy Redfern
COPYWRITER
Kim Genkinger
AGENCY
CHD
CLIENT
The Spy Factory

Where To Shop For Your Husband And His Girlfriend.

With our huge selection of surveillance and monitoring
devices, we've got a sneaking suspicion you'll find just what you're looking for.

Spy Factory

3872 Roswell Rd., Atlanta, GA 30342
(404) 814-1136

Gold/Consumer Newspaper

ART DIRECTOR
Kenny Sink

COPYWRITER
Dean Buckhorn

CREATIVE DIRECTOR
Matt Smith

AGENCY
Hawley Martin Partners

CLIENT
Adopt-A-Pet

HOW MANY TIMES DO YOU HAVE TO BE REMINDED TO GET YOUR PET FIXED?

Every year, 14 million unwanted pets are destroyed. So please, spay or neuter your pets. And call 649-6168 by July 23 to sponsor a pet in our July 30 Adopt-A-Pet ad.

Silver/Consumer Newspaper

ART DIRECTOR
Carol Henderson

COPYWRITER
Luke Sullivan

PHOTOGRAPHER
Curtis Johnson

AGENCY
Fallon McElligott

CLIENT
Star Tribune

Silver/Consumer Newspaper

ART DIRECTOR
Susan Griak

COPYWRITER
Mike Lescarbeau

PHOTOGRAPHERS
Craig Perman, Kerry Peterson

AGENCY
Fallon McElligott

CLIENT
Jim Beam Brands, Co.

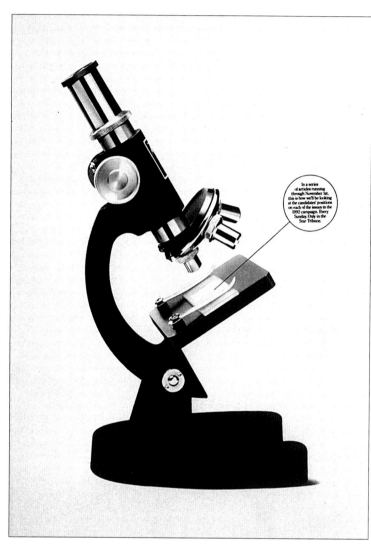

Silver/Consumer Newspaper

ART DIRECTOR
Gary Goldsmith

COPYWRITER
Dean Hacohen

PHOTOGRAPHER
Ilan Rubin

AGENCY
Goldsmith/Jeffrey

CLIENT
Bergdorf Goodman

Silver/Consumer Newspaper

ART DIRECTOR
Ellen Steinberg

COPYWRITER
David Bromberg

PHOTOGRAPHER
Mark Weiss

AGENCY
Weiss, Whitten, Carroll, Stagliano

CLIENT
The New York Restaurant Group

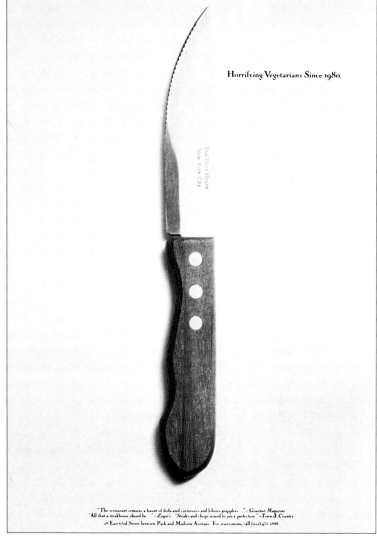

Distinctive Merit/Consumer Newspaper
ART DIRECTOR
Bob Brihn
COPYWRITER
Dean Buckhorn
PHOTOGRAPHER
Joe Lampi
AGENCY
Fallon McElligott
CLIENT
Star Tribune

Distinctive Merit/Consumer Newspaper
ART DIRECTOR
Gary Goldsmith
COPYWRITER
Dean Hacohen
AGENCY
Goldsmith/Jeffrey
CLIENT
Bergdorf Goodman

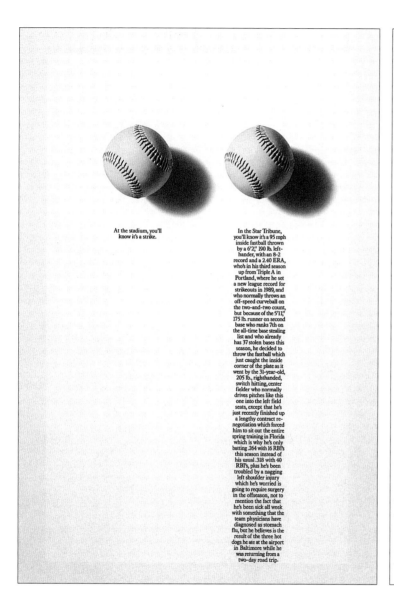

At the stadium, you'll know it's a strike.

In the Star Tribune, you'll know it's a 95 mph inside fastball thrown by a 6'2", 190 lb. left-hander, with an 8-2 record and a 2.40 ERA, who's in his third season up from Triple A in Portland, where he set a new league record for strikeouts in 1989, and who normally throws an off-speed curveball on the two-and-two count, but because of the 5'11", 175 lb. runner on second base who ranks 7th on the all-time base stealing list and who already has 37 stolen bases this season, he decided to throw the fastball which just caught the inside corner of the plate as it went by the 31-year-old, 205 lb., righthanded, switch hitting, center fielder who normally drives pitches like this one into the left field seats, except that he's just recently finished up a lengthy contract re-negotiation which forced him to sit out the entire spring training in Florida which is why he's only batting .264 with 16 RBI's this season instead of his usual .318 with 40 RBI's, plus he's been troubled by a nagging left shoulder injury which he's worried is going to require surgery in the offseason, not to mention the fact that he's been sick all week with something that the team physicians have diagnosed as stomach flu, but he believes is the result of the three hot dogs he ate at the airport in Baltimore while he was returning from a two-day road trip.

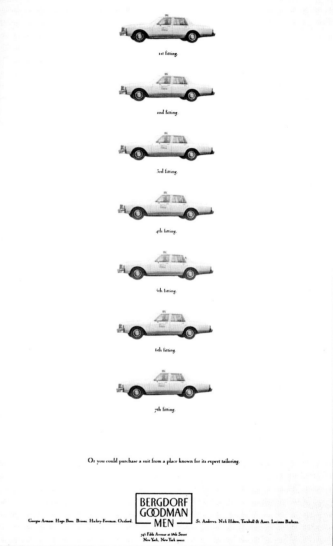

Or you could purchase a suit from a place known for its expert tailoring.

BERGDORF GOODMAN MEN

Soil can erode
at the rate of up to
one inch per year.
Now a word about
financial assets.

Taxes take a nibble here. A nibble there. Then inflation takes a lot. Little wonder the average financial portfolio gets eaten away over time. Precisely why every J.P. Morgan advisor offers a range of global investment services to balance risk and reward. Analysis, traders, and financial strategists who focus on increasing long-term reward. And generational planning services to transfer that reward. Better still, the best way to make sure your assets won't erode over time is to start a financial relationship that won't, either. If you have assets of $5 million or more, call Thomas F. Shevlin at (212) 837-1343. Private Banking **JPMorgan**

Distinctive Merit/Consumer Newspaper

ART DIRECTOR
Gary Goldsmith

COPYWRITER
Dean Hacohen

PHOTOGRAPHER
Chris Wormell

AGENCY
Goldsmith/Jeffrey

CLIENT
J.P. Morgan

Distinctive Merit/Consumer Newspaper

ART DIRECTOR
Mark Johnson

COPYWRITER
John Stingley

PHOTOGRAPHER
Jeff Zwart

AGENCY
Fallon McElligott

CLIENT
Porsche Cars North America

We would have released it sooner, but we were too busy applying for patents.

In 1948 a single, small roadster changed the course of automotive history with a wellspring of radical concepts. Hailed as a new vision, in truth it was the result of decades of development by Porsche engineers; a pilgrimage in search of the perfect car.

Every Porsche sports car hence has continued the pilgrimage. Fusing that original essence with the fruit of new thinking. Shaping the automotive world.

Now, after much anticipation, the new Porsche 968 reveals the next link in the chain.

Classic Porsche lines imbue the 968 with a familiar, timeless face. Yet, there are no fewer than seven new patents on the body alone. Stunning new aerodynamics are sculpted so that each curve, each angle serves a purpose. Design work is so detailed that airflow is even used to help direct rain spray away from the windshield.

Beneath that fluid skin, and boasting four more patents, lurks the highest torque atmospheric three litre engine in the world. Its patented new Porsche Vario-Cam continuously optimizes valve timing to burn fuel thoroughly and precisely. This increases power and provides instant throttle response, yet also helps lower emissions a dramatic 22%.

A quick browse through the continuing list of new patents reveals a headlight system using the principle of a bee's eyes. More than 1,000 reflective facets employ variable point focus to cut reflected glare. Then there's the patented new brake cooling system; the first of its kind to deflect massive volumes of air without increasing either drag or front end lift. And on and on, right down to engineering so meticulous that there are even two new patents on the spare tire system.

The 968 possesses patented Porsche ideas from past years as well. Including recent breakthroughs, like the optional Tiptronic transmission. The world's first dual-function gearbox, it allows either full automatic or clutchless manual shifting.

In fact, the car you drive now has no doubt benefited in ways that would surprise you from Porsche's history of development. We pioneered padded dashes in the '50s, a full 12 years before Federal tests prompted others to follow. And in 1961 when our race drivers complained of glare off their silver wipers, we fit our RS 61 with black ones. Try to find a car today without them.

We could continue at length. But the most intriguing gifts to the automotive world would be the newest ones, housed in the 968. To find out more, or to arrange a private viewing at your authorized Porsche dealership, call 1-800-252-4444.

The 968 may have been awhile in coming. But as always with a new Porsche, it was more than worth the wait.

Porsche 968: The next evolution.

Silver/Campaign/Consumer Newspaper

ART DIRECTOR
Gary Goldsmith

COPYWRITER
Dean Hacohen

ILLUSTRATOR
Chris Wormell

AGENCY
Goldsmith/Jeffrey

CLIENT
J.P. Morgan

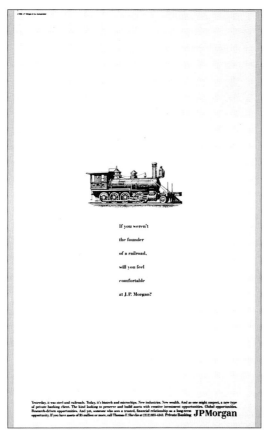

If you weren't the founder of a railroad, will you feel comfortable at J.P. Morgan?

Yesterday, it was steel and railroads. Today, it's biotech and microchips. New industries. New wealth. And as one might suspect, a new type of private banking client. The kind looking to preserve and build assets with creative investment opportunities. Global opportunities. Research-driven opportunities. And yet, someone who sees a trusted, financial relationship as a long-term opportunity. If you have assets of $5 million or more, call Thomas F. Shevlin at (212) 837-4343. Private Banking. **JPMorgan**

You've heard of all the legendary fortunes that began in a garage. But where did they go from there?

It started as just an idea. Which grew into something bigger. And something bigger still. And before long, it grew into a good-sized company. The kind we've been helping entrepreneurs build, manage and sell for over 150 years. How? By offering private banking clients everything from generational planning to employee retirement plan services with the same level of attention that serves the world's largest corporations. Not to mention the same analysts and financial strategists that serve the world's largest corporations. In hopes that one day, we'll be serving another of the world's largest corporations. If you have assets of $5 million or own a substantial company, call Thomas F. Shevlin at (212) 837-4343. Private Banking. **JPMorgan**

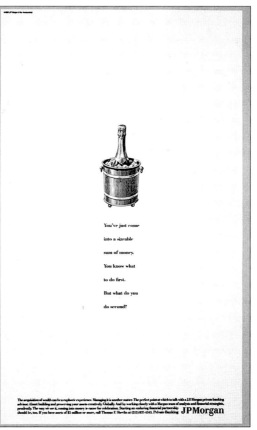

You've just come into a sizable sum of money. You know what to do first. But what do you do second?

The acquisition of wealth can be a euphoric experience. Managing it is another matter. The perfect point at which to talk with a J.P. Morgan private banking advisor. About building and preserving your assets creatively. Globally. And by working closely with a Morgan team of analysts and financial strategists, prudently. The way we see it, coming into money is cause for celebration. Starting an enduring financial partnership should be, too. If you have assets of $5 million or more, call Thomas F. Shevlin at (212) 837-4343. Private Banking. **JPMorgan**

Silver/Campaign/Consumer Newspaper

ART DIRECTOR
Mark Johnson

COPYWRITER
John Stingley

PHOTOGRAPHERS
Andreas Burz, Shawn Michienzi,
Jeff Zwart

AGENCY
Fallon McElligott

CLIENT
Porsche Cars North America

We would have released it sooner, but we were too busy applying for patents.

In 1948 a single, small roadster changed the course of automotive history with a wellspring of radical concepts. Hailed as a new vision, in truth it was the result of decades of development by Porsche engineers; a pilgrimage in search of the perfect car.

Every Porsche sports car hence has continued the pilgrimage. Fusing that original essence with the fruit of new thinking. Shaping the automotive world.

Now, after much anticipation, the new Porsche 968 reveals the next link in the chain.

Classic Porsche lines imbue the 968 with a familiar, timeless face. Yet, there are no fewer than seven new patents on the body alone. Stunning new aerodynamics are sculpted so that each curve, each angle serves a purpose. Design work is so detailed that airflow is even used to help direct rain spray away from the windshield.

Beneath that fluid skin, and boasting four more patents, lurks the highest torque atmospheric three litre engine in the world. Its patented new Porsche Vario-Cam continuously optimizes valve timing to burn fuel thoroughly and precisely. This increases power and provides instant throttle response, yet also helps lower emissions a dramatic 22%.

A quick browse through the continuing list of new patents reveals a headlight system using the principle of a bee's eyes. More than 1,000 reflective facets employ variable point focus to cut reflected glare. Then there's the patented new brake cooling system; the first of its kind to deflect massive volumes of air without increasing either drag or front end lift. And on and on, right down to engineering so meticulous that there are even two new patents on the spare tire system.

The 968 possesses patented Porsche ideas from past years as well. Including recent breakthroughs, like the optional Tiptronic transmission. The world's first dual-function gearbox, it allows either full automatic or clutchless manual shifting.

In fact, the car you drive now has no doubt benefited in ways that would surprise you from Porsche's history of development. We pioneered padded dashes in the '50s, a full 12 years before Federal tests prompted others to follow. And in 1961 when our race drivers complained of glare off their silver wipers, we fit our RS 61 with black ones. Try to find a car today without them.

We could continue at length. But the most intriguing gifts to the automotive world would be the newest ones, housed in the 968. To find out more, or to arrange a private viewing at your authorized Porsche dealership, call 1-800-252-4444. The 968 may have been awhile in coming. But as always with a new Porsche, it was more than worth the wait.

Porsche 968: The next evolution.

ADVERTISING

Silver/Campaign/Consumer Newspaper

ART DIRECTOR
Gary Goldsmith

COPYWRITER
Dean Hacohen

AGENCY
Goldsmith/Jeffrey

CLIENT
Bergdorf Goodman

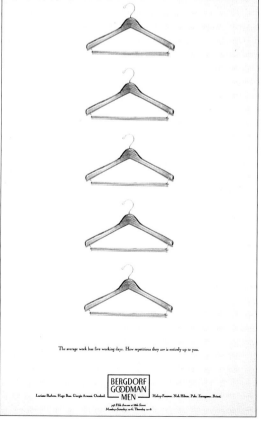

Distinctive Merit/Campaign/Consumer Newspaper

ART DIRECTOR
Mikal Reich

DESIGNER
Shalom Auslander

COPYWRITERS
Shalom Auslander, Mikal Reich,
Sharon Caplan

AGENCY
Mad Dogs & Englishmen

CLIENT
Village Voice

☐ @*!#

off, you establishment-embracing pseudo-anarchists and take your money-hungry subscription offer with you...you've all gone softer than the over-fed bellies of the crooked middle-aged babykissing handshakers you so hypocritically condemn. I mean, what ever happened to good old-fashioned anarchy, huh? You bogus "members in good standing" of the corporate cartel. Go, run your daring exposés on capitalism and democracy. Run them right beside your money-grovelling ads for subscribers and Classifieds, you pathetic overweight ex-hippies. Try playing your Grateful Dead 8-tracks a few more times. What you need is a lesson in revolution and so help me God, the minute my parents let me out of this room, I'm going to burn your weak-ass paper to a crisp.

☐ YES, I WANT TO BUY A ONE YEAR SUBSCRIPTION TO THE VILLAGE VOICE.

National Rate: $47.95 (Just 92¢ per copy)
New York Metro Rate: $44.95 (NY, NJ & CT: Just 86¢ per copy)
To order, call toll-free 1-800-336-0686 Or mail this coupon to:
The Village Voice Subscriptions, P.O. Box 1905, Marion, OH 43302.

Name_____
Address_____
City/State/Zip_____
Amount enclosed $_____ Bill me_____
Charge Me: AmEx_____ M/C_____ VISA_____
Credit Card #_____Exp Date_____
Signature_____

VOICE

Rates good in U.S. only. Canadian and foreign subscriptions $79.20 per year; must have payment with order. Allow 4-6 wks for delivery. For address changes, call 1-800-347-6969.

☐ Murderers!

Trees are being systematically swallowed up by the jaws of industry and still you insist I take part in this horror by subscribing? What could you possibly have to say that's grander than the mighty Pine or the proud Oak? This symbol of the Earth's majesty, stretching high into the air, is desperately seeking solace. Mercy! Oh please hear its cry. Perhaps you have been deafened by the volume of your own clever thoughts? You dig a knife into its belly and drag the carcass to be flayed. You strip off the skin and grind its flesh into a sappy pulp. Then you dance on its grave by printing your petty witticisms on the remains. I'd rather be nailed to the largest Elm in the forest than receive your heartless publication.

☐ YES, I WANT TO BUY A YEAR SUBSCRIPTION TO THE VILLAGE VOICE.

National Rate: $47.95 (Just 92¢ per copy) New York Metro Rate: $44.95 (NY, NJ & CT: Just 86¢ per copy)
To order, call toll-free 1-800-336-0686 Or mail this coupon to: The Village Voice Subscriptions, P.O. Box 1905, Marion, OH 43302.

Name_____Address_____City/State/Zip_____
Amount enclosed $_____Bill me_____Charge Me: AmEx_____M/C_____VISA_____
Credit Card #_____Exp Date_____Signature_____ **VOICE**

Rates good in U.S. only. Canadian and foreign subscriptions $79.20 per year; must have payment with order. Allow 4-6 wks for delivery. For address changes, call 1-800-347-6969.

☐ OHMYGAWD!

With all the to-die-for gorgeous people in the world, why would I subscribe to a paper with such El Gross-oes in it? I mean, like, instead of criminals, how about a great role model, like Debbie Gibson. She's so totally fab. Or instead of drug dealers on the block, why not The New Kids on the Block? You know, people aren't as interested in politics as you think. We're much more into Luke Perry (F.Y.I). If he ran for office, we'd be more interested. Or if say J.F.K. Jr. and Madonna got married and one of them ran? Way cool. Incidentally, the concept of reducing the city's budget without reducing expenditure on crucial social services programs is like, you know, good.

☐ YES, I WANT TO BUY A YEAR SUBSCRIPTION TO THE VILLAGE VOICE.

National Rate: $47.95 (Just 92¢ per copy) New York Metro Rate: $44.95 (NY, NJ & CT: Just 86¢ per copy)
To order, call toll-free 1-800-336-0686. Or mail this coupon to: The Village Voice Subscriptions, P.O. Box 1905, Marion, OH 43302.

Name_____Address_____City/State/Zip_____
Amount enclosed $_____Bill me_____Charge Me: AmEx_____M/C_____VISA_____
Credit Card #_____Exp Date_____Signature_____ **VOICE**

Rates good in U.S. only. Canadian and foreign subscriptions $79.20 per year; must have payment with order. Allow 4-6 wks for delivery. For address changes, call 1-800-347-6969.

Silver/Campaign/Trade Newspaper

ART DIRECTOR
John Doyle

COPYWRITER
Ernie Schenck

PHOTOGRAPHERS
Paul Clany, Curt Berner

ILLUSTRATOR
Peter Hall

AGENCY
Doyle A & D Group

CLIENT
The Dunham Company

MANY TIMES THE EFFECTS OF STRESS DON'T SHOW UP ON THE JOB.

The fact is, stress keeps close to one million people from going to work every day.

For many businesses, this is leading to expensive, long-term disabilities costing an average of $73,000 each claim.

Even when employees make it to work, stress has now become the number-one hazard in the workplace. Three out of four employees say they have frequent illness caused by stress.

Let's do something about it.

At Northwestern National Life, our disability programs specialize in the rehabilitation of stress-disabled workers. In fact, they have saved employers $38 for every $1 invested in stress rehabilitation.

To help you better measure the extent of your employees' stress, let us send you our new 1992 research— *Burnout: Causes and Cures.*

For your free copy, call or write Rick Naymark, Northwestern National Life, Box 20, Minneapolis, MN 55440, (612) 342-7137.

We want to help uncover the problems you and your employees may be having with stress.

Northwestern National Life

JUST HOW ACCURATE IS YOUR HEALTH CLAIM SERVICE?

Trouble is, a lot of claim-paying services are missing something.

It seems they're either accurate and slow, or they're fast but sometimes miss the mark.

Let's do something about it.

At Northwestern National Life, we're doing something about the inconsistencies in claim service. For example, we guarantee 98% financial and 95% payment accuracy on claims. And we guarantee 80% of all your claims will be paid within 14 calendar days. All of which are standards you asked for.

On top of that, we guarantee your complete satisfaction on everything we do, unconditionally. Or we credit your account up to 5% in each of these areas.

To help you better review your current claim service, we'd like to send you our booklet— *Getting the Most Out of Your Claim Service.*

To get your free copy, call or write Rick Naymark, Northwestern National Life, Box 20, Minneapolis, MN 55440, (612) 342-7137.

Remember, with our service guarantees you know you won't get thrown a curve.

Northwestern National Life

THAT'S NOTHING. NOW TRY TRAINING EMPLOYEES TO MAKE WISE HEALTH CARE DECISIONS.

These days, benefit managers often have to deal with a real balancing act.

Because on one hand, you're trying to give your employees health benefits they can put to good use. And on the other hand, you're trying to teach them how to use their benefits wisely.

It's a tough act to perform well.

Let's do something about it.

At Northwestern National Life, we're doing something to help employees be more active in managing their health care decisions. For example, we help design health plans that encourage employees to be better consumers of health care.

And then we support you with employee education such as our new booklet— *Helping Employees Use Health Care Wisely.*

For your free copy call or write Rick Naymark, Northwestern National Life, Box 20, Minneapolis, MN 55440, (612) 342-7137.

When it comes to helping employees use health care wisely, we've really got our act together.

Northwestern National Life

Silver/Campaign/Trade Newspaper

ART DIRECTOR
John Doyle

COPYWRITER
Ernie Schenck

PHOTOGRAPHERS
Paul Clany, Curt Berner

ILLUSTRATOR
Peter Hall

AGENCY
Doyle A & D Group

CLIENT
The Dunham Company

Gold/Trade Newspaper
ART DIRECTOR
John Doyle
COPYWRITER
Ernie Schenck
PHOTOGRAPHER
Nadav Kander
AGENCY
Doyle A & D Group
CLIENT
The Dunham Company

There are feet that have never seen a David Hockney. There are feet that have never walked the streets of Cannes. There are feet unfamiliar with beluga at midnight. Dunham. They get the job done.

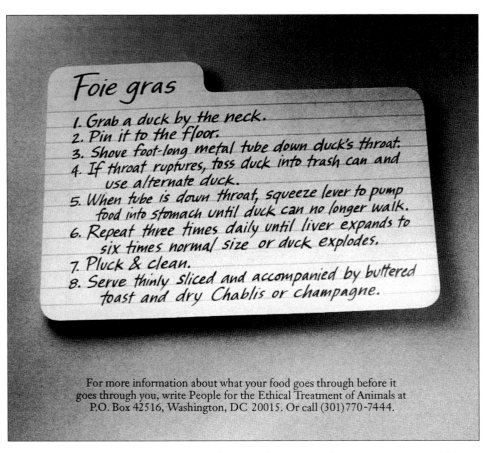

For more information about what your food goes through before it goes through you, write People for the Ethical Treatment of Animals at P.O. Box 42516, Washington, DC 20015. Or call (301)770-7444.

Silver/Public Service Newspaper
ART DIRECTOR/PHOTOGRAPHER
Bob Barrie
COPYWRITER
Jamie Barrett
AGENCY
Fallon McElligott
CLIENT
People for the Ethical Treatment of Animals

Distinctive Merit/Public Service Newspaper
ART DIRECTOR/CREATIVE DIRECTOR
John Staffen
COPYWRITER/CREATIVE DIRECTOR
Mike Rogers
EXECUTIVE CREATIVE DIRECTORS
Jack Mariucci, Bob Mackall
AGENCY
DDB Needham Worldwide
CLIENT
Earthshare

NEXT MONTH

Bless you. Recycle this newspaper and it will be used again. As tissue. Toilet paper. Paper towels.

YOU'LL BE

Or stationery. You'll be reducing solid waste. Preserving our forests. But why stop there? Use cloth

BLOWING YOUR

shopping bags. Buy energy-saving light bulbs. Compost the lawn clippings. For more ways

NOSE WITH

to help, call Earth Share 1-800-488-8887. Because the last thing a newspaper should be is trash.

THIS AD.

A Public Service of This Publication

Earth Share

Silver/Campaign/Public Service Newspaper

ART DIRECTOR
Mitch Gordon

COPYWRITER
George Gier

AGENCY
DDB Needham Worldwide

CLIENT
Lake Michigan Federation

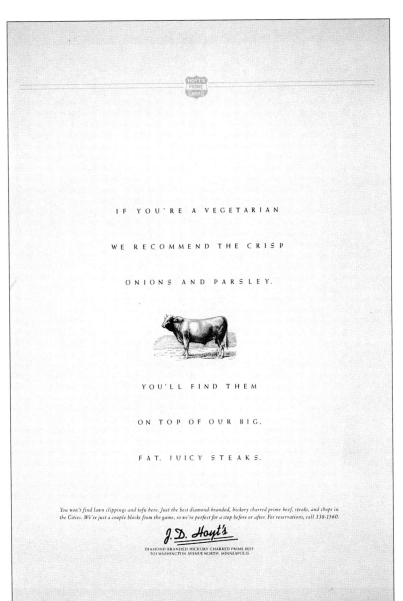

IF YOU'RE A VEGETARIAN

WE RECOMMEND THE CRISP

ONIONS AND PARSLEY.

YOU'LL FIND THEM

ON TOP OF OUR BIG.

FAT. JUICY STEAKS.

You won't find lawn clippings and tofu here. Just the best diamond-branded, hickory charred prime beef, steaks, and chops in
the Cities. We're just a couple blocks from the game, so we're perfect for a stop before or after. For reservations, call 338-1560.

J.D. Hoyt's

DIAMOND BRANDED HICKORY CHARRED PRIME BEEF
301 WASHINGTON AVENUE NORTH, MINNEAPOLIS

Distinctive Merit/Consumer Magazine
ART DIRECTOR
Susan Griek
COPYWRITER
Luke Sullivan
AGENCY
Fallon McElligott
CLIENT
J.D. Hoyt's

Silver/Consumer Magazine
COPYWRITER
Kerry Casey
PHOTOGRAPHER
Shawn Michienzi
AGENCY
Carmichael Lynch
CLIENT
Normark

It wiggles like Elvis.
It wobbles like Elvis.
Elvis, is that you?

Rapala
NORMARK
© 1991 Normark Corporation, 1710 East 78th Street, Minneapolis, Minnesota 55423

Distinctive Merit/Consumer Magazine

ART DIRECTOR
Jelly Helm

COPYWRITER
Joe Alexander

PHOTOGRAPHER
Dublin Productions

AGENCY
The Martin Agency

CLIENT
Health-tex

Distinctive Merit/Consumer Magazine

ART DIRECTOR
Jelly Helm

COPYWRITER
Joe Alexander

PHOTOGRAPHER
Dublin Productions

AGENCY
The Martin Agency

CLIENT
Health-tex

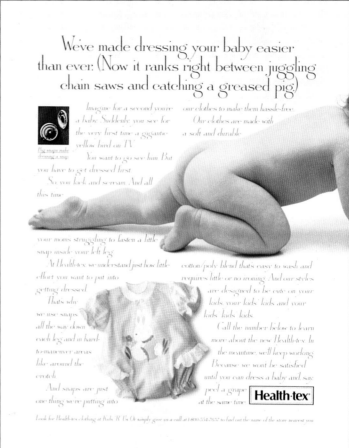

WHAT TO HAVE ON YOUR FEET WHEN THE ONLY THING DRY IS THE HEAVES.

number of leading edges exceeds the traction capacity of traditional soles by a good 50 percent. What's more, the edges are clustered in a special quadrant cut pattern, a Timberland exclusive. This new cut so amplifies grip that any comparison with the traditional wave cut (a design almost three decades old) becomes a lopsided contest. Wave cuts are obsolete, period.

Part Two of the Interactive Grip System makes sure that your foot stays in the right place so the quadrant cut sole can do its work. Your foot is secured by an Internal Fit System, a contoured sleeve that keeps your toes from jamming when the boat makes a violent lurch.

All of which may leave only one place for your old boat shoes.

Dry land.

INTERACTIVE GRIP SYSTEM

Quadrant cut sole has 50% more leading edges than standard wave cut soles.

Quadrant cut exceeds wave cut for traction, providing 360° of grip.

Internal Fit System keeps foot in correct position for comfort, balance and grip.

If you know the sea, you know there are those days when nothing will stay down.

Not breakfast. Not lunch. Not even a rum and tonic. And certainly not the boat, which the ocean seems to be trying to upchuck.

On such days the waves look like bile. They look the way your intestinal tract feels. No wonder they call it "blowing like stink."

In turbulence so extreme, there may not be a boat shoe on the face of the earth that can give the experienced sailor all the protection, agility and traction he deserves.

We'd like to introduce the one possible exception. A new class of performance boat shoes from Timberland. Shoes that are proving so superior to anything else in competitive trials we urge you to check them out.

What drives these shoes is a proprietary technology called the Interactive Grip System. So named for its ability to maximize slip resistance through the interaction of a radically advanced sole design with the hazardous surface of a storm-tossed deck.

Let us explain, starting with the sole. It has such a profusion of siping (razor cuts for traction) that the

Timberland ®
BOOTS, SHOES, CLOTHING, WIND, WATER, EARTH AND SKY.

Distinctive Merit/Consumer Magazine
ART DIRECTOR
Margaret McGovern
COPYWRITER
Paul Silverman
PHOTOGRAPHER
John Holt Studio
AGENCY
Mullen
CLIENT
The Timberland Co.

While you don't necessarily dress for men, it doesn't hurt, on occasion, to see one drool like the pathetic dog that he is.

BODYSLIMMERS™ by NANCY GANZ

Silver/Consumer Magazine
ART DIRECTOR
Noam Murro
COPYWRITER
Eddie Van Bloem
PHOTOGRAPHER
Ilan Rubin
AGENCY
Goldsmith/Jeffrey
CLIENT
Bodyslimmers

Silver/Consumer Magazine
ART DIRECTOR
Margaret McGovern
COPYWRITER
Paul Silverman
PHOTOGRAPHER
John Holt Studio
AGENCY
Mullen
CLIENT
The Timberland Co.

Silver/Consumer Magazine
ART DIRECTORS
Bill Boch, Tim Hanrahan
COPYWRITER
Ron Lawner
PHOTOGRAPHER
Kenji Toma
HAND LETTERER
John Stevens
AGENCY
Arnold Fortuna Lawner & Cabot
CLIENT
Kinney Shoes

BOAT SHOES SHOULD BE JUDGED BY HOW THEY GO WITH A BLACK SKY. NOT A BLUE BLAZER.

Silver/Consumer Magazine
ART DIRECTORS
Bill Boch, Tim Hanrahan
COPYWRITER
Ron Lawner
PHOTOGRAPHER
Robert Tardio
HAND LETTERER
John Stevens
AGENCY
Arnold Fortuna Lawner & Cabot
CLIENT
Kinney Shoes

Silver/Consumer Magazine
ART DIRECTOR
Bill Boch
DESIGNER
Tim Hanrahan
COPYWRITER
Ron Lawner
PHOTOGRAPHER
Robert Tardio
AGENCY
Arnold Fortuna Lawner &Cabot
CLIENT
Kinney Shoes

These elegant leather T-straps now open up to more fluid lines and richer hues. And you'll find them at Kinney for about forty three dollars. That's right, Kinney. The reason we didn't put a big Kinney logo on this ad is because there are some people who still don't think of Kinney as a place to buy fashionable leather shoes. Hey, fashion is where you find it.

This year black suede dances out of the dark with shimmering gold straps. You'll find them at Kinney for about thirty seven dollars. That's right, Kinney. The reason we didn't put a big Kinney logo on this ad is because there are some people who still don't think of Kinney as a place to buy fashionable leather shoes. Hey, fashion is where you find it.

Silver/Consumer Magazine

ART DIRECTOR
Gary Goldsmith

COPYWRITER
Dean Hacohen

ILLUSTRATOR
Chris Wormell

AGENCY
Goldsmith/Jeffrey

CLIENT
J.P. Morgan

Silver/Consumer Magazine

ART DIRECTOR
David Angelo

COPYWRITER
Paul Spencer

EXECUTIVE CREATIVE DIRECTORS
Jack Mariucci, Bob Mackall

PHOTOGRAPHER
Neil Slavin

AGENCY
DDB Needham Worldwide

CLIENT
New York State Lottery

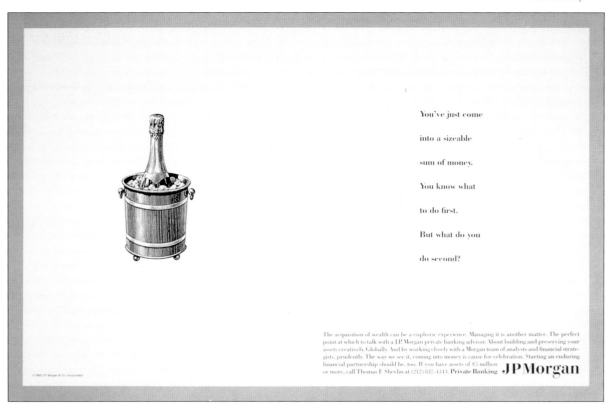

Distinctive Merit/Consumer Magazine
ART DIRECTOR
Bob Brihn
COPYWRITER
Phil Hanft
PHOTOGRAPHER
Bob Blewett
AGENCY
Fallon McElligott
CLIENT
Time Inc.

Distinctive Merit/Consumer Magazine
ART DIRECTOR
Gary Goldsmith
COPYWRITER
Dean Hacohen
ILLUSTRATOR
Chris Wormell
AGENCY
Goldsmith/Jeffrey
CLIENT
J.P. Morgan

IF ONLY IT WERE THIS EASY. In the mid-1980s, scientists believed a vaccine for AIDS would be ready in two years. Seven years later: no vaccine, no cure, and no reliable treatment. With over 150,000 dead and another 272,000 waiting to die, no American will escape the effects of this century's most deadly disease. Which is why this wasn't the first nor the last time you'll find AIDS on the cover of TIME.

If it's important to you, you'll find it in TIME.

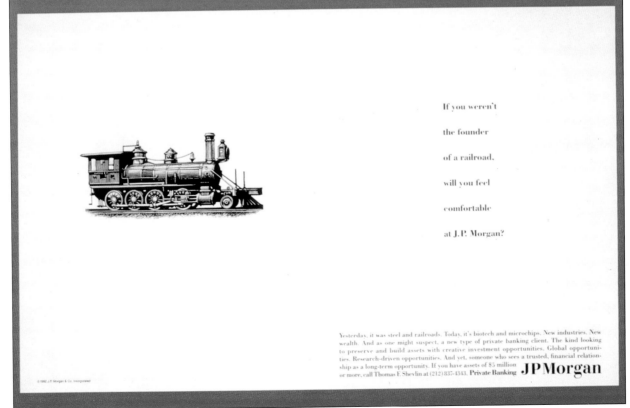

If you weren't

the founder

of a railroad,

will you feel

comfortable

at J.P. Morgan?

Yesterday, it was steel and railroads. Today, it's biotech and microchips. New industries. New wealth. And as one might suspect, a new type of private banking client. The kind looking to preserve and build assets with creative investment opportunities. Global opportunities. Research-driven opportunities. And yet, someone who sees a trusted, financial relationship as a long-term opportunity. If you have assets of $5 million or more, call Thomas E. Shevlin at (212)837-4343. **Private Banking** **JPMorgan**

Soil can erode
at the rate of up to
one inch per year.
Now a word about
financial assets.

Taxes take a nibble here. A nibble there. Then inflation takes a bite. Little wonder the average financial portfolio gets eaten away over time. Precisely why every J.P. Morgan advisor offers a range of global investment services to balance risk and reward. Analysts, traders, and financial strategists who focus on increasing long-term reward. And generational planning services to transfer that reward. Better still, the best way to make sure your assets won't erode over time is to start a financial relationship that won't, either. If you have assets of $5 million or more, call Thomas E. Shevlin at (212) 837-4343. **Private Banking** **JP Morgan**

© 1992 J.P. Morgan & Co. incorporated

Welcome to the 1992 Lee National Marketing Meeting.

June 22-26 · Marriott Plaza Hotel · Kansas City **Lee**

Distinctive Merit/Consumer Magazine

ART DIRECTOR
Gary Goldsmith

COPYWRITER
Dean Hacohen

ILLUSTRATOR
Chris Wormell

AGENCY
Goldsmith/Jeffrey

CLIENT
J.P. Morgan

Distinctive Merit/Consumer Magazine

ART DIRECTOR
Ellen Steinberg

COPYWRITER
David Statman

PHOTOGRAPHER
Guzman

AGENCY
Weiss, Whitten, Carroll, Stagliano

CLIENT
Escada USA/Apriori

Gold/Campaign/Consumer Magazine

ART DIRECTOR
Ellen Steinberg

COPYWRITERS
Ernest Lupinacci, David Statman

PHOTOGRAPHER
Guzman

AGENCY
Weiss, Whitten, Carroll, Stagliano

CLIENT
Escada USA/Apriori

The creators of Apriori clothing
take pride in the fact that other companies
have been turned on by their designs.

The creators of Apriori clothing
are always surprised by
where their designs wind up.

,Campaign/Consumer Magazine

DIRECTOR
Gary Goldsmith

COPYWRITER
Dean Hacohen

ILLUSTRATOR
Chris Wormell

AGENCY
Goldsmith/Jeffrey

CLIENT
J.P. Morgan

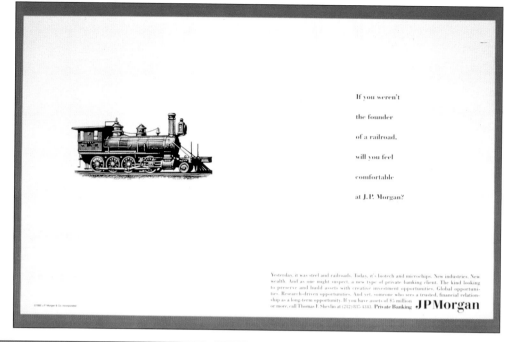

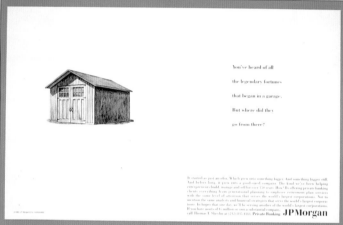

Silver/Campaign/Consumer Magazine

ART DIRECTORS
Bill Bosch, Liz Doten,
Tim Hanrahan

COPYWRITER
Ron Lawner

PHOTOGRAPHERS
Raymond Meier, Kenji Toma,
Robert Tardio

AGENCY
Arnold Fortuna Lawner & Cabot

CLIENT
Kinney Shoes

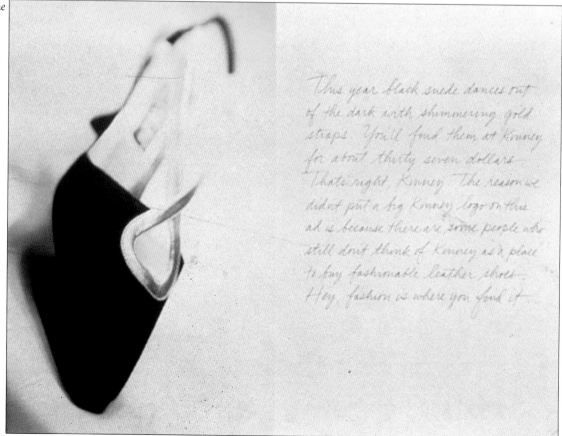

We've made dressing your baby easier than ever: (Now it ranks right between juggling chain saws and catching a greased pig.)

Babies tormented by their clothes. On the next Oprah.

Silver/Campaign/Consumer Magazine

ART DIRECTOR
Jelly Helm

COPYWRITER
Joe Alexander

PHOTOGRAPHER
Dublin Productions

AGENCY
The Martin Agency

CLIENT
Health-tex

This sleek slingback is crafted in butter soft full grain leather and sells for about thirty dollars. Flingo at Kinney. That's right, Kinney. The reason we didn't put a big Kinney logo on this ad is because there are some people who still don't think of Kinney as a place to buy fashionable leather shoes. Hey, fashion is where you find it.

This luxurious washed silk slide stands on a leather sole with a short pedestal heel. They sell for about thirty dollars at Kinney. That's right, Kinney. The reason we didn't put a big Kinney logo on this ad is because there are some people who still don't think of Kinney as a place to buy fashionable leather shoes. Hey, fashion is where you find it.

Distinctive Merit/Campaign/Consumer Magazine

ART DIRECTOR/HAND LETTERER
Tim Hanrahan

COPYWRITER
Ron Lawner

PHOTOGRAPHER
Robert Tardio

AGENCY
Arnold Fortuna Lawner & Cabot

CLIENT
Kinney Shoes

ADVERTISING

Distinctive Merit/Campaign/Consumer Magazine

ART DIRECTOR
Bill Bosch

DESIGNER
Tim Hanrahan

COPYWRITER
Ron Lawner

PHOTOGRAPHERS
Kenji Toma, Robert Tardio

AGENCY
Arnold Fortuna Lawner & Cabot

CLIENT
Kinney Shoes

Distinctive Merit/Campaign/Consumer Magazine

ART DIRECTOR
Margaret McGovern

COPYWRITER
Paul Silverman

PRODUCTION
John Holt Studio

AGENCY
Mullen

CLIENT
The Timberland Co.

Gold/Trade Magazine
ART DIRECTOR
John Vitro
COPYWRITER
John Robertson
PHOTOGRAPHER
Gary Braasch
AGENCY
Franklin Stoorza
CLIENT
Taylor Guitar

IN ONE PAIR OF HANDS,
A PIECE OF FINE WOOD
CAN BECOME A LIVING ROOM
COFFEE TABLE.

IN ANOTHER PAIR OF HANDS,
THAT PIECE OF WOOD
CAN BECOME THE SWEETEST-
SOUNDING GUITAR.

THIS IS FOR EVERYONE
WHO HAS NO DESIRE TO PLAY
THE COFFEE TABLE.

Some trees become pencils. Some trees become paper that becomes guitar magazines. Some trees become shoe trees. Some trees become Taylor guitars. Some trees have all the luck. Write us: 1040 Gillespie Way, El Cajon, CA 92020.

Distinctive Merit/Trade Magazine
ART DIRECTOR
Tom Lichtenheld
COPYWRITER
Bruce Bildsten
AGENCY
Fallon McElligott
CLIENT
Fallon McElligott

Distinctive Merit/Trade Magazine
ART DIRECTORS/COPYWRITERS
Shalom Auslander, Mikal Reich
AGENCY
Mad Dogs & Englishmen
CLIENT
Economist Magazine

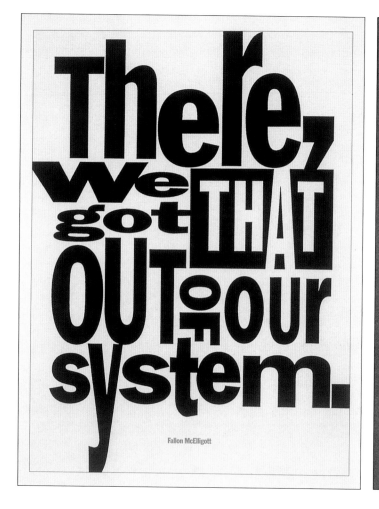

There, we got THAT OUT OF our system.

Fallon McElligott

63%
Percentage of business
magazine readers
who had lemonade stands
as children.

80%
Percentage of Economist
readers who opened
adjacent ice cube stands.

The Economist

Silver/Trade Magazine
ART DIRECTOR
John Vitro
COPYWRITER
John Robertson
PHOTOGRAPHER
Art Wolfe
AGENCY
Franklin Stoorza
CLIENT
Taylor Guitar

Silver/Trade Magazine
ART DIRECTOR
John Vitro
COPYWRITER
John Robertson
PHOTOGRAPHER
Art Wolfe
AGENCY
Franklin Stoorza
CLIENT
Taylor Guitar

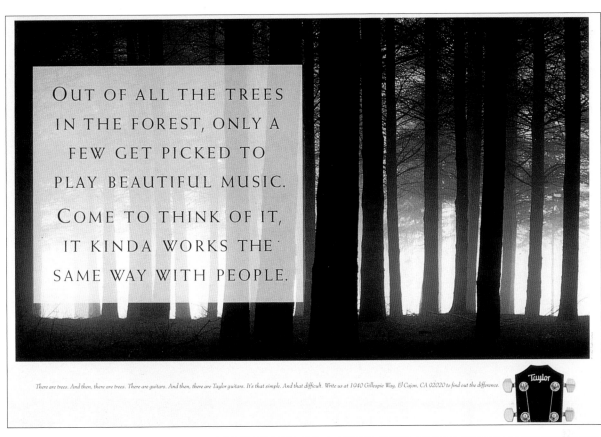

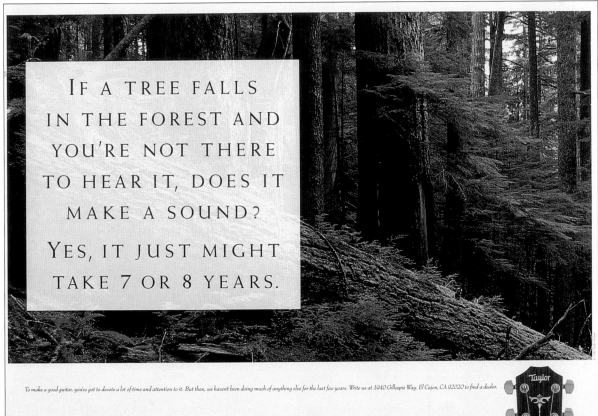

Silver/Trade Magazine
ART DIRECTOR
Margaret McGovern
COPYWRITER
Paul Silverman
PRODUCTION
John Holt Studio
AGENCY
Mullen
CLIENT
The Timberland Co.

Distinctive Merit/Trade Magazine
ART DIRECTOR
Margaret McGovern
COPYWRITER
Paul Silverman
PRODUCTION
John Holt Studio
AGENCY
Mullen
CLIENT
The Timberland Co.

WHAT TO HAVE ON YOUR FEET WHEN THE ONLY THING DRY IS THE HEAVES.

number of leading edges exceeds the traction capacity of traditional soles by a good 50 per-cent. What's more, the edges are clustered in a special quadrant cut pattern, a Timberland exclusive. This new cut so amplifies grip that any comparison with the traditional wave cut (a design almost three decades old) becomes a lopsided contest. Wave cuts are obsolete, period.

Part Two of the Interactive Grip System makes sure that your foot stays in the right place so the quadrant cut sole can do its work. Your foot is secured by an Internal Fit System, a contoured sleeve that keeps your toes from jamming when the boat makes a violent lurch.

All of which may leave only one place for your old boat shoes.

Dry land.

INTERACTIVE GRIP SYSTEM

Quadrant cut sole has 50% more leading edges than standard wave cut soles.

Quadrant cut exceeds wave cut for traction, providing 360° of grip.

Internal Fit System keeps foot in correct position for comfort, balance and grip.

If you know the sea, you know there are those days when nothing will stay down.

Not breakfast. Not lunch. Not even a rum and tonic. And certainly not the boat, which the ocean seems to be trying to upchuck.

On such days the waves look like bile. They look the way your intestinal tract feels. No wonder they call it "blowing like stink."

In turbulence so extreme, there may not be a boat shoe on the face of the earth that can give the experienced sailor all the protection, agility and traction he deserves.

We'd like to introduce the one possible exception. A new class of performance boat shoes from Timberland. Shoes that are proving so superior to anything else in competitive trials we urge you to check them out.

What drives these shoes is a proprietary technology called the Interactive Grip System. So named for its ability to maximize slip resistance through the interaction of a radically advanced sole design with the hazardous surface of a storm-tossed deck.

Let us explain, starting with the sole. It has such a profusion of siping (razor cuts for traction) that the

BOOTS, SHOES, CLOTHING. WIND, WATER, EARTH AND SKY.

BOAT SHOES SHOULD BE JUDGED BY HOW THEY GO WITH A BLACK SKY. NOT A BLUE BLAZER.

Don't get us wrong. If you want to use our new boat shoes with the Interactive Grip System to fox-trot across the yacht club dance floor, that's your choice. We guarantee you and your blazer will look good, and we promise to accept your money.

Just be aware that we engineered these shoes so you could dance on a very different surface. The storm-blackened foredeck of a boat that's bucking like a rodeo bull.

On so wet and treacherous a playing field, one slip of the foot could be one slip too many. Preventing it is what the

INTERACTIVE GRIP SYSTEM

Quadrant cut sole has 50% more leading edges than standard wave cut soles.

Quadrant cut exceeds wave cut for traction, providing 360° of grip.

Internal Fit System keeps foot in correct position for comfort, balance and grip.

Interactive Grip System is all about.

As its name implies, the System starts where the foot interacts with the boat. At the sole. Our new design gives you such a profusion of siping (razor cuts for traction) that the number of leading edges exceeds the traction capacity of traditional boat soles by a good 50%. What's more, the edges are clustered in an exclusive quadrant cut pattern. (Competitors beware.

The Timberland® quadrant cut sole so outgrips standard wave cut soles it may cause mutiny at the yacht club.)

Part Two of the Interactive Grip System makes sure that your foot stays in the right place so the quadrant cut sole can do its work. Your foot is secured for proper balance and energy distribution by an Internal Fit System, a contoured sleeve that keeps your toes from jamming when the boat makes a violent lurch.

These brand new bench-marks for marine footwear aren't just

high-tech, but true high performance for the 1990's. A new definition of authenticity that puts our imitators in an embarrassing place.

Overboard.

BOOTS, SHOES, CLOTHING. WIND, WATER, EARTH AND SKY.

Gold/Campaign/Trade Magazine
ART DIRECTOR
John Vitro
COPYWRITER
John Robertson
PHOTOGRAPHERS
Art Wolfe, Gary Braasch
AGENCY
Franklin Stoorza
CLIENT
Taylor Guitar

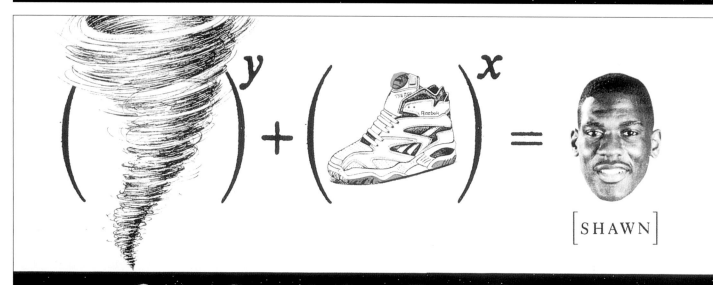

Silver/Campaign/Outdoor Poster
ART DIRECTOR/CREATIVE DIRECTOR
Tracy Wong
COPYWRITER
Rob Bagot
ILLUSTRATORS
Doug Keith, Dave Mitchell
AGENCY
Livingston & Co.
CLIENT
Seattle Supersonics

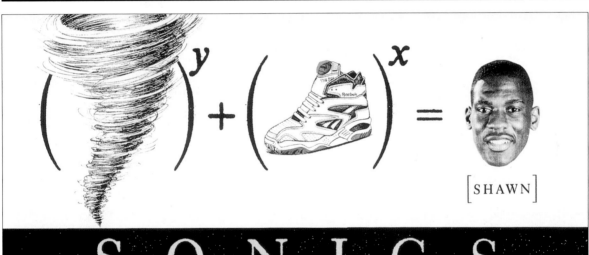

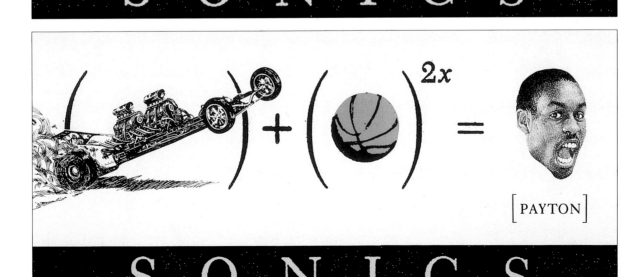

Gold/Campaign/Transit Poster
ART DIRECTOR
Kent Suter
COPYWRITER
Eric Grunbaum
PHOTOGRAPHER
Michael Jones
AGENCY
Borders, Perrin & Norrander
CLIENT
Oregon Donor Program

HAPPINESS IS BEING AN ORGAN DONOR.

OREGON DONOR PROGRAM

Feel good knowing you can help someone long after you're gone. Carry an organ donor card.

Silver/Campaign/Transit Poster

ART DIRECTOR
David Angelo

COPYWRITER
Paul Spencer

EXECUTIVE CREATIVE DIRECTORS
Jack Mariucci, Bob Mackall

PHOTOGRAPHERS
Lamb & Hall, Neil Slavin

AGENCY
DDB Needham Worldwide

CLIENT
New York State Lottery

Distinctive Merit/Transit Poster

ART DIRECTOR
David Angelo

COPYWRITER
Paul Spencer

EXECUTIVE CREATIVE DIRECTORS
Jack Mariucci, Bob Mackall

PHOTOGRAPHER
Neil Slavin

AGENCY
DDB Needham Worldwide

CLIENT
New York State Lottery

Distinctive Merit/Transit Poster

ART DIRECTOR
David Angelo

COPYWRITER
Paul Spencer

EXECUTIVE CREATIVE DIRECTORS
Jack Mariucci, Bob Mackall

PHOTOGRAPHER
Neil Slavin

AGENCY
DDB Needham Worldwide

CLIENT
New York State Lottery

Distinctive Merit/Transit Poster
ART DIRECTOR
David Angelo
COPYWRITER
Paul Spencer
EXECUTIVE CREATIVE DIRECTORS
Jack Mariucci, Bob Mackall
PHOTOGRAPHER
Lamb & Hall
AGENCY
DDB Needham Worldwide
CLIENT
New York State Lottery

Distinctive Merit/Transit Poster
ART DIRECTOR
David Angelo
COPYWRITER
Paul Spencer
EXECUTIVE CREATIVE DIRECTORS
Jack Mariucci, Bob Mackall
PHOTOGRAPHER
Joe Baraban
AGENCY
DDB Needham Worldwide
CLIENT
New York State Lottery

Distinctive Merit/Campaign/Transit Poster
ART DIRECTOR
Mike DePirro
COPYWRITER
Christina McKnight
AGENCY
J. Walter Thompson
CLIENT
Spy Magazine

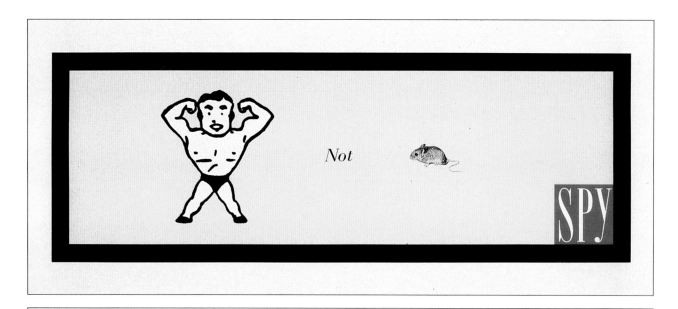

Gold/Public Service Poster

ART DIRECTOR
Mike Bevil

COPYWRITERS
Brian Brooker, Tim Bauer, Daniel Russ

AGENCY
GSD&M Advertising

CLIENT
American Civil Liberties Union

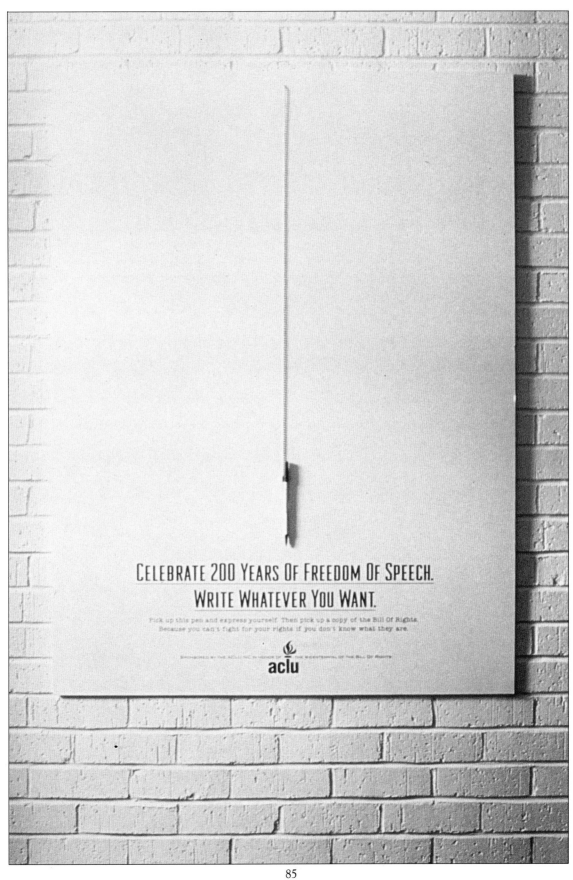

Silver/Public Service Poster

ART DIRECTOR
Chris Poulin

DESIGNER
Dana Edwards

COPYWRITER
Jonathan Plazonja

PHOTOGRAPHER
Jim Mason

AGENCY
Two Hacks and a Mac

CLIENT
CEASE

Silver/Public Service Poster

ART DIRECTOR
Dean Hanson

COPYWRITER
Doug De Groode

PHOTOGRAPHER
Shawn Michienzi

AGENCY
Fallon McElligott

CLIENT
Communities Caring for Children

Distinctive Merit/Campaign/Public Service Poster

ART DIRECTOR
Dean Hanson

COPYWRITER
Doug De Groode

ILLUSTRATOR
Mary Northrup

AGENCY
Fallon McElligott

CLIENT
Communities Caring for Children

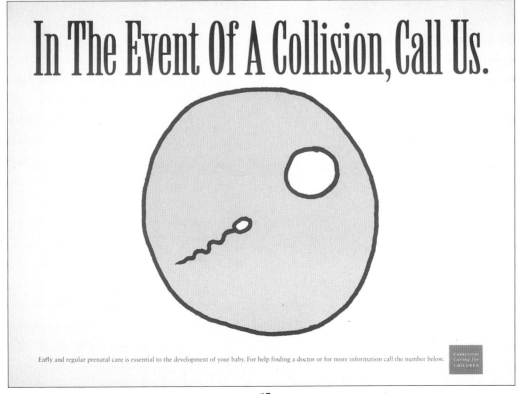

Gold/General Advertising Poster

ART DIRECTOR/COPYWRITER
Pat Harris

CREATIVE DIRECTOR
Matt Smith

PHOTOGRAPHER
Karl Stienbrenner

AGENCY
Hawley Martin Partners

CLIENT
Ace Window Cleaners

Silver/General Advertising Poster
ART DIRECTOR/COPYWRITER
Shalom Auslander
AGENCY
Mad Dogs & Englishmen
CLIENT
Village Voice

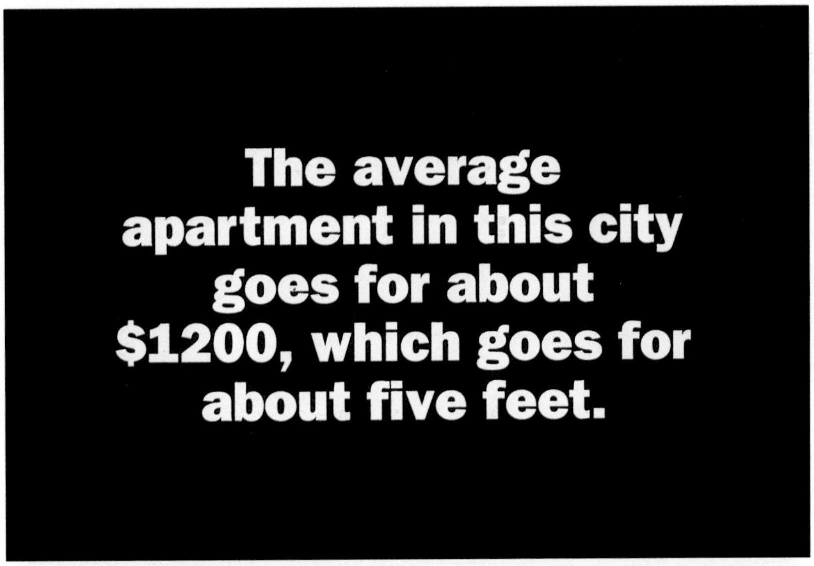

The average
apartment in this city
goes for about
$1200, which goes for
about five feet.

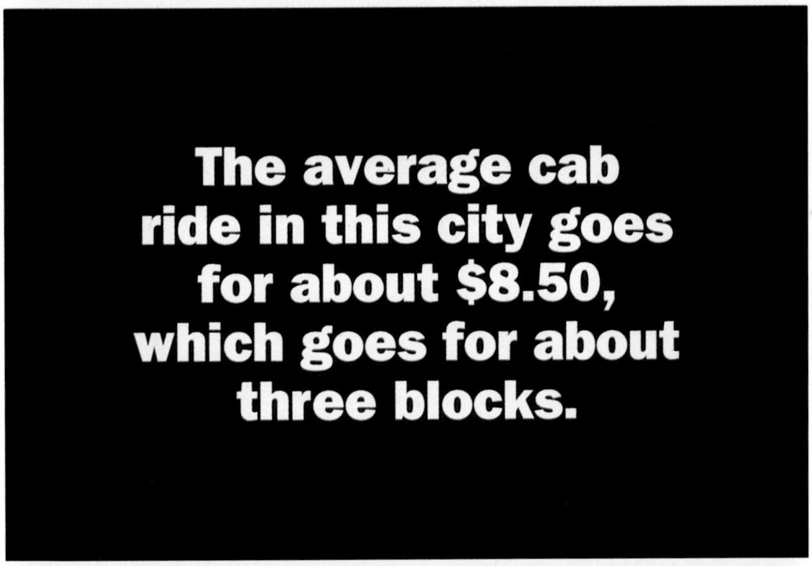

The average cab
ride in this city goes
for about $8.50,
which goes for about
three blocks.

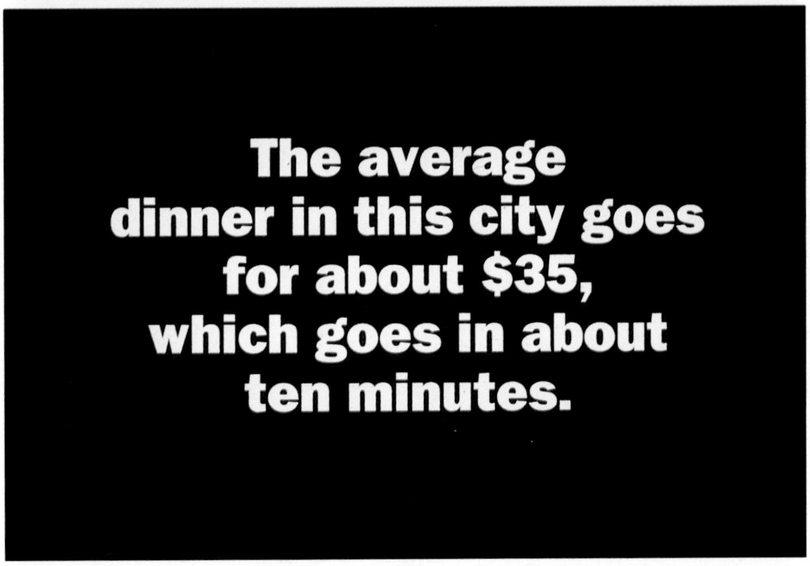

The average
dinner in this city goes
for about $35,
which goes in about
ten minutes.

Distinctive Merit/General Advertising Poster

ART DIRECTOR
Jeff Terwilliger

COPYWRITER
Kerry Casey

PHOTOGRAPHER
Pete Stone

AGENCY
Carmichael Lynch

CLIENT
Rollerblade

Distinctive Merit/General Advertising Poster

ART DIRECTOR
Margaret McGovern

COPYWRITER
Paul Silverman

PRODUCTION
John Holt Studio

AGENCY
Mullen

CLIENT
The Timberland Co.

Silver/Radio

ART DIRECTOR/COPYWRITER
Dean Hacohen

AGENCY
Goldsmith/Jeffrey

CLIENT
Crain's New York Business

Distinctive Merit/Radio

ART DIRECTOR/COPYWRITER
Dean Hacohen

AGENCY
Goldsmith/Jeffrey

CLIENT
Crain's New York Business

VO: (*spoken seriously*) Nah, nah, nah, nah, nah. You can't catch me. I'm the king of the castle. You're the dirty rascal. Missed me, missed me. Now you gotta kiss me. There's no end to the torturous remarks children will make when beating the pants off each other. Of course, at *Crain's New York Business*, we've outscooped *The New York Times* and *The Wall Street Journal* time and time again in the past year. And while we would never pour salt in a wound, we would like to mention one thing in reference to the next business story to break in this city: "Last one there's a rotten egg."

VO: The New York Metropolitan Museum of Art houses the single most extensive collection of arms and armor in the Western world. There on the main floor, are the very swords, shields, and suits of armor that safeguarded those who battled to protect their turf and expand their territory in the belligerent climate of their day. The editors of *Crain's New York Business* wish to applaud this important armory. And when the museum updates the collection to include twentieth-century artifacts, we would be happy to donate a copy of *Crain's New York Business*.

Distinctive Merit/Radio
COPYWRITER
Joe Alexander
PRODUCER
Morty Baran
AGENCY
The Martin Agency
CLIENT
Richmond Symphony

Distinctive Merit/Campaign/Radio
ART DIRECTOR/COPYWRITER
Dean Hacohen
AGENCY
Goldsmith/Jeffrey
CLIENT
Crain's New York Business

NABORS: (*singing*) Strangers in the night...
SGT. CARTER: I can't hear you!
NABORS: (*singing louder*) Strangers in the night...
SGT. CARTER: I can't hear you!
SFX: Nabors up and under.
VO: Find out how four years as Marine private Gomer Pyle
   gave a man the discipline to become one of the top
   vocalists in the world...
NABORS: (*singing even louder*): Strangers in the night...
SGT. CARTER: I can't hear you!·
SFX: Nabors up and under.
VO: Hear Jim Nabors sing with the Richmond Symphony
   Janaury 25th at the Mosque. For tickets,
   call 1-800-736-2000.

Silver/Radio

ART DIRECTOR/COPYWRITER
Dean Hacohen

AGENCY
Goldsmith/Jeffrey

CLIENT
Crain's New York Business

VO: A few years back, Frank Sinatra released his colossal hit, "New York, New York." The lyrics of which include the much repeated and ballyhooed line: "If I can make it there, I can make it anywhere." And who can forget: "I want to be A-Number-One, King of the Hill, Top of the Heap." What troubles us, is that nowhere in this song does Mr. Sinatra mention the necessity for a subscription to *Crain's New York Business*. Perhaps it was an oversight. Maybe he just forgot. Frankly, we are as surprised as you are. And sincerely hope Mr. Sinatra will consider re-recording these lyrics in the interest of making them more accurate.

Silver/Radio

COPYWRITER
Lyle Wedemeyer

PRODUCER
Mary Fran Werner

AGENCY
Martin/Williams

CLIENT
MN Department of Health

VO: A thank-you to the cigarette companies of America, from the women of America. Thank you for selecting us as a target audience of your advertising. Thank you for spending millions of advertising dollars a year to convince us that smoking makes us more attractive and more interesting. Thank you for your portrayal of us as shallow and superficial. Thank you for your condescending advertising themelines like "You've come a long way, baby." Thank you for presenting smoking as a nice break from our stressful lives. Thank you for getting us hooked. Thank you for making our hair smell like an ashtray. Thank you for staining our teeth and increasing our dry-cleaning bills. Thank you for the 52,000 cases of lung cancer you cause in women each year. Thank you for pretending you're really concerned about us, all the while you're taking in millions of dollars in profit from the cigarettes we buy. Thank you. We only hope we can return the favor some day.

Distinctive Merit/Consumer Magazine Cover

ART DIRECTOR/DESIGNER
Fred Woodward

PHOTOGRAPHER
Albert Watson

PUBLICATION
Rolling Stone Magazine

Distinctive Merit/Consumer Magazine Cover

ART DIRECTOR/DESIGNER
Fred Woodward

PHOTOGRAPHER
Herb Ritts

PUBLICATION
Rolling Stone Magazine

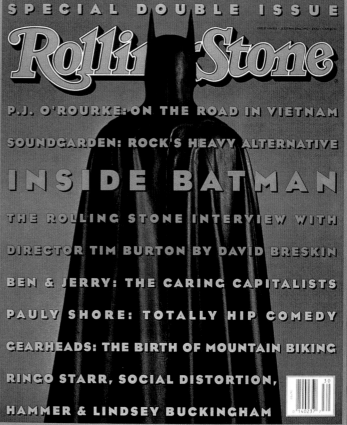

Distinctive Merit/Consumer Magazine Cover

ART DIRECTOR/DESIGNER
Fred Woodward

PHOTOGRAPHER
Herb Ritts

PUBLICATION
Rolling Stone Magazine

Distinctive Merit/Consumer Magazine Cover

ART DIRECTOR/DESIGNER
Fred Woodward

PUBLICATION
Rolling Stone Magazine

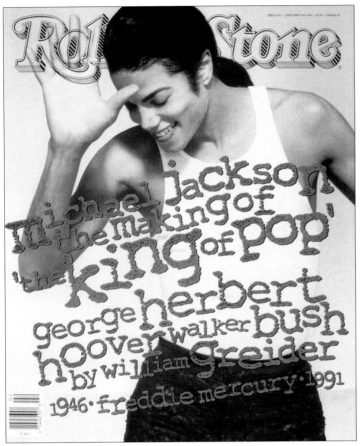

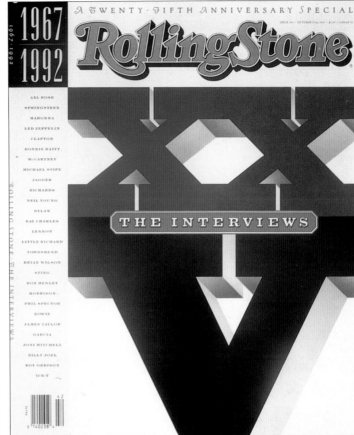

Distinctive Merit/Consumer Magazine Cover

ART DIRECTOR/DESIGNER
Fred Woodward

PHOTOGRAPHER
Albert Watson

PUBLICATION
Rolling Stone Magazine

Distinctive Merit/Consumer Magazine Cover

ART DIRECTOR
Janet Froelich

DESIGNER
Kandy Littrell

PHOTOGRAPHER
Michael O'Neill

PUBLICATION
The New York Times Magazine

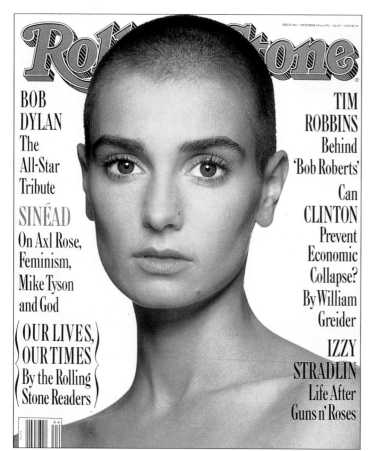

Distinctive Merit/Consumer Magazine Cover

ART DIRECTOR/WRITER/PHOTOGRAPHER
Henry Wolf
STUDIO
Henry Wolf Productions
PUBLICATION
Domus

Distinctive Merit/Consumer Magazine Cover

ART DIRECTOR
Debbie Klein
ILLUSTRATOR
Robert Saunders
PUBLICATION
Stuff Magazine

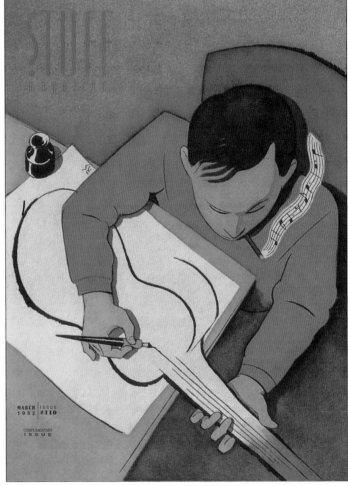

Silver/Consumer Magazine Interior

ART DIRECTOR
Fred Woodward

DESIGNER
Debra Bishop

ILLUSTRATOR
Terry Allen

PUBLICATION
Rolling Stone Magazine

Distinctive Merit/Consumer Magazine Interior

ART DIRECTOR
Fred Woodward

DESIGNER
Catherine Gilmore Barnes

WRITER
Michael Azerrad

PHOTOGRAPHER
Frank Ockenfels

PUBLICATION
Rolling Stone Magazine

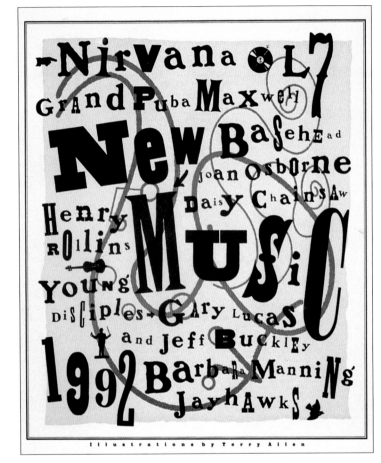

Silver/Consumer Magazine Interior
ART DIRECTOR/DESIGNER
Fred Woodward
WRITER
Patrick Goldstein
PHOTOGRAPHER
Albert Watson
PUBLICATION
Rolling Stone Magazine

Distinctive Merit/Consumer Magazine Interior
ART DIRECTOR
Fred Woodward
DESIGNER
Gail Anderson
WRITER
Jon Katz
PUBLICATION
Rolling Stone Magazine

Distinctive Merit/Consumer Magazine Interior

ART DIRECTOR
Donna M. Bonavita

WRITER
Benjamin Weiner

ILLUSTRATOR
David Shannon

STUDIO
KPMG Peat Marwick Comm.

PUBLICATION
World

Distinctive Merit/Consumer Magazine Interior

ART DIRECTOR/DESIGNER
Matthew Drace

PHOTOGRAPHER
Len Irish

PUBLICATION
Men's Journal

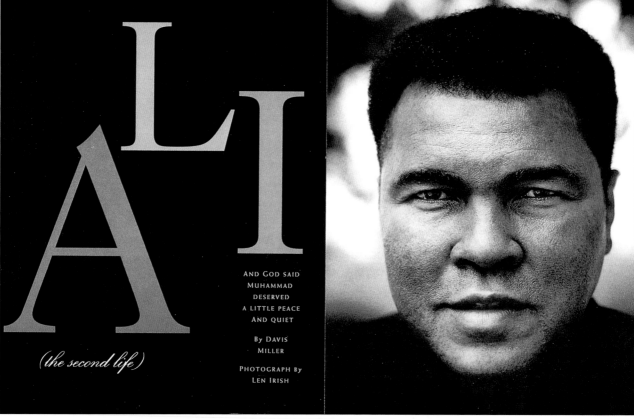

Distinctive Merit/Consumer Magazine Interior

ART DIRECTOR
Fred Woodward

DESIGNER
Debra Bishop

WRITER
Alan Light

PHOTOGRAPHER
Mark Seliger

PUBLICATION
Rolling Stone Magazine

Distinctive Merit/Consumer Magazine Interior

ART DIRECTOR
Fred Woodward

DESIGNER
Catherine Gilmore-Barnes

WRITER
Jim Henke

PHOTOGRAPHER
Herb Ritts

PUBLICATION
Rolling Stone Magazine

PHOTOGRAPHS BY MARK SELIGER

ICE

THE ROLLING STONE INTERVIEW BY ALAN LIGHT

ROLLING STONE, AUGUST 20TH, 1992 · 29

SPRINGSTEEN

The Rolling Stone Interview "In the crystal ball, I see romance, I see adventure, I see financial reward. I see those albums, man, I see them going back up the charts. I see them rising past that old Def Leppard, past that Kris Kross. I see them all the way up past 'Weird Al' Yankovic. By James Henke

PHOTOGRAPHS BY HERB RITTS

38 · ROLLING STONE, AUGUST 8TH, 1992

ROLLING STONE, AUGUST 8TH, 1992 · 39

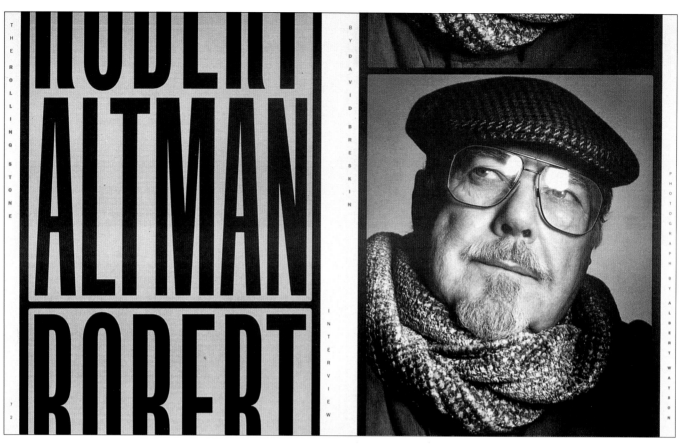

Distinctive Merit/Consumer Magazine Interior

ART DIRECTOR/DESIGNER
Fred Woodward

WRITER
David Breskin

PHOTOGRAPHER
Albert Watson

PUBLICATION
Rolling Stone Magazine

Distinctive Merit/Consumer Magazine Interior

ART DIRECTOR
Fred Woodward

DESIGNER
Angela Skouras

WRITER
Alan Light

PHOTOGRAPHER
Albert Watson

PUBLICATION
Rolling Stone Magazine

Distinctive Merit/Consumer Magazine Interior

ART DIRECTOR/DESIGNER
Fred Woodward

WRITER
Gerri Hirshey

PHOTOGRAPHER
Herb Ritts

PUBLICATION
Rolling Stone Magazine

Distinctive Merit/Consumer Magazine Interior

ART DIRECTOR/DESIGNER
Fred Woodward

COPYWRITER
Jim Squires

PHOTOGRAPHER
Philip Burke

PUBLICATION
Rolling Stone Magazine

Distinctive Merit/Consumer Magazine Interior
PUBLICATION
Creem

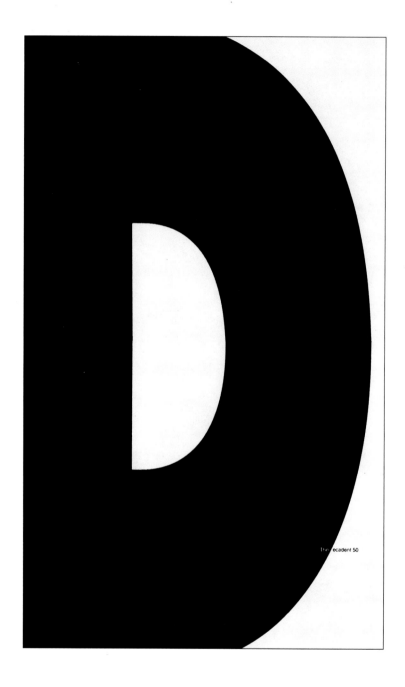

Gold/Consumer Magazine Interior Series

ART DIRECTOR

D. J. Stout

PHOTOGRAPHER

Dan Winters

PUBLICATION

Texas Monthly

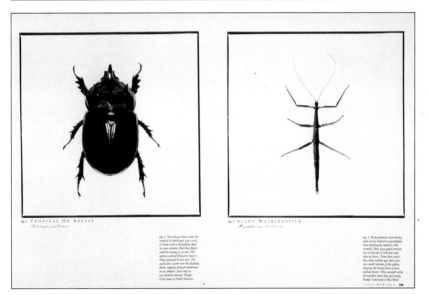

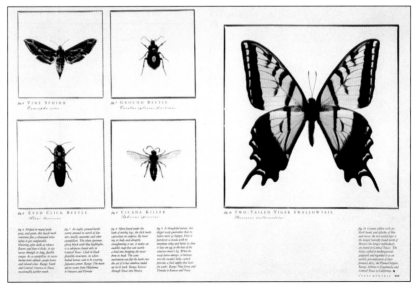

Silver/Consumer Magazine Interior Series

ART DIRECTOR
Ann Johnson

WRITER
Wendy Dubit

PHOTOGRAPHERS
Davies and Starr, Vicki Pearson

PUBLICATION
Martha Stewart Living

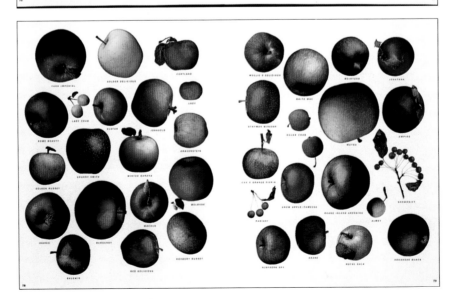

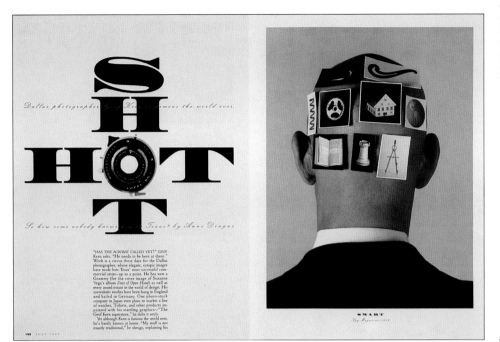

Silver/Consumer Magazine Interior Series
ART DIRECTOR
D. J. Stout
PHOTOGRAPHER
Geof Kern
PUBLICATION
Texas Monthly

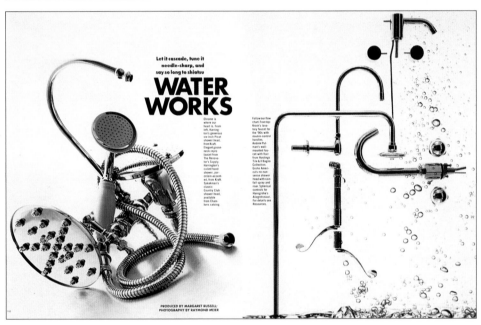

Distinctive Merit/Consumer Magazine Interior Series
ART DIRECTOR
Caroline Bowyer
DESIGNER
Jo Hay
PHOTOGRAPHER
Raymond Meier
PUBLICATION
Elle Decor

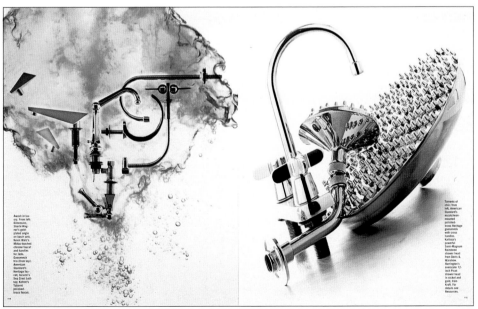

Distinctive Merit/Consumer Magazine Interior Series
ART DIRECTOR
Ann Johnson
WRITER
Corby Kummer
PHOTOGRAPHERS
Davies and Starr, Maria Robledo
PUBLICATION
Martha Stewart Living

Distinctive Merit/Consumer Magazine Interior Series
ART DIRECTOR
Fred Woodward
DESIGNER
Angela Geraldine
PHOTOGRAPHER
Steven Klein
PUBLICATION
Rolling Stone Magazine

Gold/Consumer Magazine Full Issue
ART DIRECTOR
Fred Woodward
DESIGNERS
Gail Anderson, Debra Bishop,
Catherine Gilmore Barnes,
Angela Skouras, Geraldine Hessler
PUBLICATION
Rolling Stone Magazine

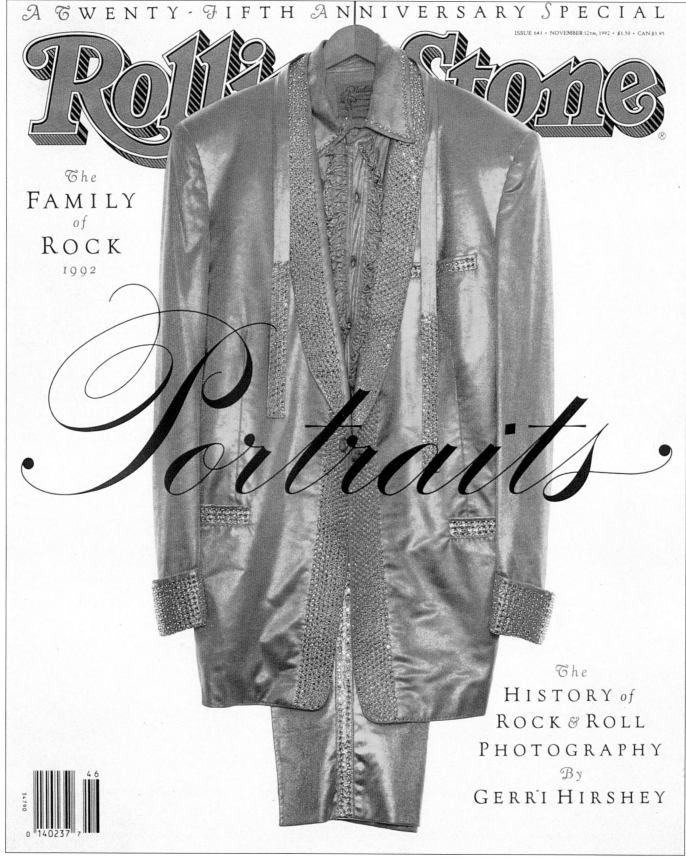

Silver/Consumer Magazine Full Issue

ART DIRECTOR
Fred Woodward

DESIGNERS
Gail Anderson, Debra Bishop,
Catherine Gilmore Barnes,
Angela Skouras, Geraldine Hessler

PUBLICATION
Rolling Stone Magazine

Distinctive Merit/Consumer Magazine Full Issue

ART DIRECTOR
Gail Towey

PUBLICATION
Martha Stewart Living

Distinctive Merit/Consumer Magazine Full Issue
ART DIRECTOR
Carl Lehmann-Haupt
DESIGNER
Nancy Cohen
PHOTOGRAPHER
Jill Greenberg
VISUAL CONTRIBUTOR
Kevin Slavin
PUBLICATION
Metropolis Magazine

Distinctive Merit/Consumer Magazine Full Issue
ART DIRECTOR/WRITER
Gary Koepke
STUDIO
Koepke Design Group
PUBLICATION
Vibe/Time Inc.

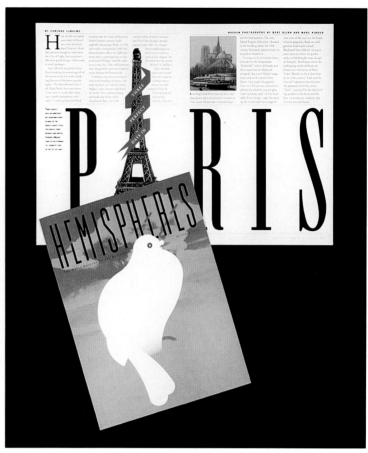

Distinctive Merit/Consumer Magazine Full Issue

ART DIRECTOR
Matthew Drace

DESIGNER
Gaemer Gutierrez

PUBLICATION
Men's Journal

Distinctive Merit/Consumer Magazine Full Issue

ART DIRECTOR
Kit Hinrichs

DESIGNER
Jackie Foshaug

STUDIO
Pentagram Design

CLIENT
United Airlines

Distinctive Merit/Consumer Magazine Full Issue

ART DIRECTOR
Fred Woodward

DESIGNERS
Gail Anderson, Debra Bishop,
Catherine Gilmore Barnes,
Angela Skouras, Geraldine Hessler

PUBLICATION
Rolling Stone Magazine

Silver/Trade Magazine Cover
ART DIRECTOR
B. Martin Pedersen
DESIGNER
Adrian Pulfer
PHOTOGRAPHER
Matthew Ralston
STUDIO
Pedersen Design Inc.
PUBLICATION
Graphis

Silver/Trade Magazine Cover

ART DIRECTOR
Adrian Pulfer

DESIGNER
B. Martin Pedersen

ILLUSTRATOR
Mick Haggerty

STUDIO
Pedersen Design Inc.

PUBLICATION
Graphis

Distinctive Merit/Trade Magazine Cover

ART DIRECTOR
B. Martin Pedersen

ILLUSTRATOR
Paul Davis

STUDIO
Pedersen Design Inc.

PUBLICATION
Graphis

Distinctive Merit/Trade Magazine Interior Series

ART DIRECTOR
B. Martin Pedersen

WRITER
Ken Coupland

PHOTOGRAPHER
Monica Lee

STUDIO
Pedersen Design Inc.

PUBLICATION
Graphis

Distinctive Merit/Trade Magazine Interior Series

ART DIRECTOR
B. Martin Pedersen

WRITER
Maggie Kinser-Saiki

PHOTOGRAPHER
Masaru Mera

STUDIO
Pedersen Design Inc.

PUBLICATION
Graphis

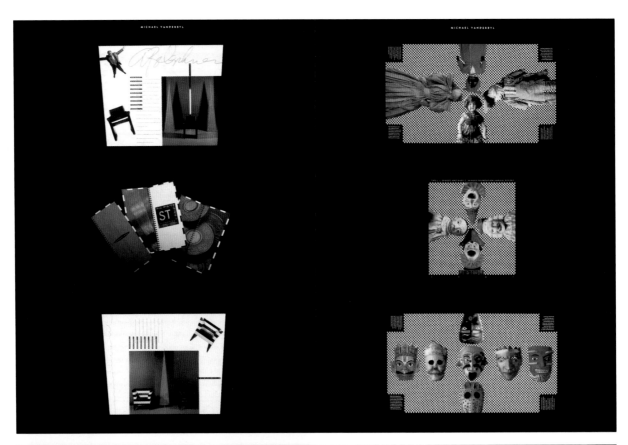

Distinctive Merit/Trade Magazine Interior Series

ART DIRECTORS
Walter Bernard, Milton Glaser

DESIGNERS
Frank Baseman, Sharon Okamoto

PHOTOGRAPHER
Matthew Klein

STUDIO
WBMG, Inc.

PUBLICATION
U&lc/International Typeface Corp.

Distinctive Merit/Trade Magazine Interior Series

ART DIRECTORS
Walter Bernard, Milton Glaser

DESIGNERS
Frank Baseman, Sharon Okamoto

WRITERS
Margaret Richardson, Joyce Rutter Kaye,
Karen Chambers, Alan Haley

STUDIO
WBMG Inc.

PUBLICATION
U&lc/International Typeface Corp.

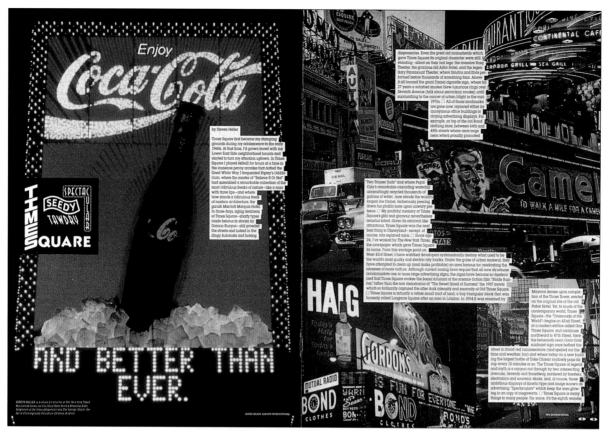

Distinctive Merit/Trade Magazine Interior Series

ART DIRECTOR
Seymour Chwast

DESIGNER
Greg Simpson

STUDIO
The Pushpin Group

PUBLICATION
International Typeface Corp.

Distinctive Merit/Trade Magazine Full Issue

ART DIRECTOR
B. Martin Pedersen

STUDIO
Pedersen Design Inc.

PUBLICATION
Graphis

Best of Show/Gold/House Publication
ART DIRECTOR/WRITER
Gary Koepke
STUDIO
Koepke Design Group
PUBLICATION
World Tour

WoRld ToUR

A REVIEW OF WORLDWIDE BUSINESS AND TECHNOLOGY NEWS PUBLISHED BY DUN & BRADSTREET SOFTWARE   VOLUME 2 NO. 1 MARCH 1992

All these people have something in common. Charles Babbage 50 Isambard Brunel 48 Chester Carlson 7 Rachel Carson 46 Confucius INSERT Nicholas Copernicus 64 Loring Crosman 29 Leonardo da Vinci INSERT Charles Darwin 42 Miles Davis 60 Simone de Beauvoir 106 Franz Fanon 106 Hugh Ferriss 85 Buckminster Fuller 91 Mahatma Gandhi 66 Joseph Glidden 89 Robert Goddard 25 Hesiod 105 Soichiro Honda 58 Raymond Hood 85 George Jenks 108 Carl Jung 62 August Kekulé 54 John Maynard Keynes 105 Charlie Klemt 21 George McGill 1 Henry Miller 38 Samuel Morse 37 Isamu Noguchi 5 Brian O'Leary 22 Gerard O'Neill 22 Donald Partridge 81 Louis Pasteur 44 Albert Pratt 33 Pierre Proudhon 104 Edwin Pynchon 99 Adam Smith 105 Robert Smithson 11 Laurence Sterne 106 Nikola Tesla 40 Frank Vester 73 Andy Warhol 52 Howard Wheeler 69 Virginia Woolf 56 **They're of the same mold, because what they set out to do was shatter the mold. They had the ability to break entrenched thought patterns in their fields, and in so doing some of them irrevocably changed the world. This issue of** *World Tour* **celebrates the act of change, sometimes called re-engineering or paradigm shifting. It's dedicated to people like these, who whether they succeed or fail, pursue visions that are often called chimeras in their generation, and reality in the next.** Technology Anti-noise 8 Artificial Islands 31 Asian TV 9 Biomass 16 Biomimicry 18 Biotechnology 10 Cartography 20 CDs 8 Computer-Aided Surgery 24 Computerized Gorilla Speech 12 DAT 36 Drug Design 26 EC Nervous System 24 Electric Cars 20 Electronic Democracy 10 Electronic Vaults 31 Eye Tracking 13 Face Interface 13 Fusion 17 Gadget Gap 26 HDTV 23 MOT Degree 24 Multimedia 10 Neural Networks 18 New Developments 6 Notebook Peripherals 18 Nuclear Power 17 Object-Oriented Programming 26 Oil 16 Patents 36 Pattern Recognition 9 Pen-Based Computers 12 Personal Communications 36 Privacy 28 Solar Fuel 16 Tech Trends 23 Teraflops 13 Turing Test 23 Wearable Computers 12 Wireless LANs 8 World Brain 9 Business Anger 79 Arms Control 101 Books 104 Capitalism 68 Corporate Espionage 101 Cuba 92 Czechoslovakia 92 Deadhead Quality 70 Deming 71 Denmark 92 Education 98 Former USSR 90 France 92 Germany 92 Global Recession 87 Great Britain 93 Green Economy 72 Hostile Takeovers 96 Hype 79 Japan 82 Korea 93 Learning Organizations 78 Maastricht 84 Marx 80 Mexico 93 Mittelstand 68 Mommy Track 78 Network Management 68 New Media 80 Offices 97 Outsourcing 72 Ozone Hole 84 Poetry 101 Populism 72 Racism 88 Self-Managed IS Teams 96 Separatism 88 Sexual Harassment 100 Spain 93 Stress 79 Total Quality 70 Tribal Knowledge 88 United States 93 Videoconferencing 96 Waste 100 Work 78 Working Smarter 97

Gold/House Publication
ART DIRECTOR/WRITER
Gary Koepke
STUDIO
Koepke Design Group
PUBLICATION
World Tour

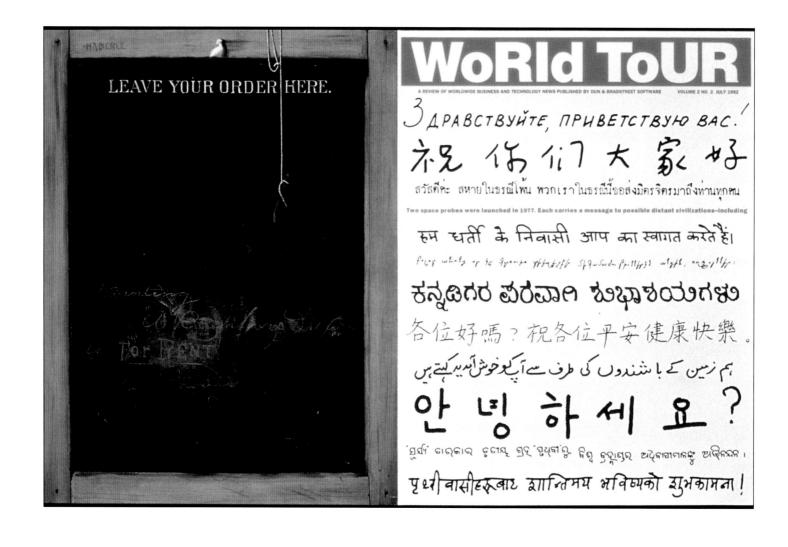

Silver/House Publication Series

ART DIRECTORS
Stephen Doyle, Paula Scher, Duane
Michals, Michael Vanderbyl, Chip Kidd

CREATIVE DIRECTORS/EDITORS
William Drenttel, Paula Scher

STUDIO
Drenttel Doyle Partners

PUBLISHER
Champion International

Silver/Book Design

ART DIRECTOR
Rita Marshall

DESIGNER
Louise Fili

ILLUSTRATOR
Gary Kelley

STUDIO
Delessert and Marshall

PUBLISHER
Creative Education

Silver/Book Design

ART DIRECTOR
Rita Marshall

ILLUSTRATOR
Christopher Wormell

STUDIO
Delessert and Marshall

PUBLISHER
Creative Education

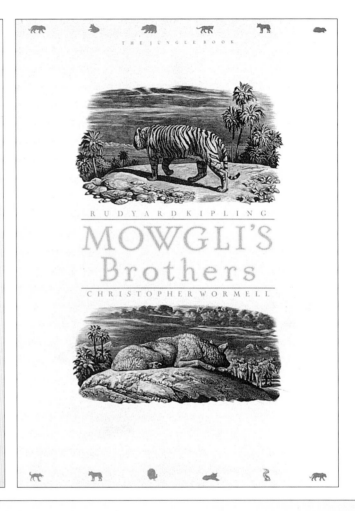

Silver/Book Design

ART DIRECTORS
Michael Gercke, Colin Forbes

WRITER
Fred Shamlian

DESIGNERS
Michael Gericke, Donna Chino,
Sharon Barel

STUDIO
Pentagram Design

PUBLISHER
Hammond Inc.

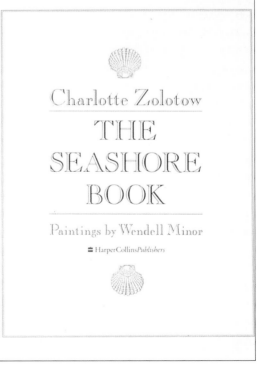

Illustrations by Etienne Delessert. Story by Rita Marshall

I Hate to Read!

All children like to read stories. The love of "the story," in some form or other, is indeed a characteristic of the human mind, and exists everywhere, in all con- ditions of life. But stories are the sweets of our mental existence, and only a few of the best and greatest have in them the ele- ments which will lead to a strong and vigor- ous mind- growth. Constant feeding upon light literature —however good that literature may be in itself— will debilitate and corrupt the men- tal appetite of the child, much the same as an un- restrained indul- gence in jam and preserves will under- mine and destroy his physi- cal health. In either case, if no result more serious occurs, the worst forms of dyspepsia will follow.

Distinctive Merit/Book Design
ART DIRECTOR
Vance Studley
CLIENT
Art Center of Design
PUBLISHER
Archetype Press

Distinctive Merit/Book Design
ART DIRECTOR
Rita Marshall
ILLUSTRATOR
Etienne Delessert
STUDIO
Delessert and Marshall
PUBLISHER
Creative Education

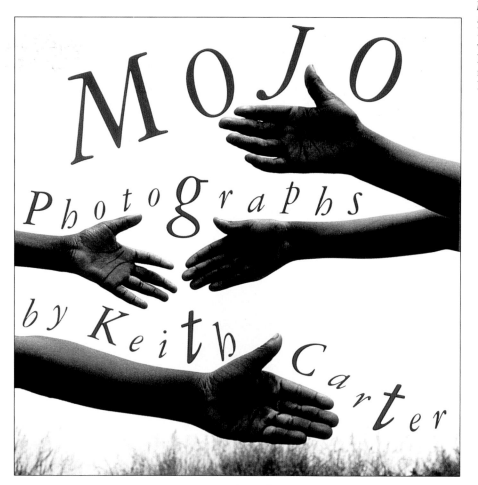

Distinctive Merit/Book Design

ART DIRECTOR
D. J. Stout

WRITER
Rosellen Brown

PHOTOGRAPHER
Keith Carter

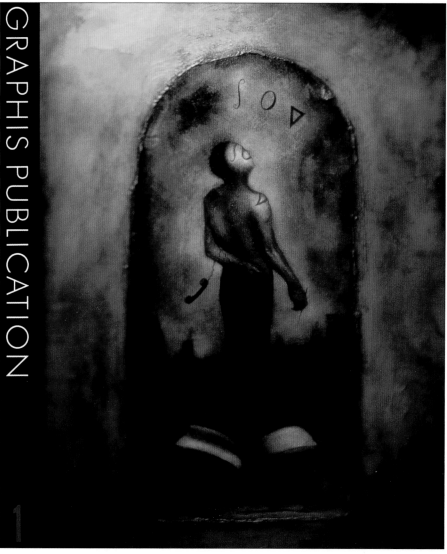

Distinctive Merit/Book Design

ART DIRECTOR
B. Martin Pedersen

DESIGNER
Adrian Pulfer

ILLUSTRATOR
Matt Mahurin

STUDIO
Pedersen Design Inc.

PUBLISHER
Graphis

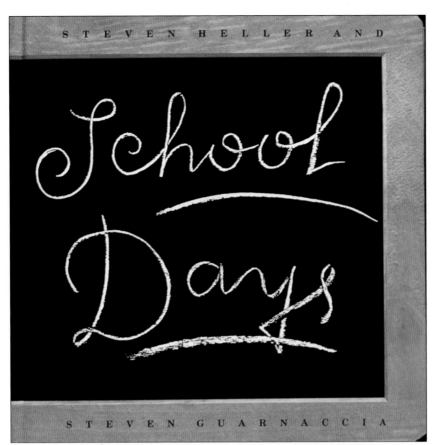

Distinctive Merit/Book Design
ART DIRECTOR
Louise Fili
WRITERS
Steven Heller, Steven Guarnaccia
PHOTOGRAPHER
William Whitehurst
PUBLISHER
Abbeville Press

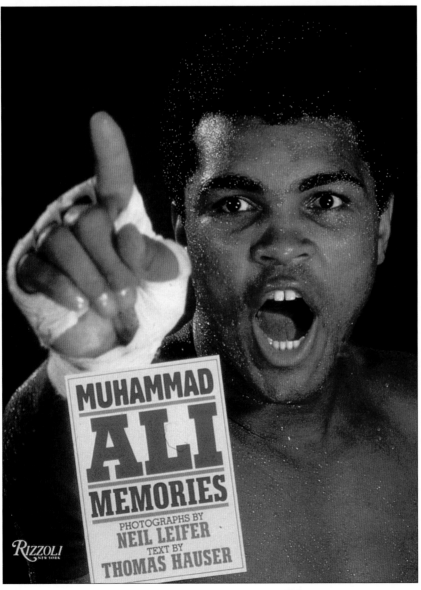

Distinctive Merit/Book Design
ART DIRECTORS
Walter Bernard, Milton Glaser
STUDIO
WBMG, Inc.

Distinctive Merit/Book Design

ART DIRECTOR
Louise Fili

DESIGNER
Lee Bearson

STUDIO
Lousie Fili

PHOTOGRAPHER
Bill Whitehurst

PUBLISHER
Abbeville Press

Distinctive Merit/Book Design

ART DIRECTORS
Paula Scher, Steven Brower

DESIGNERS
David Matt, Ron Lowe

STUDIO
Pentagram Design

PUBLISHER
Carol Publishing

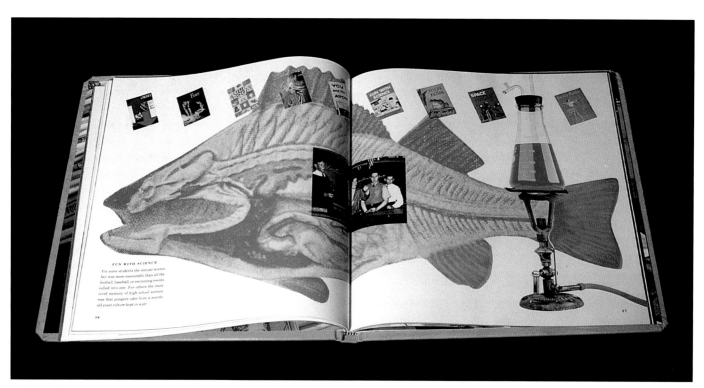

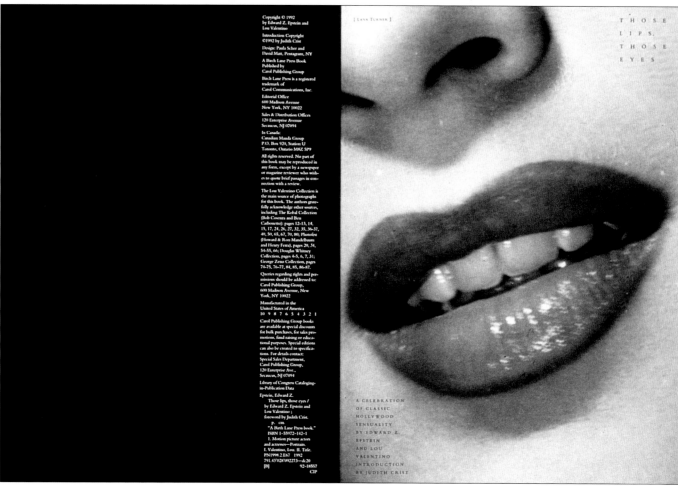

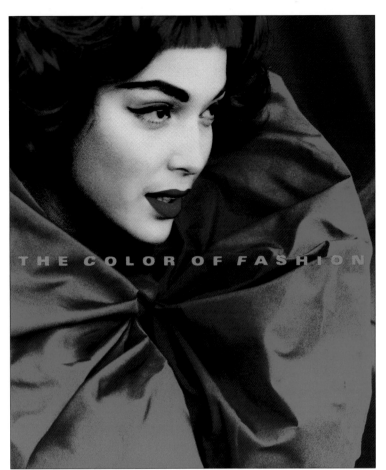

Distinctive Merit/Book Design

ART DIRECTOR
Tim Wageman

EDITORS
Lona Benny, Fran Black,
Marish Bulzone

PUBLISHER
Stewart, Tabori & Chang, Inc.

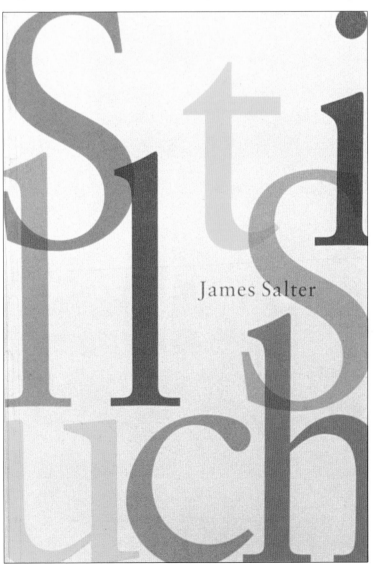

Distinctive Merit/Book Design

ART DIRECTOR
Stephen Doyle

WRITER
James Salter

PHOTOGRAPHER
Duane Michals

STUDIO
Drenttel Doyle Partners

PUBLISHER
William Drenttel

Distinctive Merit/Book Jacket Design
ART DIRECTOR
Michael Bierut
STUDIO
Pentagram Design
PUBLISHER
American Photography

Distinctive Merit/Book Jacket Design
ART DIRECTOR
Michael Bierut
STUDIO
Pentagram Design
PUBLISHER
American Photography

Distinctive Merit/Book Jacket Design

ART DIRECTOR
Stephen Doyle

PHOTOGRAPHERS
Steve Hill, Bill Gallery, Reed Davis,
Kurt Fisher, Walter Wick

STUDIO
Drenttel Doyle Partners

PUBLISHER
Harper Collins Publishers

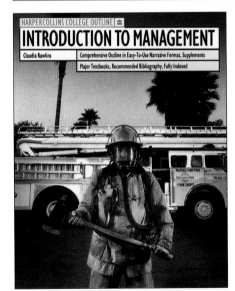

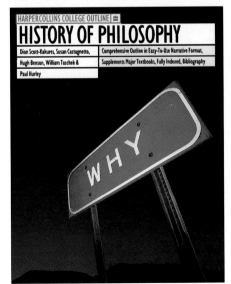

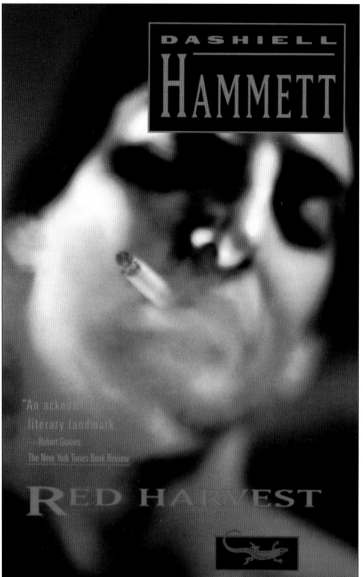

Distinctive Merit/Book Jacket Design Series
ART DIRECTOR
Susan Mitchell
DESIGNERS
Keith Sheridan, Ann Manca
PHOTOGRAPHER
Axel Crieger
STUDIO
Keith Sheridan Assoc. Inc.

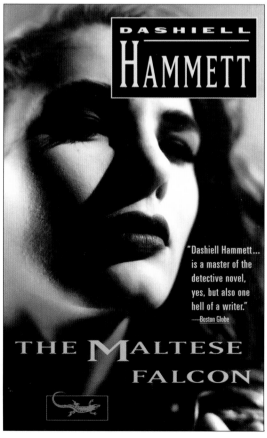

Gold/Film & Video Title Design
ART DIRECTOR
Billy Pittard
CREATIVE DIRECTOR/DIRECTOR
Judy Korin
STUDIO
Pittard/Sullivan/Fitzgerald

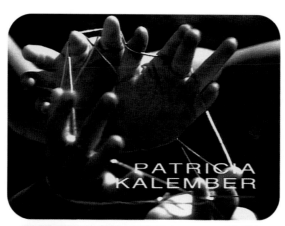

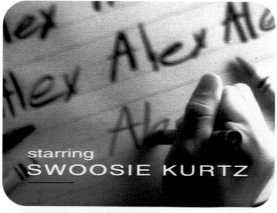

Silver/Film & Video Title Design

ART DIRECTOR
Mark Tekushan

CREATIVE DIRECTORS
Mark Tekushan, G. Griffith

DIRECTOR
Kyle Good/NBC

PRODUCER
Paul Greenberg/NBC

STUDIO
GT Group

CLIENT
NBC News

Distinctive Merit/Film & Video Title Design

ART DIRECTOR/PRODUCER
Bonnie Siegler

COPYWRITER/PRODUCER
Emily Oberman

STUDIO
MTV Network

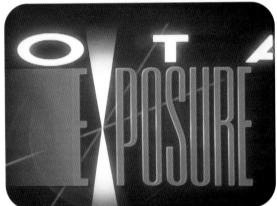

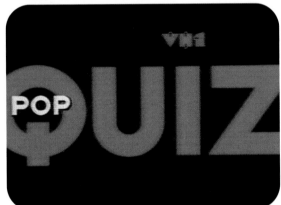

Distinctive Merit/Film & Video Title Design

ART DIRECTOR
Ed Sullian

CREATIVE DIRECTOR
Jeff Boortz

PRODUCER
John Sideropoulos

STUDIO
Pittard/Sullivan/Fitzgerald

CLIENT
John Schipp, A&E Network

Distinctive Merit/Film & Video Title Design

VP CREATIVE
Thomas Tercek

PRODUCER
Graham Mcculum

AGENCY
Mmalum Kennedy D'Auria

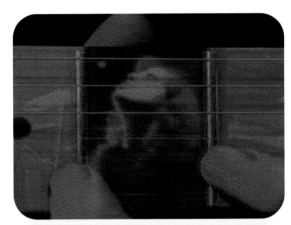

Gold/Film & Video Special Effects

ART DIRECTOR
Sam Gulisano

COPYWRITER
Scott Rosenblit

PRODUCER
Rich Carraro

DIRECTOR
John Lasseter

AGENCY
FCB/Leber Katz Partners

CLIENT
Planters/LifeSavers Co.

Gold/Film & Video Special Effects

ART DIRECTOR
David Harner

COPYWRITER
David Johnson

PRODUCER
Roseanne Horn

DIRECTOR
Barry Kinsman

AGENCY
Young & Rubicam

CLIENT
AT&T Comm.

Gold/Film & Video Special Effects

ART DIRECTOR
David Harner

COPYWRITER
David Johnson

PRODUCER
Roseanne Horn

DIRECTOR
Barry Kinsman

Gold/Film & Video Special Effects

ART DIRECTOR
Kel Andersen

COPYWRITER
Dan Gregory

PRODUCER
Louise Kirsch

DIRECTOR
Terry Windell

AGENCY
Young & Rubicam

CLIENT
First Brands Corp./Prestone

Silver/Film & Video Special Effects

ART DIRECTORS
Clement Mok, Doris Mitsch

DESIGNERS/WRITERS
Doris Mitsch, Clancy Nolan

ILLUSTRATOR/ANIMATOR
Doris Mitsch

STUDIO
Clement Mok Designs

CLIENT
Apple Computer

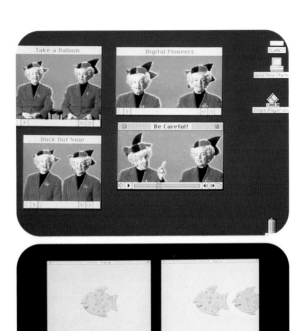

Gold/Campaign/ Film & Video Special Effects

ART DIRECTOR
John Staffen

COPYWRITER
Mike Rogers

PRODUCER
Steve Amato

DIRECTOR
Trip Gruver

AGENCY
DDB Needham Worldwide

CLIENT
Michelin

Gold/Animation
ART DIRECTOR
Roger Chouinard
STUDIO
Duck Soup Productions

Gold/Animation
ART DIRECTOR
Roger Chouinard
STUDIO
Duck Soup Productions

Distinctive Merit/Film & Video Special Effects

ART DIRECTOR
Shawn West

COPYWRITER
Sam Gulisano

PRODUCERS
Rich Carraro, Lewis Kuperman

DIRECTOR
Jon Kane/Optic Nerve

AGENCY
FCB/Leber Katz Partners

CLIENT
Planters/LifeSavers Co.

Distinctive Merit/Animation

ART DIRECTOR
Gunther Maier

COPYWRITER
Lynn Stiles

PRODUCER
Kathryn Spiess

ANIMATOR
Sue Young

AGENCY
Lord, Dentsu & Partners

CLIENT
Hitachi, Ltd.

Distinctive Merit/Series/Animation

ART DIRECTORS
Roger Chouinard, John Howley,
Mel Sommer

STUDIO
Duck Soup Productions

Distinctive Merit/Series/Animation

ART DIRECTORS
Ron Arnold, Gunther Maier

COPYWRITER
Lynn Stiles

DIRECTOR
R.O. Blechman

AGENCY
Lord, Dentsu & Partners

CLIENT
Hitachi, Ltd.

Distinctive Merit/Series/Animation

ART DIRECTORS
Ron Arnold, Gunther Maier

COPYWRITER
Lynn Stiles

DIRECTOR
R.O. Blechman

AGENCY
Lord, Dentsu & Partners

CLIENT
Hitachi, Ltd.

Silver/Exhibition & Display
ART DIRECTOR
Stephen Doyle
DESIGNER
Andrew Grey
STUDIO
Drenttel Doyle Partners
CLIENT
The Cooper-Hewitt Museum

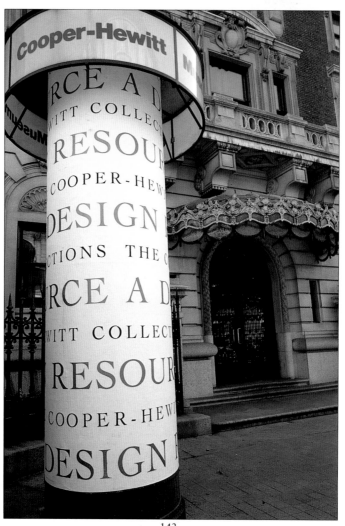

Distinctive Merit/Exhibition & Display

ART DIRECTOR
Miho

COPYWRITER
Vas Prabho

DIRECTOR
Miho

STUDIO
Design Works USA

CLIENT
Museum of Contemporary Art

Silver/Series/Environmental Graphics

ART DIRECTOR
John Bricker

DESIGNER
Tom Horton

STUDIO
Gensler and Associates/Graphics

CLIENT
KQED

Silver/Series/Environmental Graphics
ART DIRECTOR
Peter Harrison
DESIGNERS
Jim Biber, Christina Neyss,
Michael Cutch-Brenner
STUDIO
Pentagram Design

Silver/Annual Report

ART DIRECTOR
Stephen Frykholm

COPYWRITER
Clark Malcolm

ILLUSTRATORS
Guy Billout, Gould Design

CLIENT
Herman Miller, Inc.

Silver/Annual Report

ART DIRECTORS
Kevin B. Kuester, Tim Sauer

COPYWRITER
Andy Blankenburg

ILLUSTRATORS
Landon Kuester, Lauren Kuester,
Martine Lizama, Mike Lizama,
Tim Sauer

STUDIO
The Kuester Group

CLIENT
Corner House

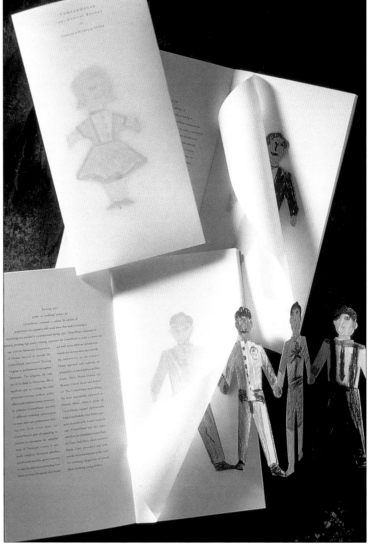

Distinctive Merit/Annual Report

ART DIRECTOR/DESIGNER
Thomas Ryan

COPYWRITER
John Baeder

PHOTOGRAPHER
McGuire

ILLUSTRATOR
Paul Ritscher

STUDIO
Thomas Ryan Design

AGENCY
Corporate Comm., Inc.

CLIENT
Cracker Barrel Old Country Store

Distinctive Merit/Annual Report

ART DIRECTORS/PHOTOGRAPHERS
Mark Schwartz, Joyce Nesnadny

ARTIST
Kay Rosen

STUDIO
Nesnadny & Schwartz

CLIENT
The Progressive Corp.

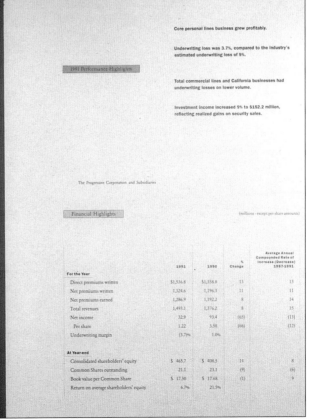

Distinctive Merit/Annual Report

ART DIRECTORS
Jan Ellis, Laurie Ellis

COPYWRITER
Peggy Lawrence

PHOTOGRAPHER
Mark Tucker

STUDIO
Ellis Design

CLIENT
Corrections Corp. of America

Silver/Booklet, Folder & Brochure

DESIGNER
Tom Wood

COPYWRITER
Mary Anne Costello

PHOTOGRAPHER
Jeff Corwin

STUDIO
Wood Design

CLIENT
Louis Dreyfus Energy

Silver/Booklet, Folder & Brochure

ART DIRECTOR
Michael Skjei

STUDIO
Michael Skjei Design Co.

CLIENT
Shay, Shea, Hsieh & Skjei

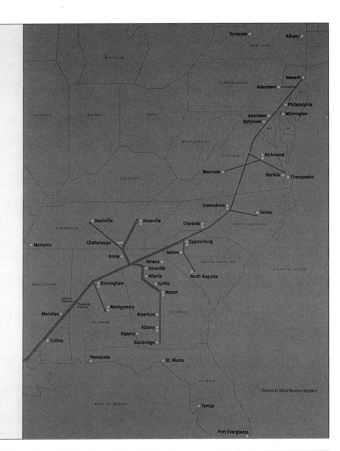

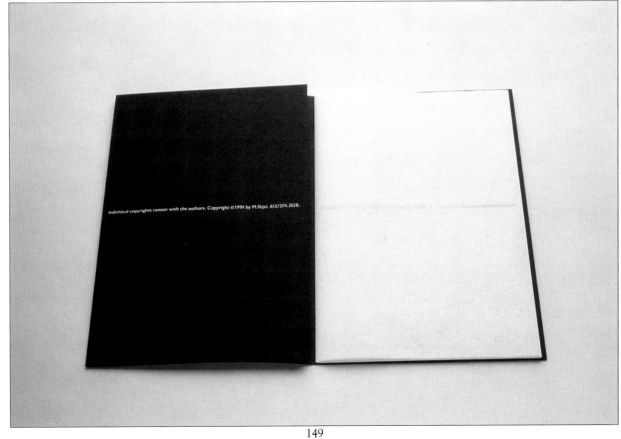

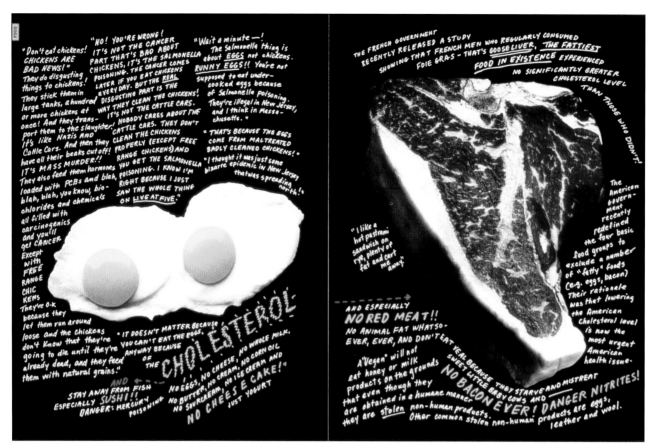

Silver/Booklet, Folder & Brochure
ART DIRECTOR/COPYWRITER/ILLUSTRATOR
Paula Scher
DESIGNER
Ron Lowe
STUDIO
Pentagram Design
CLIENT
Champion International

Distinctive Merit/Booklet, Folder & Brochure
ART DIRECTOR
Allen Weinberg
STUDIO
Sony Music
CLIENT
Sony Music

Distinctive Merit/Booklet, Folder & Brochure

ART DIRECTOR
Kit Hinrichs

DESIGNER
Bell How

COPYWRITER
Delphine Hirasuna

PHOTOGRAPHERS
Bob Esparza, Katherine Kleinman

ILLUSTRATORS
Ward Schumacher, Ingald Stermer,
Dave Stevenson

STUDIO
Pentagram Design

CLIENT
Simpson Paper

Distinctive Merit/Booklet, Folder & Brochure

ART DIRECTOR/ILLUSTRATOR
Christina Freyss

DESIGNER/ILLUSTRATOR
Ivelle Montes de Ola

COPYWRITER
Dorothy Dunn

STUDIO
Pentagram Design

CLIENT
Cooper-Hewitt Museum

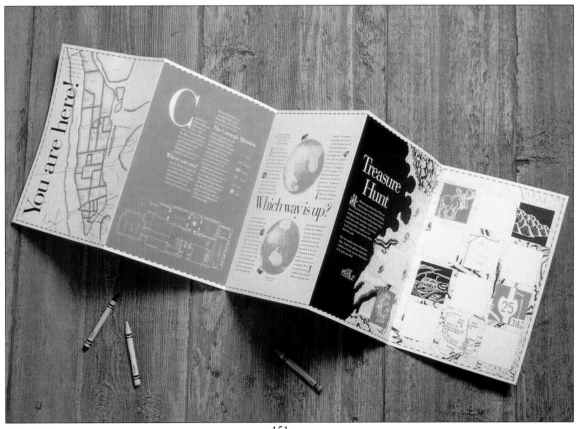

Distinctive Merit/Booklet, Folder & Brochure
ART DIRECTORS
Paula Scher, Bill Drenttel
COPYWRITER/PHOTOGRAPHER/ILLUSTRATOR
Duane Michals
STUDIO
Pentagram Design
CLIENT
Champion International

Distinctive Merit/Booklet, Folder & Brochure
ART DIRECTOR
Michael Bierut
DESIGNER
Lisa Cerveney
STUDIO
Pentagram Design
CLIENT
Mohawk Paper Mills

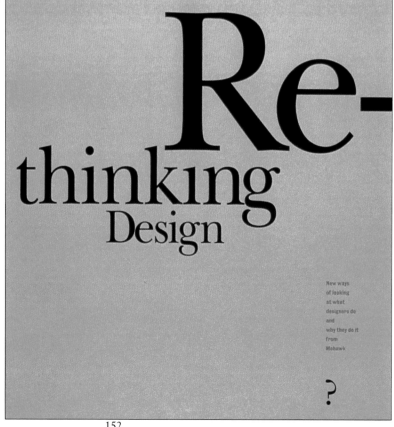

Distinctive Merit/Booklet, Folder & Brochure

DESIGNER
Tom Wood

PHOTOGRAPHER
Gloria Baker

STUDIO
Wood Design

CLIENT
Commonwealth

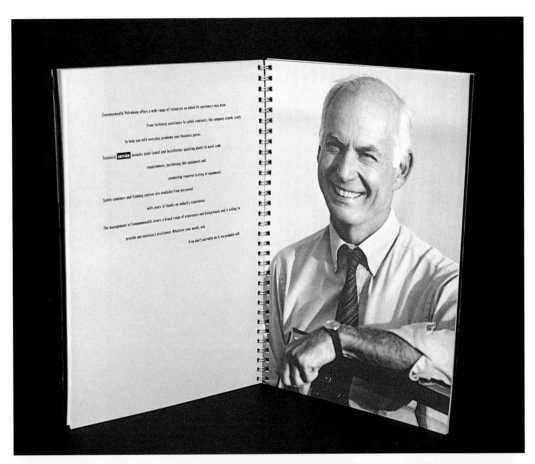

Distinctive Merit/Booklet, Folder & Brochure

DESIGNER
Tom Wood

COPYWRITER
Mary Anne Costello

PHOTOGRAPHER
Jeff Corwin

STUDIO
Wood Design

CLIENT
Louis Dreyfus Energy

independent power producer, Louis Dreyfus Energy fills that niche by combining its traditional marketing experience with new opportunities in an evolving deregulated market.

To meet the increasing demand for electric power, Louis Dreyfus is committed to providing fuel to cogeneration facilities at fixed prices for a set term. This commitment is possible through (1) the ownership and operation of gas reserve properties, (2) effective management of production and transportation costs during the contract period; and (3) global experience in merchandising and hedging activities which take advantage of volatile conditions in the marketplace.

In addition to serving the independent power market in North America, Louis Dreyfus is well positioned in the global energy market to participate in development and equity opportunities.

Louis Dreyfus Energy is a wholly owned subsidiary of the Louis Dreyfus Group, a worldwide organization of diversified companies headquartered in Paris, France. In addition to its principal operational headquarters in Paris, New York and Wilton, Connecticut, there are major offices in Zurich, Madrid, London, São Paulo, Buenos Aires, Melbourne and Tokyo with representative offices in 16 other countries.

Founded in 1851, principal activities of the parent company include the international merchandising and exporting of various commodities, ownership and management of ocean vessels, manufacturing operations and real estate development, management and ownership. In addition to petroleum and petroleum products, the Louis Dreyfus Group, through a number of subsidiaries, also merchandises all agricultural commodities, industrial alcohol, fibers and financial instruments. Annual global trading volume is approximately $25 billion.

The shipping fleet consists of 29 vessels including Lakers, Panamaxes, Cape-size dry bulk carriers, seismic research vessels and LNG carriers. Louis Dreyfus owns and operates orange juice processing plants in Brazil as well as rice milling and oilseed crushing facilities in the United States, Europe and South America. The Group's other industrial operations are located in Argentina and Brazil and involve the manufacture of particleboard wood products, modular furniture and plastic laminates. Real estate activities are conducted through Louis Dreyfus Property Group, which develops, owns and manages real properties in North America and Europe. The Property Group owns over three million square feet of premier office space as well as hotels and retail properties.

Distinctive Merit/Booklet, Folder & Brochure

ART DIRECTORS
David Sterling, Jane Kosstein,
Monica Halpert

DESIGNER
Klaus Kempenaars

COPYWRITER
Peter Mattei

STUDIO
DoubleSpace

CLIENT
Details

Distinctive Merit/Booklet, Folder & Brochure

ART DIRECTOR
Seymour Chwast

DESIGNER
Greg Simpson

STUDIO
The Pushpin Group

CLIENT
Ivy Hill Corp.

Distinctive Merit/Booklet, Folder & Brochure

ART DIRECTOR
Tyler Smith

COPYWRITER
Pat Murray

STUDIO
Tyler Smith

CLIENT
Mead

Distinctive Merit/Booklet, Folder & Brochure

ART DIRECTOR
Chris Hill

DESIGNER
Jeff Davis

COPYWRITER
Ricardo Elizondo

ILLUSTRATOR
Jack Unruh

STUDIO
Hill/A Marketing Design Group

CLIENT
Monterrey Tech University, Mexico

Distinctive Merit/Booklet, Folder & Brochure

ART DIRECTOR
David Sterling, Jane Kosstein,
Monica Halpert
DESIGNER
Jamie Oliveri/Warda Geismar
COPYWRITER
Sharon Glassman
STUDIO
DoubleSpace
CLIENT
Vibe Magazine/Time Inc.

Distinctive Merit/Booklet, Folder & Brochure

DESIGN DIRECTOR
Steff Geissbuhler
DESIGNERS
Lisette Buiani, Robert Matza
STUDIO
Chermayeff & Geismar
CLIENT
The Telemundo Group

Distinctive Merit/Series/Booklet, Folder & Brochure
ART DIRECTORS
Paula Scher, Bill Drenttel
DESIGNER
Stephen Doyle
STUDIO
Pentagram Design
PUBLISHER
Subjective Reasoning/
Champion International

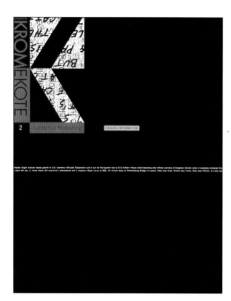

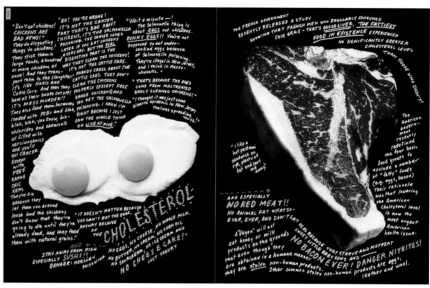

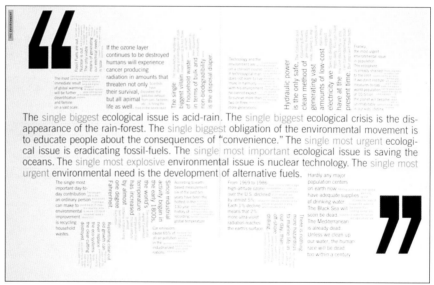

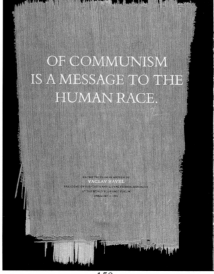

Distinctive Merit/Packaging

ART DIRECTOR
Sharon Werner

COPYWRITER
Chuck Carlson

STUDIO
Joe Duffy Design, Inc.

CLIENT
Jim Beam Brands, Co.

Distinctive Merit/Packaging

ART DIRECTOR
Allen Weinberg

STUDIO
Sony Music

CLIENT
Sony Music

Distinctive Merit/Packaging

ART DIRECTOR
Todd Waterbury

COPYWRITER
Susan Cooper

CREATIVE DIRECTOR
Helane Blumfield

ILLUSTRATOR
Todd Waterbury

STUDIO
Bloomingdale's

CLIENT
Bloomingdale's

Distinctive Merit/Packaging

ART DIRECTOR
Joe Duffy

DESIGNER
Jeff Johnson

PHOTOGRAPHER
Paul Irmiter

STUDIO
Joe Duffy Design, Inc.

CLIENT
Trail Mark

Distinctive Merit/Packaging
ART DIRECTOR
John Bricker
DESIGNER
Wendy Wells
STUDIO
Gensler and Assoc./Graphics
CLIENT
Z Gallerie

Distinctive Merit/Identity Program
ART DIRECTOR/ILLUSTRATOR
Loid Der
CREATIVE DIRECTORS
Scott Mednick, Cheryl Rudich
PHOTOGRAPHERS
Vanessa Adams, Susan Werner,
John Huet, Mark Hanauer, Loid Der
STUDIO
The Mednick Group
CLIENT
Reebok International, Ltd.

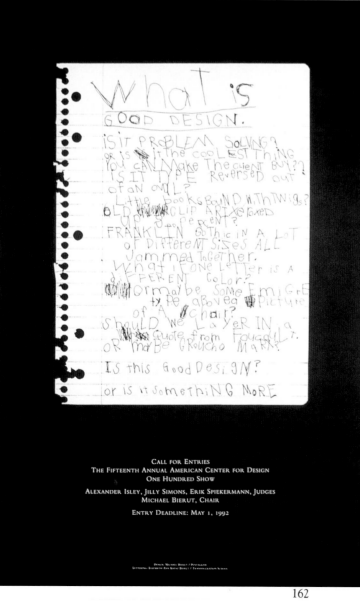

Distinctive Merit/Packaging Program
ART DIRECTOR
Jack Anderson
DESIGNERS
Jack Anderson, Julie Tanagi-Lock,
Mary Hermes, Lian Ng
ILLUSTRATOR
Julia LaPine
STUDIO
Hornall Anderson Design Works
CLIENT
Starbucks Coffee Co.

Distinctive Merit/Announcement, Invitation & Menu
ART DIRECTOR/DESIGNER
Michael Beirut
ILLUSTRATOR
Elizabeth Kresz-Beirut
STUDIO
Pentagram Design
CLIENT
American Center for Design

Distinctive Merit/Announcement, Invitation & Menu
ART DIRECTOR
Bill Porch
COPYWRITER
Jimmy Hamitter
AGENCY
Maris, West & Baker
CLIENT
Maris, West & Baker

Distinctive Merit/Announcement, Invitation & Menu
ART DIRECTOR
Robert Valentine
STUDIO
Robert Valentine Inc.
CLIENT
AIGA/NY

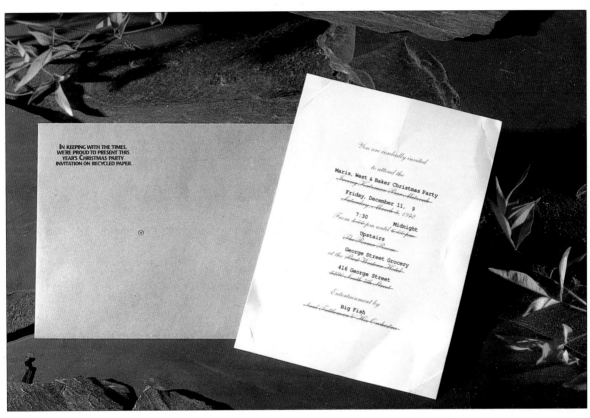

Distinctive Merit/Series/Announcement, Invitation & Menu
ART DIRECTOR/COPYWRITER
Arthur R. Rumaya
BOX DESIGN
Robert Sanders
STUDIO
The Printout
CLIENT
Arthur & Melineh Rumaya

Distinctive Merit/Logo & Trademark
ART DIRECTOR
Michael Bierut
ILLUSTRATOR
Sheila Hart
STUDIO
Pentagram Design
CLIENT
Martha Burns

Distinctive Merit/Logo & Trademark
ART DIRECTOR
Scott Mires
ILLUSTRATOR
Gerald Bustamante
STUDIO
Mires Design, Inc.
CLIENT
Full Bore Surf Shop

Silver/Letterhead, Business Card & Envelope
ART DIRECTOR
Nick Cohen
COPYWRITER
Shalom Auslander
AGENCY
Mad Dogs & Englishmen
CLIENT
Mad Dogs & Englishmen

Distinctive Merit/Letterhead, Business Card & Envelope
ART DIRECTOR
Bob Gill
STUDIO
Bob Gill
CLIENT
Bob Gill/Sara Fishko

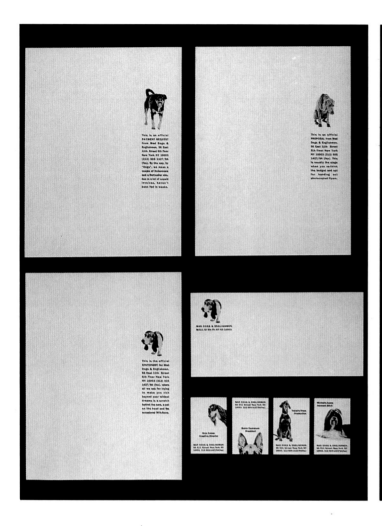

Silver/Corporate Identity

ART DIRECTORS
Paula Scher, Ron Louie

STUDIO
Pentagram Design

CLIENT
Bard College

Distinctive Merit/Corporate Identity

ART DIRECTOR
Jose Serrano

STUDIO
Mires Design, Inc.

CLIENT
Deleo Clay Tile

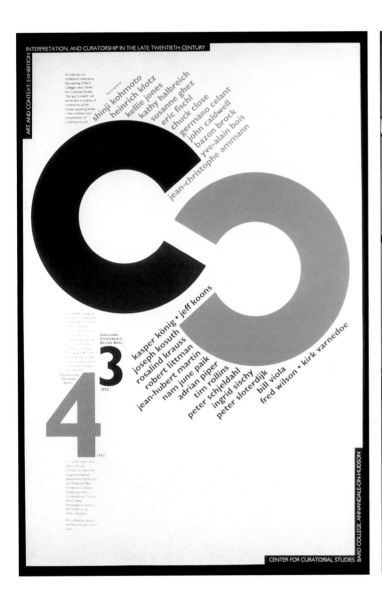

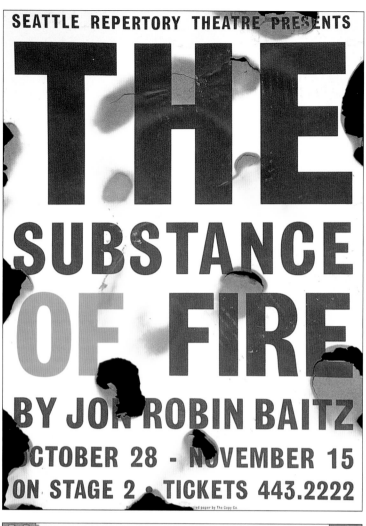

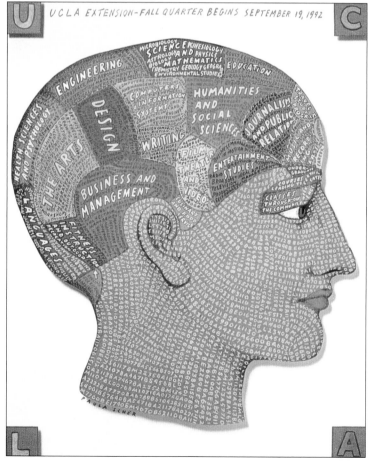

Silver/Poster

ART DIRECTOR/ILLUSTRATOR
Paula Scher
DESIGNER
Ron Lowe
STUDIO
Pentagram Design
CLIENT
Dallas Society of Visual Comm.

Silver/Poster

ART DIRECTOR
Doug Hughes
DESIGNER
Robynne Raye
COPYWRITER
Lucia Linn
STUDIO
Modern Dog
CLIENT
Seattle Repertory Theatre

Silver/Poster

ART DIRECTOR/ILLUSTRATOR
Paula Scher
STUDIO
Pentagram Design
CLIENT
UCLA

Silver/Poster
ART DIRECTOR
Kit Hinrichs
PHOTOGRAPHER
Bob Esparza
STUDIO
Pentagram Design
CLIENT
Spicers Paper

Distinctive Merit/Poster

ART DIRECTOR
Michael Gericke

STUDIO
Pentagram Design

CLIENT
AIGA/NY

Distinctive Merit/Poster

ART DIRECTOR
Morris Taub

DESIGNERS
Steven Brower, John Gall, Leah Lococo,
James Victore, Sue Walsh

STUDIO
Post No Bills

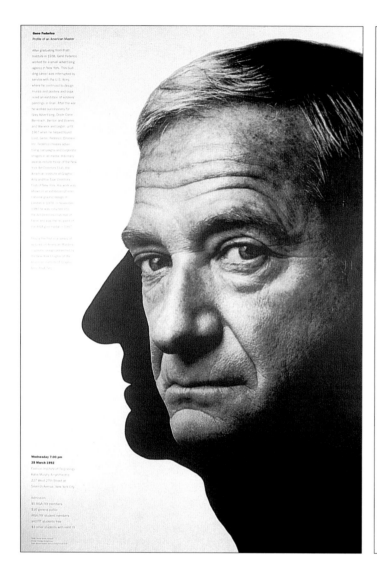

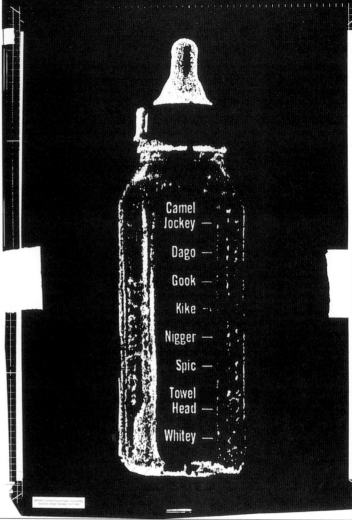

Distinctive Merit/Poster

ART DIRECTOR
Craig Frazier

DESIGNERS
Craig Frazier, Rene Rosso

STUDIO
Frazier Design

CLIENT
Frazier Design

Distinctive Merit/Advertising Photography
ART DIRECTOR/COPYWRITER/CREATIVE DIRECTOR
Cabell Harris
PHOTOGRAPHER
Vic Huber
AGENCY
Livingston + Keye
CLIENT
JBL

Distinctive Merit/Advertising Photography
ART DIRECTOR/CREATIVE DIRECTOR/COPYWRITER
Cabell Harris
PHOTOGRAPHER
Vic Huber
AGENCY
Livingston + Keye
CLIENT
JBL

Distinctive Merit/Editorial Photography
ART DIRECTOR
Matthew Drace
PHOTOGRAPHER
Len Irish
PUBLICATION
Men's Journal

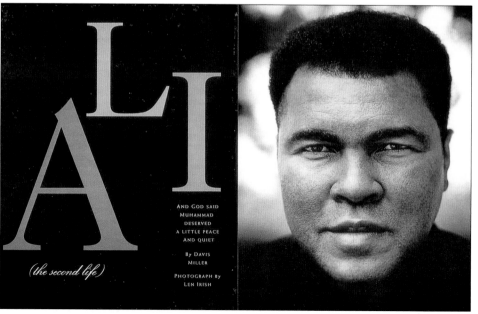

Distinctive Merit/Editorial Photography

ART DIRECTOR
Janet Froelich

DESIGNER
Kathi Rota

PHOTOGRAPHER
Dan Winters

PUBLICATION
The New York Times Magazine

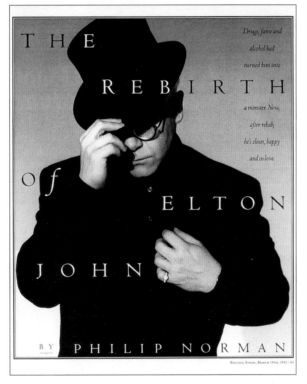

Distinctive Merit/Editorial Photography

ART DIRECTOR
Fred Woodward

DESIGNER
Debra Bishop

PHOTOGRAPHER
Herb Ritts

DIRECTOR OF PHOTOGRAPHY
Laurie Kratochvil

PUBLICATION
Rolling Stone Magazine

Distinctive Merit/Editorial Photography

ART DIRECTOR/DESIGNER
Fred Woodward

PHOTOGRAPHER
Albert Watson

DIRECTOR OF PHOTOGRAPHY
Laurie Kratochvil

PUBLICATION
Rolling Stone Magazine

Gold/Series/Editorial Photography

ART DIRECTOR/DESIGNER
Janet Froelich

PHOTOGRAPHER
James Nachtway

PUBLICATION
The New York Times Magazine

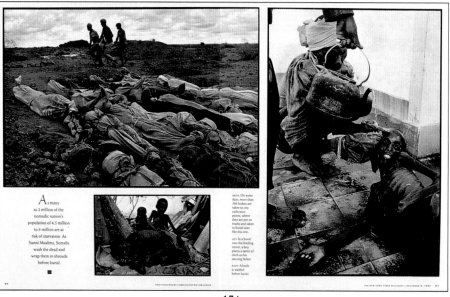

Silver/Series/Editorial Photography

ART DIRECTOR
Fred Woodward

DESIGNERS
Fred Woodward, Gail Anderson,
Catherine Gilmore-Barnes, Debra Bishop,
Angela Skouras, Geraldine Hessler

PHOTOGRAPHER
Albert Watson

DIRECTOR OF PHOTOGRAPHY
Laurie Kratochvil

PUBLICATION
Rolling Stone Magazine

Silver/Series/Editorial Photography

ART DIRECTOR
Fred Woodward

DESIGNER
Catherine Gilmore-Barnes

PHOTOGRAPHER
Herb Ritts

DIRECTOR OF PHOTOGRAPHY
Laurie Kratochvil

PUBLICATION
Rolling Stone Magazine

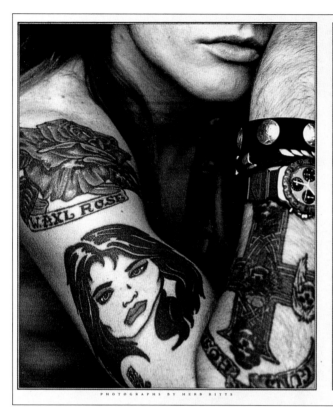

PHOTOGRAPHS BY HERB RITTS

THE ROLLING STONE INTERVIEW

ONLY A FEW MINUTES AGO, Axl Rose, sprawled on the floor of his Las Vegas hotel villa, mentioned his lack of privacy. Now, as if to prove his point, someone knocks on the door. Rose gets up to answer it, peering out into the darkness to find two breathless, carefully made-up fans who've somehow breached Guns n' Roses' security. ¶ "I HOPE YOU KNOW we went to a lot of trouble just to say hello to you," the first girl says. "I'M ONLY HERE because she dragged me here," says the second. "I'm not a very big Guns n' Roses fan or anything." ¶ GIVEN ROSE'S REPUTATION as a hothead, the predictable reaction would be irritation – or at the very least a wry, "see what I mean" smile. But Rose greets the giggly pair like a homeowner welcoming a group of trick-or-treaters. He invites them in and, smiling, begins asking them questions: Do you live here? What are your names? How did you find out where I was? As the story unravels – it turns out the two posed as call girls to extract his room number from a tight-lipped hotel clerk – Rose seems genuinely charmed. AS DO HIS VISITORS. They stick around for nearly an hour, and Rose is the perfect host – cracking jokes, offering them dinner, even laughing off their occasional barbs ("So, are you going on on time tomorrow, or what?"). By the time they leave, they've been made to feel as if it were the most natural thing in the world to barge in uninvited on a total stranger. ¶ IT'S THE EVENING before a sold-out show in late January, and Rose is in an extremely good mood. Catching the singer in this frame of mind at the scheduled time for an interview can seem like a blessing from above if you've ever been around him in the *other* mood. When Rose is feeling pressured or angry, talking to him is a lot like dodging bullets. He tends to rant, barely stopping for breath, and even the most innocent of comments can set him on edge. It is a distinctly uncomfortable feeling to be in a room alone with Axl Rose and see storm clouds suddenly gather on his face because of something you've just said. It is a feeling of wanting to get *out*, *fast*. ¶ BUT ROSE CAN BE a disarming – and formidable – conversationalist if you catch him at the right time. When he is relaxed, he seems to delight in the challenge an interview presents, and it is all but impossible to rattle him. Tell him that much of the public views him as spoiled, and he'll surprise you by agreeing. Inform him that a character in Stephen King's latest novel describes him as an asshole, and he'll ask, ever hopeful, "Was it a good character or a bad character?" The thornier the issue, the more conviction Rose displays in offering his opinion. ¶ DURING THIS CONVERSATION, Rose covered some especially rocky terrain. He talked about rhythm guitarist Izzy Stradlin's resignation from Guns n' Roses late last year. He addressed his tardiness to shows, his ongoing war with the media, his reputation as a misogynist, a homophobe, a bigot. Rose also talked in detail for the first time about childhood traumas that likely played a large part in shaping his volatile nature. He spoke about some highly disturbing memories involving his biological father that were dredged up in regression therapy and also leveled serious charges at his stepfather. (Rose's natural father could not be found for comment on the issues raised in this story; his relatives believe him to be dead. Rose's brother, his sister and a family friend corroborated the allegations concerning his stepfather. Rose's mother and stepfather declined comment.) ¶ IN TALKING ABOUT HIS EARLY YEARS, Rose grew soft-spoken and contemplative, displaying the rarely seen vulnerability that once prompted Sinéad O'Connor to remark that Rose made you want to "bring him home and give him a bowl of soup." Perhaps more than anything else, it is this surprising air of fragility, coupled with the hair-trigger temper that has all but become Rose's personal trademark, that makes him such a compelling figure. ¶ THE SAME EVENING this interview took place, Rose's sister, Amy, strolling through the Mirage Hotel, stopped to look at the royal white tigers the hotel keeps on display. She remarked how fascinating it was that a creature could be at once so ferocious and so gentle. ¶ "JUST LIKE AXL," someone said absent-mindedly. ¶ AMY LAUGHED, realizing that she had unintentionally described her brother as well.

What do you think people are thinking about you these days?
I know it's a love-hate thing. There are people that are big fans and people that really hate me.

Do you get a sense that public opinion of you has changed?
A majority of what's in the press is negative. But I think that we're also gaining more fans, people of all different ages that really like what we're doing. There's a really good vibe in the crowd, a warm vibe.

What about St. Louis? After the riot, ROLLING STONE *got letters from people saying that they were fed up with your attitude and that you don't care about your fans anymore.*
And that's why the riot happened? Is that what they're saying?
No. But I think the riot was a turning point in terms of public opinion of you.

Well, I think that the way the media covered it made me look completely responsible for it. I don't think I was the last straw. I think that the people who decided to start throwing stuff were the last straw. We have a big problem with the people that were at that concert. We gave them a ninety-minute show. We gave them what we were contracted to do, and we gave it good. They wanted more, and they felt that they could just *have* it, regardless of what happened to us or how we felt about it. When we say, "Fuck St. Louis," we're talking about the people that tore up the place. They know who they are – we're not talking about anybody else. Whether I jumped off the stage for a camera or not, that's not a good enough reason to tear the place down. It was announced that we would come back onstage, and

they were more into the riot than even the band playing.

One thing that has people exasperated is the late show times. Why do you go on so late?
I pretty much follow my own internal clock, and I perform better later at night. Nothing seems to work out for me until later at night. And it is one show I don't want to make people sit around and wait – it drives me nuts. That hour-and-a-half or two-hour time period that I'm late going onstage is living hell, because I'm wishing there was any way on earth I could get out of where I am and knowing I'm not going to be able to make it. I'm late to *everything*. I've always wanted to have it written in my will that when I die, the coffin shows up a half-hour late and says on the side, like in gold, SORRY I'M LATE.

What goes on before you take the stage? What actually makes you late?
The chiropractor we work with on the road tapes my ankles professionally. I kept twisting my ankles during shows, and it still happens now and then. I have weak ankles, always have. I used to run cross-country, and that was one of the things that got in the way of that. So I work with a chiropractor. I work with a massage therapist, because I put a lot of stress in my lower back, and with what I do onstage, there's a lot of rebuilding that has to be done. There's operatic voice exercises. And I started therapy in February [1991] and, Jesus, I'm right in the middle of stuff. I mean, if a heavy emotional issue surfaces and you've got a show in four hours, you have to figure out how to get that sorted out really quick before you get onstage so that you're not in the middle of "Jungle" and have a breakdown. The pressure of having to do the show when whatever else is going on in my life is hard to get past. We did a show in Finland where I just couldn't understand why I was doing what I was doing. I sat down while I was singing "Civil War," and I was kind of looking at my lips while I was singing and looking at the microphone and looking at the roadies, and everything just shut off. Well, that doesn't make for a very good show. We're out there to win at what we do. And if that means going on two hours late and doing a good show, I'm gonna do it. I take what I do very seriously.

Do you think that your fans take your problems seriously? Sometimes people relate to celebrities not as people but as objects or possessions – admiring the music or art isn't enough anymore. People have to feel as if they own us.
Yeah. That's a strange beast. And they don't like it when I let them know that they *don't* own me. Sometimes I don't even own myself [laughs].

Let's say a fan stopped you on the street and said, "Listen, I bought all your records, but I'm sick of your bullshit. I come to a show and you're two hours late, and I have to work the next day. You don't give a fuck about me."
If I didn't give a fuck about them, I'd come out and do a shitty show. I'd come out and tell 'em to fuck off. I'd sit down, sing the songs off-key and just not care. But I do care, and I also care too much about myself to do

BY KIM NEELY

ROLLING STONE, APRIL 2ND, 1992 · 33

ROLLING STONE, APRIL 2ND, 1992 · 35

ROLLING STONE, APRIL 2ND, 1992 · 37

Silver/Series/Editorial Photography
ART DIRECTOR
Fred Woodward
DESIGNERS
Fred Woodward, Gail Anderson,
Catherine Gilmore-Barnes, Debra Bishop,
Angela Skouras, Geraldine Hessler
PHOTOGRAPHER
Matthew Rolston
DIRECTOR OF PHOTOGRAPHY
Laurie Kratochvil
PUBLICATION
Rolling Stone Magazine

return to **form**

DARA TORRES, OLYMPIAN, RACES OUT OF RETIREMENT

In 1984, when she was seventeen years old, Dara Torres swam the fastest women's fifty-meter freestyle ever. Four years later, she set an American record in the 100-meter freestyle. She won gold and bronze medals in freestyle relays at the 1984 and 1988 Olympics. Torres retired thereafter, but two years ago she viewed a videotape of herself competing and was inspired to make a comeback. Now twenty-five, she is one of three swimmers — and the only woman — to make the U.S. Olympic team for a third successive time. Her younger colleagues call her Grandma. Maturity becomes her. ⊙ "I figured this is the last chance for me to win a gold in an individual event," she says. Only twenty weeks after giving up her job at NBC's *SportsWorld* and returning to full-time training in Gainesville, Florida, Torres swam the 100-meter freestyle in her best time ever and the world's third fastest for 1991. In the U.S. Open Swimming Championship, she won not only the meet's U.S. Swimming Comeback Award but also the women's high-point trophy. ⊙ "I have a more mature attitude this time around," she says. "I'm swimming for myself, not for coaches and parents." She says she feels comfortable training with her teenage rivals at the University of Florida. "We're all out there working for the same goal," she says. "I just try to fit in and have fun." ⊙ The daughter of a model and a Las Vegas impresario, Torres is also more focused than she was growing up in Beverly Hills. She gets up at 5:55 in the morning six days a week and swims 7000 meters, lifts weights or does aerobics, runs three or four miles and is in bed by ten at night. "No one else does the leg work I do," she claims. "I even climb the fence and swim on my own on Saturdays." ⊙ The training schedule has limited her social life to movies and college sports events. "Even though I make sacrifices, I get satisfaction from all the work I put in," she says. "Others don't know what it's like to stand up on the podium at the Olympics. Unless you're up there with the medal around your neck and the national anthem playing, you can't really know." — *Russ Ewald*

PHOTOGRAPHY BY KURT MARKUS

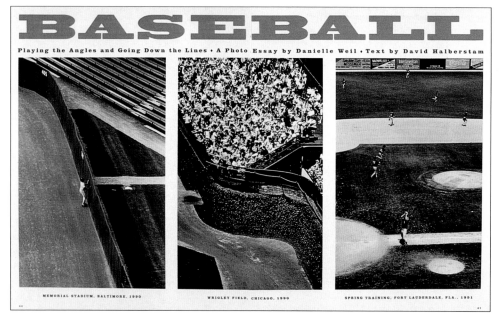

BASEBALL

Playing the Angles and Going Down the Lines • A Photo Essay by Danielle Weil • Text by David Halberstam

MEMORIAL STADIUM, BALTIMORE, 1990

WRIGLEY FIELD, CHICAGO, 1990

SPRING TRAINING, FORT LAUDERDALE, FLA., 1991

Silver/Series/Editorial Photography

ART DIRECTOR/DESIGNER
Matthew Drace

PHOTOGRAPHER
Kurt Markus

PUBLICATION
Men's Journal

Silver/Series/Editorial Photography

ART DIRECTOR
Janet Froelich

DESIGNER
Kathi Rota

PHOTOGRAPHER
Daniel Weil

PUBLICATION
The New York Times Magazine

Distinctive Merit/Series/Editorial Photography

ART DIRECTOR
Fred Woodward

DESIGNERS
Fred Woodward, Gail Anderson,
Catherine Gilmore-Barnes, Debra Bishop,
Angela Skouras, Geraldine Hessler

PHOTOGRAPHER
Kurt Markus

DIRECTOR OF PHOTOGRAPHY
Laurie Kratochvil

PUBLICATION
Rolling Stone Magazine

Distinctive Merit/Series/Editorial Photography
ART DIRECTOR
Fred Woodward
DESIGNER
Gail Anderson
PHOTOGRAPHER
Mary Ellen Mark
DIRECTOR OF PHOTOGRAPHY
Laurie Kratochvil
PUBLICATION
Rolling Stone Magazine

Distinctive Merit/Series/Editorial Photography

ART DIRECTOR
Suzanne Morin

COPYWRITER
Tina Rosenberg

PHOTOGRAPHER
Gustavo Gilabert

PUBLICATION
Audubon Magazine

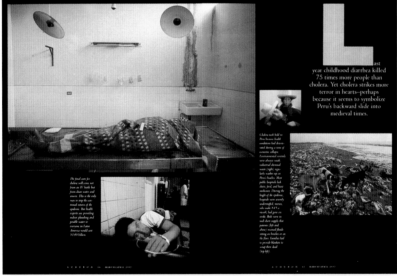

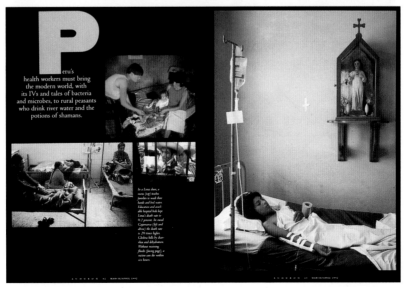

Distinctive Merit/Series/Editorial Photography

ART DIRECTOR
D.J. Stout

COPYWRITER
Skip Hollandsworth

PHOTOGRAPHER
Mary Ellen Mark

PUBLICATION
Texas Monthly

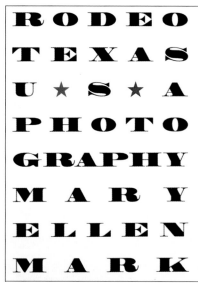

PHOTOGRAPHY & ILLUSTRATION

Distinctive Merit/Series/Editorial Photography

ART DIRECTOR
Janet Froelich

DESIGNER
Kandy Littrell

PHOTOGRAPHER
Sally Gall

PUBLICATION
The New York Times Magazine

Distinctive Merit/Series/Editorial Photography

ART DIRECTOR
Janet Froelich

DESIGNER
Kathi Rota

PHOTOGRAPHER
Sebastiao Salgado

PUBLICATION
The New York Times Magazine

Distinctive Merit/Series/Graphic Design Photography

ART DIRECTOR
Janet Froelich

PHOTOGRAPHER
Chester Higgins, Jr.

PUBLICATION
The New York Times Magazine

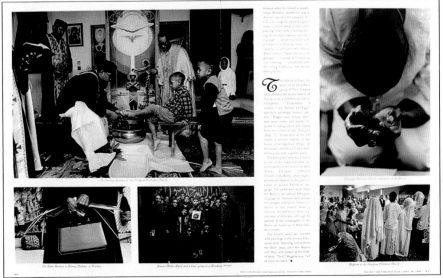

Silver/Editorial Illustration

ART DIRECTOR
Fred Woodward

ILLUSTRATOR
Braldt Bralds

PUBLICATION
Rolling Stone Magazine

Silver/Editorial Illustration

ILLUSTRATOR
Paul Davis

PUBLICATION
Rolling Stone Magazine

Silver/Series/Advertising Illustration

ART DIRECTOR
Alane Gemagen

ILLUSTRATOR
Rafal Olbinski

STUDIO
Ziff Marketing

CLIENT
New York City Opera

Distinctive Merit/Editorial Illustration

ART DIRECTOR
Stacy Drummond

DESIGN DIRECTOR
Jeffrey Keyton

DESIGNER
Steve Byram

COPYWRITER
David Felton

PHOTOGRAPHER
Robert Lewis

STUDIO
MTV Network

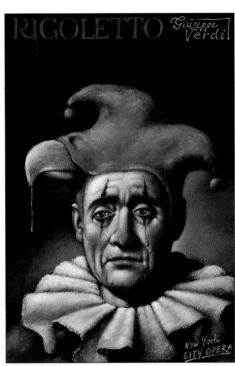

Distinctive Merit/Editorial Illustration

ART DIRECTOR/DESIGNER
Fred Woodward

COPYWRITER
William Greider

ILLUSTRATOR
C. F. Payne

PUBLICATION
Rolling Stone Magazine

Distinctive Merit/Series/Editorial Illustration

ART DIRECTOR
Fred Woodward

COPYWRITER
Peter Travers

ILLUSTRATOR
Gary Kelley

PUBLICATION
Rolling Stone Magazine

Ross Perot Talks, Washington Squawks

No matter what happens next, Ross Perot has already done a good day's work for American democracy. Like a Wall Street arbitrageur raiding a Fortune 500 company, Perot has put the two-party system "in play." With his Will Rogers wit and twang, Perot has also put the fun — and suspense — back in the campaign. With the shrewdness of a great politician, he is articulating the nation's deepest anxieties and yearnings. His cocky self-confidence is mobilizing millions to engage themselves again in the adventure of self-government.

All that is valuable and a lot more than either George Bush or Bill Clinton has contributed so far. If Perot burns out before November, as Democrats and Republicans are desperately hoping, he will still have altered the fabric of national politics substantially — both the way that candidates run for office and the way that citizens communicate with those in power. If Perot can dodge the land mines and brickbats, he may accomplish much, much more: His candidacy threatens to break up the old order and open the way for profound change.

As a result, 1992 has become a rare moment in the country's history — full of great democratic possibilities. The nation, I suspect, is entering a long period of political disarray, in which the entrenched power relationships surrounding the federal government will be challenged in imaginative new ways and perhaps broken up. The status quo must either reform itself or be replaced. Either way this historic opportunity will require poise and patience (as well as hard work) from the citizens at large. If you want real change in politics, you have to be willing to accept some chaos and uncertainty.

Right now the air is blue with slanderous accusations aimed at decapitating Perot. The governing elites, including the major media, recognize the danger he poses to their own power; they're hacking away as though the diminutive Texan were a fiery dragon at the castle

gates. Perot is a fraudulent outsider, they claim, since as a businessman, he's done the sort of deal making with political money that offends the public. Perot is a narrow-minded autocrat who will impose his own short-hair morality on the nation. Perot is a commando-style leader who will scrap the Constitution.

The New Republic, which used to idolize Bush and is now a courtier to Clinton, has already upped the ante and invoked the *f* word. Ross Perot, it announced solemnly, is an American fascist. Wow. A home-grown Mussolini from Texarkana? Fortunately, most Americans are smarter than Washington editors and reporters think they are. Everyone (including myself) has lots of unanswered questions about Perot. As he fills in the blanks in the next few months, we may decide that, indeed, he isn't up to the presidency. In the meantime, most are willing to give the man a little slack and listen to what he has to say.

For now, we know for sure that Perot is a smart character who's already achieved a serious purpose: His sudden rise confirms the bankruptcy of the status quo. The spontaneous popularity of a Texas billionaire who has never held public office reflects the fact that neither the Democrats nor the Republicans are confronting the threatening realities facing the nation and that neither party is genuinely connected to the common experience of ordinary Americans. Perot has already proved something else: The regular order is vulnerable — vulnerable to an organized insurgency from powerless citizens.

PEROT SAYS HE DOES NOT WANT THE government interfering in the reproduc-

ILLUSTRATION BY C.F. PAYNE

ROLLING STONE, AUGUST 6TH, 1992 · 31

MOVIES

PLAYING SONGS OF LOVE

The Mambo Kings

Starring Armand Assante, Antonio Banderas and Cathy Moriarty
Written by Cynthia Cidre
Directed by Arne Glimcher
Warner Bros.

By Peter Travers

FROM ITS BREATHTAKING opening shot in a Havana nightclub, where frenzied dancing muffles the backstage cries of a woman watching a man's throat cut, *The Mambo Kings* runs on pure emotion. First-time director Arne Glimcher surely does a service to Oscar Hijuelos's Pulitzer Prize-winning novel, *The Mambo Kings Play Songs of Love*, by not trying to cram it all into a two-hour movie. The book spans three decades; the film zeroes in on the years from 1952 to 1955, when two Cuban musicians — Cesar Castillo (Armand Assante) and his younger brother Nestor (Antonio Banderas) — try to make it in New York as mambo musicians. Whatever Glimcher and his astute Cuban-born screenwriter, Cynthia Cidre, lose by narrowing the book's scope, they gain by richly detailing the world that inspired the book's poetry. The extravagantly sexy and witty *Mambo Kings* is a stunner; suffused with romantic longing, the film goes beyond spectacle to honor the achievements and damned-up dreams of a culture long misunderstood by Hollywood.

Music and pain are linked for the brothers, who lead a band called the Mambo Kings. It was Cesar who was nearly killed in that club in Havana, by the jealous gangster boyfriend of Nestor's love, María (Talisa Soto). She warns Cesar to get Nestor out of Cuba. In mam-

ILLUSTRATION BY GARY KELLEY

ROLLING STONE, MARCH 19TH, 1992 · 101

ART DIRECTOR
Fred Woodward

DESIGNERS
Fred Woodward, Gail Anderson,
Catherine Gilmore-Barnes, Debra Bishop,
Angela Skouras, Geraldine Hessler

PUBLICATION
Rolling Stone Magazine

IN THE SCHEDULE they were given, the thirteen advertising judges looked at newspaper and magazine ads, transit posters, billboards, and posters to find 338 finalists in the 3200 submitted print-advertising entries. Only 7 finalists became Gold medalists, and 27 received Silver medals.

The judges also watched approximately 5.5 hours worth of commercials— or 1376 TV advertising reels (about 80% as much advertising as the average American is subjected to daily). Out of the 119 tapes selected, 9 were awarded Gold medals. Two of those were campaigns and one was produced on a budget of under $10,000. Also, one Gold medalist in this category became one of two recipients of a Best of Show citation. There were 10 Silver medal recipients.

3.3 hours worth of radio tapes were submitted. After hearing the 400 radio advertising entries, the judges found no Gold medalists in the group of 14 finalists this year, but did award 3 Silver medals.

ART DIRECTOR
Joe Baratelli
COPYWRITER
Carole Larson
DIRECTOR
Klaus Lucka
STUDIO
Luckafilm

ART DIRECTOR
Bob Meager
COPYWRITER
Tripp Westbrook
PRODUCER
Morty Baran
DIRECTOR
Amy Daniels
AGENCY
The Martin Agency
CLIENT
Kings Dominion

ART DIRECTOR
Danny Boone
COPYWRITER
Joe Alexander
PRODUCER
Pam Campagnoli
AGENCY
The Martin Agency
CLIENT
Richmond Symphony

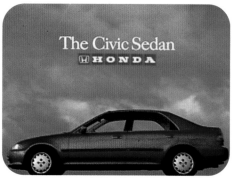

AROUND.
VO: To those who still believe that only expensive luxury cars should offer standard anti-lock brakes, a driver's airbag, and sophisticated engine technology...we think you'll come around. The Civic EX Sedan from Honda.

COASTERS.
INTERVIEWER: We're here at Kings Dominion on the Shockwave. What's the name of this roller coaster?
KID: I think it's the Rebel Yelllll!
INTERVIEWER: You know the Anaconda features six loops. We're going under water, you know that?
KID: AHHHHH!
INTERVIEWER: Now why would you be nervous, Paul?
KID: (*scream*) I'm scared, yeah!
INTERVIEWER: Something about a human being's scream, huh?
KID: AAAAAAAAAAH!
INTERVIEWER: It's kind of relaxing, don't you think?
KID: (*laughs nervously*)
INTERVIEWER: You didn't have one of those burritos did you?
KID: Uuuhhuhh. (*prolonged scream*)

JINGLE.
SUPER: How many advertisers can get Bach to do their jingle?
SFX: A famous bar of Bach.
SUPER: The Richmond Symphony. Call 788-1212.

ART DIRECTOR
David Angelo
COPYWRITER
Paul Spencer
PRODUCER
Eric Herrmann
DIRECTOR
Brent Thomas
AGENCY
DDB Needham Worldwide
CLIENT
New York State Lottery

ART DIRECTOR
David Angelo
COPYWRITER
Paul Spencer
PRODUCER
Eric Herrmann
DIRECTOR
John Lloyd
AGENCY
DDB Needham Worldwide
CLIENT
New York State Lottery

ART DIRECTOR
David Angelo
COPYWRITER
Paul Spencer
PRODUCER
Eric Herrmann
DIRECTOR
John Lloyd
AGENCY
DDB Needham Worldwide
CLIENT
New York State Lottery

GRAND BALL.
SFX: Music throughout.
BUTLER: Admiral and Lady Billingsly of Devonshire. Lord and Lady Atherton of Sussex. Sir Alfred and Lady Sheffield of Dunnsmar. And Bob of Buffalo.
VO: New York Lotto. Hey, you never know.

HELICOPTER.
SFX: Music throughout. Dog barking.
VO: New York Lotto. Hey, you never know.
SFX: Dog barking.

GRANDMA'S HERE.
SFX: Car engine.
KIDS: Grandma's here. Grandma's here.
SFX: Dog barks.
VO: New York Lotto. Hey, you never know.

ART DIRECTORS/COPYWRITERS
John Butler, Mike Shine
PRODUCER
Ben Latimer
DIRECTOR
Jeff Zwart, Colossal Pictures
AGENCY
Goodby, Berlin & Silverstein
CLIENT
Isuzu

ART DIRECTOR
Chuck Finkle
COPYWRITER
Dean Hacohen
PRODUCER
Patricia Quaglino
DIRECTOR
Henry Sandbank
AGENCY
Goldsmith/Jeffrey
CLIENT
NYNEX Business-to-Business Directory

ART DIRECTOR
Chuck Finkle
COPYWRITER
Dean Hacohen
PRODUCER
Patricia Quaglino
DIRECTOR
Henry Sandbank
AGENCY
Goldsmith/Jeffrey
CLIENT
NYNEX Business-to-Business Directory

RODEO VALUE PACK.
SFX: Music under throughout.
VO: If this were a perfect world, we'd all be driving expensive cars and living on beachfront property.
SFX: Stretching effect over animated pie chart.
VO: But in the real world you have to eat. Well, you can eat tuna once in a while. And you have to buy stuff, like socks and shoes and CDs. Well, maybe not so many CDs. Fortunately, the people at Isuzu have to buy stuff, too. That's why they've created the Rodeo, a four-wheel drive vehicle you can afford, and why they'll give you a great deal on a sound system and air-conditioning. So now you can buy more stuff. Oh, we forgot to mention taxes.

LUMBER.
MAN: Ouch! Ouch! Ooooch! Ouch! Ouch!
SFX: Tweek!
MAN: (*sigh of relief*)
VO: The NYNEX Business-to-Business Directory. Where one business finds another.

THE OZONES.
SFX: Electric guitar begins. Music is interrupted by heavy static and feedback. Electric guitar resumes rendition of "Hava Nagila."
VO: The NYNEX Business-to-Business Directory. Where one business finds another.

ART DIRECTOR
Chuck Finkle
COPYWRITER
Dean Hacohen
PRODUCER
Patricia Quaglino
DIRECTOR
Henry Sandbank
AGENCY
Goldsmith/Jeffrey
CLIENT
NYNEX Business-to-Business Directory

ART DIRECTOR
Chuck Finkle
COPYWRITER
Dean Hacohen
PRODUCER
Patricia Quaglino
DIRECTOR
Henry Sandbank
AGENCY
Goldsmith/Jeffrey
CLIENT
NYNEX Business-to-Business Directory

ART DIRECTOR
Chuck Finkle
COPYWRITER
Dean Hacohen
PRODUCER
Patricia Quaglino
DIRECTOR
Henry Sandbank
AGENCY
Goldsmith/Jeffrey
CLIENT
NYNEX Business-to-Business Directory

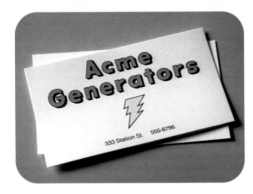

MUNICIPAL HOSPITAL.
SFX: Steady EKG beeping sound. EKG sound fades with
picture. EKG resumes steady beeping.
VO: The NYNEX Business-to-Business Directory. Where
one business finds another.

A-1 EXPLOSIVES.
SFX: Heartbeat pounding faster and faster.
MAN: (*through megaphone*) You got eight seconds,
Joe...Four seconds...Need any help?
SFX: Silence.
VO: The NYNEX Business-to-Business Directory. Where
one business finds another.

ART DIRECTOR
Chuck Finkle
COPYWRITER
Dean Hacohen
PRODUCER
Patricia Quaglino
DIRECTOR
Henry Sandbank
AGENCY
Goldsmith/Jeffrey
CLIENT
NYNEX Business-to-Business Directory

ART DIRECTOR
Chuck Finkle
COPYWRITER
Dean Hacohen
PRODUCER
Patricia Quaglino
DIRECTOR
Henry Sandbank
AGENCY
Goldsmith/Jeffrey
CLIENT
NYNEX Business-to-Business Directory

ART DIRECTOR
Chuck Finkle
COPYWRITER
Dean Hacohen
PRODUCER
Patricia Quaglino
DIRECTOR
Henry Sandbank
AGENCY
Goldsmith/Jeffrey
CLIENT
NYNEX Business-to-Business Directory

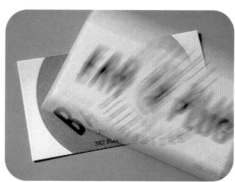

AUTO BODY.
SFX: Car parallel parking. Brakes screeching. Crashing
    sounds. Crash!
VO: The NYNEX Business-to-Business Directory. Where
    one business finds another.

ANGUS MANURE.
SFX: Sniff, sniff...sniff, sniff, sniff. Free breathing through a
    gas mask.
VO: The NYNEX Business-to-Business Directory. Where
    one business finds another.

BALLOONS.
SFX: Balloon filling up with air. Rubber stretching. Muted
    pop.
VO: The NYNEX Business-to-Business Directory. Where
    one business finds another.

ART DIRECTOR
Chuck Finkle
COPYWRITER
Dean Hacohen
PRODUCER
Patricia Quaglino
DIRECTOR
Henry Sandbank
AGENCY
Goldsmith/Jeffrey
CLIENT
NYNEX Business-to-Business Directory

ART DIRECTOR
Michael Fazende
COPYWRITER
Mike Lescarbeau
PRODUCER
Judy Brink
DIRECTOR
Eric Young/Young & Co.
AGENCY
Fallon McElligott
CLIENT
The Lee Co.

ART DIRECTOR
Bob Brihn
COPYWRITER
Phil Hanft
PRODUCERS
Char Loving, Vicki Oachs
AGENCY
Fallon McElligott
CLIENT
Time Inc.

SKI RESORT.
SFX: Swoosh of skis moving down slope. Cartoon crash sound. Chainsaw.
VO: The NYNEX Business-to-Business Directory. Where one business finds another.

FAN.
SFX: Fan turning on.
SFX: Scraping.
VO: Nothing is heavier than Lee Heavyweight Cotton Sweats.

LOSING THE BATTLE.
VO: Every war has a price. But then, after ten years of fighting this one, the bodies are still piling up. Losing the battle. If it's important to you, you'll find it in *Time*.

ART DIRECTOR
Bob Brihn
COPYWRITER
Phil Hanft
PRODUCERS
Char Loving, Vicki Oachs
DIRECTOR
Eric Young/Young & Co.
AGENCY
Fallon McElligott
CLIENT
Time Inc.

ART DIRECTOR
Michael Fazende
COPYWRITER
Mike Lescarbeau
PRODUCER
Judy Brink
DIRECTOR
Eric Young/Young & Co.
AGENCY
Fallon McElligott
CLIENT
The Lee Co.

ART DIRECTOR
Michael Fazende
COPYWRITER
Mike Lescarbeau
PRODUCER
Judy Brink
DIRECTOR
Roger Woodburn/Park Village Productions
AGENCY
Fallon McElligott
CLIENT
The Lee Co.

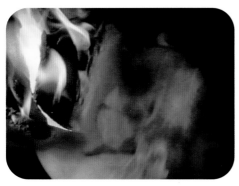

L.A. RIOTS.

VO: In the May 11th issue of *Time*, we reported what we saw during the recent riots in south-central Los Angeles. What we saw...was the enemy...and the enemy was us. All of us. Can we all get along? If it's important to you, you'll find it in *Time*.

ROLLING PICTURE.

SFX: Jazz music throughout.

BUTTON.

SFX: Background noise. TV audio.
SFX: Bang of button flying off.
SFX: Cowboy movie ricochets, etc.
VO: Need a little more room in your jeans? Try Relaxed Fit Jeans from Lee.

ART DIRECTOR
Bob Brihn
COPYWRITER
Phil Hanft
PRODUCERS
Char Loving, Vicki Oachs
DIRECTOR
Eric Young/Young & Co.
AGENCY
Fallon McElligott
CLIENT
Time Inc.

ART DIRECTOR
Bob Brihn
COPYWRITER
Phil Hanft
PRODUCERS
Char Loving, Vicki Oachs
DIRECTOR
Eric Young/Young & Co.
AGENCY
Fallon McElligott
CLIENT
Time Inc.

ART DIRECTOR
Bob Brihn
COPYWRITER
Phil Hanft
PRODUCERS
Char Loving, Vicki Oachs
DIRECTOR
Eric Young/Young & Co.
AGENCY
Fallon McElligott
CLIENT
Time Inc.

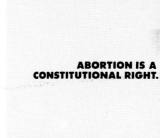

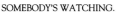

SOMEBODY'S WATCHING.
SFX: Electric drill.
VO: They already know how much you make and what you spend it on.
SFX: Keyhole saw.
VO: They know your court appearances and your business dealings. They know your health history, your marital history, your credit history.
SFX: Finger punching out hole.
VO: Next, they'll invite themselves into your bedroom. Then again, maybe they already have. Somebody's watching. If it's important to you, you'll find it in *Time*.

COLORADO RIVER.
SFX: Toilet flush.
VO: As the water of the Colorado River goes, so go the Western states. And as the Western states go...
SFX: Toilet flush.
VO:...so goes the country. We just thought you'd like to know. The Colorado... If it's important to you you'll find it in *Time*.

ROE VS. WADE.
VO: No matter which side of the abortion issue you're on, we've got news for you. It may already be decided. Why Roe v. Wade is moot. If it's important to you, you'll find it in *Time*.

ART DIRECTOR
Bob Brihn
COPYWRITER
Phil Hanft
PRODUCERS
Char Loving, Vicki Oachs
DIRECTOR
Eric Young/Young & Co.
AGENCY
Fallon McElligott
CLIENT
Time Inc.

ART DIRECTOR
Michael Fazende
COPYWRITER
Mike Lescarbeau
PRODUCER
Judy Brink
DIRECTOR
Tarsem/A+R Group
AGENCY
Fallon McElligott
CLIENT
The Lee Co.

ART DIRECTOR
Michael Fazende
COPYWRITER
Mike Lescarbeau
PRODUCER
Judy Brink
DIRECTOR
Roger Woodburn/Park Village Productions
AGENCY
Fallon McElligott
CLIENT
The Lee Co.

THE ANGRY VOTER.
SFX: Typing sound.
FVO: Congress votes itself a $23,000 pay raise. S&Ls bailed out at taxpayer expense. Unemployment shot to an eight-year high. Congress bounces thousands of bad checks.
VO: Last March, *Time* reported a major shift in voter attitudes. We just thought you'd like to know you're not alone. The angry voter. If it's important to you, you'll find it in *Time*.

BAD HAIR.
MAN: It's funny, 'cause I never have a bad hair day, ya know. Hello! I need to speak to my agent. I am not wearing this. I gotta wear a space suit? Look at me, I'm a professional model and you won't be able to see my body. How's my hair doin'? I don't need an education. Not with this face. I mean anyone looks good in jeans, but I look tough in jeans. I like space, ya know. Apollo 10 come in. One step for mankind. Martians would think I'm cool.
SFX: Crowd cheering.
MAN: I think when I'm done modeling, I'm gonna be an astronaut.
SFX: Computer space noise.

SEEN AS MEN.
VO: When most jeans makers look at women, they see men.
GUY #1: (*in a real woman's voice*) I need jeans with a little more room in the hips.
VO: Why else would they keep trying to sell men's jeans to women?
GUY #2: (*woman's voice*) ...more snug in the waist.
GUY #3: (*woman's voice*) I like a looser fit in the thighs.
GUY #4: (*woman's voice*) I need jeans designed for a woman.
VO: At Lee, we make jeans that fit the unique contours of a woman's body. Lee Relaxed Fit Jeans.

ART DIRECTOR
David Harner
COPYWRITER
David Johnson
PRODUCER
Roseanne Horn
DIRECTOR
Jim Gartner
AGENCY
Young & Rubicam
CLIENT
AT&T Communications

ART DIRECTOR
David Harner
COPYWRITER
David Johnson
PRODUCER
Roseanne Horn
DIRECTOR
Barry Kinsman
AGENCY
Young & Rubicam
CLIENT
AT&T Communications

ART DIRECTOR
Susan Griak
COPYWRITER/DIRECTOR
Jarl Olsen
CLIENT
LUNA-TIK

SILENCE.
SFX: Silence throughout.

SEAMLESS WORLDS.
VO: From one end of the earth to another. AT&T World
Connect service is here. With an AT&T card, it
makes country to country calls easy. Just dial
AT&T USADirect. AT&T World Connect. It's
all in the cards.

ART DIRECTOR
Carol Henderson
COPYWRITER
Dean Buckhorn
PRODUCER
Greg Pope
DIRECTOR
Jarl Olsen
STUDIO
Dublin Productions
AGENCY
McElligott Wright Morrison White
CLIENT
Easy Spirit

ART DIRECTOR
John Buckley
COPYWRITER
Greg Karraker
AGENCY
J. Walter Thompson/West
CLIENT
California Lottery

ART DIRECTOR
Ty Harper
COPYWRITER
Rob Schapiro
PRODUCER
Frank Soukup
DIRECTOR
Neal Slavin
AGENCY
Earle Palmer Brown
CLIENT
Water Country USA

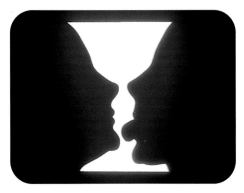

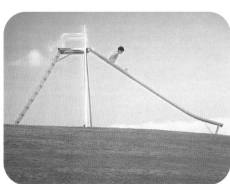

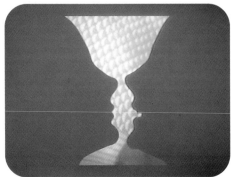

CHEESE.
TEEHEE: I heard about it Saturday night. Next day, I'm at the supermarket and it hits me. Like, I could totally afford all this cheese.
VO: Super Lotto. It could happen to anybody.

SLIDE.
SFX: Insect humming noise of a very hot day. Squeak of sweaty legs sticking on the slide.
VO: It's gonna be a long summer.
BOY: Mommmm.
VO: Take the kids to Water Country USA.

ART DIRECTOR/CREATIVE DIRECTOR
Michael Hutchinson
COPYWRITER
Larry Harris
PRODUCER
Kevin VanFleet
DIRECTOR
Osbert Parker
AGENCY
DMB&B/St. Louis
CLIENT
Annheauser-Busch, Inc./Budweiser

ART DIRECTOR
Dean Stefanides
COPYWRITER
Larry Hampel
PRODUCER
Amy Faulkner
DIRECTOR
Paul Guliner
AGENCY
Scali, McCabe, Sloves
CLIENT
Perdue

ART DIRECTORS
K.J. Bowen, Max Jerome,
Harvey Marco, Kirk Souder
COPYWRITERS
Steve Biegel, Tony Gomes
PRODUCER
Jack McWalters
AGENCY
Ammirati & Puris
CLIENT
Aetna Life and Casualty Co.

BUD SPORTS BAR.
SFX: Music and sound effects throughout.

YELLOW.
FRANK: Do not adjust your TV. This is only a test. To find out how good your chicken is, hold it up to the screen. If it doesn't match this golden-yellow color, chances are you're not getting the best chicken you can buy. A chicken that grew up healthy, eating an expensive diet of only wholesome natural foods. Always look for the chicken that matches this color. And if you have a black-and-white TV, just look for one of these. We now return to your regularly scheduled program.

PLANTING PETUNIAS.
SFX: Old Victrola playing: "We're in the Money."
SFX: Music winds down as if plug was pulled out.
SFX: Music starts up again.

ART DIRECTOR
Jeff Terwilliger
COPYWRITER
Tom Gabriel
PRODUCER
Luann Truso
DIRECTOR
Denny Carlson
AGENCY
Carmichael Lynch
CLIENT
Minnesota State Lottery

ART DIRECTOR
Tom Rosenfield
COPYWRITER
Chuck McBride
PRODUCER
Kelly Waltos
DIRECTOR
Henry Sandbank
AGENCY
Team One Advertising
CLIENT
Lexus

ART DIRECTORS
Steve Emerson, Joe Sedelmaier
COPYWRITER
Steve Emerson
PRODUCER
Shelley Winfrey
DIRECTOR
Joe Sedelmaier/Sedelmaier Productions
AGENCY
Livingston & Company
CLIENT
Alaska Airlines

THE DRIVER'S SEAT.
VO: It has four independent motors, an intricate steel frame...even an electronically-regulated temperature-control system. And that's just the driver's seat. The Lexus ES300 luxury sedan.

BUTTONS.
VO: Did you ever try to get something as simple as help on an airline? At Alaska Airlines you'll find getting help is quite simple. More often than not, you won't even need to ask for it.

ART DIRECTOR
Michael Fazende
COPYWRITER
Mike Lescarbeau
PRODUCER
Judy Brink
DIRECTOR
Tarsem/A+R Group
AGENCY
Fallon McElligott
CLIENT
The Lee Co.

Campaign
ART DIRECTOR
Chuck Finkle
COPYWRITER
Dean Hacohen
DIRECTOR
Henry Sandbank
AGENCY
Goldsmith/Jeffrey
CLIENT
NYNEX Business-to-Business Directory

Campaign
ART DIRECTOR
Chuck Finkle
COPYWRITER
Dean Hacohen
DIRECTOR
Henry Sandbank
AGENCY
Goldsmith/Jeffrey
CLIENT
NYNEX Business-to-Business Directory

WATER.
MAN: What do I need an education for? Ya know, I'm a model. Hey, can't we get any cold water over here? Of course I'm a perfectionist, look at me. Twice I've asked for cold water. What's my most attractive part? I think you get a complete package, ya know. I look good in jeans. How's my hair doing? Anyone looks good in jeans, but I look tough in jeans. Some women are intimidated by my looks. I find that exciting, ya know. I think when I'm done modeling, I'm gonna be an astronaut.

ICE RINK.
MAN: (*through megaphone*) Ladies and gentlemen. Your State Skating Champion...Patty Quaglino!
SFX: Huge splash. Silence.
VO: The NYNEX Business-to-Business Directory. Where one business finds another.

RE-ELECTION.
SFX: Police sirens approaching. Paper shredding.
VO: The NYNEX Business-to-Business Directory. Where one business finds another.

Campaign

ART DIRECTOR
Chuck Finkle

COPYWRITER
Dean Hacohen

DIRECTOR
Henry Sandbank

AGENCY
Goldsmith/Jeffrey

CLIENT
NYNEX Business-to-Business Directory

Campaign

ART DIRECTOR
Chuck Finkle

COPYWRITER
Dean Hacohen

DIRECTOR
Henry Sandbank

AGENCY
Goldsmith/Jeffrey

CLIENT
NYNEX Business-to-Business Directory

Campaign

ART DIRECTOR
Chuck Finkle

COPYWRITER
Dean Hacohen

DIRECTOR
Henry Sandbank

AGENCY
Goldsmith/Jeffrey

CLIENT
NYNEX Business-to-Business Directory

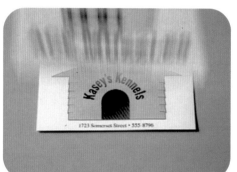

MARRIAGE COUNSELORS.
MAN: Now I want you both to be open and honest with each other. Share your true feelings.
SFX: Things being thrown back and forth. Crashes grow louder and louder. Continues throughout.
VO: The NYNEX Business-to-Business Directory. Where one business finds another.

KASEY'S KENNELS.
SFX: Small dog barking incessantly. Muted yelps.
VO: The NYNEX Business-to-Business Directory. Where one business finds another.

WXYZ.
DJ: (*sleepy voice*) We're here with you all night (*yawn*) playin' your favorites, like this...(*hyper, top-40 voice*)...mega-hit blast from the past! Comin' right atcha, comin' right now! Crank it up, babe, I love ya...
VO: The NYNEX Business-to-Business Directory. Where one business finds another.

Campaign

ART DIRECTOR
Chuck Finkle

COPYWRITER
Dean Hacohen

DIRECTOR
Henry Sandbank

AGENCY
Goldsmith/Jeffrey

CLIENT
NYNEX Business-to-Business Directory

Campaign

ART DIRECTORS
Bill Schwab, Dick Sittig,
Lee Clow, Gill Witt

COPYWRITERS
Dion Hughes, Dick Sittig,
Lee Clow, George Logothetides

AGENCY
Chiat/Day/Mojo

CLIENT
Reebok

Campaign

ART DIRECTOR/DIRECTOR
Jeremy Postaer

COPYWRITER/DIRECTOR
Steve Simpson

PRODUCER
Ben Latimer

AGENCY
Goodby, Berlin & Silverstein

CLIENT
Chevys Restaurant

DAN & DAVE'S MOMS.

VO: Dan's mom.
MRS. O'BRIEN: Dan.
VO: Dave's mom.
MRS. JOHNSON: Dave.
VO: Dan's coach.
COACH: Dan.
VO: Dave's coach.
COACH: Dave.
VO: Dan's dentist.
DENTIST: Dan.
VO: Dave's mailman.
MAILMAN: Dave.
VO: Dan's paperboy.
PAPERBOY: Dan.
VO: Dave's pastor.
PASTOR: Dave.
VO: Dan's girlfriend.
GIRLFRIEND: Dan.
VO: Dave's mom.
MRS. JOHNSON: Dave.
EX-GIRLFRIEND: Definitely Dave.
VO: To be settled in Barcelona.

Campaign

ART DIRECTOR
Michael Fazende

COPYWRITER
Mike Lescarbeau

PRODUCER
Judy Brink

DIRECTOR
Eric Young/Young & Co.

AGENCY
Fallon McElligott

CLIENT
The Lee Co.

Campaign

ART DIRECTOR
Michael Fazende

COPYWRITER
Mike Lescarbeau

PRODUCER
Judy Brink

DIRECTOR
Tarsem/A+R Group

AGENCY
Fallon McElligott

CLIENT
The Lee Co.

Campaign

ART DIRECTOR
Bob Brihn

COPYWRITER
Phil Hanft

PRODUCERS
Char Loving, Vicki Oachs

DIRECTOR
Eric Young/Young & Co.

AGENCY
Fallon McElligott

CLIENT
Time Inc.

SODA CAN.
SFX: Dramatic music throughout.
VO: Just in time for the recycling craze?
SFX: Crunch.
VO: Lee Heavyweight Cotton Sweats.

WATER.
MAN: What do I need an education for? Ya know, I'm a model. Hey, can't we get any cold water over here? Of course I'm a perfectionist, look at me. Twice I've asked for cold water. What's my most attractive part? I think you get a complete package, ya know. I look good in jeans. How's my hair doing? Anyone looks good in jeans, but I look tough in jeans. Some women are intimidated by my looks. I find that exciting, ya know. I think when I'm done modelling I'm gonna be an astronaut.

L.A. RIOTS.
VO: In the May 11th issue of *Time*, we reported what we saw during the recent riots in south-central Los Angeles. What we saw...was the enemy...and the enemy was us. All of us. Can we all get along? If it's important to you, you'll find it in *Time*.

Campaign

ART DIRECTOR
Leslie Caldwell

COPYWRITER/CREATIVE DIRECTOR
Mike Koelker

PRODUCER
Anna Frost

DIRECTOR
Joe Pytka

AGENCY
Foote, Cone and Belding

CLIENT
Levi Strauss

Campaign

ART DIRECTOR
Ty Harper

COPYWRITER
Rob Schapiro

PRODUCER
Frank Soukup

DIRECTOR
Neal Slavin

AGENCY
Earle Palmer Brown

CLIENT
Water Country USA

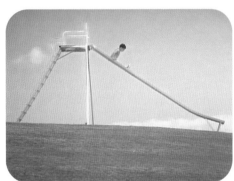

Campaign

ART DIRECTORS
Terre Nichols, Mark Hughes

COPYWRITERS
Tom Cunniff, Mike Herlehy

PRODUCER
Elise Baruch

DIRECTOR
Peter Lauer

AGENCY
Lord, Denstu & Partners/New York

CLIENT
Lea & Perrins

BROWN.

SFX: Music in.
VO: Brown. The only color born in September. (*music up and under*) Warm. Big shoulders. Brown. (*music up, music under*) Strong. Earthy...Color with both feet on the ground (*music up, music under*) and nobody does brown like Dockers.

SLIDE.

SFX: Insect humming noise of a very hot day. Squeak of sweaty legs sticking on the slide.
VO: It's gonna be a long summer.
BOY: Mommmm.
VO: Take the kids to Water Country USA.

NIGHTMARE.

VO: Lea & Perrins Steak Sauce. Great on beef, beef, beef (*echo*). Lea & Perrins Steak Sauce. Great on beef. Great on beef. Great on beef.
COW: Umpf!
VO: Lea & Perrins. The steak sauce only a cow could hate.

Campaign

ART DIRECTOR
Paul Rubenstein

COPYWRITER
James Cohen

PRODUCER
Tom Dakin

AGENCY
Bozell

CLIENT
Jim Cutie

Campaign

ART DIRECTOR
Paul Janas

COPYWRITER
William Mericle

AGENCY
Hal Riney & Partners

CLIENT
Subway Restaurants

ART DIRECTOR
Bob Brihn

COPYWRITER
Phil Hanft

PRODUCERS
Char Loving, Vicki Oachs

DIRECTOR
Eric Young/Young & Co.

AGENCY
Fallon McElligott

CLIENT
Time Inc.

INTERVIEW.

VO: Finding writers to join the best new sports section in New York hasn't been easy.
MAN: Most triples in a season, New York Mets.
KID: 10, Mookie Wilson.
MAN: First draft choice of the Knicks in '67.
KID: Walt Frazier.
MAN: Most shutouts, New York Yankees.
KID: Whitey Ford.
MAN: How far down the left field line in Wrigley field?
KID: 350 feet.
MAN: 355, get outta here.
VO: The bigger, bolder sports section of *The Times*. Every day. Everything New York. Everything sports. Now in *The New York Times*.

EVERYTHING'S FRESH.

OWNER: I hope when people see Subway, bells go off and they think good sandwich. We don't deep fry or freeze dry—everything's fresh. Each morning, I slice tomatoes, onions. I even bake the bread. These days, people think a lot about what foods to eat. Nothing's more honest than a good sandwich. So if the body's a temple, this is the place to come when the temple gets hungry.
VO: For twenty-five years, Subway has quietly made some of the best sandwiches anywhere, starting at a dollar sixty-nine. For more information, visit the Subway near you.

L.A. RIOTS.

VO: In the May 11th issue of *Time*, we reported what we saw during the recent riots in south-central Los Angeles. What we saw...was the enemy...and the enemy was us. All of us. Can we all get along? If it's important to you, you'll find it in *Time*.

ART DIRECTOR
Michael Fazende
COPYWRITER
Mike Lescarbeau
PRODUCER
Judy Brink
DIRECTOR
Tarsem/A+R Group
AGENCY
Fallon McElligott
CLIENT
The Lee Co.

Campaign
ART DIRECTOR
Frank Costantini
COPYWRITER
J.J. Jordan
PRODUCER
Linda Rafoos
AGENCY
J. Walter Thompson
CLIENT
Warner Lambert/E.P.T.

Public Service
ART DIRECTORS/COPYWRITERS/DIRECTORS
Peter Cohen, Leslie Sweet
AGENCY
Streetsmart Advertising
CLIENT
Coalition for the Homeless

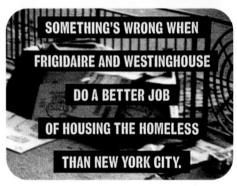

**COALITION FOR THE HOMELESS
695-8700**

BRAIN.
WOMAN: I'm a model, but that doesn't mean other girls should be jealous. I mean it's hard work staying perfect.
SFX: Clock gong.
WOMAN: For whom the bell tolls. I wanna be an actress, but I wanna be a serious actress. I want to play the life of Mother Theresa. Ahhhh! My goals? To end violence throughout the world, and find a really easy-to-manage hairstyle. I love dogs. I love little small ones that you can take to work with you. You walk in with your dog leash and you look very cool. You look very chic. I love spending money. Spend, spend, spend, spend, spend. Um, a cappucino. I look good in jeans, but most everybody looks good in jeans, but I look perfect. You know if mascara is not important, how come there's a rear-view mirror in every car? I don't like reading books. I think that it's very boring and if it's work I mean, reading, then make it into a movie. Excuse me but I'd like an espresso. You can't be a model your whole life. I mean its not like oh, my brain hurts, but...you can't eat anything. Cellulite is not my cup of tea. Speaking of tea, where's my waiter? Can I change my order?
SFX: Dog growling.

PADOVAN. MURPHY. FREDERICK/MARTIN.
WOMAN: My body tells me I might be but then you know a woman's body is kind of, you know, you never know, symptoms you could have for just a regular monthly cycle type thing.
MAN: And we're at a very nice age to start having kids, 34. I'm 34. I'm ready.
WOMAN: I've always been ready!! (*laughs*)
MAN: Um, besides myself and her, the most important thing is my family and that is having a child.
WOMAN: It's negative.
MAN: Ah, bummer!
WOMAN: I could have sworn it was positive.
MAN: Don't get worried, man. We're going to keep trying.

CARDBOARD BOXES.
SFX: Street noises, garbage trucks, horns honking, etc. throughout.

Public Service
ART DIRECTOR
Kirk Souder
COPYWRITER
Court Crandall
PRODUCER
Vincent Joliet
DIRECTOR
Joe Pytka
AGENCY
Stein Robaire Helm
CLIENT
Museum of Contemporary Art

Public Service
ART DIRECTOR/COPYWRITER
Jeremy Postaer
PRODUCER
Cindy Fluitt
DIRECTOR
Jeff Goodby
AGENCY
Goodby, Berlin & Silverstein
CLIENT
Partnership for a Drug Free America

Public Service
ART DIRECTOR
Jamie Mahoney
COPYWRITER
Ken Hines
PRODUCER
Jim Vaile
AGENCY
The Martin Agency
CLIENT
United Way

TV DINNER.
SFX: Game show playing on a television in background.

LONG WAY HOME.
SFX: Music under throughout.
VO #1: My teacher tells us all we gotta do is just say no. And the other day a policeman came to our class talking about say no, too. Well, my teacher doesn't have to walk home through this neighborhood. And maybe the dealers are scared of the police...but they're not scared of me. And they sure don't take no for an answer.
VO #2: To Kevin Scott...and all the other kids who take the long way home, we hear you...don't give up.

LOOK AROUND.
SFX: Disjointed sounds of bottles crashing, bangs, bumps, crashes. Footsteps. Sirens. Loud car music. Child cries. Discordant piano. Pop goes the weasel. Tragic music. Camera click.

Film & TV Art Direction

ART DIRECTOR
David Angelo

COPYWRITER
Paul Spencer

PRODUCER
Eric Herrmann

DIRECTOR
John Lloyd

AGENCY
DDB Needham Worldwide

CLIENT
New York State Lottery

Low-Budget

ART DIRECTOR
Jeremy Postaer

COPYWRITER
Bob Kerstetter

PRODUCER
Elizabeth O'Toole

DIRECTOR
Jeff Goodby

AGENCY
Goodby, Berlin & Silverstein

CLIENT
San Francisco Museum of Modern Art

Promotional Video

ART DIRECTOR
Steve Miller

COPYWRITER
Rob Slosberg

PRODUCER
Penny Cohen

TYPOGRAPHER
Graham Clifford

AGENCY
Chiat/Day/Mojo

CLIENT
Reebok Pro-Bono

CABLE.
SFX: Birds. Outside noises.
MAN: Does it come with cable?
AGENT: Ah, well...
VO: New York Lotto. Hey, you never know.

TOM'S POT ROAST.
SFX: Music under throughout. It sounds like it's coming over an old-fashioned radio.
WIFE: Joe, how do you feel about pot roast?
JOE: I feel a rational sense of guilt pervading an otherwise mandatory denial of sardonic bliss, which seems to question the very·nature of my emerging responsibility as a human being. But whatever you want would be fine.
VO: You're never quite the same after a trip to the Modern.

WITNESS VIDEO.
All visual supers: You can say a story was fabricated. You can say the jury was corrupt. You can say a document is false. You can say a person is lying. You can even say you don't trust newspapers. But you can't say what you just saw never happened. Take pictures. Shoot a film. Make a video. Help us give cameras to the world. Expose injustice. Show us what's wrong with the world. And maybe we can help make it right.

Promotional Video

ART DIRECTORS/COPYWRITERS
Hank Perlman, Frank Todaro,
Bryan Buckley, Robert Wong

PRODUCER
Valerie Edwards

DIRECTOR
Laura Belse

AGENCY
Frankfurt Gips Balkind

CLIENT
Adobe Systems, Inc.

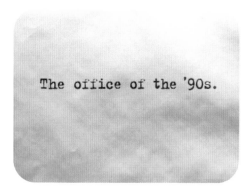

THE OFFICE AND ME.

MAN #1: Of course it could. Everything could, but, uh, we're really proud of the way we are managing it and the way we solve our problems.

WOMAN #1: Well, in the company, everyone has the same basic computer, but only two are compatible. And that's mine and Tracy's.

WOMAN #2: That's me, Tracy.

MAN #1: Well, we've got a couple of computers that talk to each other. Um, that was a major breakthrough for us.

WOMAN #1: We use the exact same applications.

WOMAN #2: When she gets an upgrade, I get an upgrade.

WOMAN #1: And that's not what everyone has. So this makes ours unique.

WOMAN #2: We're like two little twins.

MAN #2: I send text from my computer to other computers all over the world in ASCII of course. Sometimes people complain about losing formatting things, um, like font, and font size, and outlines, and underlines, and italics. But my writing doesn't need that. Bold. Bold. Bold. One doesn't need bold. Bold is to make up for not being able to use a properly placed exclamation point (*sniffs*) and I think it's deplorable.

MEN #3 & #4: Hum.

MAN #3: In my workstation they do have a way where you can—I can fax myself a graph or spreadsheet. Then, I can take that spreadsheet and attach it to a file that I want to send out. And within the E-Mail program, I usually like to take it, fax it to myself, and then I fax it to myself. So I can see what the other person is going to get. It's confusing 'cause it's all coming from the same computer, but I have to put it through certain stages. I have to distill it into a final product that I can send out.

WOMAN #3: It's fabulous. You send it out one night, and the next day, it's there. It's saved my job many times. I can get things there, wherever it needs to be, overnight. So, sometimes, when things are really important, I send it by two different overnight carriers. Just to cover myself.

WOMAN #4: He's gone.

WOMAN #3: Oh sh—

MAN #4: Well, I mean everyone just faxes stuff now. I, well—you can't fax the page. So what we do is just make copies and fax the copies. The copier will give you good quality photos or it'll give you good quality text, but it never gives you good quality of both. So we want to make two copies of—and the paper's jammed right now. We just—well, this thing's all screwed up again. This isn't working at all, right now. So if it were working, I'd make two copies. I'll show you with this. Here's a good example of good photo quality. So I just cut them out. You have to kind of make a sandwich out of them both. You take the photo from one, and the type from the other one and that gives you a good enough original that will work fine over the fax. So this is about the best we can do. I don't think anyone has ever thanked us, but nobody really complains much about it either. So it works pretty well.

WOMAN #5: You know, I work in a large office with a lot of people and they all need copies of everything. Sometimes more than one. Many of them, they either lost it or they forget where they put it. Some of them even take it home, and when they take it home they forget to bring it back. So I always make it a practice to have at least two or three dozen extra because I don't like to stay after five o'clock. I love to be home in time for "Jeopardy."

WOMAN #6: It's a lot of paper and we handle it well. I can break it down six different ways for one company. I just call my assistant...Matt, could you come in please?

MAN #5: Yes?

WOMAN #6: Matt, I need you to find a letter for me. It's really important. It's concerning that bank that we had relations with in 1988. The RTC is looking for a document that I sent to them in September/October...It could take a few days 'cause we'll have to go to cold storage and retrieve it. I always get what I want but it's never been more than a week.

MAN #6: As you can see this place is pretty crowded. But, that's the way it is and I work with it alright. Here are the important files. We don't have anything for it today, but the red files are the important files. I used to like to think that I'd be an engineer, and that probably got me into filing this way, because it's logical for me. I can find them quicker and the people upstairs keep asking me for things. Nobody knows where they are except for me.

Film & TV Art Direction

ART DIRECTOR
David Angelo

COPYWRITER
Paul Spencer

PRODUCER
Eric Herrmann

DIRECTOR
Brent Thomas

AGENCY
DDB Needham Worldwide

CLIENT
New York State Lottery

Film & TV Art Direction

ART DIRECTOR
David Angelo

COPYWRITER
Paul Spencer

PRODUCER
Eric Herrmann

DIRECTOR
Brent Thomas

AGENCY
DDB Needham Worldwide

CLIENT
New York State Lottery

Film & TV Art Direction

ART DIRECTOR
David Angelo

COPYWRITER
Paul Spencer

PRODUCER
Eric Herrmann

DIRECTOR
Brent Thomas

AGENCY
DDB Needham Worldwide

CLIENT
New York State Lottery

GRAND BALL.
SFX: Music throughout.
BUTLER: Admiral and Lady Billingsly of Devonshire. Lord and Lady Atherton of Sussex. Sir Alfred and Lady Sheffield of Dunnsmar. And Bob of Buffalo.
VO: New York Lotto. Hey, you never know.

BACKSEAT DRIVER.
MAN: Faster...Faster. Faster!!!!
VO: New York Lotto. Hey, you never know.

OPERA.
SFX: Opera music. Music stops.
WOMAN: Thank you.
SFX: Music continues.
VO: New York Lotto. Hey, you never know.

Film & TV Art Direction

ART DIRECTORS
Donna Weinheim, Kevin Donovan

COPYWRITERS
Cliff Freeman, Rick LeMoine

PRODUCER
Jean Kelly

DIRECTOR
Bruce Dowad

AGENCY
Cliff Freeman & Partners

CLIENT
Little Caesars

Film & TV Art Direction

ART DIRECTORS/COPYWRITERS
Donna Weinheim, Cliff Freeman

PRODUCER
Melanie Klein

DIRECTOR
Mark Story

AGENCY
Cliff Freeman & Partners

CLIENT
Little Caesars

Film & TV Art Direction

ART DIRECTOR
Terre Nichols

COPYWRITER
Mike Herlehy

PRODUCER
Elise Baruch

DIRECTOR
Peter Lauer

AGENCY
Lord, Dentsu & Partners/New York

CLIENT
Lea & Perrins, Inc.

SOUNDS OF SUMMER.
VO: Aaah, the sounds of summer.
SFX: Birds chirping, wind rustling. Expandable jug opening. Jug noises from other nearby families. Jug noises and nature sounds grow into a cacophony of summer sounds. Little girl giggles.
VO: Two pizzas, two Crazy Breads, and this jug with Kool-Aid for $8.98. It's Little Caesar's.
LITTLE CAESAR: Picnic! Picnic!

TOOZY DOOZY.
VO: Upon learning Little Caesars is offering two pizzas for $5.99...
SFX: Old projector, large clicking.
VO: ...the mind enters five stages...shock...disbelief...confusion...
SFX: Shoes stomping on floor.
VO: ...denial...and finally acceptance.
SFX: 1930s style music plays.
VO: Now let's watch the subject registering denial again in extreme slow motion.

NIGHTMARE.
VO: Lea & Perrins Steak Sauce. Great on beef, beef, beef (*echo*). Lea & Perrins Steak Sauce. Great on beef. Great on beef. Great on beef.
COW: Umpf!
VO: Lea & Perrins. The steak sauce only a cow could hate.

Film & TV Copywriting

ART DIRECTOR
John Staffen

COPYWRITER
Mike Rogers

PRODUCER
Steve Amato

DIRECTOR
Emily Oberman

AGENCY
DDB Needham Worldwide

CLIENT
Earthshare

ALL TYPE.
SFX: Tape noise throughout.

Film & TV Copywriting

ART DIRECTOR
David Angelo

COPYWRITER
Paul Spencer

PRODUCER
Eric Herrmann

DIRECTOR
John Lloyd

AGENCY
DDB Needham Worldwide

CLIENT
New York State Lottery

CABLE.
SFX: Birds. Outside noises.
MAN: Does it come with cable?
AGENT: Ah, well...
VO: New York Lotto. Hey, you never know.

Film & TV Copywriting

ART DIRECTOR
David Harner

COPYWRITER
David Johnson

PRODUCER
Roseanne Horn

DIRECTOR
Jim Gartner

AGENCY
Young & Rubicam

CLIENT
AT&T Communications

TED.
GIRL: Dad, we need to talk. Dad, we need to talk.
VO: I know you don't like Ted very much but...he's...he's asked me to be his...w-wife...he's...he's asked me to be his...w-wife
SFX: Busy signal
GIRL: I'm getting married. Your daughter...no...I know you don't like him but...
SFX: Busy signal.
GIRL: Daddy, I'm gonna marry Ted...Daddy, I'm gonna marry Ted...He's intelligent. He makes great spaghetti...
SFX: Busy signal.
GIRL: Dad, you're not losing a daughter you're gaining...Ted.
VO: When you're overseas, even a busy signal is no problem with AT&T USA Direct. All you have to do is send a message that'll get through later.

Film & TV Copywriting

ART DIRECTORS
K.J. Bowen, Max Jerome,
Harvey Marco, Kirk Souder

COPYWRITERS
Steve Biegel, Tony Gomes

PRODUCER
Jack McWalters

AGENCY
Ammirati & Puris Inc.

CLIENT
Aetna Life and Casualty Co.

Film & TV Copywriting

ART DIRECTOR
Scott O'Leary

COPYWRITERS
John Krueger, Bob Powers

PRODUCER
John Seaton

DIRECTOR
Dennis Manarchy

AGENCY
DMB&B/St. Louis

CLIENT
Anheuser-Bush, Inc./Budweiser

Call: Retirement Made Easy
1-800-AETNA60

ROCKET SCIENCE.
SFX: Advanced lecture in lecture hall in differential equations throughout. Chalkboard sounds. Ridiculously complicated.

GOING TO THE FRIDGE.
SFX: Background sound of a sporting event. Footsteps. Sound of refrigerator door opening. Sound of a bottle opening. Pouring into glass.

ART DIRECTOR
Bob Adsit

COPYWRITER
Thom Baginski

PRODUCER
Lora Nelson

DIRECTOR
Bob Giraldi

AGENCY
DDB Needham Worldwide

CLIENT
Ads Against AIDS

ART DIRECTOR
Kevin Mote

COPYWRITER
Alex Lasker

PRODUCER
Linda Stewart

DIRECTOR/PHOTOGRAPHER
Danny Ducovny

STUDIO
Cucoloris Films

CLIENT
Farm Aid

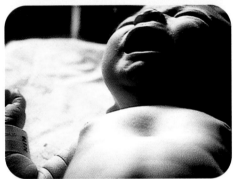

EYES.

VO: There are two ways to look at AIDS. It's their problem.
MAN: Well, that's true.
VO: Or it's everyones.
MAN: They never become famous until they're dead.
WOMAN: I adored his work even when he was alive.
VO: It's in the streets.
BEGGAR: You wouldn't have a dollar? I wouldn't ask if I didn't need it. Don't pass me up.
VO: Or right next door.
SFX: Alarm clock. Sound of church bells.
VO: They asked for it.
SFX: Gong sound. Baby crying.
VO: Nobody asked for it. You can close your eyes to AIDS. But you can never look the other way.

FARM AID.

MAN: For five generations my family's taken great pride in the beauty of this life. We've never asked or wanted for anything. My dad was smart enough to see some of what was coming—the pitfalls of the modern marketplace, as Mr. Thibeau the banker puts it. So I became the first Wheeler to go to college. I hope to send my children to college one day. What their businesses will be is up to them, of course, but I know it won't be farming. The last of my heavy equipment was sold off by the bank yesterday. Tomorrow, [the] land itself goes up for auction. It gives me very little comfort to say: "At least my father wasn't around to see it."

Consumer Newspaper
ART DIRECTOR
Jamie Mahoney
COPYWRITER
Raymond McKinney
AGENCY
The Martin Agency
CLIENT
Center for Cosmetic Plastic Surgery

Consumer Newspaper
ART DIRECTOR
Jerry Torchia
COPYWRITER
Mike Hughes
ILLUSTRATOR
Scott Sawyer
AGENCY
The Martin Agency
CLIENT
Signet Bank

Consumer Newspaper
ART DIRECTOR
Jerry Torchia
COPYWRITER
Mike Hughes
ILLUSTRATOR
Scott Sawyer
AGENCY
The Martin Agency
CLIENT
Signet Bank

WE REMOVE CROWS FEET.
(FORGIVE US, ASPCA.)

Our facelifts will smooth out all the wrinkles around your eyes and forehead. Give us a call at 804-481-5151. We'll be glad to set up an appointment for a consultation.

Center for Cosmetic Plastic Surgery

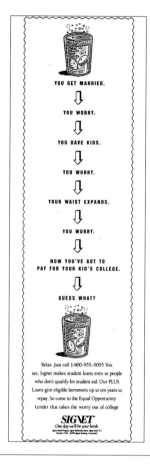

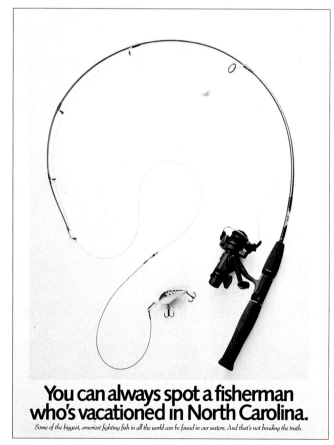

You can always spot a fisherman who's vacationed in North Carolina.

Some of the biggest, orneriest fighting fish in all the world can be found in our waters. And that's not bending the truth.

BOSOM BUDDY.

Dr. Mladick has been using saline breast implants for 17 years. Not silicone. Call 804-481-5151 to set up an appointment for a consultation.

Center for Cosmetic Plastic Surgery

Consumer Newspaper
ART DIRECTOR
Jim Mountjoy
COPYWRITER
Ed Jones
PHOTOGRAPHER
MARVY!
AGENCY
Loeffler Ketchum Mountjoy
CLIENT
North Carolina Travel & Tourism

Consumer Newspaper
ART DIRECTOR
Jamie Mahoney
COPYWRITER
Raymond McKinney
AGENCY
The Martin Agency
CLIENT
Center for Cosmetic Plastic Surgery

Consumer Newspaper
ART DIRECTOR
Gordon Smith
COPYWRITER
Steve Lasch
AGENCY
Loeffler Ketchum Mountjoy
CLIENT
WTVI

Consumer Newspaper
ART DIRECTOR
Tom Lichtenheld
COPYWRITER
Luke Sullivan
PHOTOGRAPHER
Shawn Michienzi
AGENCY
Fallon McElligott
CLIENT
Jim Beam Brands, Co.

AT LEAST ONE STREET IN AMERICA WILL ALWAYS BE SAFE FOR KIDS.

"Sesame Street" weekdays at 8am and 4pm on WTVI.

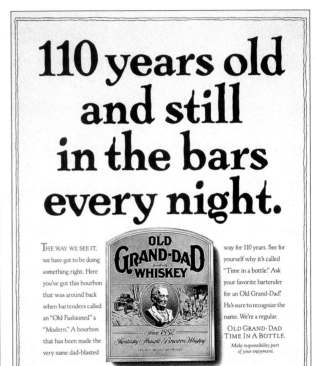

Statistics show that your father spent about $134,000 raising you. Here's a nice way to pay back about fifty bucks of it.

Timex. It takes a licking and keeps on ticking. **TIMEX**

Consumer Newspaper
ART DIRECTOR
Dean Hanson
COPYWRITER
Bruce Bildsten
AGENCY
Fallon McElligott
CLIENT
Timex Corp.

Consumer Newspaper
ART DIRECTOR
Kevin Lippy
COPYWRITER
Rankin Mapother
AGENCY
Two Guys Advertising

A NEW YEAR'S EVE YOU'LL REMEMBER.

"St. Mary's alcohol-free New Year's Eve party," call 249-1031.

Consumer Newspaper
ART DIRECTOR
Mike Murray
COPYWRITER
Kristine Larsen
PHOTOGRAPHER
Arndt Photography
AGENCY
Hunt Murray
CLIENT
Mystic Lake Casino

Consumer Newspaper
COPYWRITER
Jim Copacino
CREATIVE DIRECTOR
Jim Walker
AGENCY
McCann-Erickson
CLIENT
Washington Mutual

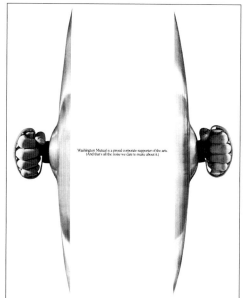

Consumer Newspaper
ART DIRECTOR
Eric Tilford
COPYWRITER
Todd Tilford
CREATIVE DIRECTOR
Stan Richards
AGENCY
The Richards Group
CLIENT
The Spy Factory

Consumer Newspaper
ART DIRECTOR
Tim Parker
COPYWRITER
Dave Newman
ILLUSTRATOR
George Vogt
AGENCY
Borders, Perrin & Norrander
CLIENT
Oregon Dairy Products Commission

Consumer Newspaper

ART DIRECTOR
Arty Tan

COPYWRITER
Mike Lescarbeau

PHOTOGRAPHER
Kerry Peterson

AGENCY
Fallon McElligott

CLIENT
Star Tribune

Consumer Newspaper

ART DIRECTOR
Susan Griak

COPYWRITER
Mike Lescarbeau

PHOTOGRAPHERS
Craig Perman, Kerry Peterson

AGENCY
Fallon McElligott

CLIENT
Jim Beam Brands, Co.

Consumer Newspaper

ART DIRECTOR
Noam Murro

COPYWRITER
Dean Hacohen

ILLUSTRATOR
Mike Samuels

AGENCY
Goldsmith/Jeffrey

CLIENT
El Al Airlines

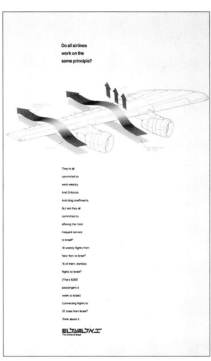

Consumer Newspaper

ART DIRECTOR
Gary Goldsmith

COPYWRITER
Dean Hacohen

PHOTOGRAPHER
Ilan Rubin

AGENCY
Goldsmith/Jeffrey

CLIENT
Bergdorf Goodman

Consumer Newspaper

ART DIRECTOR
Gary Goldsmith

COPYWRITER
Dean Hacohen

PHOTOGRAPHER
Chris Wormell

AGENCY
Goldsmith/Jeffrey

CLIENT
J.P. Morgan

Consumer Newspaper

ART DIRECTOR
Cliff Sorah

COPYWRITER
Ken Hines

PHOTOGRAPHER
Richard Ustinich

AGENCY
The Martin Agency

CLIENT
Residence Inn

Consumer Newspaper

ART DIRECTOR
Randy Hughes

COPYWRITER
Josh Denberg

PHOTOGRAPHER
Curtis Johnson, Arndt Photography

AGENCY
Clarity Coverdale Rueff

CLIENT
St. Paul Pioneer Press

Consumer Newspaper

ART DIRECTOR
Clem McCarthy

COPYWRITER
Bill McCullam

AGENCY
Ammirati & Puris Inc.

CLIENT
Aetna Life & Casualty Company

Consumer Newspaper

ART DIRECTOR
Melinda Kanipe

COPYWRITER
Scott Zacaroli

PHOTOGRAPHER
Brett Froomer

AGENCY
Ammirati & Puris Inc.

CLIENT
BMW of North America, Inc.

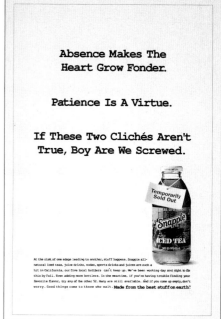

Consumer Newspaper

ART DIRECTOR
Mike Mazza

COPYWRITER
Steve Silver

CREATIVE DIRECTOR
Tom Cordner

PHOTOGRAPHERS
Joe Dominic, Michael Raasch, R. Leech

AGENCY
Team One Advertising

CLIENT
Lexus

Consumer Newspaper

ART DIRECTOR
Brenda Dziadzio

COPYWRITER
Paul Silverman

PHOTOGRAPHER
Clint Clemens

AGENCY
Mullen

CLIENT
Rolls-Royce Motor Cars, Inc.

Consumer Newspaper

ART DIRECTOR
Kathryn Windley

COPYWRITERS
R. Klein, J. O'Neill, J. Kerin

PHOTOGRAPHER
Douglas Whyte

AGENCY
Hal Riney & Partners

CLIENT
Snapple

Consumer Newspaper

ART DIRECTOR
Danny Boone

COPYWRITER
Jack Mahoney

AGENCY
The Martin Agency

CLIENT
Capitol Forum

Consumer Newspaper

ART DIRECTOR
Mark Fuller

COPYWRITER
Joe Alexander

PHOTOGRAPHER
Michael Furman

AGENCY
The Martin Agency

CLIENT
Mercedes Benz

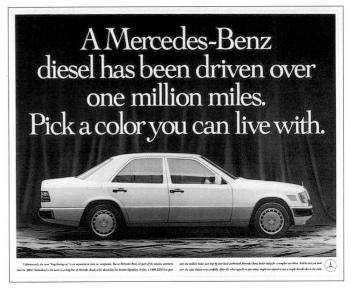

Consumer Newspaper

ART DIRECTOR
Shari Hindman

COPYWRITERS
Jack Mahoney, Bill Westbrook

PHOTOGRAPHER
David LeBon

AGENCY
The Martin Agency

CLIENT
Mercedes Benz

Consumer Newspaper

ART DIRECTOR
Shari Hindman

COPYWRITER
Jack Mahoney

PHOTOGRAPHERS
David LeBon, John Early

AGENCY
The Martin Agency

CLIENT
Mercedes Benz

Consumer Newspaper

ART DIRECTOR
Mark Johnson

COPYWRITER
John Stingley

PHOTOGRAPHER
Andreas Burz

AGENCY
Fallon McElligott

CLIENT
Porsche Cars North America

Consumer Newspaper

ART DIRECTOR
Mark Johnson

COPYWRITER
John Stingley

PHOTOGRAPHER
Jeff Zwart

AGENCY
Fallon McElligott

CLIENT
Porsche Cars North America

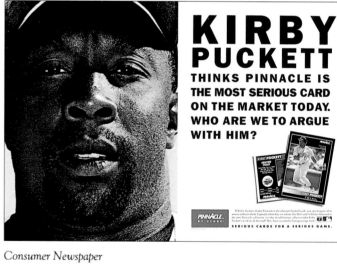

Consumer Newspaper

ART DIRECTOR
Andrea D'Aquino

COPYWRITER
Nat Whitten

PHOTOGRAPHER
Major League Marketing

AGENCY
Weiss, Whitten, Carroll, Stagliano

CLIENT
Score Group, Inc.

Consumer Newspaper

ART DIRECTOR
Jim Mountjoy

COPYWRITER
Ed Jones

PHOTOGRAPHER
Tim Olive

AGENCY
Loeffler Ketchum Mountjoy

CLIENT
Duke Power

Consumer Newspaper/Campaign

ART DIRECTOR
Steve Pollack

COPYWRITER
Scott Lusbador

AGENCY
Arnold Fortuna Lawner & Cabot

CLIENT
Toro Loco

Consumer Newspaper/Campaign

ART DIRECTOR
Michael Kadin

COPYWRITER
Jim Garaventi

AGENCY
Leonard Monahan Lubars & Kelly

CLIENT
The Narragansett

Consumer Newspaper/Campaign

ART DIRECTOR/ILLUSTATOR
Randy Hughes

COPYWRITER
Josh Denberg

PRODUCER
Jan Miller

AGENCY
Clarity Cloverdale Rueff

CLIENT
Moose & Sadie's Coffee House

WE'D SEND YOUR COMPLIMENTS TO THE CHEF, BUT HE DOESN'T SPEAK ENGLISH.

Authentic Mexican cuisine made by an authentic Mexican chef.

TORO LOCO
Mexican Restaurant
23 Valley St., South Orange 761-1515

SAVE UP TO 80% DURING OUR GOING OUT OF BUSINESS SALE.

(Oh sure, now you'll come in.)

the narragansett

COME TRY TODAY'S FRESH BREW. OR MAYBE TRY SOME ESPRESSO. TELL US WHAT YOU THINK. AND DON'T WORRY, THERE'S NO HIDDEN CAMERA.

We've secretly replaced Folgers Crystals with real coffee.

212 THIRD AVENUE NORTH.
WAREHOUSE DISTRICT.
MINNEAPOLIS.
371-0464.
MOOSE & SADIE'S
COFFEE
HOUSE

TO TRULY APPRECIATE OUR FOOD, WE RECOMMEND EATING AT TACO BELL.

Mexican food that may be different from what you're used to. It's authentic.

TORO LOCO
Mexican Restaurant
23 Valley St., South Orange 761-1515

AT 50-80% OFF THE ONLY THING YOU CAN'T SAVE IS OUR STORE.

The dresses are going. The skirts are going. The fixtures are going. Shouldn't you be going too?

the narragansett

COME HANG OUT AND HAVE A GOOD CUP OF COFFEE. OR MAYBE AN ESPRESSO. BECAUSE WHILE SLEEPING WITH STRANGERS MAY BE DANGEROUS, WAKING UP WITH THEM ISN'T.

Wake up with people you don't know.

212 THIRD AVENUE NORTH.
WAREHOUSE DISTRICT.
MINNEAPOLIS.
371-0464.
MOOSE & SADIE'S
COFFEE
HOUSE

YOU CAN EITHER MAKE RESERVATIONS WITH US OR MEXICANA AIRLINES.

Experience authentic Mexican cuisine without going all the way to Mexico.

TORO LOCO
Mexican Restaurant
23 Valley St., South Orange 761-1515

WE WROTE THE BOOK ON FASHION. UNFORTUNATELY, IT ENDS WITH CHAPTER 11.

At our going out of business sale you'll save 80% on European fashions. Au-revoir and Arrivederci.

the narragansett

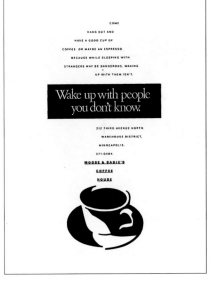

SURE, OUR COFFEE IS ABOUT A DOLLAR A CUP ESPRESSO, A LITTLE MORE. BUT FACE IT. IF THE STUFF AT WORK WERE ANY GOOD, THEY WOULDN'T BE GIVING IT AWAY. NOW WOULD THEY?

One taste and you'll know why office coffee is free.

212 THIRD AVENUE NORTH.
WAREHOUSE DISTRICT.
MINNEAPOLIS.
371-0464.
MOOSE & SADIE'S
COFFEE
HOUSE

Consumer Newspaper/Campaign

ART DIRECTOR
Bryan Burlison

COPYWRITER
Todd Tilford

CREATIVE DIRECTOR
Stan Richards

PHOTOGRAPHER
Richard Reens

AGENCY
The Richards Group

CLIENT
Harley-Davidson of Dallas

Consumer Newspaper/Campaign

ART DIRECTOR
Everett Young Wilder

COPYWRITER
Todd Tilford

PHOTOGRAPHER
Julio Castaner

AGENCY
The Richards Group

CLIENT
Auto Exam

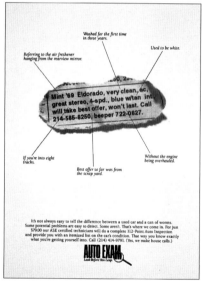

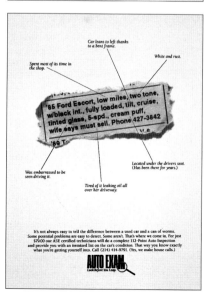

Consumer Newspaper/Campaign
ART DIRECTOR
Jim Mountjoy
COPYWRITER
Ed Jones
AGENCY
Loeffler Ketchum Mountjoy
CLIENT
Opera

Consumer Newspaper/Campaign
ART DIRECTOR/COPYWRITER
Ellen Steinberg
PHOTOGRAPHER
Mark Weiss
PRODUCER
Vickie Gillis
AGENCY
Weiss, Whitten, Carroll, Stagliano
CLIENT
Ghurka

Attractive, fabulously wealthy widow seeks dashing, eligible bachelor for evening filled with sizzling repartee, dancing and sexual intrigue. Appreciation of fine music a definite plus. In fact, am thinking the opera would be a good place for us to meet-say 8pm on November 12 or 14 at Ovens Auditorium?
Reply: 372-3626. Ask for **"The Merry Widow."**

PLEASE NOTE:

A Ghurka handbag would greatly complement many items advertised in this section.

GHURKA

41 East 57th Street, New York City · 1-800-852-9796 · Also available at other fine stores.

Wealthy, saucy widow still seeking dapper bachelor for romantic encounter-maybe even matrimony. Ideal rendezvous spot: the opera-say 8ish on November 12 or 14 at Ovens Auditorium? Don't worry, you can't miss me. I'm the one with the great pair of lungs.
Reply: 372-3626. Ask for **"The Merry Widow."**

PLEASE NOTE:

Today's issue of the Times will fit conveniently into a Ghurka briefcase.

GHURKA

41 East 57th Street, New York City · 1-800-852-9796 · Also available at other fine stores.

Rich, increasingly desperate widow still seeking to make beautiful music with playboy bachelor. I'll be at the opera at Ovens Auditorium, 8pm, November 12 and 14. Will you? Don't want to pressure you by saying this could be your last chance. But I will say this: it won't be long until the fat lady sings.
Reply: 372-3626. Ask for **"The Merry Widow."**

PLEASE NOTE:

If you've turned to this section to find out what's in style, we recommend a Ghurka tote.

GHURKA

41 East 57th Street, New York City · 1-800-852-9796 · Also available at other fine stores.

Consumer Newspaper/Campaign

ART DIRECTOR
Gary Goldsmith

COPYWRITER
Dean Hacohen

AGENCY
Goldsmith/Jeffrey

CLIENT
Bergdorf Goodman

Consumer Newspaper/Campaign

ART DIRECTOR
Hal Curtis

COPYWRITER
Steve Skibba

CREATIVE DIRECTOR
Cabell Harris

PHOTOGRAPHER
Mark Gervase

AGENCY
Work

CLIENT
Beverly Hills Baseball Card Shop

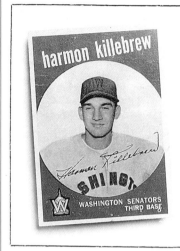

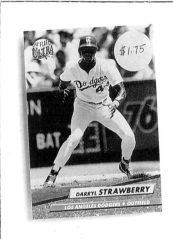

Consumer Newspaper/Campaign

ART DIRECTOR
Dean Hanson

COPYWRITER
Bruce Bildsten

AGENCY
Fallon McElligott

CLIENT
Timex Corp.

Consumer Newspaper/Campaign

ART DIRECTOR
Bob Barrie

COPYWRITER
Bruce Bildsten

PHOTOGRAPHERS
Vic Huber, Andreas Burz

AGENCY
Fallon McElligott

CLIENT
Porsche Cars North America

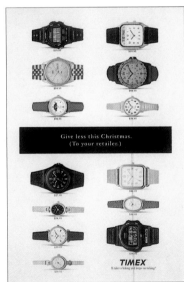

Consumer Newspaper/Campaign

ART DIRECTOR
Mike Murray

COPYWRITER
Jennifer Blair

AGENCY
Hunt Murray

CLIENT
Mystic Lake Casino

Consumer Newspaper/Campaign

ART DIRECTOR
Bob Brihn

COPYWRITER
Dean Buckhorn

PHOTOGRAPHER
Joe Lampi

AGENCY
Fallon McElligott

CLIENT
Star Tribune

Trade Newspaper/Campaign

ART DIRECTOR
Dabni Harvey

COPYWRITER
Steve Price

AGENCY
Saatchi & Saatchi Advertising

CLIENT
Salomon North America

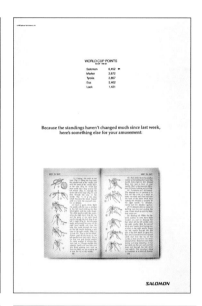

Trade Newspaper
ART DIRECTOR
Sharon Mushahwar
COPYWRITER
Dave Pullar
PHOTOGRAPHER
Keith Berr
AGENCY
Wyse Advertising
CLIENT
Cleveland Society of Communicating Arts

Public Service Newspaper
ART DIRECTOR
Mike Rylander
COPYWRITER
Tom Witt
AGENCY
The Ivory Tower
CLIENT
Earth Island Institute

Public Service Newspaper
ART DIRECTOR
Mike Rylander
COPYWRITER
Tom Witt
AGENCY
The Ivory Tower
CLIENT
Earth Island Institute

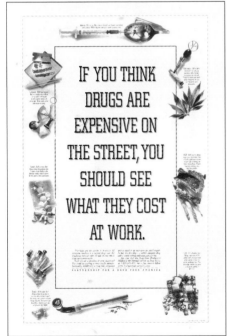

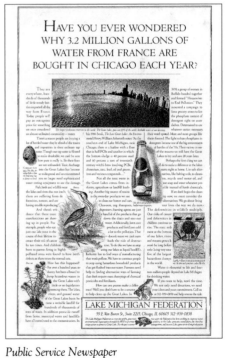

Public Service Newspaper
ART DIRECTOR
Darrell Credeur
COPYWRITER
Tom Darbyshire
PHOTOGRAPHER
Dan Mullen
AGENCY
Earle Palmer Brown
CLIENT
Partnership for a Drug-Free America

Public Service Newspaper
ART DIRECTOR
Mitch Gordon
COPYWRITER
George Gier
AGENCY
DDB Needham Worldwide
CLIENT
Lake Michigan Federation

Public Service Newspaper
ART DIRECTOR
Mitch Gordon
COPYWRITER
George Gier
AGENCY
DDB Needham Worldwide
CLIENT
Lake Michigan Federation

Public Service Newspaper

ART DIRECTORS/COPYWRITERS
Peter Cohen, Leslie Sweet

AGENCY
Streetsmart Advertising

CLIENT
Coalition for the Homeless

Public Service Newspaper/Campaign

ART DIRECTOR
Kevin Kearns

COPYWRITER
Jay Nelson

PHOTOGRAPHER
Marcus Halevi

AGENCY
Arnold Fortuna Lawner & Cabot

CLIENT
Free Romania

Public Service Newspaper

ART DIRECTOR
Kevin Lippy

COPYWRITER
Ed Neary

PHOTOGRAPHER
Geoffrey Carr

AGENCY
Doe-Anderson Advertising

CLIENT
Kentucky Literacy Commission

Public Service Newspaper/Campaign

ART DIRECTOR
Mike Rylander

COPYWRITER
Tom Witt

AGENCY
The Ivory Tower

CLIENT
Earth Island Institute

Consumer Magazine

ART DIRECTOR
David Angelo

COPYWRITER
Doug Raboy

AGENCY
Smith/Greenland

CLIENT
Citizens for Racial Harmony

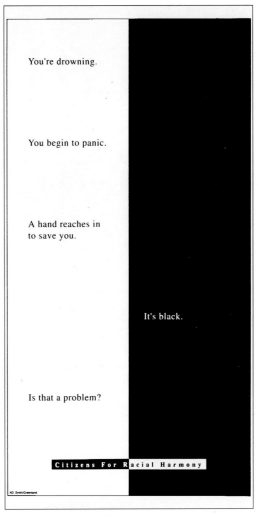

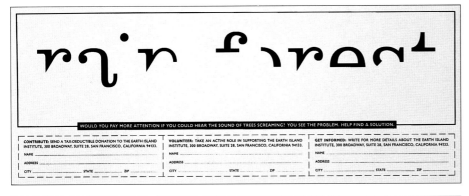

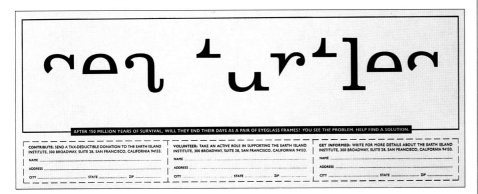

Consumer Magazine

ART DIRECTOR
David Angelo

COPYWRITER
Doug Raboy

AGENCY
Smith/Greenland

CLIENT
Citizens for Racial Harmony

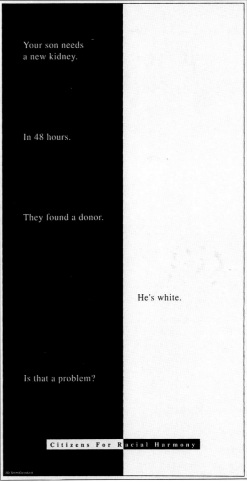

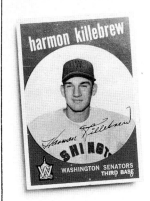

**RELIVE THE DAYS
WHEN BEING A
WASHINGTON SENATOR
WAS NOTHING
TO BE ASHAMED OF.**

Unlike their congressional namesakes, there's nothing scandalous about these
senators. So visit Beverly Hills Baseball Card Shop. We'll help you remember
when a senator could actually play the field and not end up in the tabloids.

BEVERLY HILLS BASEBALL CARD SHOP

Consumer Magazine
ART DIRECTOR
Hal Curtis
COPYWRITER
Steve Skibba
CREATIVE DIRECTOR
Cabell Harris
PHOTOGRAPHER
Mark Gervase
AGENCY
Work
CLIENT
Beverly Hills Baseball Card Shop

**YOUR WIFE HAS A
COMPLETE SET OF SILVER.
CERTAINLY YOU'RE
ENTITLED TO A COMPLETE
SET OF '63 DODGERS.**

If your better half has taken the lead in the family heirloom department,
it's time you visited Beverly Hills Baseball Card Shop. We'll set you up with
the cards you've always dreamed of. The way we see it, it's only fair.

BEVERLY HILLS BASEBALL CARD SHOP

Consumer Magazine
ART DIRECTOR
Hal Curtis
COPYWRITER
Steve Skibba
CREATIVE DIRECTOR
Cabell Harris
PHOTOGRAPHER
Mark Gervase
AGENCY
Work
CLIENT
Beverly Hills Baseball Card Shop

**HOW MANY
OTHER INVESTMENTS
COME WITH
A STICK OF GUM?**

If you're looking for an investment, here's something to chew on: Baseball card
values are soaring. So pick up a few packs from Beverly Hills Baseball Card Shop.
Besides, they're not just filled with investment potential. They're filled with gum.

BEVERLY HILLS BASEBALL CARD SHOP

Consumer Magazine
ART DIRECTOR
Hal Curtis
COPYWRITER
Steve Skibba
CREATIVE DIRECTOR
Cabell Harris
PHOTOGRAPHER
Mark Gervase
AGENCY
Work
CLIENT
Beverly Hills Baseball Card Shop

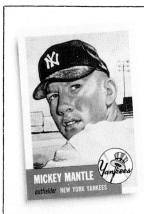

**WHERE GROWN MEN
COME TO SPEND THEIR
ALLOWANCES.**

At Beverly Hills Baseball Card Shop, the cards you always wanted as a kid are
still available. And best of all, now you can spend your money on them without even
asking for your Mom's permission. Although you might have to ask for your wife's.

BEVERLY HILLS BASEBALL CARD SHOP

Consumer Magazine
ART DIRECTOR
Hal Curtis
COPYWRITER
Steve Skibba
CREATIVE DIRECTOR
Cabell Harris
PHOTOGRAPHER
Mark Gervase
AGENCY
Work
CLIENT
Beverly Hills Baseball Card Shop

Consumer Magazine
ART DIRECTOR
Mike Fetrow
COPYWRITER
Doug DeGroode
PHOTOGRAPHER
Steve Umland
AGENCY
Hunt Murray
CLIENT
Hed Design

Consumer Magazine
ART DIRECTOR
Bob Brihn
COPYWRITER
Doug DeGroode
AGENCY
Fallon McElligott
CLIENT
Vescio's

Consumer Magazine
ART DIRECTOR
Arty Tan
COPYWRITER
Luke Sullivan
PHOTOGRAPHER
Shawn Michienzi
AGENCY
Fallon McElligott
CLIENT
Art Center

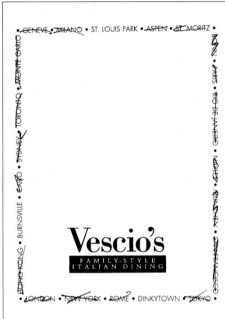

Consumer Magazine
ART DIRECTOR
Bob Brihn
COPYWRITER
Doug DeGroode
AGENCY
Fallon McElligott
CLIENT
Vescio's

Consumer Magazine
ART DIRECTOR
Mark Johnson
COPYWRITER
Luke Sullivan
PHOTOGRAPHER
Jack Malloy
AGENCY
Fallon McElligott
CLIENT
B.K. Cypress Log Homes

Consumer Magazine

ART DIRECTOR
Michael Kadin

COPYWRITER
Jim Garaventi

AGENCY
Leonard Monahan Lubars & Kelly

CLIENT
The Naragansett

Consumer Magazine

ART DIRECTOR
Jelly Helm

COPYWRITER
Joe Alexander

PHOTOGRAPHERS
Kerry Peterson, Rick Dublin

AGENCY
The Martin Agency

CLIENT
Health-tex

SAVE UP TO 80% DURING OUR GOING OUT OF BUSINESS SALE.

(Oh sure, now you'll come in.)

the narragansett

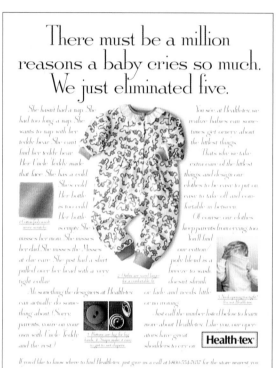

NAKED GIRLS AND FLAMING SKULLS
DON'T MAKE A GUITAR WORK BETTER.
UNFORTUNATELY.

YAMAHA
RGZ

ITS FATHER WAS A SCIENTIST.
ITS MOTHER WAS A TREE.

YAMAHA
APX Electric Acoustics

TO SURVIVE YOU NEED FOUR THINGS:
FOOD. SEX. SHELTER. GUITARS.
MAKE THAT TWO THINGS.

YAMAHA
Pacifica

Consumer Magazine

ART DIRECTOR
Al Christensen

COPYWRITER
Harry Cociollo

ILLUSTRATOR
Buc Rodgers

AGENCY
dGWB

CLIENT
Yamaha Guitars

Consumer Magazine

ART DIRECTOR
Al Christensen

COPYWRITER
Harry Cociollo

ILLUSTRATOR
Andrew Portwood

PHOTOGRAPHER
Jack Freed

AGENCY
dGWB

CLIENT
Yamaha Guitars

Consumer Magazine

ART DIRECTOR
Al Christensen

COPYWRITER
Harry Cociollo

ILLUSTRATOR
Dave Stevenson

AGENCY
dGWB

CLIENT
Yamaha Guitars

Consumer Magazine

ART DIRECTOR
Tom Lichtenheld

COPYWRITER
John Stingley

PHOTOGRAPHERS
Craig Perman, Dave Jordano

AGENCY
Fallon McElligott

CLIENT
Jim Beam Brands, Co.

Consumer Magazine

ART DIRECTOR
Carol Henderson

COPYWRITER
Doug DeGroode

PHOTOGRAPHERS
Shawn Michienzi, Rick Dublin

AGENCY
Fallon McElligott

CLIENT
Jim Beam Brands, Co.

Consumer Magazine

ART DIRECTOR
Tom Lichtenheld

COPYWRITER
John Stingley

PHOTOGRAPHERS
Rob Goebel, Dave Jordano

AGENCY
Fallon McElligott

CLIENT
Jim Beam Brands, Co.

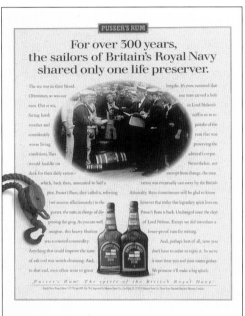

Consumer Magazine

ART DIRECTOR
Curt Johnson

COPYWRITER
Amelia Rosner

PHOTOGRAPHER
Chris Collins

AGENCY
Angotti, Thomas, Hedge, Inc.

CLIENT
Austin Nichols & Co.

Consumer Magazine

ART DIRECTOR
Allen Richardson

COPYWRITER
Gary Cohen

PHOTOGRAPHER
Carl Furuta

AGENCY
Grace & Rothschild

CLIENT
Land Rover North America

Consumer Magazine

ART DIRECTOR
Dean Fueroghne

COPYWRITER
Brian McMahon

AGENCY
Ogilvy & Mather

CLIENT
Hyatt Regency Waikiki/Ciao Mein

Consumer Magazine

ART DIRECTOR
Kevin Weidenbacher

COPYWRITER
Judith Atwood

PHOTOGRAPHER
Stephen Hellerstein

AGENCY
Scali, McCabe, Sloves

CLIENT
Rollscreen Co.

Consumer Magazine

ART DIRECTOR
Jim Mountjoy

COPYWRITER
Ed Jones

PHOTOGRAPHER
MARVY!

AGENCY
Loeffler Ketchum Mountjoy

CLIENT
North Carolina Travel & Tourism

Consumer Magazine

ART DIRECTOR
Mark Hughes

COPYWRITER
Rich Middendorf

PHOTOGRAPHER
Steve Hellerstein

AGENCY
Lord, Dentsu & Partners

CLIENT
TDK Electronics Corp.

Consumer Magazine

ART DIRECTOR
Tom Resenfield

COPYWRITER
Chuck McBride

PHOTOGRAPHER
Jody Dole

ILLUSTRATOR
Gregory M. Derth

AGENCY
Team One Advertising

CLIENT
Roederer

Consumer Magazine

ART DIRECTOR
Keith Weinman

COPYWRITER
Jack Fund

ILLUSTRATOR
Brian Callanan

AGENCY
Rubin Postaer & Associates

CLIENT
Lands' End, Inc.

Consumer Magazine

ART DIRECTORS/COPYWRITERS
Gerard Vaglio, Brian Wright

CREATIVE DIRECTOR
Sal DeVito

PHOTOGRAPHER
Cailor/Resnick

AGENCY
Follis/DeVito/Verdi

CLIENT
Daffy's

Consumer Magazine

ART DIRECTOR
Craig Tanimoto

COPYWRITERS
Hillary Jordan, Eric Grunbaum

PHOTOGRAPHER
Lamb & Hall

AGENCY
Chiat/Day/Mojo

CLIENT
Mitsubishi Electronics Sales

Consumer Magazine

ART DIRECTOR
Shari Hindman

COPYWRITER
Raymond McKinney

PHOTOGRAPHER
Jamie Cook

AGENCY
The Martin Agency

CLIENT
Wrangler

Consumer Magazine

ART DIRECTOR
Jelly Helm

COPYWRITER
Joe Alexander

PHOTOGRAPHER
Dublin Productions

AGENCY
The Martin Agency

CLIENT
Health-tex

Consumer Magazine

ART DIRECTOR
Mark Fuller

COPYWRITER
Steve Bassett

PHOTOGRAPHER
Kerry Peterson

AGENCY
The Martin Agency

CLIENT
Health-tex

Consumer Magazine

ART DIRECTOR
Jelly Helm

COPYWRITER
Joe Alexander

PHOTOGRAPHER
Rick Dublin

AGENCY
The Martin Agency

CLIENT
Health-tex

Consumer Magazine

ART DIRECTOR
Michael Fazende

COPYWRITER
Mike Gibbs

PHOTOGRAPHER
Michael Johnson

AGENCY
Fallon McElligott

CLIENT
The Lee Co.

Consumer Magazine

ART DIRECTOR
Bob Brihn

COPYWRITER
Phil Hanft

PHOTOGRAPHER
Joe Lampi

AGENCY
Fallon McElligott

CLIENT
Time Inc.

Consumer Magazine

ART DIRECTOR
Bob Brihn

COPYWRITER
Phil Hanft

AGENCY
Fallon McElligott

CLIENT
Time Inc.

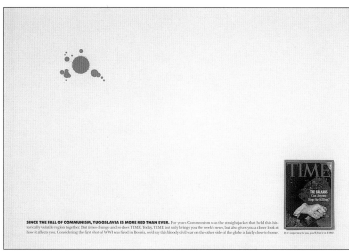

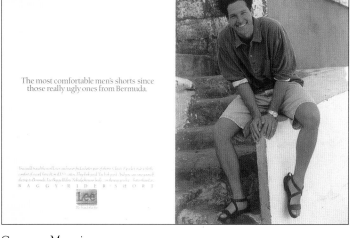

Consumer Magazine

ART DIRECTOR
Bob Brihn

COPYWRITER
Phil Hanft

PHOTOGRAPHER
Joe Lampi

AGENCY
Fallon McElligott

CLIENT
Time Inc.

Consumer Magazine

ART DIRECTOR
Michael Fazende

COPYWRITER
Mike Gibbs

PHOTOGRAPHER
Michael Johnson

AGENCY
Fallon McElligott

CLIENT
The Lee Co.

Consumer Magazine

ART DIRECTOR
Michael Fazende

COPYWRITER
Mike Gibbs

PHOTOGRAPHER
Michael Johnson

AGENCY
Fallon McElligott

CLIENT
The Lee Co.

Consumer Magazine

ART DIRECTOR
Bob Brihn

COPYWRITER
Phil Hanft

PHOTOGRAPHER
Carl Cedergren

AGENCY
Fallon McElligott

CLIENT
Time Inc.

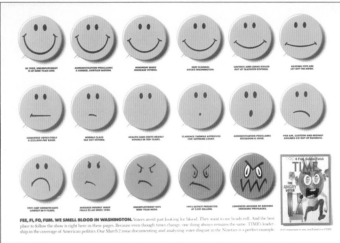

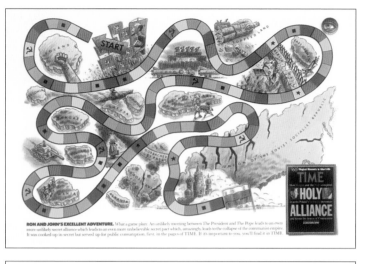

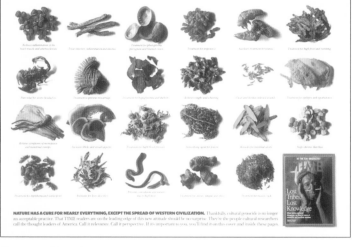

Consumer Magazine

ART DIRECTOR
Bob Brihn

COPYWRITER
Phil Hanft

PHOTOGRAPHER
Joe Lampi

AGENCY
Fallon McElligott

CLIENT
Time Inc.

Consumer Magazine

ART DIRECTOR
Bob Brihn

COPYWRITER
Phil Hanft

PHOTOGRAPHER
Joe Lampi

AGENCY
Fallon McElligott

CLIENT
Time Inc.

Consumer Magazine

ART DIRECTOR
Bob Brihn

COPYWRITER
Phil Hanft

AGENCY
Fallon McElligott

CLIENT
Time Inc.

Consumer Magazine

ART DIRECTOR
Bob Barrie

COPYWRITER
Bruce Bildsten

PHOTOGRAPHER
Shawn Michienzi

AGENCY
Fallon McElligott

CLIENT
Porsche Cars North America

Consumer Magazine

ART DIRECTOR
Michael Fazende

COPYWRITER
Mike Lescarbeau

PHOTOGRAPHER
Michael Johnson

AGENCY
Fallon McElligott

CLIENT
The Lee Co.

Consumer Magazine

ART DIRECTOR/HAND LETTERER
Tim Hanrahan

COPYWRITER
Ron Lawner

PHOTOGRAPHER
Robert Tardio

AGENCY
Arnold Fortuna Lawner & Cabot

CLIENT
Kinney Shoes

Consumer Magazine

ART DIRECTOR
Jerry Gentile

COPYWRITER
Rob Feakins

PHOTOGRAPHERS
Charles Hopkins, Jim Haefner,
David LeBon, Smith/Nelson,
Daniels & Daniels

AGENCY
Chiat/Day/Mojo

CLIENT
Nissan Motor Corp.

Consumer Magazine

ART DIRECTOR
Yvonne Smith

COPYWRITER
Rob Siltanen

PHOTOGRAPHERS
Bob Grigg, Smith/Nelson

AGENCY
Chiat/Day/Mojo

CLIENT
Nissan Motor Corp.

Consumer Magazine

ART DIRECTOR
Ian Potter

COPYWRITER
Steve Rabosky

PHOTOGRAPHER
Dennis Waugh

AGENCY
Chiat/Day/Mojo

CLIENT
Eveready Batteries

Consumer Magazine

ART DIRECTOR
Steve Sweitzer

COPYWRITER
Bob Rice

PHOTOGRAPHER
Dennis Ashlock

AGENCY
Chiat/Day/Mojo

CLIENT
Nissan Motor Corp.

Consumer Magazine

ART DIRECTOR
Craig Tanimoto

COPYWRITER
Hillary Jordan

PHOTOGRAPHER
Jim Arndt , Lamb & Hall

AGENCY
Chiat/Day/Mojo

CLIENT
Mitsubishi

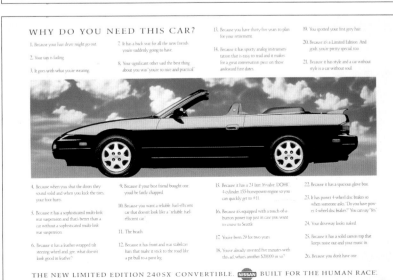

Consumer Magazine

ART DIRECTOR
Yvonne Smith

COPYWRITER
Rob Siltanen

PHOTOGRAPHER
Charles Hopkins, Lamb & Hall

AGENCY
Chiat/Day/Mojo

CLIENT
Nissan Motor Corp.

Consumer Magazine
ART DIRECTOR/CREATIVE DIRECTOR
Cabell Harris
COPYWRITER
Larry Johnson
PHOTOGRAPHER
Dennis Manarchy
AGENCY
Livingston+Keye
CLIENT
JBL

Consumer Magazine
ART DIRECTOR/CREATIVE DIRECTOR/COPYWRITER
Cabell Harris
PHOTOGRAPHER
Vic Huber
AGENCY
Livingston+Keye
CLIENT
JBL

Consumer Magazine
ART DIRECTOR/CREATIVE DIRECTOR/COPYWRITER
Cabell Harris
PHOTOGRAPHER
Vic Huber
AGENCY
Livingston+Keye
CLIENT
JBL

Consumer Magazine
ART DIRECTOR/HAND LETTERER
Tim Hanrahan
COPYWRITER
Ron Lawner
PHOTOGRAPHER
Robert Tardio
AGENCY
Arnold Fortuna Lawner & Cabot
CLIENT
Kinney Shoes

Consumer Magazine

ART DIRECTOR
Richard Bess

COPYWRITER
David Smith

PHOTOGRAPHER
Jim Hall, Lamb & Hall

AGENCY
Rubin Postear & Assoc.

CLIENT
American Honda Motor Co., Inc.

Consumer Magazine

ART DIRECTOR
Keith Weinman

COPYWRITER
Jack Fund

PHOTOGRAPHER
Jim Hall, Lamb & Hall

AGENCY
Rubin Postear & Assoc.

CLIENT
American Honda Motor Co., Inc.

Consumer Magazine

ART DIRECTOR
Gary Goldsmith

COPYWRITER
Dean Hacohen

ILLUSTRATOR
Chris Wormell

AGENCY
Goldsmith/Jeffrey

CLIENT
J.P. Morgan

Consumer Magazine

ART DIRECTOR
Jim Keane

COPYWRITER
Joe Nagy

PHOTOGRAPHER
John Mason

AGENCY
Carmichael Lynch

CLIENT
Harley-Davidson

Consumer Magazine
ART DIRECTOR
Jim Keane
COPYWRITER
Joe Nagy
PHOTOGRAPHER
John Mason
AGENCY
Carmichael Lynch
CLIENT
Harley-Davidson

Consumer Magazine
ART DIRECTOR/ILLUSTRATOR
K.J. Bowen
COPYWRITER
Tony Gomes
AGENCY
Ammirati & Puris Inc.
CLIENT
Aetna Life and Casualty Co.

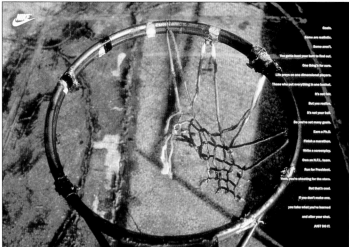

Consumer Magazine
ART DIRECTOR
Wilky Lau
COPYWRITER
Jimmy Smith
CREATIVE DIRECTOR
Julian Ryder
PHOTOGRAPHER
Carl Furuta
AGENCY
Muse Cordero Chen
CLIENT
Nike

Consumer Magazine
ART DIRECTOR
Howard Title
COPYWRITER
Wayne Winfield
CREATIVE DIRECTOR
James Caporimo
PHOTOGRAPHER
Nadav Kander
AGENCY
Waring & LaRosa, Inc.
CLIENT
Heublein, Inc.

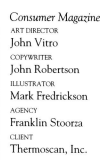

Consumer Magazine

ART DIRECTOR
John Vitro

COPYWRITER
John Robertson

ILLUSTRATOR
Mark Fredrickson

AGENCY
Franklin Stoorza

CLIENT
Thermoscan, Inc.

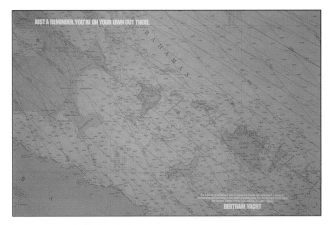

Consumer Magazine

ART DIRECTOR
Tim Ryan

COPYWRITER
Christina Gordet

PHOTOGRAPHER
Randy Miller

AGENCY
McFarland &Drier

CLIENT
Bertram Yacht

Consumer Magazine

ART DIRECTOR
Jim Mountjoy

COPYWRITER
Ed Jones

AGENCY
Loeffler Ketchum Mountjoy

CLIENT
Verbatim

Consumer Magazine

ART DIRECTOR
Ellen Steinberg

COPYWRITER
Ernest Lupinacci

PHOTOGRAPHER
Guzman

AGENCY
Weiss, Whitten, Carroll, Stagliano

CLIENT
Escada USA/Apriori

Consumer Magazine

ART DIRECTOR
Ellen Steinberg

COPYWRITER
Ernest Lupinacci

PHOTOGRAPHER
Guzman

AGENCY
Weiss, Whitten, Carroll, Stagliano

CLIENT
Escada USA/Apriori

Consumer Magazine/Campaign

ART DIRECTOR
Scott Krahn

COPYWRITERS
Gary Mueller, Pete Kellen

PHOTOGRAPHERS
Jeff Eising, John Stewart

AGENCY
Birdsall-Voss & Kloppenburg

CLIENT
Blackhawk Farms

Consumer Magazine/Campaign

ART DIRECTOR
Al Christensen

COPYWRITER
Harry Cociollo

ILLUSTRATOR
Buc Rodgers

AGENCY
dGWB

CLIENT
Yamaha

Consumer Magazine/Campaign
ART DIRECTOR
Bob Brihn
COPYWRITER
Bruce Bildsten
PHOTOGRAPHER
Rocky Schenck
AGENCY
Fallon McElligott
CLIENT
Jim Beam Brands, Co.

Consumer Magazine/Campaign
ART DIRECTOR
Dean Hanson
COPYWRITER
Bruce Bildsten
PHOTOGRAPHER
Miro
AGENCY
Fallon McElligott
CLIENT
Timex Corp.

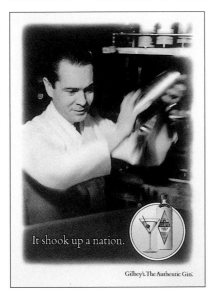

Consumer Magazine/Campaign

ART DIRECTOR
Bob Barrie

COPYWRITER
Bruce Bildsten

PHOTOGRAPHERS
Andreas Burtz, David Torreano, Jeff Zwart

AGENCY
Fallon McElligott

CLIENT
Porsche Cars North America

Consumer Magazine/Campaign

ART DIRECTOR
Michael Fazende

COPYWRITER
Mike Lescarbeau

PHOTOGRAPHER
Michael Johnson

AGENCY
Fallon McElligott

CLIENT
The Lee Co.

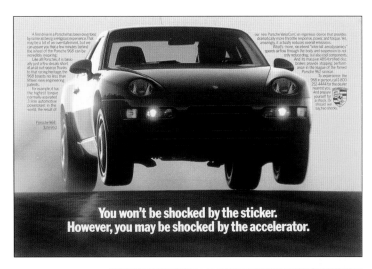

Consumer Magazine/Campaign

ART DIRECTOR
Tom Lichtenheld

COPYWRITER
John Stingley

PHOTOGRAPHERS
**Rob Goebel, Frank Fahey,
Craig Perman, Dave Jordano**

AGENCY
Fallon McElligott

CLIENT
Jim Beam Brands, Co.

Consumer Magazine/Campaign

ART DIRECTOR
Bob Brihn

COPYWRITER
Phil Hanft

PHOTOGRAPHER
Joe Lampi

ILLUSTRATOR
Bob Blewett

AGENCY
Fallon McElligott

CLIENT
Time Inc.

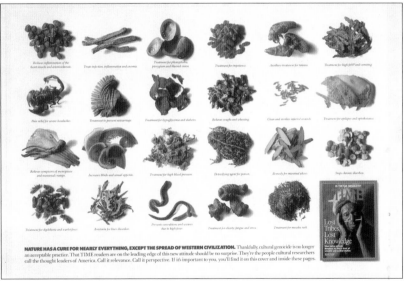

PRINT ADVERTISING

Consumer Magazine/Campaign

ART DIRECTOR
Steve Stone

COPYWRITER
David Fowler

PHOTOGRAPHERS
**Dan Escobar, Anne Crump,
Gary Hush, Peter Drake**

AGENCY
Ammirati & Puris, Inc.

CLIENT
Nikon Inc.

Consumer Magazine/Campaign

ART DIRECTOR
Jeremy Postaer

COPYWRITERS
Bob Kerstetter, Rob Bagot

PHOTOGRAPHER
Duncan Sim

AGENCY
Goodby, Berlin & Silverstein

CLIENT
Finlandia Vodka

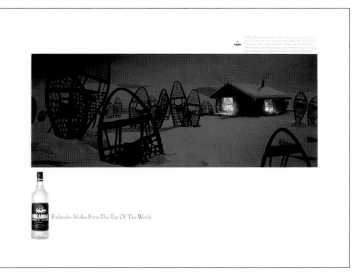

Consumer Magazine/Campaign

ART DIRECTOR
David Angelo

COPYWRITER
Paul Spencer

EXECUTIVE CREATIVE DIRECTORS
Jack Mariucci, Bob Mackall

PHOTOGRAPHER
Neil Slavin, Lamb & Hall

AGENCY
DDB Needham Worldwide

CLIENT
New York State Lottery

Consumer Magazine/Campaign

AGENCY
Leo Burnett Company

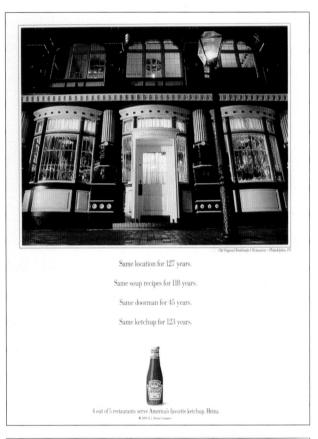

Same location for 127 years.

Same soup recipes for 118 years.

Same doorman for 45 years.

Same ketchup for 123 years.

4 out of 5 restaurants serve America's favorite ketchup. Heinz.

Hours: Always open.

Attire: Black leather to black tie.

Entertainment: Jazz pianist (daily).

Motto: "Bureaucrats are the meatloaf of humanity."

Ketchup: The slow one.

4 out of 5 restaurants serve America's favorite ketchup. Heinz.

Consumer Magazine/Campaign
ART DIRECTOR
David Carlson
COPYWRITER
Jonathan Hoffman
AGENCY
Leo Burnett Company

Consumer Magazine/Campaign
ART DIRECTOR
Jim Mountjoy
COPYWRITER
Ed Jones
AGENCY
Loeffler Ketchum Mountjoy
CLIENT
Verbatim

A pie in the face of flight delays, long commutes and endless campaign speeches.

Be a star quarterback, especially if you're all thumbs.

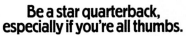

"Oh wow! A Formula 1 car, two golf courses and a professional football team. Just what I've always wanted."

Consumer Magazine/Campaign

ART DIRECTOR
Margaret McGovern

COPYWRITER
Paul Silverman

PRODUCTION
John Holt Studio

AGENCY
Mullen

CLIENT
The Timberland Co.

Consumer Magazine/Campaign

ART DIRECTORS
Clark Frankel, Hank Champion, Gloria Kapral

COPYWRITER
Sue Karenio

AGENCY
Young & Rubicam, NY

CLIENT
Sugar Free Jell-O/Kraft General Foods, Inc.

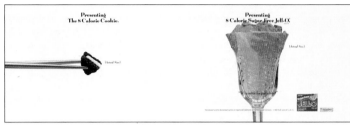

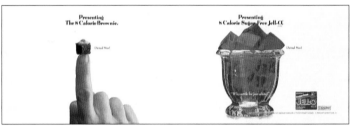

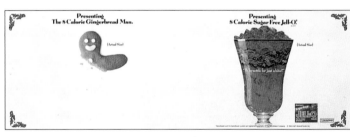

Consumer Magazine

ART DIRECTOR
Hal Curtis

COPYWRITER
Tom Camp

CREATIVE DIRECTOR
Cabell Harris

PHOTOGRAPHER
Mark Gervase

AGENCY
Work

CLIENT
Hypnotic Hats, Ltd.

Trade Magazine

ART DIRECTOR
Karen Lynch

COPYWRITER
Roger Baldacci

AGENCY
Mullen

CLIENT
Mullen

Trade Magazine
ART DIRECTOR
Randy Hughes
COPYWRITER
Josh Denberg
AGENCY
Clarity Coverdale Rueff
CLIENT
Art Directors & Copywriters Club

Trade Magazine
ART DIRECTOR/COPYWRITER
David Wojdyla
AGENCY
Ammirati & Puris, Inc.
CLIENT
Jim Gonzales Retouching

Trade Magazine

ART DIRECTOR
Robert Rich

COPYWRITER
Michael Sheehan

AGENCY
Clarke Goward Fitts Matteson

CLIENT
Locate in Scotland

Trade Magazine

ART DIRECTOR
David Angelo

COPYWRITER
Paul Spencer

EXECUTIVE CREATIVE DIRECTORS
Jack Mariucci, Bob Mackall

PHOTOGRAPHER
Carl Fischer

AGENCY
DDB Needham Worldwide

CLIENT
The Art Directors Club

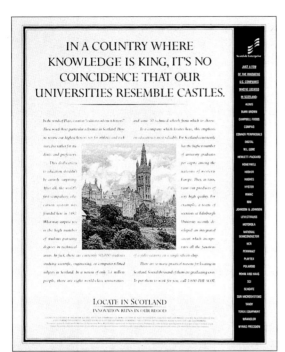

Trade Magazine

ART DIRECTOR
Bob Barrie

COPYWRITER
Bruce Bildsten

PHOTOGRAPHER
Jeff Zwart

AGENCY
Fallon McElligot

CLIENT
Porsche Cars North America

Trade Magazine

ART DIRECTOR
Susan Griak

COPYWRITER
Dean Buckhorn

PHOTOGRAPHER
Shawn Michienzi

AGENCY
Fallon McElligott

CLIENT
The Lee Co.

Trade Magazine
ART DIRECTOR
Arty Tan
COPYWRITER
Luke Sullivan
PHOTOGRAPHER
Kerry Peterson
AGENCY
Fallon McElligott
CLIENT
Penn Racquet Sports

Trade Magazine
ART DIRECTOR
Bob Barrie
COPYWRITER
Mike Gibbs
PHOTOGRAPHER
Joe Lampi
AGENCY
Fallon McElligott
CLIENT
Hush Puppies Shoes

Trade Magazine
ART DIRECTOR
Noam Murro
COPYWRITER
Dean Hacohen
PHOTOGRAPHER
Ilan Rubin
AGENCY
Goldsmith/Jeffrey
CLIENT
Crain's New York Business

Trade Magazine
ART DIRECTOR
Henriette Lienke
COPYWRITER
Dean Hacohen
AGENCY
Goldsmith/Jeffrey
CLIENT
Crain's New York Business

Trade Magazine
ART DIRECTOR
Noam Murro
COPYWRITER
Dean Hacohen
PHOTOGRAPHER
Ilan Rubin
AGENCY
Goldsmith/Jeffrey
CLIENT
Crain's New York Business

Trade Magazine
ART DIRECTOR
Noam Murro
COPYWRITER
Dean Hacohen
PHOTOGRAPHER
Ilan Rubin
AGENCY
Goldsmith/Jeffrey
CLIENT
Crain's New York Business

Trade Magazine
ART DIRECTOR
Henriette Lienke
COPYWRITER
Dean Hacohen
AGENCY
Goldsmith/Jeffrey
CLIENT
Crain's New York Business

Trade Magazine
ART DIRECTOR
Henriette Lienke
COPYWRITER
Dean Hacohen
AGENCY
Goldsmith/Jeffrey
CLIENT
Crain's New York Business

Trade Magazine
ART DIRECTOR
Mark Hughes
COPYWRITER
Rich Middendorf
PHOTOGRAPHER
Steve Hellerstein
AGENCY
Lord, Dentsu & Partners
CLIENT
TDK Electronics Corp.

With all
due respect to
Alan Greenspan,
we feel we're
the one offering
the prime rate.

If you're sharing
this copy of Crain's,
we'd like to
remind you that
private ownership
is the cornerstone
of capitalism.

24
Average age when a
typical businessman buys
his first home.

24
Average age when a
typical Economist reader
sells it to him.

The Economist

6
Net number
of shapes a typical
Economist reader
can make from
a single paper clip
during any given
Board meeting.

The Economist

1205
Annual number of
political speeches
which suspiciously
correspond to
Economist articles.

The Economist

Trade Magazine
ART DIRECTORS/COPYWRITERS
Mikal Reich, Shalom Auslander
AGENCY
Mad Dogs & Englishmen
CLIENT
Economist Magazine

Trade Magazine
ART DIRECTORS/COPYWRITERS
Shalom Auslander, Mikal Reich
AGENCY
Mad Dogs & Englishmen
CLIENT
Economist Magazine

Trade Magazine
ART DIRECTORS/COPYWRITERS
Shalom Auslander, Mikal Reich
AGENCY
Mad Dogs & Englishmen
CLIENT
Economist Magazine

Trade Magazine
ART DIRECTORS
Shalom Auslander, Mikal Reich
COPYWRITER
Nick Cohen
AGENCY
Mad Dogs &Englishmen
CLIENT
Economist Magazine

Trade Magazine
ART DIRECTOR
Bob Meagher
COPYWRITER
Joe Alexander
PHOTOGRAPHERS
Cathy Groth, Dean Hawthorne
AGENCY
The Martin Agency
CLIENT
The Martin Agency

Trade Magazine
ART DIRECTOR
Robb Burnham
COPYWRITER
Alan Marcus
AGENCY
Martin/Williams

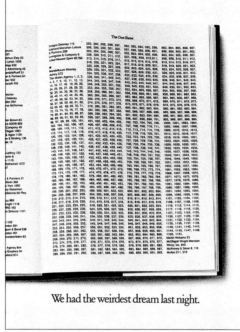

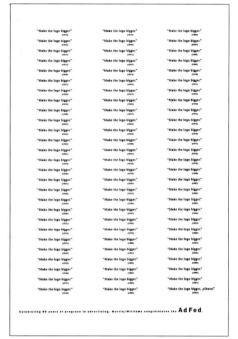

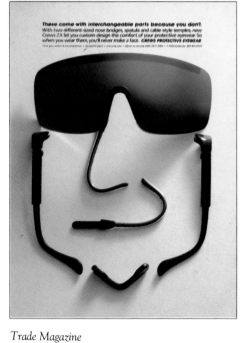

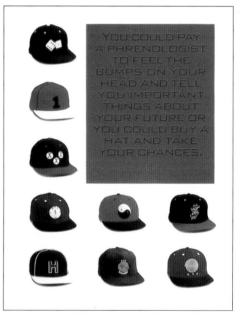

Trade Magazine
ART DIRECTOR
Bill Ainsworth
CREATIVE DIRECTORS
Trace Hallowell, Michael H. Thompson
COPYWRITER
Sheperd Simmons
PHOTOGRAPHER
Bill Dawson
AGENCY
Thompson & Co.
CLIENT
Crews

Trade Magazine
ART DIRECTOR
Andrea D'Aquino
COPYWRITER
David Bromberg
PHOTOGRAPHER
Mark Weiss
AGENCY
Weiss, Whitten, Carroll, Stagliano
CLIENT
Harvard Business Review

Trade Magazine
ART DIRECTOR
Hal Curtis
COPYWRITER
Tom Camp
CREATIVE DIRECTOR
Cabell Harris
PHOTOGRAPHER
Mark Gervase
AGENCY
Work
CLIENT
Hypnotic Hats, Ltd.

Trade Magazine
ART DIRECTOR
Hal Curtis
COPYWRITER
Tom Camp
CREATIVE DIRECTOR
Cabell Harris
PHOTOGRAPHER
Mark Gervase
AGENCY
Work
CLIENT
Hypnotic Hats, Ltd.

Trade Magazine
ART DIRECTOR
Tom Roth
COPYWRITER
Mark Ledermann
PHOTOGRAPHER
Fred Vanderpoel
AGENCY
Anderson & Lembke
CLIENT
Fred Vanderpoel

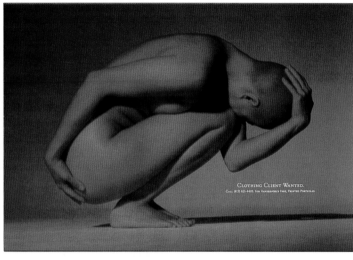

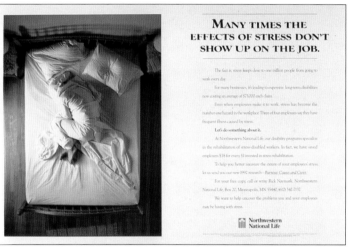

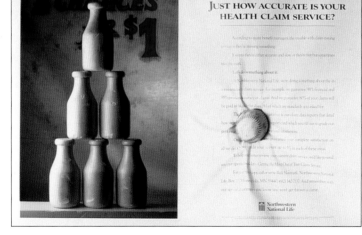

Trade Magazine
ART DIRECTOR
Hal Curtis
COPYWRITER
Tom Camp
CREATIVE DIRECTOR
Cabell Harris
PHOTOGRAPHER
Mark Gervase
AGENCY
Work
CLIENT
Hypnotic Hats, Ltd.

Trade Magazine
ART DIRECTOR
Jac Coverdale
COPYWRITER
Jerry Fury
PHOTOGRAPHERS
Shawn Michienzi, MARVY!
AGENCY
Clarity Coverdale Rueff
CLIENT
Northwestern National Life
Insurance

Trade Magazine
ART DIRECTOR
Jac Coverdale
COPYWRITER
Jerry Fury
PHOTOGRAPHER
Steve Umland
AGENCY
Clarity Coverdale Rueff
CLIENT
Northwestern National Life
Insurance

Trade Magazine
ART DIRECTOR
Dean Hanson
COPYWRITER
Phil Hanft
AGENCY
Fallon McElligott
CLIENT
Weyerhaeuser Paper Co.

Trade Magazine
ART DIRECTOR
Dean Hanson
COPYWRITER
Phil Hanft
ILLUSTRATOR
Christian Wesp
AGENCY
Fallon McElligott
CLIENT
Weyerhaeuser Paper Co.

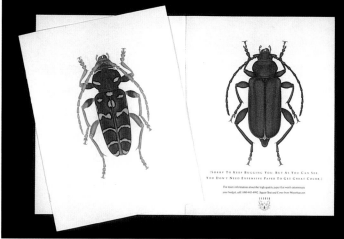

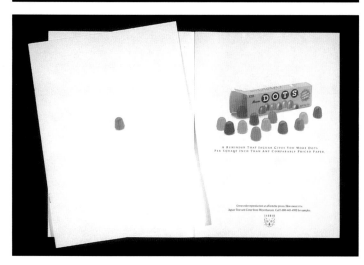

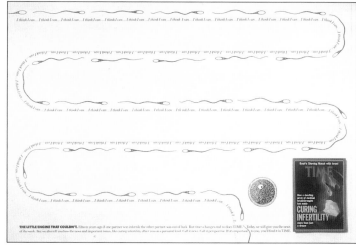

Trade Magazine
ART DIRECTOR
Dean Hanson
COPYWRITER
Phil Hanft
PHOTOGRAPHER
Shawn Michienzi
AGENCY
Fallon McElligott
CLIENT
Weyerhaeuser Paper Co.

Trade Magazine
ART DIRECTOR
Bob Brihn
COPYWRITER
Phil Hanft
AGENCY
Fallon McElligott
CLIENT
Time Inc.

Trade Magazine

ART DIRECTOR
Bob Brihn

COPYWRITER
Phil Hanft

ILLUSTRATOR
Bob Blewett

AGENCY
Fallon McElligott

CLIENT
Time Inc.

Trade Magazine

ART DIRECTOR
Bob Brihn

COPYWRITER
Phil Hanft

AGENCY
Fallon McElligott

CLIENT
Time Inc.

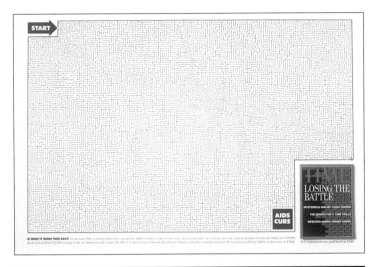

Trade Magazine

ART DIRECTOR
Bob Barrie

COPYWRITER
Mike Gibbs

AGENCY
Fallon McElligott

CLIENT
Continental Bank

Trade Magazine

ART DIRECTOR
Mark Johnson

COPYWRITER
Bill Miller

PHOTOGRAPHER
Shawn Michienzi

AGENCY
Fallon McElligott

CLIENT
Rolling Stone Magazine

Trade Magazine

ART DIRECTOR
Bob Barrie

COPYWRITER
Mike Gibbs

PHOTOGRAPHER
Shawn Michienzi

AGENCY
Fallon McElligott

CLIENT
Continental Bank

Trade Magazine

ART DIRECTOR/COPYWRITER
Gary Goldsmith

PHOTOGRAPHER
Ilan Rubin

AGENCY
Goldsmith/Jeffrey

CLIENT
US/Rolling Stone Magazine

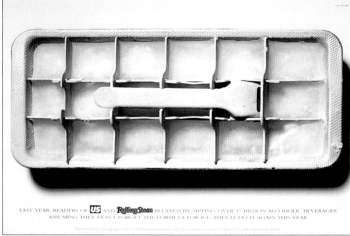

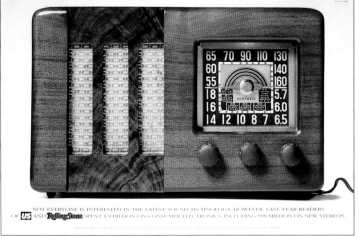

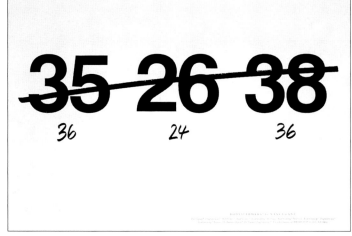

Trade Magazine

ART DIRECTOR/COPYWRITER
Gary Goldsmith

PHOTOGRAPHER
Ilan Rubin

AGENCY
Goldsmith/Jeffrey

CLIENT
US/Rolling Stone Magazine

Trade Magazine

ART DIRECTOR
Noam Murro

COPYWRITER
Eddie Van Bloem

AGENCY
Goldsmith/Jeffrey

CLIENT
Bodyslimmers

Trade Magazine

ART DIRECTOR
Jeremy Postaer

COPYWRITER
Steve Simpson

PHOTOGRAPHER
Bruce Davidson

AGENCY
Goodby, Berlin & Silverstein

CLIENT
The New Yorker Magazine

Trade Magazine

ART DIRECTOR
Tim Galles

COPYWRITER
Lynn Stiles

AGENCY
Lord, Dentsu & Partners

CLIENT
British Open Sportswear

Trade Magazine

ART DIRECTOR
Margaret McGovern

COPYWRITER
Paul Silverman

PHOTOGRAPHER
Michelle MacDonald

PRODUCTION
John Holt Studio

AGENCY
Mullen

CLIENT
The Timberland Co.

Trade Magazine/Campaign

ART DIRECTOR
Robert Rich

COPYWRITER
Michael Sheehan

PHOTOGRAPHER
Mike Ryan

ILLUSTRATOR
Laurie Johnson

AGENCY
Clarke Goward Fitts Matteson

CLIENT
Locate in Scotland

Trade Magazine/Campaign

ART DIRECTOR
I Jian Lin

COPYWRITER
Jonathan Plazonja

AGENCY
Encompass Comm.

CLIENT
Typographic House

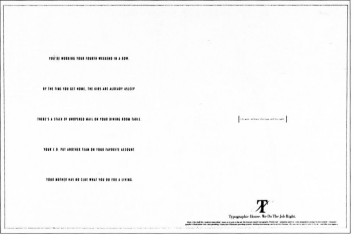

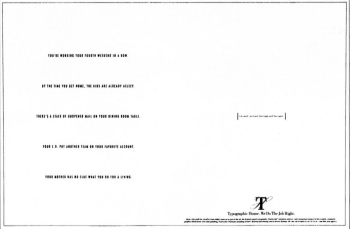

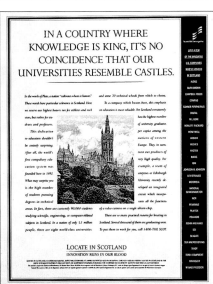
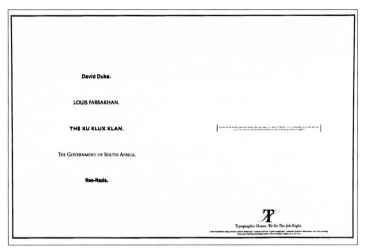

Trade Magazine/Campaign

ART DIRECTOR
Dean Hanson

COPYWRITER
Phil Hanft

PHOTOGRAPHER
Shawn Michienzi

ILLUSTRATOR
Christain Wesp

AGENCY
Fallon McElligott

CLIENT
Weyerhaeuser Paper Co.

Trade Magazine/Campaign

ART DIRECTOR
Henriette Lienke

COPYWRITER
Dean Hacohen

AGENCY
Goldsmith/Jeffrey

CLIENT
Crain's New York Business

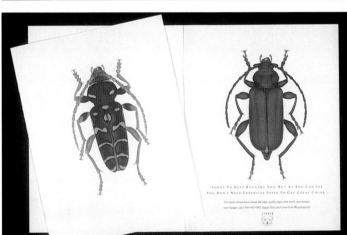

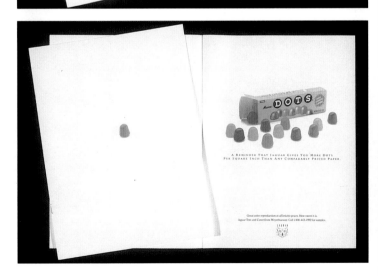

Trade Magazine/Campaign

ART DIRECTOR
Henriette Lienke

COPYWRITER
Dean Hacohen

AGENCY
Goldsmith/Jeffrey

CLIENT
Crain's New York Business

Trade Magazine/Campaign

ART DIRECTOR
Steve Stone

COPYWRITER
Bob Kerstetter

PHOTOGRAPHER
Dan Escobar

ILLUSTRATOR
Varitel Select

AGENCY
Goodby, Berlin & Silverstein

CLIENT
Norwegian Cruise Line

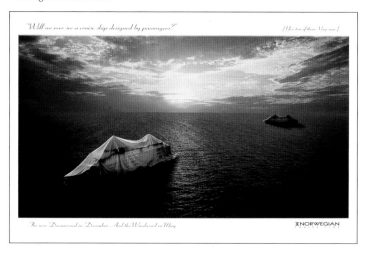

Trade Magazine/Campaign
ART DIRECTOR
Steve Stone
COPYWRITERS
Rob Bagot, Steve Simpson
PHOTOGRAPHER
Greg Dearth
AGENCY
Goodby, Berlin & Silverstein
CLIENT
Clarks of England

Trade Magazine/Campaign
ART DIRECTOR
Hal Curtis
COPYWRITERS
Brian Quennell, Tom Camp
CREATIVE DIRECTOR/DIRECTOR
Cabell Harris
PHOTOGRAPHER
Gary McGuire
AGENCY
Livingston + Keye

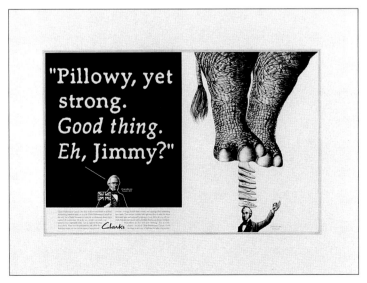

Trade Magazine

ART DIRECTORS/COPYWRITERS
Shalom Auslander, Mikal Reich

AGENCY
Mad Dogs & Englishmen

CLIENT
Economist Magazine

Public Service Magazine

ART DIRECTOR
Jim Mountjoy

COPYWRITER
Ed Jones

ILLUSTRATOR
John Burgoyne

AGENCY
Loeffler Ketchum Mountjoy

CLIENT
North Carolina Zoo

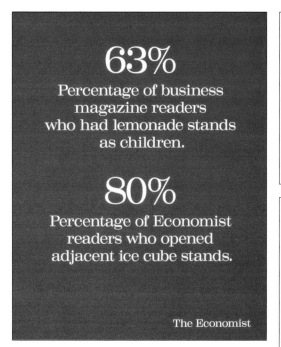

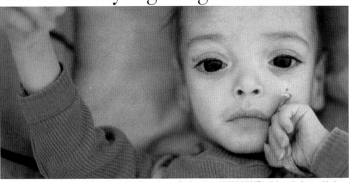

Public Service Magazine

ART DIRECTOR
Bob Meagher

COPYWRITER
Joe Alexander

AGENCY
The Martin Agency

CLIENT
National AIDS Hotline

Public Service Magazine

ART DIRECTOR
Carol Henderson

COPYWRITER
Doug DeGroode

PHOTOGRAPHER
Jim Arndt

AGENCY
Fallon McElligott

CLIENT
Children's Defense Fund

Public Service Magazine

ART DIRECTOR
Sally Wagner

COPYWRITER
Christopher Wilson

AGENCY
Martin/Williams

CLIENT
American Humane Assoc.

Public Service Magazine

ART DIRECTOR
Ed Segura

COPYWRITER
Jimmy Smith

CREATIVE DIRECTOR
Julian Ryder

AGENCY
Muse Cordero Chen

CLIENT
Advertising Anonymous

Public Service Magazine/Campaign

COPYWRITER
Mary Webb

PHOTOGRAPHER
Erik Gronlund

AGENCY
Anderson & Lembke

CLIENT
Ad Council-Points of Light Foundation

Outdoor Poster

ART DIRECTOR
Frank Haggerty

COPYWRITER
Kerry Casey

PHOTOGRAPHER
Shawn Michienzi

AGENCY
Carmichael Lynch

CLIENT
Normark

Outdoor Poster

ART DIRECTOR
Warren Johnson

COPYWRITER
Joe Nagy

AGENCY
Carmichael Lynch

CLIENT
Harley-Davidson

Outdoor Poster

ART DIRECTOR
Dave Cook

COPYWRITER
Dion Hughes

PHOTOGRAPHER
Rick Dublin

AGENCY
Chiat/Day/Mojo

CLIENT
NYNEX Yellow Pages

Outdoor Poster

ART DIRECTOR
Susan Griak

COPYWRITER
Luke Sullivan

AGENCY
Fallon McElligott

CLIENT
J.D. Hoyt's

Public Service Poster

ART DIRECTOR
Leslie Sweet

COPYWRITER
Barton Landsman

AGENCY
McElligott Wright Morrison White

CLIENT
Memorial Blood Center

Public Service Poster/Campaign

ART DIRECTOR
Chris Poulin

COPYWRITER
Jonathan Plazonja

AGENCY
Two Hacks and a Mac

CLIENT
CEASE

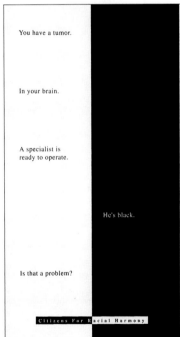

Public Service Poster

ART DIRECTOR
David Angelo

COPYWRITER
Doug Raboy

AGENCY
Smith/Greenland

CLIENT
Citizens for Racial Harmony

Public Service Poster/Campaign
ART DIRECTOR
Susan Griak
COPYWRITER
Dean Buckhorn
PHOTOGRAPHER
Jim Arndt
AGENCY
Fallon McElligott
CLIENT
The National Kidney Foundation

Public Service Poster/Campaign
ART DIRECTOR
Dean Hanson
COPYWRITER
Doug DeGroode
PHOTOGRAPHERS
Shawn Michienzi, Dan Halsey
ILLUSTRATOR
Mary Northrup
AGENCY
Fallon McElligott
CLIENT
Communities Caring for Children

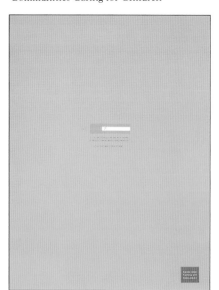

Public Service Poster/Campaign
ART DIRECTOR
Jim Amadeo
COPYWRITERS
Jim Amadeo, George Goetz
AGENCY
Ingalls Quinn & Johnson
CLIENT
New England Anti-Vivisection Society

Public Service Poster/Campaign
ART DIRECTOR
Leslie Sweet
COPYWRITER
Barton Landsman
PHOTOGRAPHER
Ben Saltzman
AGENCY
McElligott Wright Morrison White
CLIENT
Memorial Blood Center

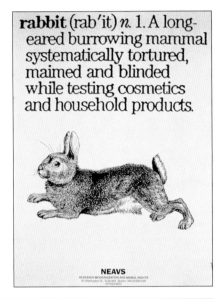

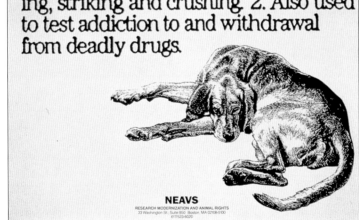

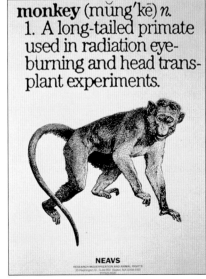

General Poster
ART DIRECTORS
George Capuano, Leo Fiorica
COPYWRITER
Helene Rosenthal
AGENCY
Bozell/New York
CLIENT
Charles Mangano

General Poster
ART DIRECTOR
Jim Keane
COPYWRITER
Joe Nagy
AGENCY
Carmichael Lynch
CLIENT
Clint Clemens

General Poster
ART DIRECTOR
Greg Wood
COPYWRITER
Mick O'Brien
AGENCY
Devine & Pearson
CLIENT
DiCenso's

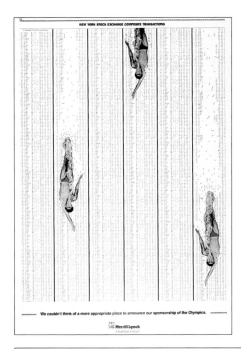

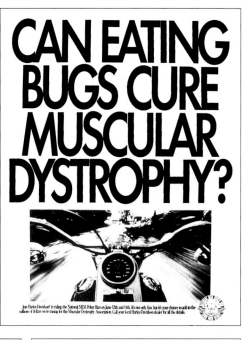

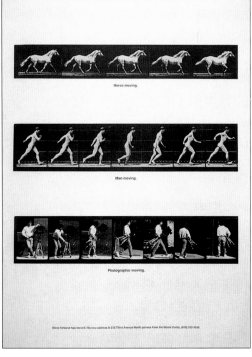

General Poster
ART DIRECTOR/COPYWRITER
Carol Henderson
PHOTOGRAPHERS
Steve Umland, Edward Muybridge
AGENCY
Fallon McElligott
CLIENT
Steve Umland

General Poster
ART DIRECTOR
Tom Lichtenheld
COPYWRITER
John Stingley
PHOTOGRAPHER
Shawn Michienzi
AGENCY
Fallon McElligott
CLIENT
The Lee Co.

General Poster
ART DIRECTORS
Gary Goldsmith, Henriette Lienke
COPYWRITER
Dean Hacohen
PHOTOGRAPHER
Robert Ammirati
AGENCY
Goldsmith/Jeffrey
CLIENT
NYNEX Business-to-Business Directory

General Poster

ART DIRECTOR
Doug Trapp

COPYWRITER
Jeff Turner

AGENCY
Martin/Williams

CLIENT
Dr. Greg Dahl

Before.   *After.*

Dr. Greg Dahl, Chiropractor

General Poster

ART DIRECTOR
Danny Boone

COPYWRITER
Joe Alexander

PHOTOGRAPHER
Dean Hawthorne

AGENCY
The Martin Agency

CLIENT
Richmond Symphony

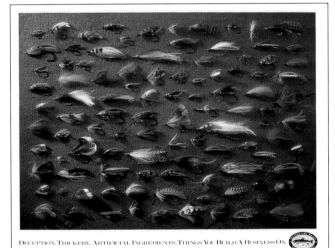

General Poster

ART DIRECTOR
Mark Fuller

COPYWRITER
Jack Mahoney

PHOTOGRAPHER
Tony Sylvestro

AGENCY
The Martin Agency

CLIENT
Farm at Mt. Walden

Rare Photos Of Jim Palmer, Fully Clothed.

Crown Hill Stamp & Coin 8343 15th Avenue NW 789-5363

General Poster

ART DIRECTOR
Kevin Nolan

COPYWRITER
Jim Copacino

CREATIVE DIRECTOR
Jim Walker

AGENCY
McCann-Erickson

CLIENT
Crown Hill Stamp & Coin

General Poster

ART DIRECTOR
Margaret McGovern

COPYWRITER
Paul Silverman

PRODUCTION
John Holt Studio

AGENCY
Mullen

CLIENT
The Timberland Co.

General Poster/Campaign

ART DIRECTOR
Wade Koniakowsky

COPYWRITER
Bob Kerstetter

ILLUSTRATOR
Mark Lyon

AGENCY
dGWB

CLIENT
STA Travel

General Poster

ART DIRECTOR
Tom Lichtenheld

COPYWRITER
Luke Sullivan

AGENCY
Fallon McElligott

CLIENT
Porsche Cars North America

Sales Promotion Poster

ART DIRECTOR
Tom Lichtenheld

COPYWRITER
Luke Sullivan

PHOTOGRAPHER
Vic Huber

AGENCY
Fallon McElligott

CLIENT
Porsche Cars North America

Sales Promotion Poster
ART DIRECTOR
Susan Griak
COPYWRITER
Tina Hall
AGENCY
Fallon McElligott
CLIENT
Fallon McElligott

Sales Promotion Poster
ART DIRECTOR
Sakol Mongkolkasetarin
COPYWRITER
Jsada Mongkolkasetarin
ILLUSTRATOR
Sumith Mongkolkasetarin
AGENCY
M Group
CLIENT
The Rainbow Connection

ART DIRECTOR/COPYWRITER
Dean Hacohen
AGENCY
Goldsmith/Jeffrey
CLIENT
NYNEX Business-to-Business Directory

ART DIRECTOR
Grant Richards
COPYWRITER
Todd Tilford
PRODUCER
Karen Junkins
AGENCY
The Richards Group
CLIENT
Memorex

PETRY MUSIC.
SFX: Muzak plays in background.
MAN: Paul Petry here at Petry Piped-in Music. We run a music studio that specializes in re-orchestrating Top-40 rock hits into light and breezy music. You know, for elevators. Hey, it's a living. Anyhow, the other day this guy stops and asks me to put an ad in the NYNEX Business-to-Business Directory. Says they distribute over half a million copies in the New York Metro area. And I'm thinking, wow. That's a lot of elevators. But now I'm questioning the whole thing. See, what I really want to do is concentrate on a career in rap. And now I'll be stuck in this studio Monday through Friday making E-Z listening tapes for every dentist's office this side of Hoboken. More happy harps. More zippy xylophones. You know what happens if you record this stuff for months on end? You need a lobotomy. There I'll be flipping through the NYNEX Business-to-Business Directory myself. I'll be looking up "Electro-Shock Therapy Equipment." I had to be out of my mind.
VO: The NYNEX Business-to-Business Directory. Where one business finds another.

GLASS HOUSES.
SFX: Opera music. Shatttering glass that builds to a crescendo along with the music.
VO: It turns out there are two things people who live in glass houses shouldn't do. One of them is buy Memorex cassette tapes. Is it live or is it Memorex?

ART DIRECTOR/COPYWRITER
Dean Hacohen
AGENCY
Goldsmith/Jeffrey
CLIENT
NYNEX Business-to-Business Directory

ART DIRECTOR/COPYWRITER
Dean Hacohen
AGENCY
Goldsmith/Jeffrey
CLIENT
Crain's New York Business

ART DIRECTOR/COPYWRITER
Dean Hacohen
AGENCY
Goldsmith/Jeffrey
CLIENT
NYNEX Business-to-Business Directory

ART DIRECTOR/COPYWRITER
Dean Hacohen
AGENCY
Goldsmith/Jeffrey
CLIENT
Crain's New York Business

ART DIRECTOR
Randy Hughes
COPYWRITERS
Josh Denberg, Jerry Fury
PRODUCER
Jenee Schmidt
AGENCY
Clarity Coverdale Rueff
CLIENT
St. Paul Pioneer Press

COPYWRITER
Thomas Hripko
PRODUCER
Harvey Lewis
AGENCY
The Richards Group
CLIENT
Motel 6

MILQUETOAST.

VO: Some people like to read the Sunday paper. Some don't have much time to read the paper. And some have so much time all they do is read the paper. Some people like columnists who make them think. Some people don't like to think. There are those people who like to read about politics. And those who like entertainment. And of course those who think politics is entertainment. Some people like to read the opinions. Some people are milquetoast and have no opinions. Some people have turned this advertisement off already and will never know its conclusion. Some people have listened attentively and will learn there's a new Sunday Pioneer Press for people who want to keep up on all kinds of things. Some like the improved Showtime section with weekly planning guide. Others like it for the only Sunday business section in the Twin Cities. Some people will hear this ad and call 291-1888 for a subscription to Sunday's Pioneer Press. Some people will not. That's unfortunate. The Pioneer Press. Words to Live By.

TIRE PRESSURE GAUGE.

TOM: Hi. Tom Bodett for Motel 6 with "Tom's Tips for Summer Trips." Just a couple of things to help separate the real traveler from the weekend warrior. Always take along a tire pressure gauge. They usually never work right, but the attendants at the station are sure impressed when you pull out your own. I usually clip mine onto my shirt pocket, just like they do. Lets them know they're not dealing with a rookie. Toss a cooler in the back, stick a compass on the dash, and hang a litter bag from the radio knob. Then before you hit the road, call 505-891-6161 and make reservations at Motel 6. We've got nearly 700 locations from coast to coast and no matter where you go, you'll get a clean, comfortable room where the kids stay free for around twenty-five bucks in most places. More in some, less in others, but always the lowest prices of any national chain. So now that you're a real traveler, get out on the road and come see us. I'm Tom Bodett for Motel 6. Keep those hands at ten and two and we'll leave the light on for you.

BEHAVIOR MODIFICATION.

TOM: Hi. Tom Bodett for Motel 6 with an idea for the 90s. It's kind of a behavior modification program for anyone who wants to uncomplicate their life. Here's how it works. Come spend the night at Motel 6 and discover how to survive comfortably with only the bare essentials. Afterall, material things are just a burden we place on ourselves, creating an endless pursuit to make more, so we can get more. And at Motel 6 you won't find any material things around burden you. No, you get just what you need. A clean, comfortable room, where you can relax, take a hot shower, and put things in perspective. And unlike those trendy Zen stress-relief clincs, a night at Motel 6 doesn't mean taking a second mortgage on the house. No, all this reality will cost you around twenty-five bucks. More in some places, less in others, but always the lowest prices of any national chain. So get out of the fast lane and come spend the night with us. I'm Swami Tommy for Motel 6 and we'll leave the light on for you.

GREENER AMERICA.

TOM: Hi. Tom Bodett for Motel 6 here with "Tom's Tips for a Greener America." Instead of plugging in an electric hedge trimmer around the house and then going to the gym for a workout, why not pick up a pair of manual clippers. They don't use any electricity and they're great for your pecs. Just picture it, you've got your heart rate up into your training zone, getting in a workout and getting your yard work done at the same time. Why not? And while we're at it, why not do away with the sixty pounds of coupons that fall out of Sunday's paper. If everyone would just charge less to begin with, we could save a whole forest instead of printing coupons. That's why you'll never see a coupon for Motel 6. We've already got the lowest prices of any national chain. So come see us. Enjoy a clean, comfortable room for around twenty-five bucks. More in some places, less in others, so not only will you save money, but if you recycle all those coupons that are cluttering up your refrigerator, you could even make a little, too. I'm Tom Bodett for Motel 6, and we'll leave the light on for you.

ART DIRECTOR/COPYWRITER
Dean Hacohen
AGENCY
Goldsmith/Jeffrey
CLIENT
NYNEX Business-to-Business Directory

COPYWRITER
Lyle Wedemeyer
PRODUCER
Mary Fran Werner
AGENCY
Martin/Williams
CLIENT
MN Department of Health

BIG TIME BALLOONS.

MAN: Barney Bowler, here. Big Time Balloons. (*balloon filling up*) I've got this small balloon store. Two helium tanks. Two types of balloons. We do birthday parties. The other day, this guy comes in and asks me to buy an ad in the NYNEX Business-to-Business Directory. Says it's the book that reaches businesses all over the New York Metro area. Over half a million copies in distribution. And I'm thinking, I've always wanted to do office parties. Why not? Well, now that I've thought about it, I'll tell you why not. Businesses give you big balloon orders. Massive orders. You see how many balloons were dropped at those political conventions? (*pop*) Now when you've got a small balloon business and pop a few, that goes with the territory. But if you're filling 10,000 a day? (*pop, pop*) Talk about migraines. And if I expand into hot air balloons and corporate blimps? Oooh, imagine popping one of those puppies. And there I'll be. Flipping through the NYNEX Business-to-Business Directory myself. Looking up "Ear Plugs, Industrial Suppliers..." (*pop*) I gotta be nuts.

VO: The NYNEX Business-to-Business Directory. Where one business finds another.

WHAT IS IT ABOUT WOMEN?

VO: What is it about us women? What is it about us that makes us feel guilty when we vacuum around furniture, instead of under it? What is it about women that makes us never take the last piece of anything from a plate? What is it that makes us lick Kleenex and scrub kids faces with it. Even kids that aren't our own? What makes us do that? What is it that makes us fifty percent better than men at locating misplaced socks? What is it that makes us buy canned goods and put them in our cupboards...and then never use them? Is that heredity or environment that makes us do that? I'd like to know. And what is it that makes us smoke cigarettes even more than men? I'd like to know that, too. And what is it that makes cigarette companies spend millions of dollars in advertising each year to get us to keep smoking? Could it be the millions in profits they make? What is it about that fact that makes you so mad? And now that you know, what is it you're gonna do to quit?

SIXTEEN JUDGES reviewed 885 editorial design entries. 286 newspaper, magazine, book, and house organ covers and interiors became finalists. One of the 4 Gold medalists also received a Best of Show citation. 10 Silver medals were awarded.

Consumer Newspaper
ART DIRECTOR
Galie Jean-Louis
WRITER
David Breskin
PHOTOGRAPHER
The Douglas Brothers
PUBLICATION
Anchorage Daily News

Consumer Newspaper
ART DIRECTOR
Galie Jean-Louis
WRITER
Nicholas Krystof
ILLUSTRATOR
Scott Menchin
PUBLICATION
Anchorage Daily News

Consumer Newspaper
ART DIRECTOR
Cynthia Hoffman
COPYWRITER
Matthew Gilbert
PUBLICATION
The Boston Globe

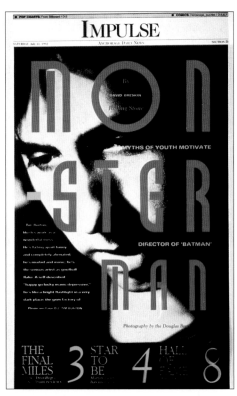

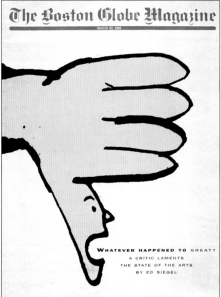

Consumer Newspaper
ART DIRECTOR
Lucy Bartholomay
PHOTOGRAPHER
Michele McDonald
PUBLICATION
The Boston Globe

Consumer Newspaper
ART DIRECTOR
Lucy Bartholomay
PUBLICATION
The Boston Globe

Consumer Newspaper
ART DIRECTOR
Lucy Bartholomay
ILLUSTRATOR
Scott Menchin
PUBLICATION
The Boston Globe

Consumer Newspaper

ART DIRECTOR
Robert Newman

PHOTOGRAPHERS
UPI/Bettmann

PUBLICATION
The Village Voice

Consumer Newspaper

ART DIRECTOR
Robert Newman

DESIGNER
Florian Bachlera

ILLUSTRATOR
Philip Burke

PUBLICATION
The Village Voice

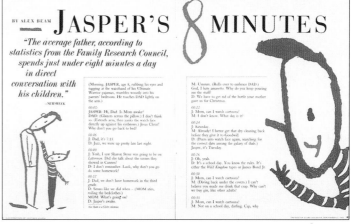

Consumer Newspaper

ART DIRECTOR
Lucy Bartholomay

PHOTOGRAPHER
Victoria Blewer

PUBLICATION
The Boston Globe

Consumer Newspaper

ART DIRECTOR
Lucy Bartholomay

ILLUSTRATOR
Santiago Cohen

PUBLICATION
The Boston Globe

Consumer Newspaper

ART DIRECTOR
Rena Sokolow

ILLUSTRATOR
Anthony Russo

PUBLICATION
The Boston Globe

Consumer Newspaper

ART DIRECTOR
Lucy Bartholomay

ILLUSTRATOR
J. W. Stewart

PUBLICATION
The Boston Globe

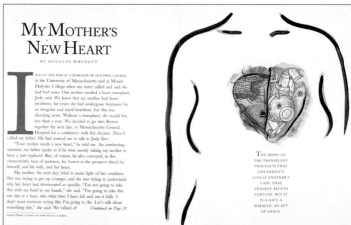

Consumer Newspaper

ART DIRECTOR
Cynthia Hoffman

COPYWRITER
Jean Fain

ILLUSTRATOR
John Hersey

PUBLICATION
The Boston Globe

Consumer Newspaper

ART DIRECTOR
Lucy Bartholomay

ILLUSTRATOR
Patrick Blackwell

PUBLICATION
The Boston Globe

Consumer Magazine Cover

ART DIRECTOR
Suzanne Morin

DESIGN DIRECTOR
Michael Bierut

PHOTOGRAPHER
Ken Regan

PUBLICATION
Audubon Magazine

Consumer Magazine Cover

ART DIRECTOR
Suzanne Morin

PHOTOGRAPHER
Eugene Richards

PUBLICATION
Audubon Magazine

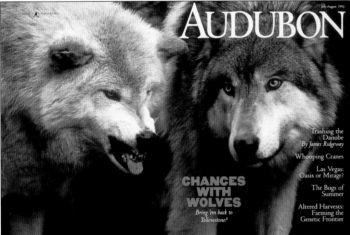

Consumer Magazine Cover

ART DIRECTOR
Suzanne Morin

PHOTOGRAPHER
Tom & Pat Leeson

PUBLICATION
Audubon Magazine

Consumer Magazine Cover

PUBLICATION
Witness

Consumer Magazine Cover

ART DIRECTOR
Jane Palecek

PHOTOGRAPHER
Matt Mahurin

PUBLICATION
Health

Consumer Magazine Cover

ART DIRECTOR
Jane Palecek

PHOTOGRAPHER
Geof Kern

PUBLICATION
Health

Consumer Magazine Cover

ART DIRECTOR/DESIGNER
Fred Woodward

PHOTOGRAPHER
Mark Seltser

PUBLICATION
Rolling Stone Magazine

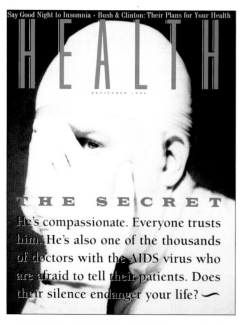

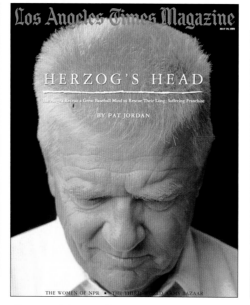

Consumer Magazine Cover

ART DIRECTOR
Nancy Duckworth

ILLUSTRATOR
Gary Baserman

PUBLICATION
L. A. Times Magazine

Consumer Magazine Cover

ART DIRECTOR
Nancy Duckworth

PHOTOGRAPHER
Mark Seliger

PUBLICATION
L. A. Times Magazine

Consumer Magazine Cover

ART DIRECTOR
Jessica Helfand

WRITER
Judy Bachrach

PHOTOGRAPHER
William Wegman

PUBLICATION
Philadelphia Inquirer Magazine

Consumer Magazine Cover

ART DIRECTOR
Jessica Helfand

WRITER
Henry Goldman

ILLUSTRATOR
Scott Menchin

PUBLICATION
Philadelphia Inquirer Magazine

Consumer Magazine Cover

ART DIRECTOR
Audrey Satterwhite

WRITER
John Wilburn

ILLUSTRATOR
Philip Burke

PUBLICATION
Houston Press

Consumer Magazine Cover

ART DIRECTOR
Jessica Helfand

WRITER
Stephan Salisbury

ILLUSTRATOR
Jessica Helfand

PUBLICATION
Philadelphia Inquirer Magazine

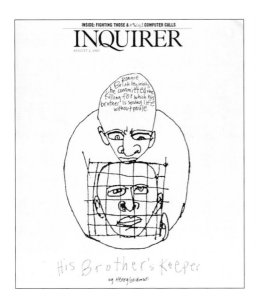

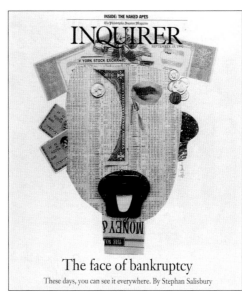

Consumer Magazine Cover

ART DIRECTOR
Audrey Satterwhite

WRITER
John Wilburn

ILLUSTRATOR
Steve Brodner

PUBLICATION
Houston Press

Consumer Magazine Cover

ART DIRECTOR
Donna M. Bonavita

WRITER
Robert Strozier

ILLUSTRATOR
Seymour Chwast

STUDIO
KPMG Peat Marwick Comm.

PUBLICATION
World

Consumer Magazine Cover

ART DIRECTOR
Carl Lehmann-Haupt

DESIGNER
Nancy Cohen

PHOTOGRAPHER
Kristine Larsen

PUBLICATION
Metropolis Magazine

Consumer Magazine Interior

ART DIRECTOR
Andrzej Jankera

PUBLICATION
House Beautiful Magazine

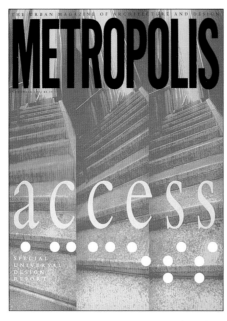

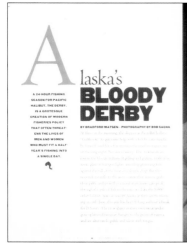

Consumer Magazine Interior

ART DIRECTOR
Suzanne Morin

WRITER
Bradford Matsen

PHOTOGRAPHER
Bob Sacha

PUBLICATION
Audubon Magazine

Consumer Magazine Interior

ART DIRECTOR
Suzanne Morin

WRITER
Tina Rosenberg

PHOTOGRAPHER
Gustavo Gilabert

PUBLICATION
Audubon Magazine

Consumer Magazine Interior

ART DIRECTOR
Suzanne Morin

WRITER
Pamela Weintraub

ILLUSTRATOR
James Marsh

PUBLICATION
Audubon Magazine

Consumer Magazine Interior

ART DIRECTOR
Suzanne Morin

WRITER
Fred Pearce

PHOTOGRAPHER
Eugene Richards

PUBLICATION
Audubon Magazine

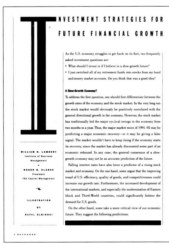

Consumer Magazine Interior

ART DIRECTOR
Suzanne Morin

DESIGN DIRECTOR
Michael Bierut

WRITER
Peter Steinhart

PHOTOGRAPHER
K&K Ammann

AGENCY
Audubon Magazine

Consumer Magazine Interior

DESIGNER
Bruce Patrick

WRITERS
William Lambert, Roger Clarke

ILLUSTRATOR
Rafal Olbinski

STUDIO
BYU Graphics

PUBLICATION
Exchange Magazine

Consumer Magazine Interior

DESIGNER
David Eliason

WRITER
Robert G. Crawford

ILLUSTRATOR
Alan E. Cober

STUDIO
BYU Graphics

PUBLICATION
Exchange Magazine

Consumer Magazine Interior

DESIGN DIRECTOR
Diana LaGuardia

DESIGNER
Chris Gangi

PHOTOGRAPHER
Nadav Kander

PUBLICATION
Condé Nast Traveler

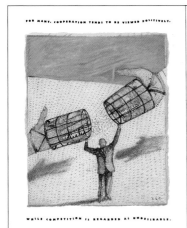

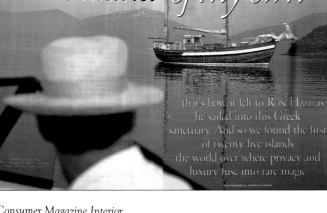

Consumer Magazine Interior

DESIGN DIRECTOR
Diana LaGuardia

DESIGNER
Mike Powers

PHOTOGRAPHER
Anthony Gordon

PUBLICATION
Condé Nast Traveler

Consumer Magazine Interior

ART DIRECTOR
Olivia Bradrutt-Giron

DESIGNER
Matt Berman

PHOTOGRAPHER
Hans Feurer

PUBLICATION
Elle Magazine

Consumer Magazine Interior

ART DIRECTOR

Olivia Bradrutt-Giron

PHOTOGRAPHER

Tyen

PUBLICATION

Elle Magazine

Consumer Magazine Interior

ART DIRECTOR

Olivia Bradrutt-Giron

PHOTOGRAPHER

Edouard Sicot

PUBLICATION

Elle Magazine

Consumer Magazine Interior

ART DIRECTOR

Olivia Bradrutt-Giron

PHOTOGRAPHER

Francis Giacobetti

PUBLICATION

Elle Magazine

Consumer Magazine Interior

ART DIRECTOR

Olivia Bradrutt-Giron

PHOTOGRAPHER

Michel Comte

PUBLICATION

Elle Magazine

Consumer Magazine Interior

ART DIRECTOR
Olivia Bradrutt-Giron

DESIGNER
Matt Berman

PHOTOGRAPHER
Gilles Bensimon

PUBLICATION
Elle Magazine

Consumer Magazine Interior

ART DIRECTOR
Caroline Bowyer

DESIGNER
Jo Hay

PUBLICATION
Elle Decor

Consumer Magazine Interior

ART DIRECTOR
Caroline Bowyer

DESIGNER
Jo Hay

PHOTOGRAPHER
Nedjeljko Matura

PUBLICATION
Elle Decor

Consumer Magazine Interior

ART DIRECTOR
Audrey Satterwhite

DESIGNER
Ted Keller

WRITER
John Wilburn

PUBLICATION
Houston Press

Consumer Magazine Interior

ART DIRECTOR
Audrey Satterwhite

DESIGNER
Ted Keller

WRITER
John Wilburn

PHOTOGRAPHER
Mark Seliger

PUBLICATION
Houston Press

Consumer Magazine Interior

ART DIRECTOR
Audrey Satterwhite

DESIGNER
Ted Keller

WRITER
John Wilburn

PHOTOGRAPHER
Mark Seliger

PUBLICATION
Houston Press

Consumer Magazine Interior

ART DIRECTOR
Audrey Satterwhite

WRITER
John Wilburn

PHOTOGRAPHER
Keith Carter

PUBLICATION
Houston Press

Consumer Magazine Interior

ART DIRECTOR
Audrey Satterwhite

DESIGNER
Ted Keller

WRITER
John Wilburn

ILLUSTRATOR
Steve Brodner

PUBLICATION
Houston Press

Consumer Magazine Interior

ART DIRECTOR
Jane Palecek

DESIGNER
Dorothy Marschall

ILLUSTRATOR
C. F. Payne

PUBLICATION
Health

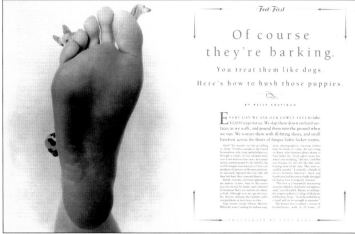

Consumer Magazine Interior

ART DIRECTOR
Jane Palecek

DESIGNER
Dorothy Marschall

PHOTOGRAPHER
Geof Kern

PUBLICATION
Health

Consumer Magazine Interior

ART DIRECTOR
Donna M. Bonavita

WRITER
Nancy Adriance

ILLUSTRATOR
Bill Nelson

STUDIO
KPMG Peat Marwick Comm.

PUBLICATION
World

Consumer Magazine Interior

ART DIRECTOR
Donna M. Bonavita

WRITER
Robert W. Casey

ILLUSTRATOR
Koichi Sato

STUDIO
KPMG Peat Marwick Comm.

PUBLICATION
World

Consumer Magazine Interior

ART DIRECTOR
Donna M. Bonavita

WRITER
Margery Stein

PHOTOGRAPHER
Manfred Kage

STUDIO
KPMG Peat Marwick Comm.

PUBLICATION
World

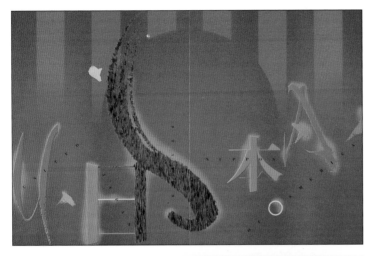

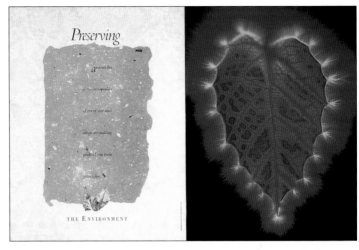

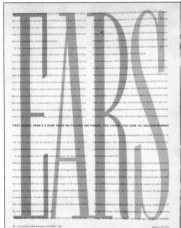

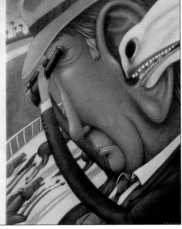

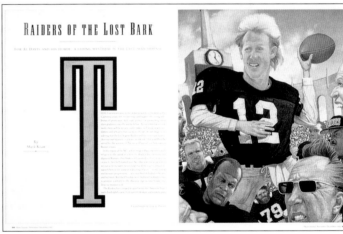

Consumer Magazine Interior

ART DIRECTOR
Nancy Duckworth

ILLUSTRATOR
Keith Graves

PUBLICATION
L. A. Times Magazine

Consumer Magazine Interior

ART DIRECTOR
Matthew Drace

DESIGNER
Giovanni Russo

ILLUSTRATOR
C. F. Payne

PUBLICATION
Men's Journal

Consumer Magazine Interior

ART DIRECTOR
Janet Froelich

DESIGNER
Kathi Rota

PHOTOGRAPHER
Danielle Weil

PUBLICATION
The New York Times Magazine

Consumer Magazine Interior

ART DIRECTOR
Jessica Helfand

WRITER
Art Carey

PUBLICATION
Philadelphia Inquirer Magazine

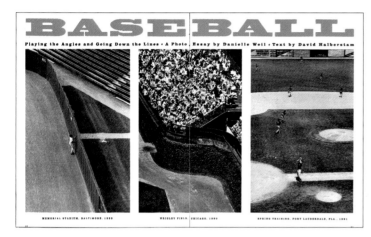

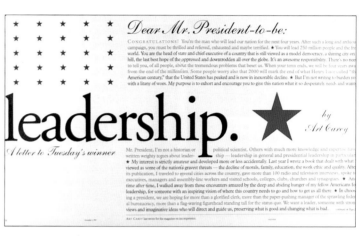

Consumer Magazine Interior

ART DIRECTOR/DESIGNER
Fred Woodward

WRITER
David Breskin

PHOTOGRAPHER
Albert Watson

PUBLICATION
Rolling Stone Magazine

Consumer Magazine Interior

ART DIRECTOR
Fred Woodward

DESIGNER
Gail Anderson

WRITER
Joe Wood

PHOTOGRAPHER
Albert Watson

PUBLICATION
Rolling Stone Magazine

Consumer Magazine Interior

ART DIRECTOR
Fred Woodward

DESIGNER
Gail Anderson

WRITER
P. J. O'Rourke

ILLUSTRATOR
Everett Peck

PUBLICATION
Rolling Stone Magazine

Consumer Magazine Interior

ART DIRECTOR
Fred Woodward

DESIGNER
Gail Anderson

WRITER
Alan Light

PHOTOGRAPHER
Frank Ockenfels

PUBLICATION
Rolling Stone Magazine

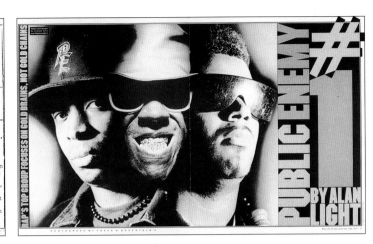

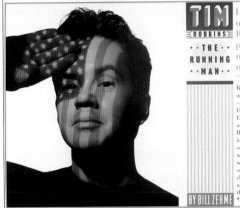

Consumer Magazine Interior

ART DIRECTOR
Fred Woodward

DESIGNER
Debra Bishop

WRITER
Bill Zehme

PHOTOGRAPHER
Albert Watson

PUBLICATION
Rolling Stone Magazine

Consumer Magazine Interior

PUBLICATION
Creem

Consumer Magazine Interior

ART DIRECTOR
D. J. Stout

PHOTOGRAPHER
Dan Winters

PUBLICATION
Texas Monthly

Consumer Magazine Interior Series

ART DIRECTOR
Suzanne Morin

WRITER
Bruce Stutz

PHOTOGRAPHER
Richard Misrach

PUBLICATION
Audubon Magazine

Consumer Magazine Interior Series

DESIGN DIRECTOR
Diana LaGuardia

DESIGNER
Chris Gangi

PHOTOGRAPHER
Knut Bry

ILLUSTRATORS
John Grimwade, Greg Wakabayashi

PUBLICATION
Condé Nast Traveler

Consumer Magazine Interior Series

DESIGN DIRECTOR
Diana LaGuardia

DESIGNER
Mike Powers

PHOTOGRAPHERS
Paul Warchol, Barry Iverson

ILLUSTRATOR
John Grimwade

PUBLICATION
Condé Nast Traveler

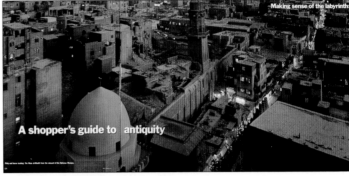

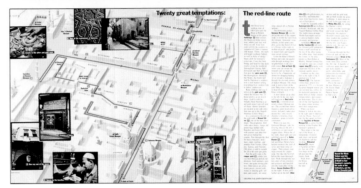

Consumer Magazine Interior Series

ART DIRECTOR
David Armario

DESIGNER
James Lambertus

PHOTOGRAPHER
Dan Winters

ILLUSTRATOR
Dana Berry

PUBLICATION
Discover Magazine

Consumer Magazine Interior Series

ART DIRECTOR
David Armario

PHOTOGRAPHER
Tim Simmons

PUBLICATION
Discover Magazine

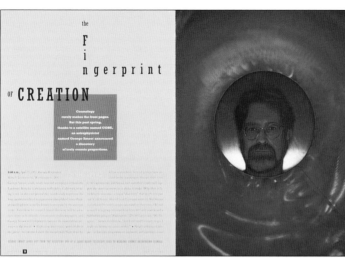

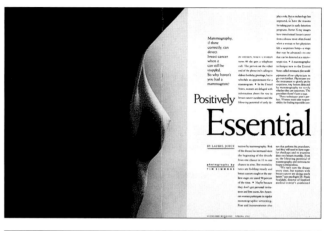

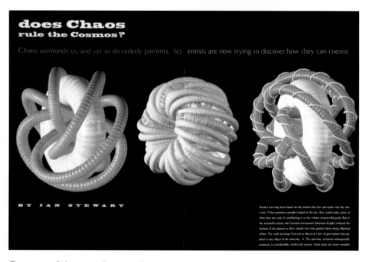

Consumer Magazine Interior Series

ART DIRECTORS
David Armario, James Lambertus

DESIGNER
James Lambertus

PUBLICATION
Discover Magazine

Consumer Magazine Interior Series

ART DIRECTOR
James Lambertus, David Armario

DESIGNER
James Lambertus

ILLUSTRATOR
Alan Cober

PUBLICATION
Discover Magazine

Consumer Magazine Interior Series

ART DIRECTOR
James Lambertus

PUBLICATION
Discover Magazine

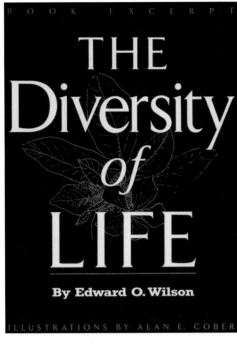

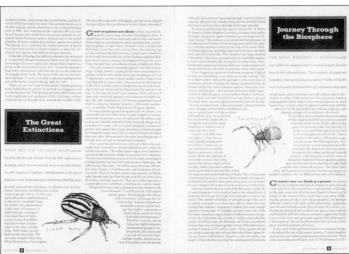

Consumer Magazine Interior Series

ART DIRECTOR
Joannah Ralston

ILLUSTRATOR
Michael Klein

PUBLICATION
Eating Well Magazine

Consumer Magazine Interior Series

ART DIRECTOR
Caroline Bowyer

DESIGNER
Jo Hay

PHOTOGRAPHER
Raymond Meier

PUBLICATION
Elle Decor

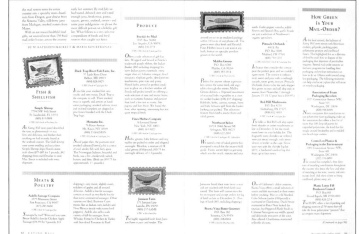

Consumer Magazine Interior Series
ART DIRECTOR
Olivia Bradrutt-Giron
PHOTOGRAPHER
Gilles Bensimon
PUBLICATION
Elle Magazine

Consumer Magazine Interior Series
ART DIRECTOR
Olivia Bradrutt-Giron
PHOTOGRAPHER
Gilles Bensimon
PUBLICATION
Elle Magazine

Consumer Magazine Interior Series

ART DIRECTOR
Olivia Bradrutt-Giron

PHOTOGRAPHER
Gilles Bensimon

PUBLICATION
Elle Magazine

Consumer Magazine Interior Series

ART DIRECTOR
Olivia Bradrutt-Giron

DESIGNER
Matt Berman

PHOTOGRAPHER
Serge Lutens

PUBLICATION
Elle Magazine

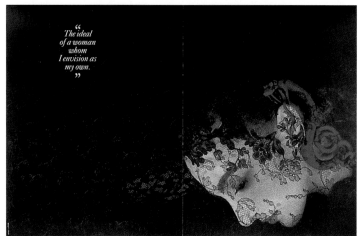

Consumer Magazine Interior Series

ART DIRECTOR
Olivia Bradrutt-Giron

PHOTOGRAPHERS
Gilles Bensimon, Lothar Schmid

ILLUSTRATORS
Angelo Tarlazzi, Karl Lagerfeld

PUBLICATION
Elle Magazine

Consumer Magazine Interior Series

ART DIRECTOR
Andrzej Janerka

PUBLICATION
House Beautiful Magazine

Consumer Magazine Interior Series

ART DIRECTOR
Andrzej Janerka

PHOTOGRAPHER
Paul Warchol

PUBLICATION
House Beautiful Magazine

Consumer Magazine Interior Series

ART DIRECTOR
Donna M. Bonavita

WRITER
Benjamin Weiner

ILLUSTRATOR
Lane Smith

STUDIO
KPMG Peat Marwick Comm.

PUBLICATION
World

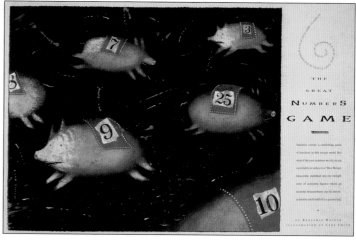

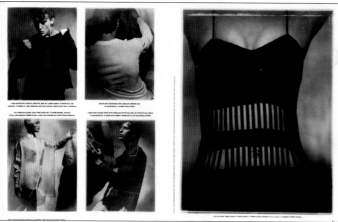

Consumer Magazine Interior Series

ART DIRECTOR
Janet Froelich

DESIGNER
Kathi Rota

PHOTOGRAPHER
Michele Clement

PUBLICATION
The New York Times Magazine

Consumer Magazine Interior Series

ART DIRECTOR
Jennifer Wavereck

COPYWRITER
Sarah Medford

PHOTOGRAPHER
Todd Eberle

PUBLICATION
Martha Stewart Living

Consumer Magazine Interior Series

ART DIRECTOR
Jennifer Wavereck

PHOTOGRAPHER
Grant Peterson

PUBLICATION
Martha Stewart Living

Consumer Magazine Interior Series

ART DIRECTOR
Gael Towey

COPYWRITER
Celia Barbour

PHOTOGRAPHER
Victoria Pearson

PUBLICATION
Martha Stewart Living

Consumer Magazine Interior Series

ART DIRECTOR
Jennifer Wavereck

COPYWRITER
Sarah Medford

PHOTOGRAPHER
Bruce Wolf

PUBLICATION
Martha Stewart Living

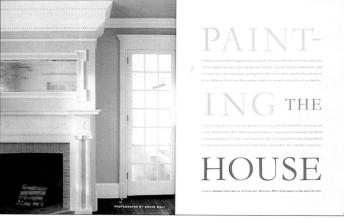

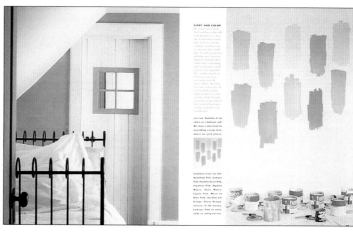

Consumer Magazine Interior Series

ART DIRECTOR
Laura Harrigan

COPYWRITER
Corby Kummer

PHOTOGRAPHER
Maria Robledo

PUBLICATION
Martha Stewart Living

Consumer Magazine Interior Series

ART DIRECTOR
Gael Towey

COPYWRITER
Anmarie Iversen

PHOTOGRAPHER
Grant Peterson

PUBLICATION
Martha Stewart Living

Consumer Magazine Interior Series

ART DIRECTOR
Matthew Drace

DESIGNER
Giovanni Russo

PHOTOGRAPHER
Neal Rogers

PUBLICATION
Men's Journal

Consumer Magazine Interior Series

ART DIRECTOR/DESIGNER
Matthew Drace

PHOTOGRAPHER
Dan Borris

PUBLICATION
Men's Journal

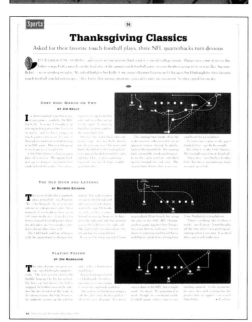

Consumer Magazine Interior Series

ART DIRECTOR/DESIGNER
Jane Palacek

ILLUSTRATOR
Gene Greif

PUBLICATION
Health

Consumer Magazine Interior Series

ART DIRECTOR/DESIGNER
Jane Palecek

ILLUSTRATORS
Anita Kunz, Matt Mahurin

PUBLICATION
Health

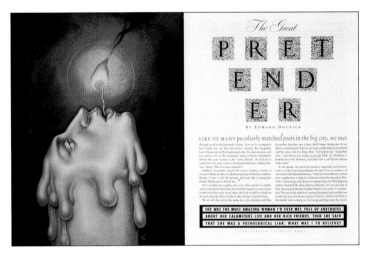

Consumer Magazine Interior Series

ART DIRECTOR
D. J. Stout

PHOTOGRAPHER
Mary Ellen Mark

PUBLICATION
Texas Monthly

Consumer Magazine Interior Series

ART DIRECTOR
D. J. Stout

PHOTOGRAPHER
Keith Carter

PUBLICATION
Texas Monthly

Consumer Magazine Interior Series

ART DIRECTOR
D. J. Stout

PHOTOGRAPHER
Lee Crum

PUBLICATION
Texas Monthly

Consumer Magazine Full Issue

ART DIRECTOR
Suzanne Morin

PUBLICATION
Audubon Magazine

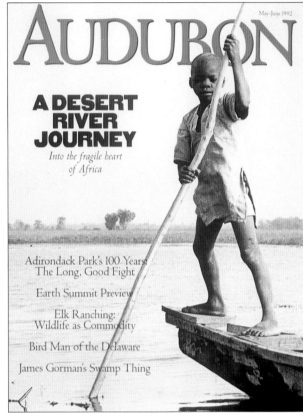

Consumer Magazine Full Issue

ART DIRECTOR
Donna M. Bonavita

ASSISTANT ART DIRECTOR
Heidi Gross

WRITER
Robert M. Strozier

STUDIO
KPMG Peat Marwick Comm.

PUBLICATION
World Magazine

Consumer Magazine Full Issue

ART DIRECTOR
Donna M. Bonavita

ASSISTANT ART DIRECTOR
Heidi Gross

WRITER
Robert M. Strozier

STUDIO
KPMG Peat Marwick Comm.

PUBLICATION
World Magazine

Consumer Magazine Full Issue

ART DIRECTORS
Matthew Drace, Giovani Russo,
Gaemer Gutierrez

DESIGNER
Matthew Drace

PUBLICATION
Men's Journal

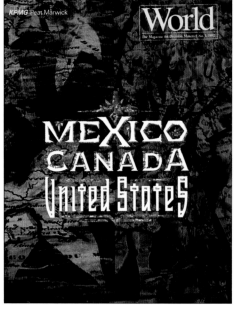

Trade Magazine Cover

ART DIRECTOR
Andrew Kner

DESIGNER/ILLUSTRATOR
Gabor Domján

PUBLICATION
Print Magazine

Trade Magazine Cover

ART DIRECTOR
B. Martin Pedersen

PHOTOGRAPHER
John Mattos

STUDIO
Pedersen Design Inc.

PUBLICATION
Graphis

Trade Magazine Cover

ART DIRECTORS
Walter Bernard, Milton Glaser,
Frank Baseman, Sharon Okamoto

AGENCY
WBMG, Inc.

PUBLICATION
Magazine Week

Trade Magazine Interior

ART DIRECTOR
Mark Geer

WRITER
Charles Bankhead

ILLUSTRATOR
James Endicott

STUDIO
Geer Design, Inc.

PUBLICATION
Caring/Memorial Healthcare System

Trade Magazine Interior

ART DIRECTOR
B. Martin Pedersen

WRITER
Paola Antonelli

STUDIO
Pedersen Design Inc.

PUBLICATION
Graphis

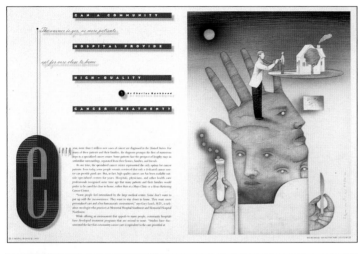

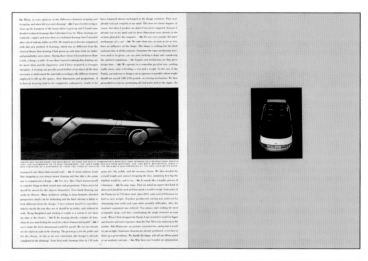

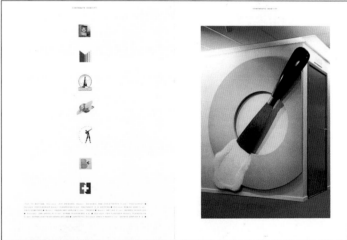

Trade Magazine Interior

ART DIRECTOR
B. Martin Pedersen

PHOTOGRAPHER
Masaru Mera

STUDIO
Pedersen Design Inc.

PUBLICATION
Graphis

Trade Magazine Interior

ART DIRECTOR
B. Martin Pedersen

STUDIO
Pedersen Design Inc.

PUBLICATION
Graphis

Trade Magazine Interior

ART DIRECTOR
B. Martin Pedersen

WRITER
Brendan Gill

PHOTOGRAPHER
Arnold Newman

STUDIO
Pedersen Design Inc.

PUBLICATION
Graphis

Trade Magazine Interior

ART DIRECTOR
Dania Martinez Davey

PUBLICATION
HG/Condé Nast Publications

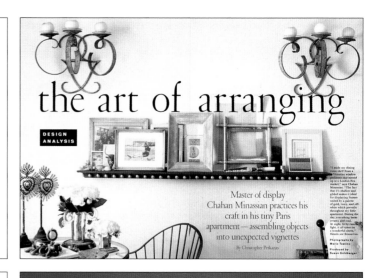

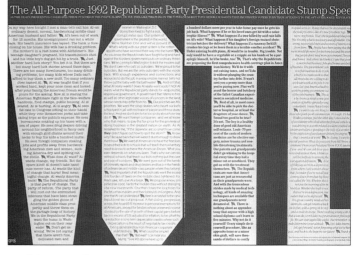

Trade Magazine Interior

ART DIRECTORS
Dania Martinez Davey, Marcos Gago

PUBLICATION
HG/Condé Nast Publications

Trade Magazine Interior

ART DIRECTOR
Seymour Chwast

DESIGNER
Greg Simpson

WRITER
Tony Hendra

STUDIO
The Pushpin Group

PUBLICATION
U&lc/International Typeface Corp.

Trade Magazine Interior

ART DIRECTOR
Seymour Chwast

DESIGNER
Greg Simpson

WRITER
Allan Haley

STUDIO
The Pushpin Group

PUBLICATION
U&lc/International Typeface Corp.

Trade Magazine Interior

ART DIRECTOR
B. Martin Pedersen

WRITER
Ken Coupland

STUDIO
Pedersen Design Inc.

PUBLICATION
Graphis

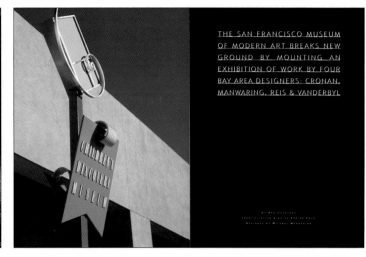

Trade Magazine Interior

ART DIRECTOR
B. Martin Pedersen

DESIGNER
Adrian Pulfer

WRITER
Sally Beardsley

PHOTOGRAPHER
Poul I.B. Henriksen

STUDIO
Pedersen Design Inc.

PUBLICATION
Graphis

Trade Magazine Interior

ART DIRECTOR
B. Martin Pedersen

WRITER
Richard B. Woodward

PHOTOGRAPHER
Hiro

STUDIO
Pedersen Design Inc.

PUBLICATION
Graphis

Trade Magazine Interior
ART DIRECTOR
B. Martin Pedersen
WRITER
Christopher Petkanas
PHOTOGRAPHER
Dean Chamberlain
STUDIO
Pedersen Design Inc.
PUBLICATION
Graphis

Trade Magazine Interior
ART DIRECTOR
Alexander Isley
WRITER
Allan Haley
PHOTOGRAPHER
Monica Stevenson
STUDIO
Alexander Isley Design
PUBLICATION
U&lc/International Typeface Corp.

House Publication
ART DIRECTOR
Stephen Doyle
WRITER
Vaclav Havel
CREATIVE DIRECTOR
William Drenttel
EDITOR
Paula Scher
STUDIO
Drenttel Doyle Partners
PUBLICATION
Subjective Reasoning
PUBLISHER
Champion International

House Publication

ART DIRECTORS
Mark Geer, Morgan Bomar

DESIGNER
Heidi Flynn Allen

WRITERS
Jolynn Rogers, Karen Kephart

STUDIO
Geer Design, Inc.

CLIENT
Memorial Healthcare System

House Publication

ART DIRECTOR
Donna M. Bonavita

DESIGNERS
Donna M. Bonavita, Heidi Gross

WRITERS
Nancy Adriance, Sally Smith

STUDIO
KMPMG Peat Marwick Comm.

PUBLICATION
Inside Track

Book Design

ART DIRECTOR
Stephen Doyle

WRITER
James Salter

PHOTOGRAPHER
Duane Michals

STUDIO
Drenttel Doyle Partners

PUBLISHER
William Drenttel

Book Design

ART DIRECTOR
Stephen Doyle

DESIGNER
Andrew Gray

STUDIO
Drenttel Doyle Partners

PHOTOGRAPHERS
Dawoud Bey, Scott Frances, Peter Moore

PUBLISHER
The Museum of Modern Art, New York

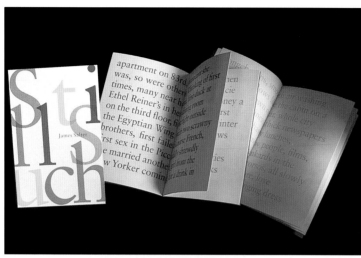

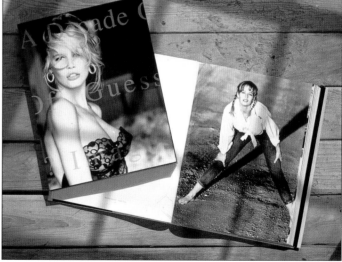

Book Design

ART DIRECTOR
B. Martin Pedersen

DESIGNER
Adrian Pulfer

STUDIO
Pedersen Design Inc.

PUBLISHER
Graphis

Book Design

ART DIRECTOR
Paul Marciano

DESIGNER
Samantha Gibson

COPYWRITER
Emily Corey

STUDIO
Guess?, Inc.

PUBLISHER
Guess?, Inc.

Book Design

ART DIRECTOR/AUTHOR/PHOTOGRAPHER
Hara

DESIGNER
Tom Lewis

CLIENT
Harry N. Abrams

Book Design

ART DIRECTOR
John Fontana

DESIGNER
Heidi North

PUBLISHER
Harmony

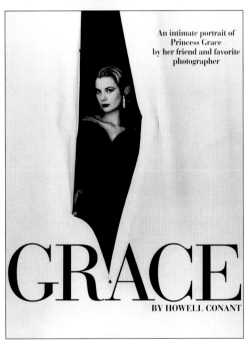

Book Design

ART DIRECTOR
Mary K. Baumann

DESIGNER
Will Hopkins

STUDIO
Hopkins/Baumann

PUBLISHER
Random House

Book Design

ART DIRECTOR
Robert Shapazian

DESIGNER
Jeffrey Mueller

ILLUSTRATOR
Toni Zeto

PUBLISHER
The Lapis Press

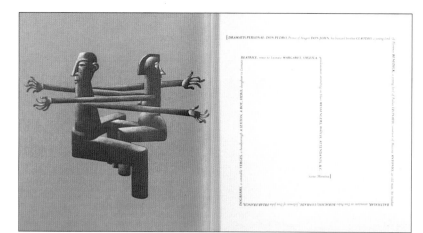

Book Design
AGENCY
Martin Solomon

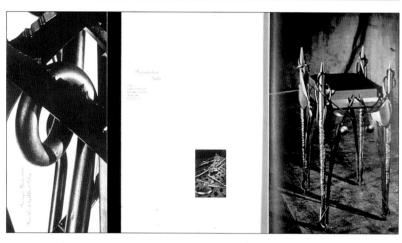

Book Design
ART DIRECTOR
Michael Beirut
WRITERS
P. Joseph, J.R. Gruber, M. Westby
DESIGNER
Dorit Lev
PHOTOGRAPHER
Michael Galatis
STUDIO
Pentagram Design
PUBLISHER
Peter Joseph Gallery

Book Design
ART DIRECTOR
Robin Rickabaugh
DESIGNER
Kim Lew
WRITER/ARTIST
Willa Shalit
PHOTOGRAPHER
David Gorsek
STUDIO
Principia Graphica
PUBLISHER
Beyond Words Publishing

Book Design
ART DIRECTOR
Robin Rickabaugh
DESIGNER
Jon Olsen
PHOTOGRAPHER
Robert Clayton
STUDIO
Principia Graphica
PUBLISHER
Beyond Words Publishing

Book Design

ART DIRECTOR
Miho

WRITER
Larry Frank

PHOTOGRAPHERS
Michael O'Shaughnessy,
Nancy Hunter Warren

PUBLISHER
Red Crane Books

Book Design

ART DIRECTOR
Lynn Pieroni Fowler

AUTHOR
Louise Pickford

PHOTOGRAPHER
Gus Filgate

PUBLISHER
Stewart, Tabori & Chang, Inc.

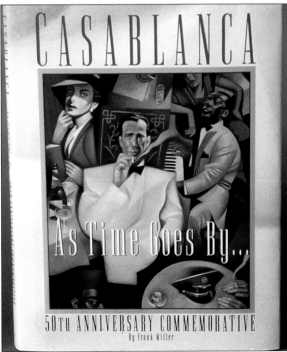

Book Design
ART DIRECTOR
Al Cetta

DESIGNER
Wendell Minor

STUDIO
Wendell Minor Design

Book Design
ART DIRECTOR
Michael J. Walsh

DESIGNERS
Karen E. Smith, Elaine Streithof

PUBLISHER
Turner Publishing, Inc.

Book Design
ART DIRECTOR
Al Cetta
DESIGNER
Wendell Minor
STUDIO
Wendell Minor Design

Book Design
ART DIRECTOR
Ben Gasner
PHOTOGRAPHER
Mickey Koren
STUDIO
Erwin Lefkowitz & Associates
CLIENT
Els Bendheim

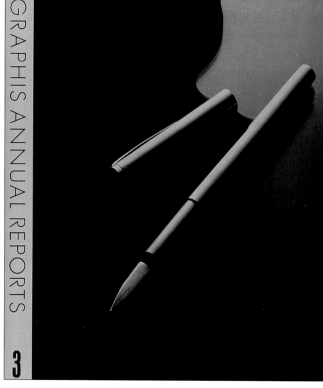

Book Design
ART DIRECTOR/DESIGNER
Julie Duquet
COPYWRITER
Sylvia Watanabe
ILLUSTRATOR
Stephen Rydberg
PUBLISHER
Doubleday

Book Design
ART DIRECTOR
Adrian Pulfer
DESIGNER
B. Martin Pedersen
PHOTOGRAPHER
Dennis Blachut
STUDIO
Pedersen Design Inc.
PUBLISHER
Graphis Annual Reports

Book Design
ART DIRECTOR
B. Martin Pedersen
PHOTOGRAPHER
Greg Gorfkle
STUDIO
Pedersen Design Inc.
PUBLISHER
Graphis

Book Design
ART DIRECTOR
B. Martin Pedersen
STUDIO
Pedersen Design Inc.
PUBLISHER
Graphis

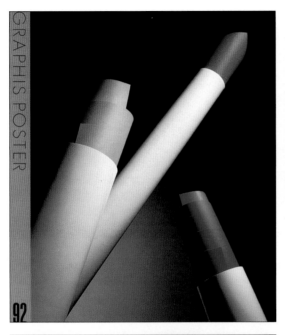

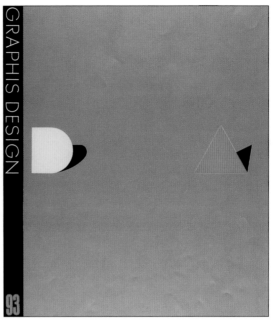

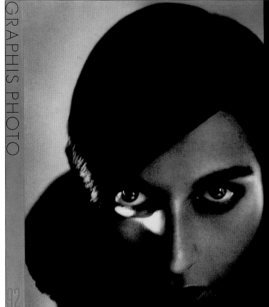

Book Design
ART DIRECTOR
B. Martin Pedersen
DESIGNER
Adrian Pulfer
PHOTOGRAPHER
Javier Vallhonrat
STUDIO
Pedersen Design Inc.
PUBLISHER
Graphis

Book Design
ART DIRECTOR
Victor Weaver
DESIGNER
Jo Bonney
STUDIO
Jo Bonney Design
PUBLISHER
Hyperion

Book Design

ART DIRECTOR
Susan Mitchell

DESIGNER
Heidi North

PHOTOGRAPHER
Mark Newman

PUBLISHER
Vintage Books

Book Design

ART DIRECTOR
Steven Brower

DESIGNER
Morris Taub

PHOTOGRAPHER
Barry King

PUBLISHER
Carol Publishing

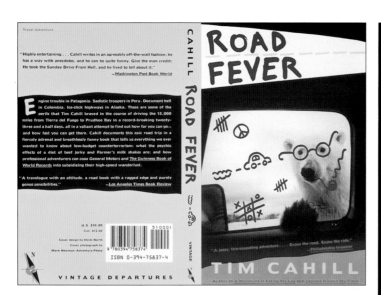

Book Design

ART DIRECTOR
John Muller

PHOTOGRAPHER
Michael Regnier

AGENCY
Muller + Co.

PUBLISHER
American Institute of Graphic Arts

Book Design

ART DIRECTOR/DESIGNER
Fred Woodward

PUBLISHER
Rolling Stone Magazine

Book Design Series

ART DIRECTOR
Krystyna Skalski

DESIGNER
Jo Bonney

STUDIO
Jo Bonney Design

PUBLISHER
Grove Press

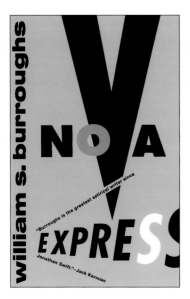

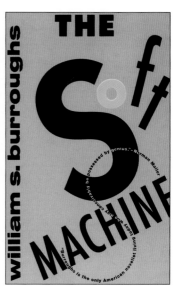

THERE WERE 247 finalists out of 1579 graphic design submissions. Although there were no Gold medalists, 15 Silver medals were awarded.

The sixteen editorial/graphic design judges viewed a new category for the Annual—TV & film design which covers such areas as title design, special effects, and animation. Out of 64 entries, 21 became finalists. Of these, the judges felt that 6 achieved Gold awards and 3 merited Silver.

Film & Video Special Effects

ART DIRECTOR/CREATIVE DIRECTOR
Michael Hutchinson

COPYWRITER
Larry Harris

PRODUCER
Kevin VanFleet

DIRECTOR
Osbert Parker

AGENCY
DMB&B/St. Louis

CLIENT
Anheuser-Busch, Inc./Budweiser

Film & Video Special Effects

ART DIRECTOR/COPYWRITER/CREATIVE DIRECTOR
Jim Borcherdt

PRODUCER
Jane Liepschutz

DIRECTOR
Osbert Parker

AGENCY
DMB&B/St.Louis

CLIENT
Anheuser-Busch, Inc./ Budweiser

Film & Video Special Effects
ART DIRECTOR
Dennis Hammer
COPYWRITER
Ray McAnallen
PRODUCER
Michael Windler
DIRECTOR
Steve Chase
AGENCY
DMB&B
CLIENT
Anheuser-Busch, Inc./Budweiser

Film & Video Special Effects
ART DIRECTOR/COPYWRITER/CREATIVE DIRECTOR
Jim Borcherdt
PRODUCER
Jane Liepschutz
DIRECTOR
Osbert Parker
AGENCY
DMB&B
CLIENT
Anheuser-Busch, Inc./Budweiser

Animation
ART DIRECTOR/CREATIVE DIRECTOR
Michael Hutchinson
COPYWRITER
Larry Harris
PRODUCER
Kevin VanFleet
DIRECTOR
Osbert Parker
AGENCY
DMB&B
CLIENT
Anheuser-Busch, Inc./Budweiser

Animation

ART DIRECTOR/COPYWRITER/CREATIVE DIRECTOR
Jim Borcherdt

PRODUCER
Jane Liepschutz

DIRECTOR
Osbert Parker

AGENCY
DMB&B

CLIENT
Anheuser-Busch, Inc./ Budweiser

Animation

ART DIRECTOR
Craig Yoe

PRODUCER
J.J. Sedelmaier

DIRECTOR
Tom Pomposello

ANIMATOR
Tony Eastman

STUDIO
J.J. Sedelmaier

CLIENT
MTV Network

Environmental Graphics
ART DIRECTOR/SCULPTOR
Tony Palladino

Environmental Graphics
ART DIRECTOR
Joe Duffy
PHOTOGRAPHER
Paul Irmiter
STUDIO
Joe Duffy Design
CLIENT
Trail Mark

Annual Report
CREATIVE DIRECTORS
Danny Abelson, Aubrey Balkind, Kent Hunter
DESIGNER
Riki Sethiadi
COPYWRITERS
Michael Clive, Danny Abelson
AGENCY
Frankfurt Gips Balkind
CLIENT
Comcast Corp.

Annual Report
ART DIRECTOR
Bryan L. Peterson
COPYWRITER
Marsha Coburn
PHOTOGRAPHER
Robb Debenport
AGENCY
Peterson & Co.
CLIENT
Mothers Against Drunk Driving

Annual Report

CREATIVE DIRECTORS
Kent Hunter, Aubrey Balkind

DESIGNERS
Ruth Diener, Kent Hunter

PHOTOGRAPHER
Dan Borris

ILLUSTRATORS
Josh Gosfield, J.D. King

AGENCY
Frankfurt Gips Balkind

CLIENT
Time Warner, Inc.

Annual Report

ART DIRECTOR
Rick Landesberg

COPYWRITER
Elinore S. Thomas

PHOTOGRAPHER
Scott Goldsmith (cover)

STUDIO
Landesberg Design Assoc.

CLIENT
Alcoa Foundation

Annual Report

ART DIRECTOR
David Stoyan Wooters

PHOTOGRAPHER
Al Nomura

ILLUSTRATOR
Tim Lewis

STUDIO
Stoyan Design

CLIENT
Rainbow Technologies

Annual Report

CREATIVE DIRECTORS
Aubrey Balkind, Kent Hunter

DESIGNER
Ruth Diener

COPYWRITER
Jim Donohue

PHOTOGRAPHER
Michael Llewellyn

AGENCY
Frankfurt Gips Balkind

CLIENT
Duracell International Inc.

Annual Report

ART DIRECTOR
David Citomowicz

COPYWRITER
Vicki Karp

PHOTOGRAPHER
Annie Liebovitz

STUDIO
Channel 13/WNET-TV

CLIENT
Channel 13/WNET-TV

Annual Report

ART DIRECTOR
Kit Hinrichs

DESIGNER
Piper Murakami

PHOTOGRAPHER
Jeff Corwin

ILLUSTRATORS
Max Seabaugh, Helene Moore

STUDIO
Pentagram Design

CLIENT
Norcen Energy Resources

Annual Report

ART DIRECTOR
Sara Bernstein

COPYWRITER
John Sargent

PHOTOGRAPHER
James Rudnick

STUDIO
Sara Bernstein Design

CLIENT
American Maize Corp.

Annual Report

ART DIRECTOR
Lana Rigsby

DESIGNER
Troy S. Ford

COPYWRITER
JoAnn Stone

PHOTOGRAPHERS
C. Shinn, J. Sims, J. Baraban

ILLUSTRATOR
Andy Dearwater

STUDIO
Rigsby Design, Inc.

CLIENT
Serv-Tech, Inc.

Annual Report
ART DIRECTOR
Woody Pirtle
DESIGNER
John Klotnia
STUDIO
Pentagram Design
CLIENT
The Rockefeller Foundation

Booklet, Folder & Brochure
ART DIRECTOR
Warren Johnson
COPYWRITER
Jim Nelson
PRODUCER
Brenda Clemons
AGENCY
Carmichael Lynch
CLIENT
Harley-Davidson

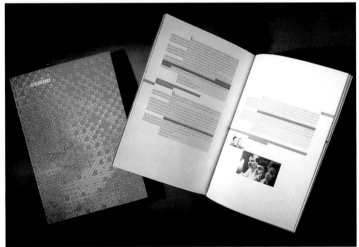

Booklet, Folder & Brochure
DESIGN DIRECTOR
Tom Geismar
DESIGNER
Cathy Schaefer
COPYWRITER
Terry Brown
PHOTOGRAPHERS
Michael Lutch, Chuck Gathard
STUDIO
Chermayeff & Geismar
CLIENT
Gemini Consulting

Booklet, Folder & Brochure
DESIGN DIRECTOR
Tom Geismar
DESIGNER
Cathy Schaefer
STUDIO
Chermayeff & Geismar
CLIENT
The Knoll Group

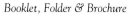

Booklet, Folder & Brochure
ART DIRECTOR
Kit Hinrichs
DESIGNER
Amy Chan
COPYWRITER
Delphine Hirasuna
PHOTOGRAPHERS
Bob Esparaza, Terry Heffernan
STUDIO
Pentagram Design
CLIENT
Simpson Paper

Booklet, Folder & Brochure
ART DIRECTOR
Kit Hinrichs
DESIGNER
Belle How
COPYWRITER
Delphine Hirasuna
ILLUSTRATORS
Barbara Benthian, John Hersey, Dave Stevenson, Will Nelson
STUDIO
Pentagram Design
CLIENT
Simpson Paper

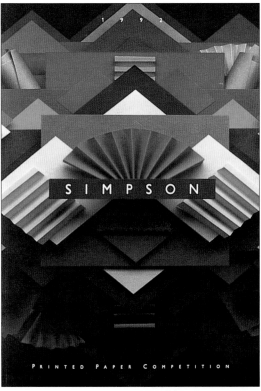

Booklet, Folder & Brochure
ART DIRECTOR
Lowell Williams
DESIGNER
Bill Carson
PHOTOGRAPHER
Bob Harr
ILLUSTRATOR
Andy Dearwater
STUDIO
Pentagram Design
CLIENTS
Cousins Properties, C&S, Sorran

Booklet, Folder & Brochure
ART DIRECTOR
Kit Hinrichs
DESIGNER
Amy Chan
COPYWRITER
Susan Sharpe
PHOTOGRAPHERS
Bob Esparza, Bill Zemanek
COMPUTER DESIGNER
Lisa Miller
STUDIO
Pentagram Design
CLIENTS
San Francisco Advertising Club,
San Francisco Creative Alliance

Booklet, Folder & Brochure
ART DIRECTOR/COPYWRITER
Michael Bierut
DESIGNERS
Dorit Lev, Anne Cowin
PHOTOGRAPHER
Reven T. C. Wurman
STUDIO
Pentagram Design
PUBLISHER
Gilbert Paper

Booklet, Folder & Brochure
ART DIRECTOR/ILLUSTRATOR
Milchael Bierut
DESIGNER
Agnethe Glatved
STUDIO
Pentagram Design
CLIENT
Cactus

Booklet, Folder & Brochure
ART DIRECTOR
Tom Kaminsky
DESIGNERS
Alex Barthelemy, Donald Suthard
COPYWRITER
Craig Walker
ARTIST
Frederic Remington
AGENCY
Kaminsky Design
CLIENT
Daniels Printing Co.

Booklet, Folder & Brochure
ART DIRECTOR
Louise Fili
STUDIO
Louise Fili Ltd.
CLIENT
Richard Solomon

Booklet, Folder & Brochure
ART DIRECTOR/ILLUSTRATOR
Andy Dearwater
COPYWRITER
JoAnn Stone
STUDIO
Dearwater Design
CLIENT
Anglo Shipping & Trading Inc.

Booklet, Folder & Brochure
ART DIRECTOR
Tony Palladino
DESIGNER/COPYWRITER
Kate Palladino
STUDIO
Palladino Comm.

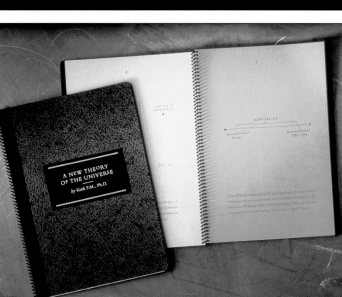

Booklet, Folder & Brochure
ART DIRECTOR/ILLUSTRATOR
Steve Sandstrom
COPYWRITER/ILLUSTRATOR
Peter Wegner
STUDIO
Sandstrom Design
CLIENT
KINK FM 102

Booklet, Folder & Brochure
ART DIRECTOR/COPYWRITER
Robert Valentine
DESIGNER
Dina Dell'Arciprete
PHOTOGRAPHER
Maria Robledo
STUDIO
Robert Valentine Inc.
CLIENT
Maria Robledo Photography

Booklet, Folder & Brochure
ART DIRECTOR
Joe Ivey
COPYWRITER
Anne Moss Rogers
PHOTOGRAPHER
Bernard Phillips
ILLUSTATOR
Barbara Banthien
AGENCY
Howard, Merrell & Partners
CLIENT
Ciba-Geigy Turf & Ornamental Products

Booklet, Folder & Brochure
ART DIRECTOR
Robert Valentine
DESIGNER
Wayne Wolf
PHOTOGRAPHER
Henny Garfunkel
ILLUSTRATORS
Harry Bates, Regan Dunnick
STUDIO
Robert Valentine Inc.
CLIENT
Gilbert Paper

Booklet, Folder & Brochure
ART DIRECTOR
Allen Weinberg
STUDIO
Sony Music

Booklet, Folder & Brochure
ART DIRECTOR
Chris Hill
DESIGNER
Jeff Davis
COPYWRITER
Joann Mitchell
PHOTOGRAPHER
Beryl Striewski
STUDIO
Hill/A Marketing Design Group
CLIENT
Texas Children's Hospital

Booklet, Folder & Brochure
ART DIRECTOR
Bruce Crocker
DESIGNER
Martin Sorger
COPYWRITER
Betsy Clark
ILLUSTRATORS
Lee Busch, Michael Maslin
STUDIO
Crocker Inc.
CLIENT
Boston Acoustics

Booklet, Folder & Brochure
ART DIRECTOR
Elizabeth Dziersk
DESIGNER
Michael Scricco
COPYWRITER
Mel Maffei
PHOTOGRAPHERS
Jeff Corwin, Craig Cutler, Bob Day,
Yuri Dojc, Nadav Kander,
Jeffrey Newbury, Scott Witte,
Rieder & Walsh
STUDIO
Keiler Design Group
CLIENT
Strathmore Paper

Booklet, Folder & Brochure
ART DIRECTORS
Michelle Novak, Steve Tomkiewicz, George Tscherny
COPYWRITERS
George Tscherny, Sonia Tscherny
PHOTOGRAPHERS
George Tscherny, Michelle Novak
STUDIO
George Tscherny, Inc.
CLIENT
Champion International Corp.

Booklet, Folder & Brochure
ART DIRECTOR
John Harris
STUDIO
Sarah Lawrence College
CLIENT
Sarah Lawrence College in Paris

Booklet, Folder & Brochure
ART DIRECTOR
Aaron Booher
COPYWRITER
Students
STUDIO
Sarah Lawrence College
CLIENT
Sarah Lawrence College

Booklet, Folder & Brochure
ART DIRECTOR
J.P. Williams
PHOTOGRAPHER
Albert Watson
STUDIO
Bergdorf Goodman
CLIENT
Bergdorf Goodman

Booklet, Folder & Brochure
ART DIRECTOR
Rex Peteet
COPYWRITER
Mary Keck
STUDIO
Sibley/Peteet Design
CLIENT
James River Corp.

Booklet, Folder & Brochure
ART DIRECTOR
Stacy Drummond
DESIGNER
Steve Byram
DESIGN DIRECTOR
Jeffrey Keyton
COPYWRITERS
Sharon Glassman, Cheryl Family
STUDIO
MTV Network
CLIENT
MTV Network

Booklet, Folder & Brochure
ART DIRECTOR
Lou Fiorentino
COPYWRITER
Hilberth Leibe
STUDIO
Fiorentino Leibe Associates
CLIENT
KBA-Planeta North America

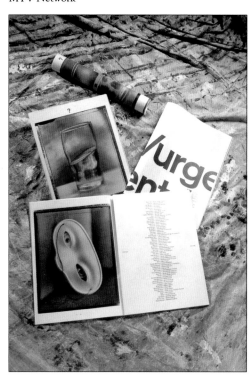

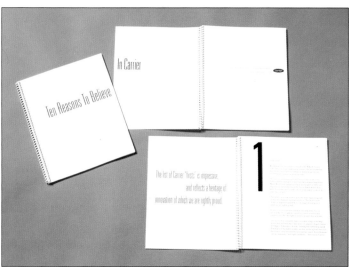

Booklet, Folder & Brochure
ART DIRECTOR
William Wondriska
ILLUSTRATOR
Merle Nacht
STUDIO
Wondriska Associates
CLIENT
Carrier Corp.

Booklet, Folder & Brochure
ART DIRECTOR/CREATIVE DIRECTOR
Helane Blumfield
COPYWRITER
Susan Cooper
PHOTOGRAPHER
Albert Watson
STUDIO
Bloomingdale's
CLIENT
Bloomingdale's

Booklet, Folder & Brochure

ART DIRECTOR
Peter Harrison

COPYWRITERS
Lucy Fellowes, Denis Wood

PHOTOGRAPHER
Ken Pelka

STUDIO
Pentagram Design

CLIENT
Cooper-Hewitt Museum

Booklet, Folder & Brochure

ART DIRECTOR
Tyler Smith

COPYWRITER
Geoff Currier

PHOTOGRAPHER
John Huet

STUDIO
Tyler Smith

CLIENT
Louis Boston, Inc.

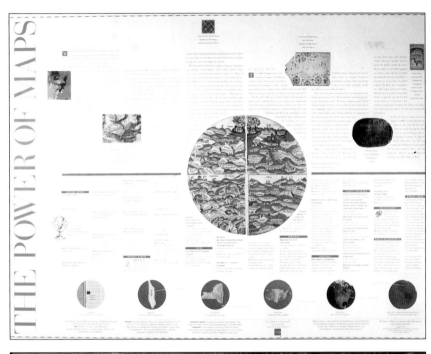

Booklet, Folder & Brochure

ART DIRECTOR
Steve Sandstrom

COPYWRITER
David Brooks

PHOTOGRAPHER
Steve Bonini

STUDIO
Sandstrom Design

CLIENT
Derby Cycle Corp.

Booklet, Folder & Brochure/Series

DESIGN DIRECTOR
Tom Geismar

DESIGNER
Weston Bingham

PHOTOGRAPHER
Karen Yamauchi

STUDIO
Chermayeff & Geismar

CLIENT
The Knoll Group

Booklet, Folder & Brochure/Series
ART DIRECTOR
Rex Peteet
COPYWRITER
Mary Keck
STUDIO
Sibley/Peteet Design
CLIENT
James River Corp.

Booklet, Folder & Brochure/Series
ART DIRECTORS
Scott Bremner, Tom Saputo, Mike Mazza
DESIGNERS
Tom Saputo, Scott Brenner
CREATIVE DIRECTOR
Tom Cordner
COPYWRITER
Steve Silver
PHOTOGRAPHER
Michael Ruppert
AGENCY
Team One Advertising

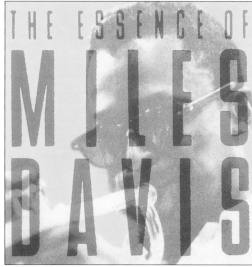

Booklet, Folder & Brochure/Series
ART DIRECTOR
Allen Weinberg
STUDIO
Sony Music
CLIENT
Sony Music

Booklet, Folder & Brochure/Series
ART DIRECTOR/ILLUSTRATOR
Paul Davis
STUDIO
Paul Davis Studio
CLIENT
New York Shakespeare Festival

Booklet, Folder & Brochure/Series

ART DIRECTOR
Bruce Crocker

DESIGNER
Martin Sorger

COPYWRITERS
Stona Fitch, Ira Friedman

PHOTOGRAPHERS
Bill Gallery, Gallen Mei, John Shotwell

STUDIO
Crocker Inc.

CLIENT
Boston Acoustics

Booklet, Folder & Brochure/Series

ART DIRECTOR
Toni Bowerman

COPYWRITER
Lee Nash

ILLUSTRATOR
Jean-Christian Knaff

AGENCY
Cipriani Kremer Design

CLIENT
Wang Laboratories Inc.

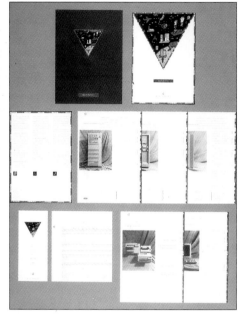

Packaging

ART DIRECTOR
Jack Anderson

DESIGNERS
Jack Anderson, Mary Hermes, Leo Raymundo

COPYWRITER
Paul Suzman

ILLUSTRATORS
Larry Jost, George Tanagi

STUDIO
Joe Duffy Design, Inc.

Packaging

ART DIRECTOR
Joe Duffy

DESIGNER
Jeff Johnson

PHOTOGRAPHER
Paul Irmiter

STUDIO
Joe Duffy Design, Inc.

CLIENT
Trail Mark

Packaging

ART DIRECTOR/COPYWRITER
Steve Curran

DESIGNER
John Tombley

ILLUSTRATOR
Elwood Smith

STUDIO
Gametek

CLIENT
Trail Mark

Packaging

ART DIRECTOR
Nicky Lindeman

PHOTOGRAPHER
Michael Halsband

STUDIO
Sony Music

CLIENT
Sony Music

Packaging

ART DIRECTOR
Jim Christie

CREATIVE DIRECTOR
John C. Jay

PHOTOGRAPHER
Phillipe Lardy

STUDIO
Bloomingdale's

CLIENT
Bloomingdale's

Packaging

ART DIRECTOR
Bruce Crocker

COPYWRITER
Jonathan Plazonja

PHOTOGRAPHER
Bill Gallery

STUDIO
Crocker Inc.

CLIENT
Boston Acoustics

Packaging

ART DIRECTOR/PACKAGE DESIGNER
Kim Champagne

PHOTOGRAPHER
George Adins

ILLUSTRATOR
Josh Gosfield

STUDIO
Warner Brothers Records

CLIENT
Capricorn Records

Packaging

ART DIRECTOR
Stacy Drummond

PHOTOGRAPHERS
J. Denner Jr., Fabio Nosotti

STUDIO
Sony Music

CLIENT
Sony Music

Packaging

ART DIRECTOR
Allen Weinberg

PRODUCER
Dave Brubeck

STUDIO
Sony Music

CLIENT
Sony Music

Packaging

ART DIRECTOR
Jeri Heiden

PHOTOGRAPHER
Glen Erler

TYPOGRAPHER
Donald Young

STUDIO
Warner Bros. Records

CLIENT
Warner Brothers/Sire Records

Packaging
ART DIRECTOR
Ted Nuttall
COPYWRITER
Steve Hutchison
CREATIVE DIRECTOR
Toni Young
ILLUSTRATOR
Dugald Stermer
STUDIO
Young Associates
CLIENT
Software Marketing Corp.

Packaging
ART DIRECTOR/COPYWRITER
Michael Strassburger
DESIGNERS
Robynne Raye, Vittorio Costarella
STUDIO
Modern Dog
CLIENT
Modern Dog

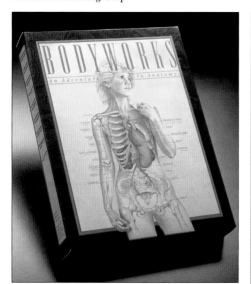

Packaging
ART DIRECTOR
Patti Britton
COPYWRITER
Sam Sebastiani
PHOTOGRAPHER
Thea Schrack
ILLUSTRATOR
Evans and Brown Co.
STUDIO
Britton Design
CLIENT
Viansa Winery

Packaging
ART DIRECTORS
Tom Recchion, Michael Stipe, Jeff Gold, Jim Ladwig
DESIGNERS
Tom Recchion, Michael Stipe
PHOTOGRAPHER
Anton Corbijn
STUDIO
Warner Bros. Records
CLIENT
R.E.M. Athens Ltd./Warner
Brothers Records

Packaging

ART DIRECTOR
Bob Garland

AGENCY
J. Walter Thompson

CLIENT
Kellogg Frosted Bran Flakes

Packaging

ART DIRECTOR
Laura LiPuma-Nash

DESIGNER
B. Middleworth

PHOTOGRAPHER
Ron Keith

STUDIO
Warner Brothers Records

Packaging

ART DIRECTOR
Nicky Lindeman

PHOTOGRAPHER/ILLUSTRATOR
Amy Quip

STUDIO
Sony Music

CLIENT
Sony Music

Packaging

ART DIRECTORS
Patricia Ziegler, Nancy Bauch, Vic Zauderer

COPYWRITER
Mel Ziegler

ILLUSTRATORS
Patricia Ziegler, Faye Rosenzweig

CLIENT
The Republic of Tea

Packaging

ART DIRECTOR
Henry Vizcarra

STUDIO
30Sixty Design Inc.

CLIENT
Gorky's Russian Brewery

Announcement, Invitation & Menu

ART DIRECTOR
Gordon Mortensen

ILLUSTRATOR
John Craig

STUDIO
Mortensen Design

CLIENT
Mortensen Design/Z Prepress

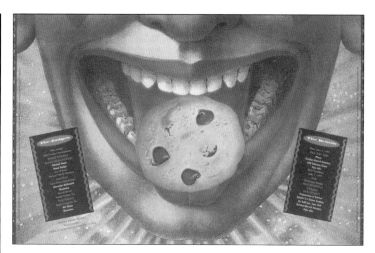

Packaging

ART DIRECTOR
Joe Duffy

DESIGNERS
Sharon Werner, Neil Powell

COPYWRITERS
Chuck Carlson, Haley Jonson

STUDIO
Joe Duffy Design, Inc.

CLIENT
Jim Beam Brands, Co.

Announcement, Invitation & Menu

ART DIRECTOR/DESIGNER/COPYWRITER/ILLUSTRATOR
Tony Palladino
STUDIO
Palladino Comm.

Announcement, Invitation & Menu

ART DIRECTOR
Michael Gericke
STUDIO
Pentagram Design
CLIENT
Hammond Inc.

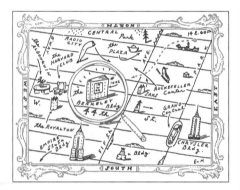

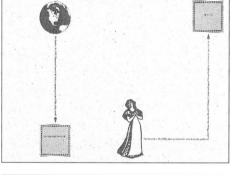

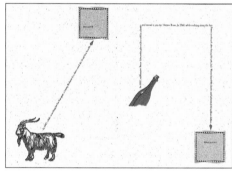

Announcement, Invitation & Menu
ART DIRECTOR
Robert Valentine
DESIGNER
Wayne Wolf
ILLUSTRATOR
Eric Hanson
STUDIO
Robert Valentine Inc.
CLIENT
Authors & Artists Group

Announcement, Invitation & Menu
ART DIRECTOR/DESIGNER/COPYWRITER/ILLUSTRATOR
Tony Palladino
STUDIO
Palladino Comm.
CLIENT
School of Visual Arts

Announcement, Invitation & Menu
ART DIRECTOR
Jack Anderson
DESIGNERS
Jack Anderson, David Bates, Lian Ng,
Leo Raymundo
COPYWRITER
Pamela Mason-Davey
ILLUSTRATOR
Yutaka Sasaki
STUDIO
Hornall Anderson Design Works

Announcement, Invitation & Menu
ART DIRECTOR
Lowell Williams
COPYWRITER
JoAnn Stone
DESIGNER
Bill Carson
ILLUSTRATOR
Michael Schwab
STUDIO
Pentagram Design
CLIENT
James M. Montgomery

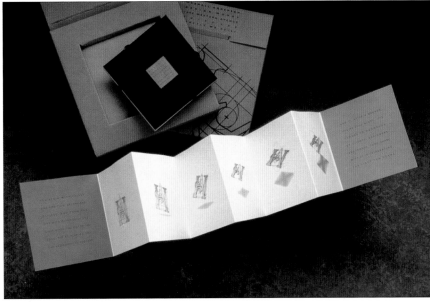

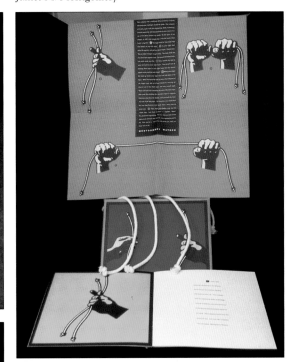

Announcement, Invitation & Menu
ART DIRECTOR
Carol A. Dronsfield
COPYWRITER
Michele Paccione
AGENCY
Carol A. Dronsfield

Announcement, Invitation & Menu
ART DIRECTOR
Rick Vaughn
STUDIO
Vaughn/Wedeen Creative
CLIENT
QC Graphics

Calendar & Appointment Book

ART DIRECTOR
Peter Harrison

DESIGNER
Harold Burch

STUDIO
Pentagram Design

CLIENT
Applied Graphics

Calendar & Appointment Book

ART DIRECTOR/ILLSUTRATOR
Michael Beirut

DESIGNER
Christina Freyss

STUDIO
Pentagram Design

CLIENT
Simpson Paper

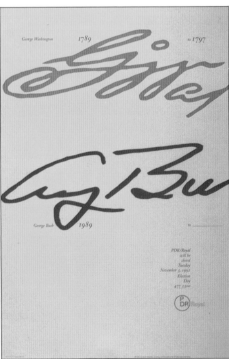

Calendar & Appointment Book

ART DIRECTOR
Neil Shakery

DESIGNER
Mark Selfe

COPYWRITERS
Peterson, Skolnick, Dodge

ILLUSTRATOR
Mark Summers

STUDIO
Pentagram Design

CLIENT
Royal Viking Line

Calendar & Appointment Book

ART DIRECTOR
Harold Burch

ILLUSTRATOR
Seymour Chwast

STUDIO
Pentagram Design

CLIENT
Applied Graphics, Inc.

Announcement, Invitation & Menu/Series

ART DIRECTOR
Martin Solomon

DESIGNER
Alexa Nosal

STUDIO
Martin Solomon

CLIENT
PDR/Royal

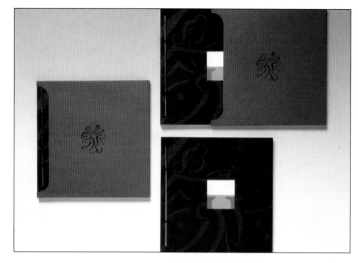

Calendar & Appointment Book

ART DIRECTOR
Brooks Branch

DESIGNER
Vu Tran

ILLUSTRATOR
Charles Anderson

STUDIO
30Sixty Design Inc.

CLIENT
Paramount Licensing

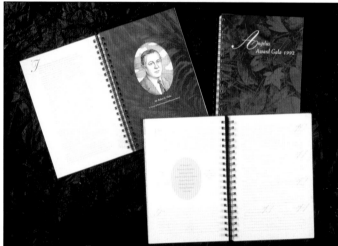

Calendar & Appointment Book

ART DIRECTOR
Julia Wyant

DESIGNER
Jennifer Deitz

COPYWRITERS
St. Vincent's Development Staff

ILLUSTRATOR
Julie Berson

AGENCY
The Wyant Group, Inc.

CLIENT
St. Vincent's Hospital of New York

Logo & Trademark

DESIGN DIRECTOR
Steff Geissbuhler

DESIGNER
Lisette Buiani

STUDIO
Chermayeff & Geismar

CLIENT
The Telemudo Group

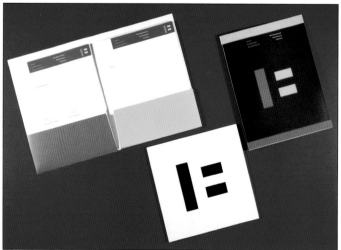

Logo & Trademark

ART DIRECTOR
Michael Meade

STUDIO
GTE Graphic Comm.

CLIENT
GTE Corp.

Logo & Trademark
ART DIRECTOR
Frank D'Astolfo
STUDIO
Frank D'Astolfo Design
CLIENT
XYZ Productions

Logo & Trademark
ART DIRECTOR
Joe Duffy
DESIGNER
Jeff Johnson
COPYWRITER
Greg Rothweller
PHOTOGRAPHER
Paul Irmiter
STUDIO
Joe Duffy Design, Shea Architects
CLIENT
Mark III

Logo & Trademark
ART DIRECTOR
Jeff Larson
DESIGNER
Scott Dvorak
STUDIO
Larson Design Assoc.
CLIENT
Larson Design Assoc.

Logo & Trademark
ART DIRECTOR
Dave Kottler
DESIGNERS
Bart Welch, Paul Caldera
STUDIO
The Knottler Caldera Group
CLIENT
Frogskin, Inc.

Logo & Trademark
ART DIRECTOR
John Ball
PHOTOGRAPHER
Chris Wimpey
STUDIO
Mires Design, Inc.
CLIENT
Mercy Hospital

Logo & Trademark
ART DIRECTOR
Jennifer Morla
DESIGNERS
Jennifer Morla, Craig Bailey
STUDIO
Morla Design
CLIENT
Ristorante Ecco

Logo & Trademark
ART DIRECTOR
Erik Svenson MacPeek
ILLUSTRATOR
David Zabenko
STUDIO
Mystic MarineLife Aquarium
CLIENT
Mystic MarineLife Aquarium

Logo & Trademark
ART DIRECTOR
Michael Bierut
ILLUSTRATOR
Dorit Lev
STUDIO
Pentagram Design
CLIENT
Gotham Equities

Logo & Trademark
ART DIRECTOR
Seymour Chwast
DESIGNER
William Bevington
STUDIO
The Pushpin Group
CLIENT
Arch Assoc.

Logo & Trademark
ART DIRECTOR
Mike Salisbury
ILLUSTRATOR
Regina Grosveld
STUDIO
Mike Salisbury Comm.
CLIENT
Gotcha

Logo & Trademark
ART DIRECTOR
Jennifer Lyon
ILLUSTRATOR
Michael Halbert
STUDIO
Sandstrom Design
CLIENT
Portland Civic Stadium

Logo & Trademark
ART DIRECTOR
Joe Vax
DESIGNER
May Key Chung
ILLUSTRATOR
Dug Waggoner
STUDIO
Vaxworks
CLIENT
California Cut Flower Commission

Logo & Trademark

ART DIRECTOR
Woody Pirtle

DESIGNER
John Klotnia

STUDIO
Pentagram Design

CLIENT
Noonan Russo (PR)

Logo & Trademark

ART DIRECTOR
Steve Sandstorm

ILLUSTRATOR
Nancy Stahl

STUDIO
Sandstorm Design

CLIENT
Derby Cycle Corp.

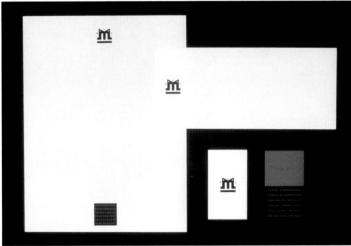

Letterhead, Business Card & Envelope

ART DIRECTOR/ILLUSTRATOR
Thomas Vasquez

STUDIO
Brainstorm, Inc.

CLIENT
George Mecca

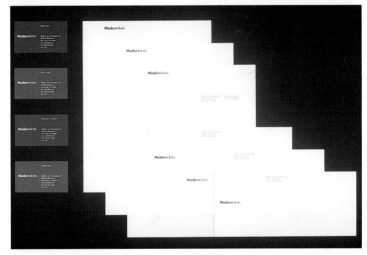

Letterhead, Business Card & Envelope

ART DIRECTORS
James Sebastian, Margaret Biedel

DESIGNER
Brian Fingeret

STUDIO
Designframe Inc.

CLIENT
Modern Arts Packaging Inc.

Letterhead, Business Card & Envelope

ART DIRECTOR/COPYWRITER
Doug Trapp

AGENCY
Martin/Williams

CLIENT
Dr. Greg Dahl, Chiropractor

Letterhead, Business Card & Envelope
ART DIRECTOR
Scott Mires
ILLUSTRATOR
Seymour Chwast
STUDIO
Mires Design, Inc.
CLIENT
Brian Meredith

Letterhead, Business Card & Envelope
ART DIRECTOR
Kevin Weidenbacher
AGENCY
Scali, McCabe, Sloves
CLIENT
National Cultural Alliance

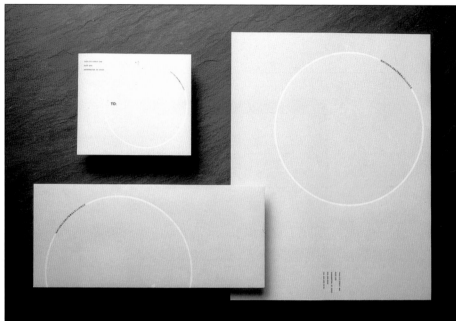

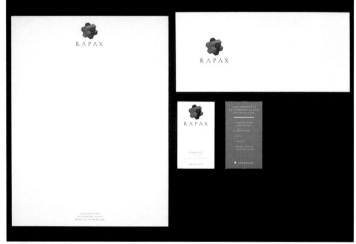

Letterhead, Business Card & Envelope
ART DIRECTOR
Henry Vizcarra
DESIGNER
William Heustis, Estay Heustis
STUDIO
30Sixty Design Inc.
CLIENT
Rapax

Corporate Identity
ART DIRECTORS
Paula Scher, Ron Lowe
STUDIO
Pentagram Design
CLIENT
One Fifth Avenue

Corporate Identity

ART DIRECTOR
Chris Hill

DESIGNER
Jeff Davis, Laura Menega

PHOTOGRAPHER
Mark Green

ILLUSTRATOR
Andy Dearwater

STUDIO
Hill/A Marketing Design Group

CLIENT
Hines Interests Limited Partnership

Corporate Identity

ART DIRECTOR
Robert Valentine

DESIGNER
Dina Dell'Arciprete, Wayne Wolf

ILLUSTRATOR
David Sheldon

STUDIO
Robert Valentine Inc.

CLIENT
The Fashion Group International

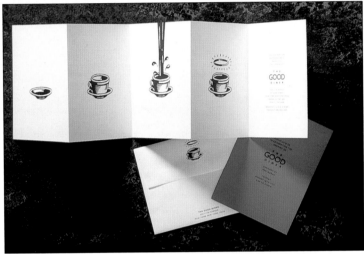

Corporate Identity

ART DIRECTOR
Michael Beirut

ILLUSTATOR
Woody Pirtle

STUDIO
Pentagram Design

CLIENT
Gotham Equities

Poster

ART DIRECTOR/ILLUSTRATOR
Woody Pirtle

DESIGNERS
John Klotnial, Ivette Montes de Oca

STUDIO
Pentagram Design

CLIENT
Royal Society of Arts

Poster
ART DIRECTOR
Jurek Wajdowicz
DESIGNERS
Lisa LaRochelle, Jurek Wajdowicz
PHOTOGRAPHER
Henri Cartier-Bresson
STUDIO
Emerson, Wajdowicz Studios, Inc.
CLIENT
Freedom House

Poster
ART DIRECTOR/ILLUSTATOR
Woody Pirtle
DESIGNER
John Klotnia
STUDIO
Pentagram Design
CLIENT
Creative Club of Tampa Bay

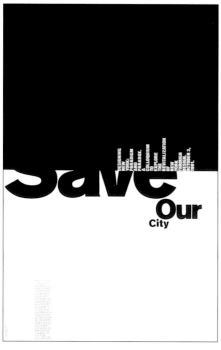

Poster
ART DIRECTOR/COPYWRITER
Michael Bierut
STUDIO
Pentagram Design
CLIENT
Designing New York Commitee

Poster
ART DIRECTOR
Tim Thompson
DESIGNER/ILLUSTRATOR
Dave Plunkert
STUDIO
Graffito
CLIENT
Intelsat

Poster
ART DIRECTOR
Ronni Ascagni
DESIGNER
Jim Streacker
COPYWRITER
Susan Cooper
CREATIVE DIRECTOR
Helane Blumfield
PHOTOGRAPHER
José Picayo
CLIENT
Bloomingdale's

Poster

ART DIRECTOR
McRay Magleby

COPYWRITER
Norm Darais

ILLUSTRATORS
McRay Magleby, Dave Eliason

STUDIO
BYU Graphics

CLIENT
Brigham Young University

Poster

ART DIRECTOR
Todd Waterbury

COPYWRITER
Susan Cooper

CREATIVE DIRECTOR
Helane Blumfield

STUDIO
Bloomingdale's

CLIENT
Bloomingdale's

Poster

ART DIRECTOR
Lanny Sommese

AGENCY
Sommese Design

CLIENT
Central Pennsylvania Festival of the Arts

Poster

ART DIRECTOR
Rachel Wear

DESIGNER
Terry Irwin

PHOTOGRAPHER
Nemai Ghosh

STUDIO
Landor Design Assoc.

CLIENT
San Francisco Film Society

Poster

ART DIRECTOR/ILLUSTRATOR
McRay Magleby

COPYWRITER
Norm Darais

AGENCY
BYU Graphics

CLIENT
Brigham Young University

Poster

ART DIRECTOR
Jeff Larson

COPYWRITER
Keith Christianson

ILLUSTRATOR
Rhonda Nass

STUDIO
Larson Design Assoc.

CLIENT
Litho Productions

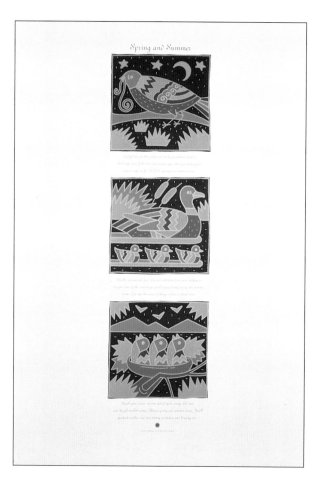

Self-Promotion

ART DIRECTOR
Rick Marciniak

COPYWRITER
John Fatteross

PHOTOGRAPHERS
Scott Morgan, Laurie Rubin, Hans Neleman

AGENCY
Clarion Marketing and Comm.

CLIENT
Clarion Marketing and Comm.

Self-Promotion

ART DIRECTOR
B. Martin Pedersen

PHOTOGRAPHER
Jody Dole

STUDIO
Pedersen Design Inc.

CLIENT
Jody Dole

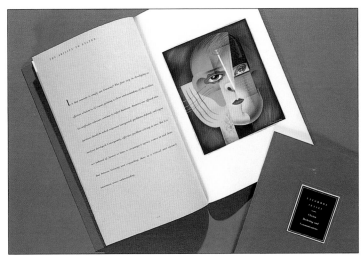

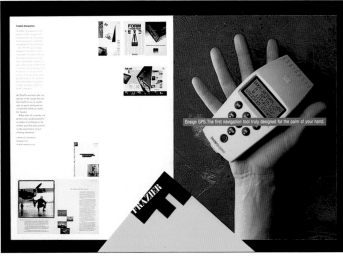

Self-Promotion

ART DIRECTOR
Todd Hart

DESIGNER
Shawn Freeman

COPYWRITER
Bill Baldwin

PHOTOGRAPHER
Phil Hollenbeck

STUDIO
Focus 2

CLIENT
Dallas Society of Visual Comm.

Self-Promotion

ART DIRECTOR/COPYWRITER
Craig Frazier

DESIGNERS
Craig Frazier, Rene Rosso

STUDIO
Frazier Design

CLIENT
Frazier Design

Self-Promotion

ART DIRECTOR
Tom Kaminsky

COPYWRITER
Craig Walker

DESIGNERS
Donald Suthard, Alicia Zampitella

ILLUSTRATOR
Seymour Chwast

STUDIO
Kaminsky Design

CLIENT
Daniels Printing Co.

Self-Promotion

ART DIRECTOR
Doreen Caldera

DESIGNER
Kim Gee

COPYWRITER
Donna Rascona

PHOTOGRAPHER
Rodney Rascona

STUDIO
The Kottler Caldera Group

CLIENT
Rascona Studio, Inc.

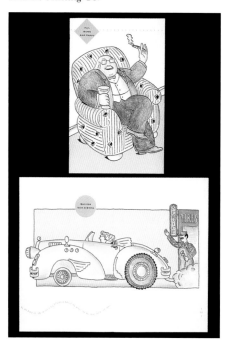

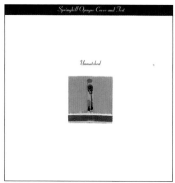

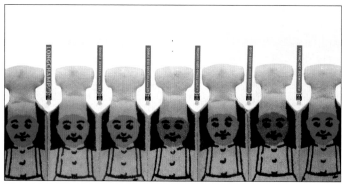

Self-Promotion

ART DIRECTOR
Tom Kaminsky

DESIGNERS
Alex Barthelemy, Donald Suthard

COPYWRITER
Craig Walker

STUDIO
Kaminsky Design

CLIENT
Springhill Paper/International Paper Co.

Self-Promotion

ART DIRECTOR
Mark Oldach

DESIGNER
Don Emery

COPYWRITERS
David Oldach, Don Emery

PHOTOGRAPHER
David Ormesher

STUDIO
Mark Oldach Design

CLIENT
Closer Look Video Group, Inc.

Self-Promotion

ART DIRECTOR
Scott Wadler

DESIGNERS/COPYWRITERS
Sharon Glassman, Laurie Rosenwold

ILLUSTRATOR
Laurie Rosenwold

STUDIO
MTV Network

CLIENT
Comedy Central

Self-Promotion

ART DIRECTOR
Laurie Kelliher

ILLUSTRATOR
John Pirman

STUDIO
MTV Network

CLIENT
Nick at Nite

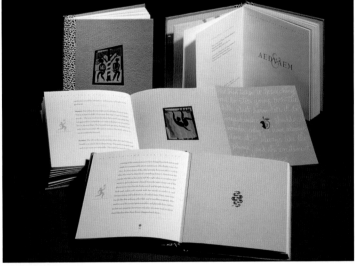

Self-Promotion

ART DIRECTOR
Kurt Hollomon

COPYWRITER
Peter Wegner

PHOTOGRAPHER
Mark Hooper

ILLUSTRATOR
Ward Schumaker

STUDIO
Sandstrom Design

CLIENT
Sandstrom Design

Self-Promotion

ART DIRECTOR
Rex Peteet

DESIGNER
Don Sibley

COPYWRITER
Lee Herrick

ILLUSTRATORS
Rex Peteet, Don Sibley, David Beck

CALLIGRAPHY
David Beck, Tom Hough

STUDIO
Sibley/Peteet Design

CLIENT
Heritage Press

234 PHOTOGRAPHIC entries were viewed. 62 finalists were selected. In
the final edit, 1 Gold and 5 Silver medalists emerged.

157 illustrators submitted entries hoping to become part of the 38 finalists. No Golds were achieved, but 4 were awarded Silver medals.

Advertising Photography

ART DIRECTOR
Dennis Stevens

COPYWRITER
Joanna Templeton

EXECUTIVE CREATIVE DIRECTORS
Jack Mariucci, Bob Mackall

PHOTOGRAPHER
Philip Dixon

AGENCY
DDB Needham Worldwide

CLIENT
Joseph E. Seagram Cordon Rouge Mumm

Advertising Photography

ART DIRECTOR
John Doyle

COPYWRITER
Ernie Schenck

PHOTOGRAPHER
Nadav Kander

STUDIO
Doyle A&D Group

CLIENT
The Dunham Co.

Advertising Photography

ART DIRECTOR/CREATIVE DIRECTOR/COPYWRITER
Cabell Harris

PHOTOGRAPHER
Vic Huber

AGENCY
Livingston + Keye

CLIENT
JBL

Advertising Photography

ART DIRECTOR/CREATIVE DIRECTOR
Cabell Harris

COPYWRITER
Larry Johnson

PHOTOGRAPHER
Dennis Manarchy

AGENCY
Livingston + Keye

CLIENT
JBL

Advertising Photography/Series

ART DIRECTOR
Paul Guayante

COPYWRITER
Dan Brooks

EXECUTIVE CREATIVE DIRECTORS
Jack Mariucci, Bob Mackall

PHOTOGRAPHER
Charles Purvis

AGENCY
DDB Needham Worldwide

CLIENT
Clairol/Logics

Advertising Photography/Series

ART DIRECTOR
David Angelo

COPYWRITER
Paul Spencer

EXECUTIVE CREATIVE DIRECTORS
Jack Mariucci, Bob Mackall

PHOTOGRAPHER
Neil Slavin, Lamb & Hall

AGENCY
DDB Needham Worldwide

CLIENT
New York State Lottery

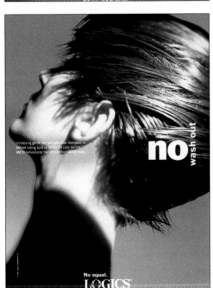

Advertising Photography/Series
ART DIRECTOR
Chuck Creasy
COPYWRITER
Randy Horick
PHOTOGRAPHER
Michael W. Rutherford
AGENCY
Charles Creasy Creative
CLIENT
Middle Tennessee Valley Boy Scouts
of America

Editorial Photography
ART DIRECTOR
Tom Poth
COPYWRITER/PHOTOGRAPHER
Joe Baraban
STUDIO
Hixo
CLIENT
Austin A.S.M.P.

Editorial Photography
ART DIRECTOR
B. Martin Pedersen
PHOTOGRAPHER
Arnold Newman
STUDIO
Pedersen Design
PUBLICATION
Graphis

Editorial Photography
ART DIRECTOR
B. Martin Pedersen
PHOTOGRAPHER
Phil Sauer
STUDIO
Pedersen Design
PUBLICATION
Graphis

Editorial Photography
ART DIRECTOR
B. Martin Pedersen
PHOTOGRAPHER
Monica Lee
STUDIO
Pedersen Design
PUBLICATION
Graphis

Editorial Photography

PHOTOGRAPHER
Wilt/Stern

DIRECTOR OF PHOTOGRAPHY
David Friend

PUBLICATION
Life Magazine

Editorial Photography

ART DIRECTOR
Matthew Drace

DESIGNER
Giovanni Russo

PHOTOGRAPHER
George Holtz

PUBLICATION
Men's Journal

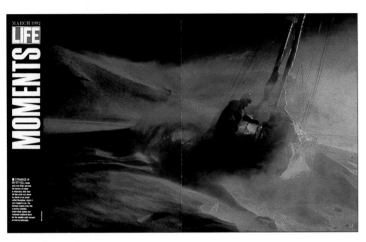

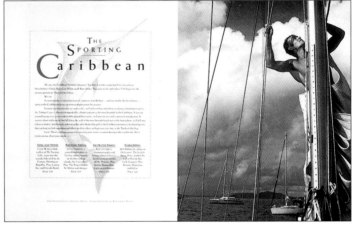

Editorial Photography

ART DIRECTOR
Janet Froelich

DESIGNER
Kathi Rota

PHOTOGRAPHER
Danielle Weil

PUBLICATION
The New York Times Magazine

Editorial Photography

ART DIRECTOR
Fred Woodward

DESIGNER
Debra Bishop

PHOTOGRAPHER
Albert Watson

DIRECTOR OF PHOTOGRAPHY
Laurie Kratochvil

PUBLICATION
Rolling Stone Magazine

Editorial Photography

ART DIRECTOR/DESIGNER
Fred Woodward

PHOTOGRAPHER
Albert Watson

DIRECTOR OF PHOTOGRAPHY
Laurie Kratochvil

PUBLICATION
Rolling Stone Magazine

Editorial Photography

ART DIRECTOR/DESIGNER
Fred Woodward

PHOTOGRAPHER
Albert Watson

DIRECTOR OF PHOTOGRAPHY
Laurie Kratochvil

PUBLICATION
Rolling Stone Magazine

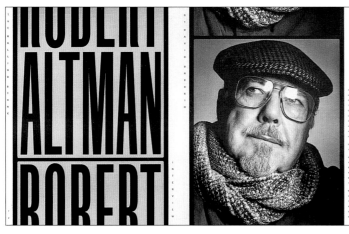

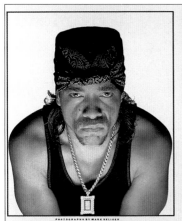

Editorial Photography

ART DIRECTOR
Fred Woodward

DESIGNER
Debra Bishop

PHOTOGRAPHER
Mark Seliger

DIRECTOR OF PHOTOGRAPHY
Laurie Kratochvil

PUBLICATIONS
Rolling Stone Magazine

Editorial Photography

ART DIRECTOR
Fred Woodward

DESIGNER
Debra Bishop

PHOTOGRAPHER
Mark Seliger

DIRECTOR OF PHOTOGRAPHY
Laurie Kratochvil

PUBLICATION
Rolling Stone Magazine

Editorial Photography

ART DIRECTOR/DESIGNER
Fred Woodward

PHOTOGRAPHER
Albert Watson

DIRECTOR OF PHOTOGRAPHY
Laurie Kratochvil

PUBLICATION
Rolling Stone Magazine

Editorial Photography

ART DIRECTOR
Fred Woodward

DESIGNER
Angela Skouras

PHOTOGRAPHER
Dan Winters

DIRECTOR OF PHOTOGRAPHY
Laurie Kratochvil

PUBLICATION
Rolling Stone Magazine

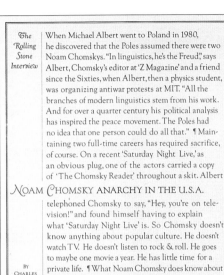

The Rolling Stone Interview

When Michael Albert went to Poland in 1980, he discovered that the Poles assumed there were two Noam Chomskys. "In linguistics, he's the Freud," says Albert, Chomsky's editor at 'Z Magazine' and a friend since the Sixties, when Albert, then a physics student, was organizing antiwar protests at MIT. "All the branches of modern linguistics stem from his work. And for over a quarter century his political analysis has inspired the peace movement. The Poles had no idea that one person could do all that." ¶ Maintaining two full-time careers has required sacrifice, of course. On a recent 'Saturday Night Live,' as an obvious plug, one of the actors carried a copy of 'The Chomsky Reader' throughout a skit. Albert

NOAM CHOMSKY ANARCHY IN THE U.S.A.

telephoned Chomsky to say, "Hey, you're on television!" and found himself having to explain what 'Saturday Night Live' is. So Chomsky doesn't know anything about popular culture. He doesn't watch TV. He doesn't listen to rock & roll. He goes to maybe one movie a year. He has little time for a private life. ¶ What Noam Chomsky does know about is how the human brain creates language. Consider

BY CHARLES M. YOUNG

42 · Rolling Stone, May 28th, 1992

PHOTOGRAPH BY DAN WINTERS

Editorial Photography/Series

ART DIRECTOR
Fred Woodward

DESIGNERS
Fred Woodward, Gail Anderson,
Catherine Gilmore-Barnes, Debra Bishop,
Angela Skouras, Geraldine Hessler

PHOTOGRAPHER
Herb Ritts

DIRECTOR OF PHOTOGRAPHY
Laurie Kratochvil

PUBLICATION
Rolling Stone Magazine

Editorial Photography/Series

ART DIRECTOR
Suzanne Morin

COPYWRITER
Brad Matsen

PHOTOGRAPHER
Bob Sacha

PUBLICATION
Audubon Magazine

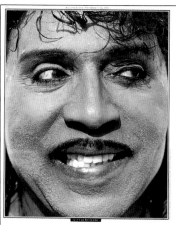

Editorial Photography/Series
ART DIRECTOR
Diana LaGuardia
PHOTOGRAPHER
Richard Misrach
DIRECTOR OF PHOTOGRAPHY
Kathleen Klech
PUBLICATION
Condé Nast Traveler Magazine

Editorial Photography/Series
ART DIRECTOR
Diana LaGuardia
PHOTOGRAPHER
Philip-Lorca Dicorcia
DIRECTOR OF PHOTOGRAPHY
Kathleen Klech
PUBLICATION
Condé Nast Traveler Magazine

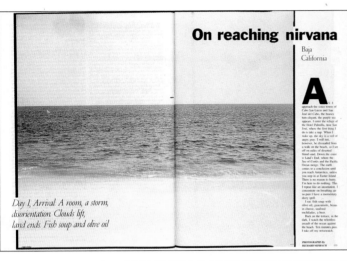

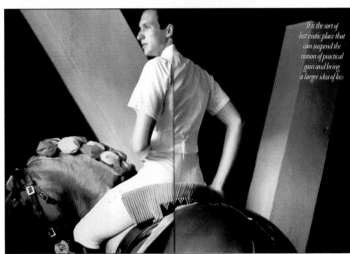

Editorial Photography/Series

ART DIRECTOR
David Armario

ILLUSTRATOR
Ruven Afanaour

PUBLICATION
Discover Magazine

Editorial Photography/Series

DIRECTOR OF PHOTOGRAPHY
David Friend

PUBLICATION
Life Magazine

There's a lot of disagreement about how it functions in people, and whether it can be built into anything else.

what is

consciousness?

SOME PEOPLE SPEND A LOT OF TIME THINKING ABOUT OTHER PEOPLE THINKING ABOUT THEM-SELVES. THE MYSTERY OF SELF-AWARENESS ENGAGED THE ENERGIES OF SCIENTISTS AND PHILOSO-PHERS LONG BEFORE RENE DESCARTES CLAIMED THAT EXISTENCE DEPENDED UPON IT, AND IT'S CERTAINLY GARNERED A LOT OF ATTENTION SINCE THEN. CONSCIOUSNESS DOES APPEAR TO BE A HALLMARK OF HUMANITY, BUT WHAT EXACTLY IS IT? AND IF IT'S SOMETHING INNATELY HUMAN AND ALIVE, CAN IT BE GIVEN TO A MACHINE? DISCOVER ASKED CHRISTOF KOCH, A NEURAL-SYSTEMS EXPERT AT CALTECH, HOW OUR BRAINS TURN THIS PARTICULAR TRICK, THEN WE TURNED TO TERRY WINOGRAD, A COMPUTER SCIENTIST AT STANFORD, TO FIND OUT IF HIS MACHINES AND PROGRAMS WOULD EVER BECOME CONSCIOUS. FINALLY WE PUT THE SAME QUESTION TO HANS MORAVEC, WHO BUILDS ROBOTS AT CARNEGIE-MELLON AND WHO GAVE US A VERY SURPRISING ANSWER.

PHOTOGRAPHS BY RUVEN AFANADOR

"THESE ARE THE BODIES OF THE PREVIOUS NIGHT'S DEAD.

"I THINK THIS IS A GIRL — IT'S HARD TO TELL WHEN THEY ARE SO SKELETAL.

The Connected Brain

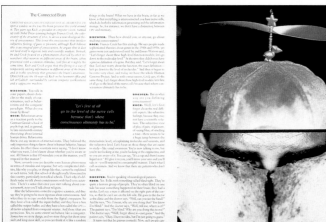

"Let's first of all go to the level of the nerve cells because that's where consciousness adamantly has to be."

"THIS MOTHER AND CHILD ARE EXTREMELY FORTUNATE.

Minds With Mobility

Editorial Photography/Series

PHOTOGRAPHER
Cristina Garcia Rodero

DIRECTOR OF PHOTOGRAPHY
David Friend

PUBLICATION
Life Magazine

Editorial Photography/Series

DIRECTOR OF PHOTOGRAPHY
David Friend

PUBLICATION
Life Magazine

Editorial Photography/Series

ART DIRECTOR
Suzanne Morin

WRITER
Elizabeth Royte

PHOTOGRAPHER
Alex Webb

PUBLICATION
Audubon Magazine

Graphic Design Photography

ART DIRECTOR
Stacy Drummond

DESIGN DIRECTOR
Jeffrey Keyton

DESIGNER
Steve Byram

COPYWRITER
Cheryl Family

PHOTOGRAPHER
Robert Lewis

STUDIO
MTV Network

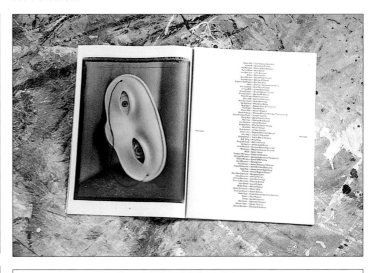

Graphic Design Photography

ART DIRECTOR
Terry Gutbellet

COPYWRITER
Ken Lassiter

PHOTOGRAPHER
Jay Maisel

STUDIO
Ice Comm.

Graphic Design Photography

ART DIRECTOR/PHOTOGRAPHER
Chris Collins

CLIENT
Chris Collins Studio

Graphic Design Photography

ART DIRECTOR
B. Martin Pedersen

DESIGNER
Adrian Pulfer

PHOTOGRAPHER
Dennis Blachut

STUDIO
Pedersen Design Inc.

PUBLICATION
Graphis Annual Reports

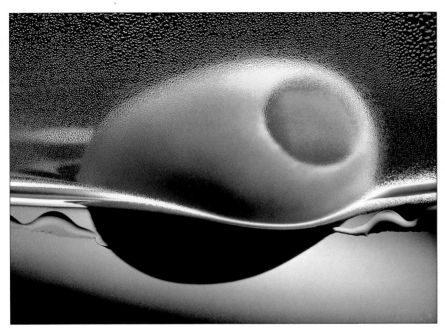

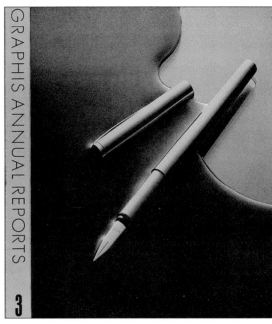

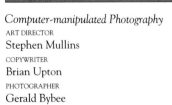

Computer-manipulated Photography

ART DIRECTOR
Stephen Mullins

COPYWRITER
Brian Upton

PHOTOGRAPHER
Gerald Bybee

Computer-manipulated Photography

PHOTOGRAPHER
Bobby Neel Adams

DIRECTOR OF PHOTOGRAPHY
David Friend

PUBLICATION
Life Magazine

Advertising Illustration

ART DIRECTOR/ILLUSTRATOR
Robert Kopecky

STUDIO
Robert Kopecky

CLIENT
Ian Schrager/Paramount Hotel

Advertising Illustration

AGENCY
DMB&B

Advertising Illustration

ART DIRECTOR
Dru Ouellette

DESIGNER
Kevin O'Donoghue

AGENCY
Young & Rubicam

CLIENT
United States Army

Advertising Illustration/Series

ART DIRECTOR
Guy Marino

ILLUSTRATOR
Brad Holland

AGENCY
Doremus & Co.

CLIENT
Bankers Trust

Advertising Illustration/Series

ART DIRECTORS
Tony Hitchcock, Gene Lindgren

DESIGNERS
M. Paraskevas, Alex Hargrave

ILLUSTRATOR
M. Paraskevas

STUDIO
M. Paraskevas

CLIENT
The Hampton Classic

Advertising Illustration/Series

ART DIRECTOR
Arnie Arlow

COPYWRITER/ILLUSTRATOR
Braldt Bralds

AGENCY
T.B.W.A. Advertising

CLIENT
Carillon Importers

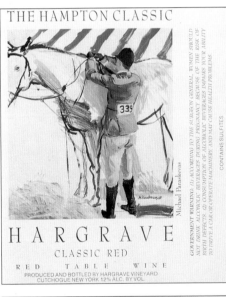

Advertising Illustration/Series

ART DIRECTOR
Arnie Arlow

COPYWRITER
Michel Roux

ILLUSTRATORS
Rev. Howard Finster, Gary Kelley,
George Rodrigue, Charles Becker,
Gordon Sherman

AGENCY
TBWA

CLIENT
Carillon Importers

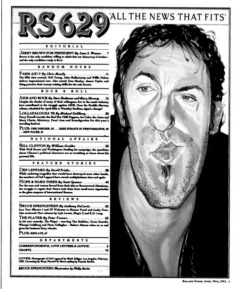

Editorial Illustration

ART DIRECTOR
Fred Woodward

ILLUSTRATOR
Philip Burke

PUBLICATION
Rolling Stone Magazine

Editorial Illustration

ART DIRECTOR
Fred Woodward

COPYWRITER
Peter Travers

ILLUSTRATOR
Jonathon Rosen

PUBLICATION
Rolling Stone Magazine

Editorial Illustration

ART DIRECTOR
Fred Woodward

COPYWRITER
Peter Travers

ILLUSTRATOR
Jack Unruh

PUBLICATION
Rolling Stone Magazine

Editorial Illustration

ART DIRECTOR/ILLUSTRATOR
Don Weller

WRITER
Gary Kimball

STUDIO
The Weller Institue for the Cure of Design

PUBLICATION
Park City Lodestar Magazine

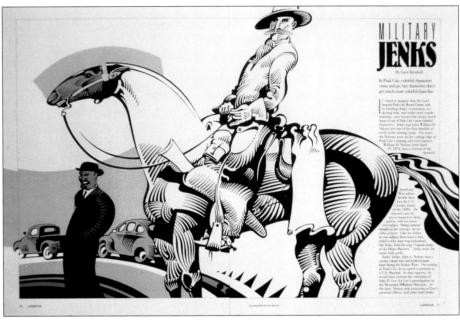

Editorial Illustration

ART DIRECTOR
Fred Woodward

WRITER
Alan Light

ILLUSTRATOR
Charles Burns

PUBLICATION
Rolling Stone Magazine

Editorial Illustration

ART DIRECTOR
Fred Woodward

WRITER
Elysa Gardner

ILLUSTRATOR
Brian Cronin

PUBLICATION
Rolling Stone Magazine

Editorial Illustration

ART DIRECTOR
Fred Woodward

WRITER
Anthony De Curtis

ILLUSTRATOR
Peter Sis

PUBLICATION
Rolling Stone Magazine

Editorial Illustration

ART DIRECTOR
Fred Woodward

WRITER
Peter Travers

ILLUSTRATOR
Edward Solel

PUBLICATION
Rolling Stone Magazine

Editorial Illustration

DESIGNER/ILLUSTRATOR
Ivan Chermayeff

STUDIO
Chermayeff & Geismar Inc.

CLIENT
UCLA

Editorial Illustration

ART DIRECTOR
Kerig Pope

WRITER
Alex Haley

ILLUSTRATOR
Brad Holland

STUDIO
Brad Holland

PUBLICATION
Playboy

Editorial Illustration

ART DIRECTOR/DESIGNER
Matthew Drace

ILLUSTRATOR
Elwood Smith

PUBLICATION
Men's Journal

Editorial Illustration/Series

ART DIRECTOR
James Lambertus, David Armario

DESIGNER
James Lambertus

WRITER
Edward O. Wilson

ILLUSTRATOR
Alan Cober

PUBLICATION
Discover Magazine

Editorial Illustration/Series

ART DIRECTOR
David Armario

DESIGNER
James Lambertus

ILLUSTRATOR
Henrik Drescher

PUBLICATION
Discover Magazine

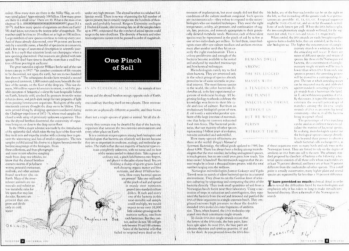

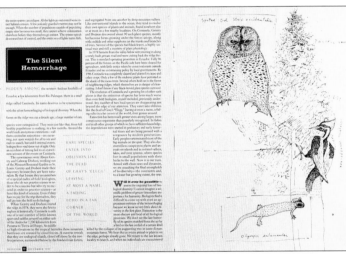

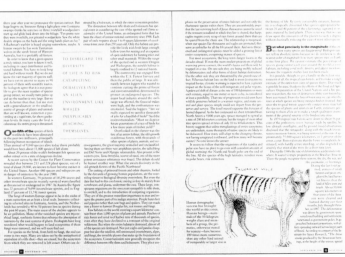

Editorial Illustration/Series

ART DIRECTOR
Lance Matusek

ILLUSTRATOR
Brad Holland

CLIENT
Aetna Life and Casualty Insurance Co.

Editorial Illustration/Series

ART DIRECTOR
Michael Grossman

ILLUSTRATOR
Scott Menchin

PUBLICATION
Entertainment Weekly

Graphic Design Illustration
ART DIRECTOR
Jacqueline Ghosin
DESIGNERS
James Fash, Franz Platte
ILLUSTRATOR
André François
CLIENT
Tastemaker

Graphic Design Illustration
ART DIRECTOR/ILLUSTRATOR
Paul Davis
STUDIO
Paul Davis Studio
PUBLICATION
City University of New York
Freshman Admissions Guide

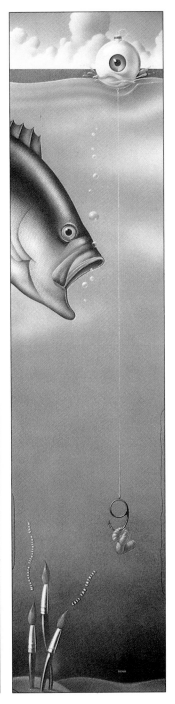

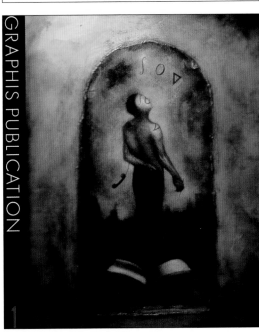

Graphic Design Illustration
ART DIRECTOR
B. Martin Pedersen
DESIGNER
Adrian Pulfer
ILLUSTRATOR
Matt Mahurin
STUDIO
Pedersen Design Inc.
PUBLICATION
Graphis Publication

Graphic Design Illustration
ART DIRECTOR
José Serrano
ILLUSTRATOR
Tracy Sabin
STUDIO
Mires Design
CLIENT
Peninsula Family YMCA

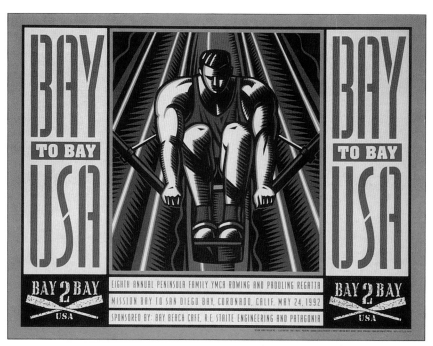

Graphic Design Illustration
ART DIRECTOR
Lynn Phelps
COPYWRITER
Lauren Paige Kennedy
ILLUSTRATOR
Theo Rudnak
CLIENT
AIGA/Minnesota

Graphic Design Illustration/Series
ART DIRECTOR
Rocco Callari
DESIGNER
Tony Fouracre
ILLUSTRATOR
Braldt Bralds
CLIENT
United Nations Postal Service

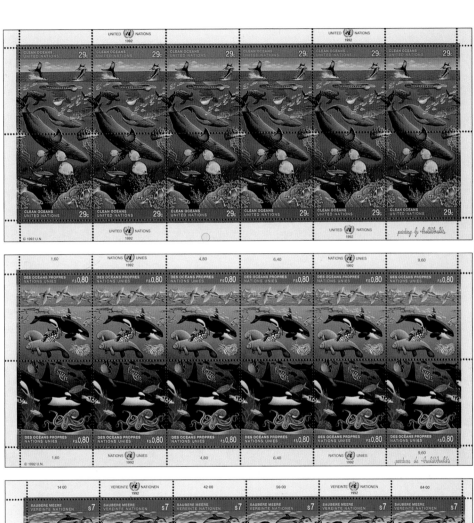

CHAIRPERSON

Karl Steinbrenner

STEINBRENNER ASSOCIATES

CO-CHAIRPERSONS

Andy Kner

R.C. PUBLICATIONS

Minoru Morita

CREATIVE CENTER, INC.

B. Martin Pedersen

PEDERSEN DESIGN, INC.

JUDGES

Per Arnoldi

DENMARK

Fred Buhler

GERMANY

Barry Day

UNITED KINGDOM

Rudolph de Harak

ADC HALL OF FAME, UNITED STATES

M.J. Demner

AUSTRIA

Gene Federico

ADC HALL OF FAME, UNITED STATES

Jean Feldman

FRANCE

Renzie Hanham

NEW ZEALAND

Mutsuo Katsui

JAPAN

Chaz Maviyane-Davies

ZIMBABWE

Pedro Tabernero

SPAIN

Felipe Taborda

BRAZIL

SEVEN YEARS AGO I was given the honor and the opportunity to create the Art Directors Club International Exhibition of advertising, design, and graphic communications. It has been seven years of pure excitement and gratifying growth.

Even in the face of proliferating award shows and a marked decline in the size of our businesses in some countries, the ADC International has proven to be a showcase for the increasingly expert and effective work being dome around the world. Now that our industry is growing into ever more countries in an expanding worldwide free market, we expect an ever greater representation in succeeding years.

My thanks and that of my co-chairmen go to this year's judges who selected the small but excellent show of graphic design and advertising you will see in the International section of this book.

For each of the past seven years the New York Art Directors Club has invited a panel of leading designers, creative directors, and communications writers from at least ten countries on seven continents or sub-continents. It has ben exciting, to say the least. Exciting and exhausting to review so much work and to judge it all in the contexts within which they were conceived and executed. No simple task, yet very satisfying.

I'd like to pass on a thought that has recurred almost every year, voiced by virtually every one of our International judges. They have all been of the opinion that we see only a fraction of the great work being done worldwide. This may be due to there being too little timely awareness of the competition and its deadlines. Should this be the case, I invite the readers and perusers of this 72nd Annual to contact is for the entry information and deadlines necessary to enter the upcoming English version of our International Competition—and to help us spread the word to those who may as yet not have heard about it.

KARL H. STEINBRENNER

CHAIRMAN, SEVENTH ANNUAL INTERNATIONAL EXHIBITION

Silver/Television

ART DIRECTOR
Takuya Onuki

COPYWRITER
Tonomi Maeda

PRODUCER
Seiichiro Horii

DIRECTOR
Shinya Nakajima

AGENCY
Hakuhodo Inc.

CLIENT
Nissin Food Products Co., Ltd.

Gold/Television

ART DIRECTOR
Takuya Onuki

COPYWRITER
Tonomi Maeda

PRODUCER
Seiichiro Horii

DIRECTOR
Shinya Nakajima

AGENCY
Hakuhodo Inc.

CLIENT
Nissin Food Products Co., Ltd.

SFX: Ocean wave sounds throughout. Stalking sounds in
 the wet sand. Babble of shrieking hunters. Stalking sounds.
VO: Hungry? Summer is Seafood Cup Noodle time. Nissin.

Distinctive Merit/Public Service

ART DIRECTOR
Luis Christello

COPYWRITERS
J. Carlos Campos, Daniel R. Torin

PRODUCER
Jodaf Filmes

DIRECTOR
João Daniel

AGENCY
Y&R Portugal

CLIENT
Super Som

Distinctive Merit/Art Direction

ART DIRECTOR
Tom Notman

COPYWRITER
Alastair Wood

PRODUCER
Barry Stephenson

DIRECTOR
Richard Dean

AGENCY
BSB Dorland Ltd.

CLIENT
Woolworths

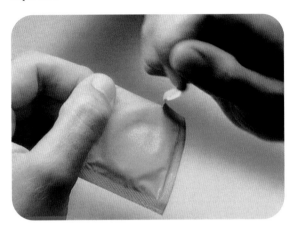

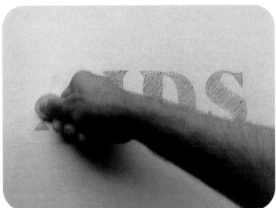

Distinctive Merit/Newspaper

ART DIRECTOR
Kevin Bratley

COPYWRITER
John Townshend

TYPOGRAPHER
Leonie Brierle

PHOTOGRAPHER
Barry Lategan

AGENCY
DMB&B

CLIENT
Digital Service

Once a company has learned to solve its own problems,
it never forgets.

Two inches of water. All it takes to sink a company.

Distinctive Merit/Newspaper

ART DIRECTOR
Seiki Takahasi

DESIGNER
Yuji Furuya

COPYWRITER
Akihiro Sekine

PHOTOGRAPHERS
T. Watanabe, T. Kakutani

AGENCY
Dentsu Inc./Japan Graphics Corp.

CLIENT
Fujitsu Ltd.

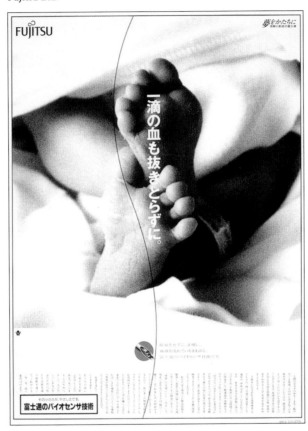

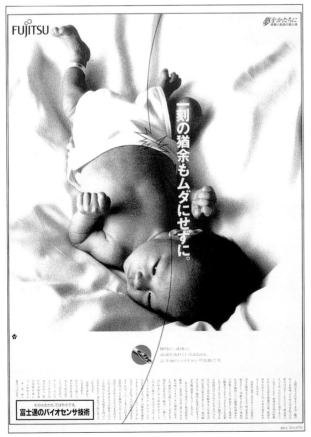

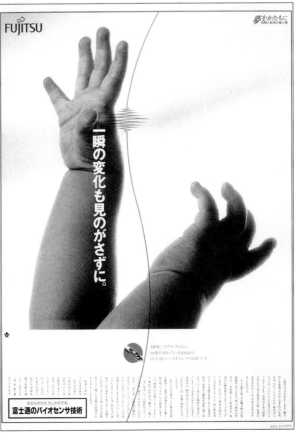

Silver/Magazine

ART DIRECTOR

Hans-Georg Pospischil

COPYWRITERS

Poala Piglia, Peter Breul, Bernadette Gotthardt

ILLUSTRATOR

Paola Piglia

PUBLICATION

Frankfurter Allgemeine Magazin

Gold/Annual Report

ART DIRECTOR/DESIGNER
Michael Johnson

PHOTOGRAPHERS
Martin Barraud, Evan Hurd,
Michael Harding

STUDIO
Smith & Martin Ltd.

AGENCY
Johnson Banks

CLIENT
The Watch Gallery

Silver/Annual Report

ART DIRECTOR
Adelaide Acerbi

COPYWRITER
Fulio Irace

STUDIO
Adelaide Acerbi

CLIENT
Gemm

Silver/Annual Report

ART DIRECTOR
Ken Bridger

DESIGNER
Lisa Farmer

COPYWRITER
Luigi Lodi

STUDIO
Bridger & Bridger Graphic Comm.

CLIENT
Alpi

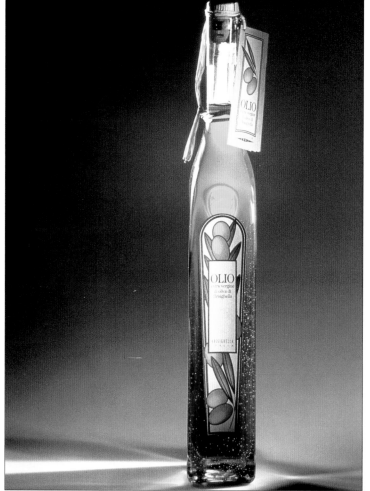

Silver/Annual Report

ART DIRECTOR/TYPOGRAPHER
Will de l'Ecluse

DESIGNERS
Will de l'Ecluse, Hans Bockting,
Fredericke Bouten

PHOTOGRAPHER/ILLUSTRATOR
Erik van Gurp, Henk Hoebé

STUDIO
UNA Amsterdam

CLIENT
ACF Holding

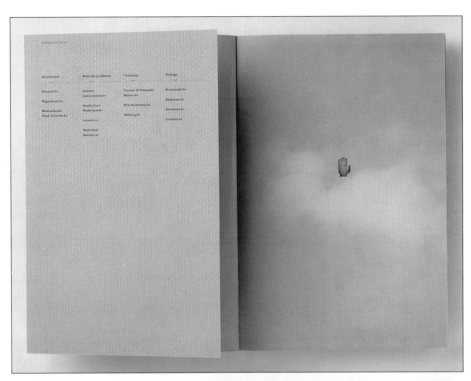

Distinctive Merit/Annual Report

ART DIRECTOR
Ken Mihi

STUDIO
Ken Mihi Assoc.

Gold/Annual Report

ART DIRECTOR/COPYWRITER
Uwe Loesch

DESIGNERS
Michael Gais, Iris Utikal

PHOTOGRAPHER
Udo Bechmann

STUDIO
Arbeitsgemeinschaft für Visuelle
und Verbale Kommunication

CLIENT
Zanders Feinpapiere AG

Distinctive Merit/Packaging

ART DIRECTOR/CREATIVE DIRECTOR
Kenzo Matsui

DESIGNERS
Kenzo Matsui, Yuko Araki

STUDIO
Kenzo Matsui & Assoc.

CLIENT
Ehime Prefecture

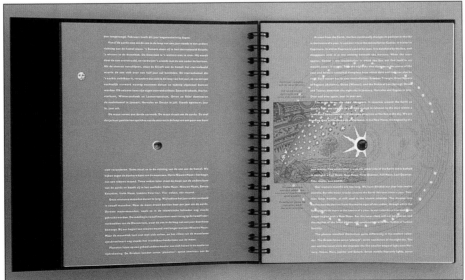

Silver

ART DIRECTORS
Hans Bockting, Will de l'Ecluse

DESIGNERS
Will de l'Ecluse, Hans Bockting,
Véro Crickx

CARTOGRAPHER
Dirk Fortuin/Global View

STUDIO
UNA Amsterdam

CLIENT
UNA/Bloem/Ando

Distinctive Merit/Calendar

ART DIRECTOR/DESIGNER/
PHOTOGRAPHER
Susumu Endo

CLIENT
Audio-Technica

Distinctive Merit/Packaging

ART DIRECTOR/DESIGNER
Minoru Shiokawa

CREATIVE DIRECTORS
Shunsaku Suguira, Serge Lutans

STUDIO
Shiseido Co., Ltd.

CLIENT
Shiseido Co., Ltd.

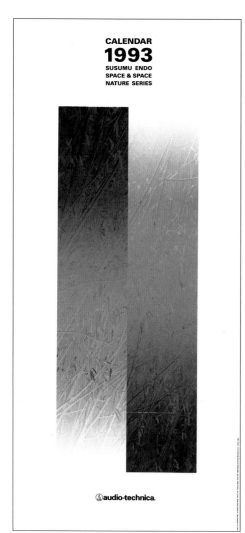

Distinctive Merit/Packaging

ART DIRECTOR
Yoichirou Fujii

DESIGNERS
Yoichirou Fujii, Keiko Maeka

PHOTOGRAPHER
Masao Ohta

STUDIO
Sony Music Communications, Inc.

CLIENT
Alfa Records, Inc.

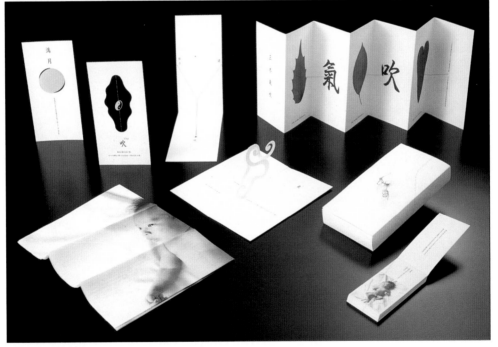

ART DIRECTOR/DESIGNER
Ken Miki

COPYWRITERS
Ken Miki, Tomoko Miki

AGENCY
Ken Miki & Assoc.

Silver/Poster

ART DIRECTOR
Tsuyoshi Kamiyama
COPYWRITER
Shinji Uchida
PHOTOGRAPHER/ILLUSTRATOR
Noriyuki Hashida, Kanbei Seki
AGENCY
Dentsu, Young & Rubicam
CLIENT
The Nikka Whisky Distilling Co., Ltd.

Distinctive Merit/Poster

ART DIRECTOR/DESIGNER
Akio Okumura

STUDIO
Packaging Create Inc.

CLIENT
Japan Graphic Designers Association Inc.

Distinctive Merit/Public Service Poster

ART DIRECTOR/DESIGNER/COPYWRITER/ILLUSTRATOR
Takashi Akiyama

STUDIO
Takashi Akiyama Studio

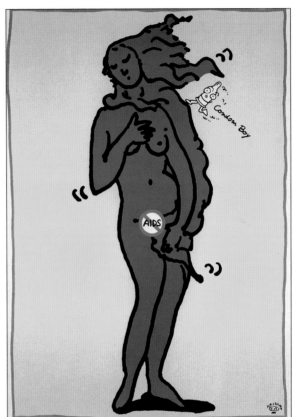

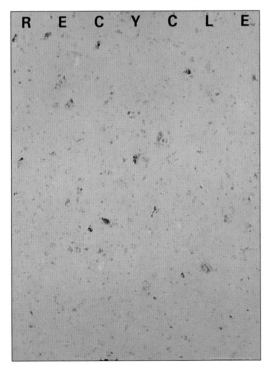

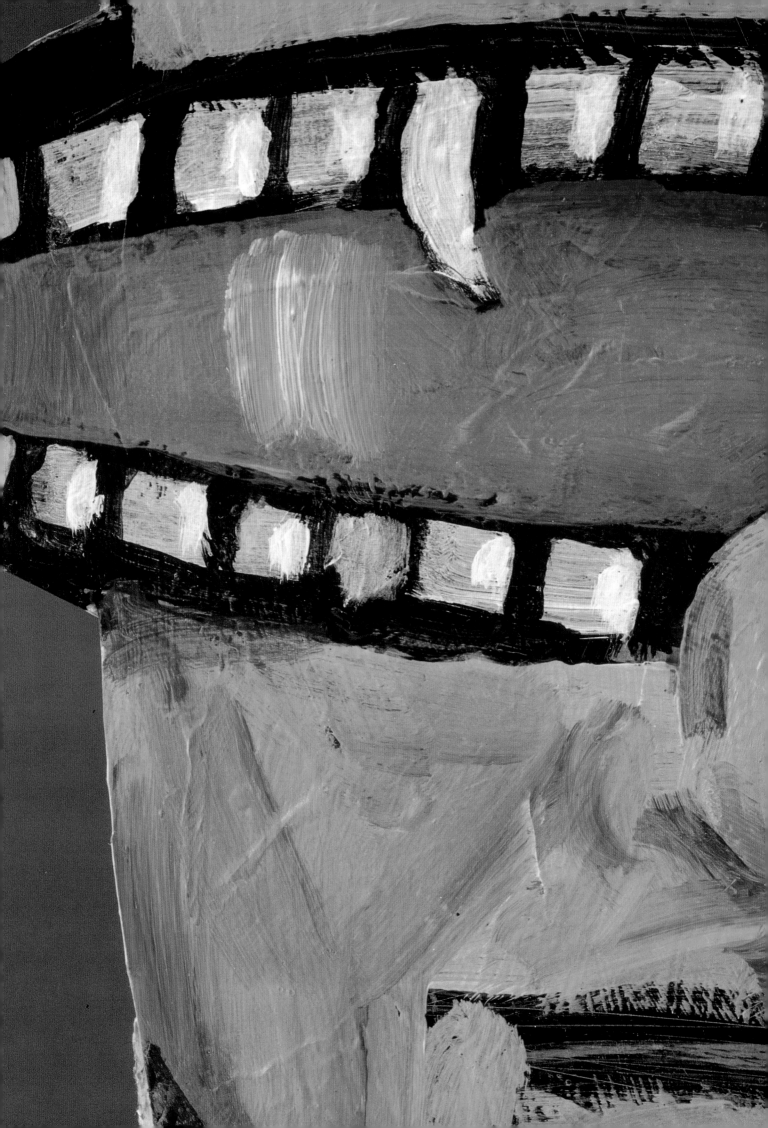

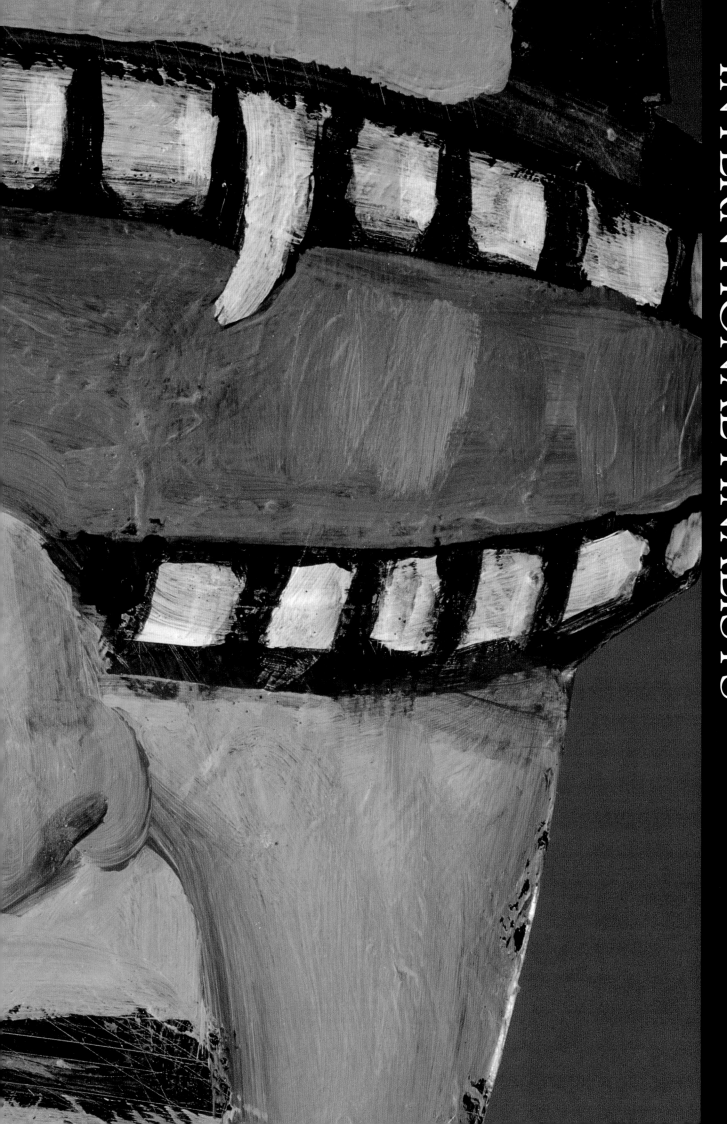

ART DIRECTOR
Philip Ingevics
COPYWRITERS
Jan Kempski, Marc Stoiber
PRODUCER
Jürgen Heide
DIRECTOR
Andreas Kayales
AGENCY
BBDO Düsseldorf, Interteam Design
CLIENT
VPRT

ART DIRECTOR
Pieter van Velsen
COPYWRITER
Wim Ubachs
AGENCY
Saatchi & Saatchi

CREATIVE DIRECTOR
Fernano Vega Olmos
AGENCY
Casares Grey & Associados

FISH.
VO: Ladies and gentlemen, we're about to show you the difference between press advertising...and television advertising. Commercial television...brings life into advertising.

BOXER.
VO: This man drives an Audi. He believes in keeping his work and private life strictly separate.

ART DIRECTOR
Enrique Faillace
COPYWRITER
Alberto Hernandez
PRODUCER
Laura Garcia
DIRECTOR
William Teale
AGENCY
JMC/Young & Rubicam
CLIENT
Sony de Venezuela

CREATIVE DIRECTOR
Fernano Vega Olmos
AGENCY
Casares Grey & Associados

AGENCY
Miller Myers Bruce Dallacosta

A new channel is born.

BUTTERFLY.
SFX: Music under.
VO: At Sony, we're constantly remaking ourselves. To achieve the new Trinitron XBR2, we gave it picture and sound so sharp, and clear; so clean and true, you won't believe it. The remarkable Sony Trinitron XBR2. See it, hear it, feel it. You'll agree it's not just a thing of beauty but television reborn.

ART DIRECTOR
Urs Schneider

COPYWRITER
Johannes Krammer

DIRECTOR
David Deveson

STUDIO
Film Factory

AGENCY
Demner & Merlicek

CLIENT
Kastner & Öhler

ART DIRECTOR
Marc Huber

COPYWRITER
Johannes Krammer

DIRECTOR
Bady Minck, Stefan Stratil

STUDIO
Film Factory

AGENCY
Demner & Merlicek

CLIENT
Profil Magazine

ART DIRECTOR
Rolf Elsner

COPYWRITER
Ole Krogh

PHOTOGRAPHER
N. Bruel

PRODUCER
Filmfabrikken

DIRECTOR
Christian Lyngbye

AGENCY
Young & Rubicam

SPORTSHOUSE.
VO: A jogger going beyond the speed limit and promptly getting a ticket. Something that can only happen with quality-proofed jogging boots by Kastner & Öhler.

SAD MOOD.
CHANCELLOR: (*singing*) I'm in a sad mood...
VO: Sorry, *Profil* will be out again on Monday.

FIRST DATE.
YOUNG LADY: Ehmm...Don't you think you'd better take some precautions?
YOUNG MAN: Well, we've only just...What now?
YOUNG LADY: The sooner the better, darling. Anyway you'll get more out of it if you get on to it right away.
YOUNG MAN: Well, I...er.
YOUNG LADY: You might as well get it over with. Anyway, you've got to be careful—what with kids and all that.
YOUNG MAN: Ehmm...well, okay, I'll er...just slip out for a minute.
YOUNG LADY: What on earth for? The bank's closed now!
VO: It's easy to take precautions with a pension plan from Den Danske Bank. You can start for only 200 kr. a month, which is cheaper than the alternatives.

ART DIRECTOR/CREATIVE DIRECTOR
Beat Keller
PRODUCER
G.L.A.S.S.
DIRECTOR
Rudi Lienhard
STUDIO
GGK Zürich

ART DIRECTOR
Masao Miyashita
COPYWRITER
Kenichiro Sakaguchi
CREATIVE DIRECTORS
Douglas Biro, Masayuki Aoki, Peter James
DIRECTOR
Koh Sakata
AGENCY
McCann-Erickson Hakuhodo Inc.
CLIENT
Coca-Cola Corp.

ART DIRECTOR/COPYWRITER
Faruk Cassis
PRODUCER
Laura Garcia
DIRECTOR
James O'Dea
AGENCY
JMC/Young & Rubicam
CLIENT
Pirelli

LIVE AND LET LIVE.
VO: We see the famous Einstein, Brecht, Chaplin, and Lenin. One day or another they all came, at a different age for different reasons to Switzerland. Then we see a dead junkie in a toilet who left Switzerland at eighteen years—much too early. Let's think of them. Live and let live. GGK.

MY FIRST COKE.
FRIENDS: How's it going Kenji?
FRIEND #1: Kenji.
KENJI: Hey, *Oni-chan* [big brother], what's Coca-Cola taste like?
BROTHER: It's cold and fizzy...
FRIEND #1: And refreshing! You've tasted it before, right?
KENJI: Nope.
FRIEND #1: You never tried it before?
FRIENDS: Never? He never tried it before!
GIRL: That's okay. Here, Coca-Cola.
FRIEND #2: First time!
BROTHER: How is it?
KENJI: It tickles my throat and it tastes good.
GIRL: And?
KENJI: It's refreshing!
FRIEND #1: Refreshing! Did you hear it?
FRIEND #2: He's a grown-up now.
VO: The moment that refreshes.

ART DIRECTOR/CREATIVE DIRECTOR
Mark Denton
COPYWRITER/CREATIVE DIRECTOR
Chris Palmer
PRODUCER
Paul Fenton
DIRECTOR
Tony Kaye
AGENCY
Simons Palmer
CLIENT
Nike

ART DIRECTOR
Jun-ichiro Akiyoshi
COPYWRITER
Shinji Takahashi
PRODUCER
Kenji Funai
DIRECTOR
Shoji Kuwabara
AGENCY
Hakuhodo Inc.
CLIENT
Matsushita Electric Industrial Co., Ltd.

ART DIRECTOR
Tadahiko Fujii
COPYWRITERS
Toshiaki Seto, Miki Matstui
PRODUCER
Satoshi Takeuchi
DIRECTOR
Takashi Shimoji
AGENCY
Hakahudo Inc.
CLIENT
Ezaki Glico Co., Ltd.

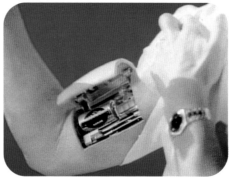

KICK IT.
SFX: "Can I Kick It" plays throughout.
VO#1: Can I kick it?
VO: #2: Yes you can...

EDBERG'S SECRET.
VO: Tennis player Stefan Edberg always turns the world on. Is it really true that the secret behind his power is a Panasonic dry cell?

GLICO & BISKO.
SONG: Yo-heave-ho!
    Yo-heave-ho!
    I should be able to do anything.
    This time I can do it for sure
    ... one, two, three.
    A bit more, a little bit more to go,
    A bit more, a little bit more to go.
    I should be able to do anything.
    Cheer up, ... one, two, three.
    (*repeat*)
VO: Grow up slowly. Glico & Bisko.

ART DIRECTORS/COPYWRITERS
Yasumichi Uwagawa, Sho Akiyama
CREATIVE DIRECTOR
Yukio Oshima
PRODUCER
Fumikazu Kawaguchi
DIRECTOR
Toshiaki Nakano
AGENCY
Dentsu Inc., Taiyo Kikaku Co., Ltd.
CLIENT
Toyota Motor Corp.

Campaign
ART DIRECTOR
Philip Ingevics
COPYWRITERS
Jan Kempski, Marc Stoiber
PRODUCER
Jürgen Heide
DIRECTOR
Andreas Kayales
AGENCY
BBDO Düsseldorf, Interteam Design
CLIENT
VPRT

DOG. SUMO. FISH.
VO: Ladies and gentlemen, we're about to show you the difference between press advertising...and television advertising. Commercial television. Brings life into advertising.

Campaign
ART DIRECTOR
Peter van den Engel
COPYWRITER
Martijn Horvath
PRODUCER
Christel Hofstee
DIRECTOR
Thed Lenssen
AGENCY
DMB&B Advertising B.V.
CLIENT
Royal PTT Netherlands N.V.

VACANCY.
VO: The president of a big French corporation fails to interest a highly-qualified Dutchman in the position of International Marketing Manager. He chooses Royal PTT Netherlands N.V.

THE PITCH.
VO: Against all odds an American enterprise loses an expected order to Royal PTT Netherlands N.V.

TAKE OVER.
VO: Japanese businessmen see their aggressive, expansion policy fail because the ideal company is not for sale: Royal PTT Netherlands N.V.

Campaign

ART DIRECTOR
Tomek Luczynski

COPYWRITER
Johannes Krammer

PRODUCER
Waltraud Bròz

DIRECTOR
Wolfgang Glück

AGENCY
Demner & Merlicek

CLIENT
ORF-Blue Danube Radio

Campaign

ART DIRECTOR
Barbara Poxleitner

COPYWRITER
Werner Busam

PRODUCER
Jörg Bauer

DIRECTOR
Kevin Molony

AGENCY
Grey Düsseldorf

CLIENT
B.A.T.

Campaign

ART DIRECTOR
Humberto Lopardo

COPYWRITER/CREATIVE DIRECTOR
Fernando Vega Olmos

PRODUCER
Armando Morando

DIRECTOR
Alfredo Stuart

AGENCY
Casares Grey & Associados

CLIENT
Cepas Argentinas

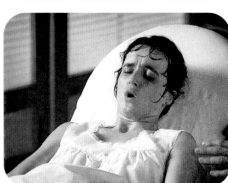

RADIO.
PRESENTER: This is a radio. This is a blue radio. And this is Blue Danube Radio. Sounds great!
VO: Blue Danube Radio. Sounds great!

PRESIDENT.
PRESENTER: The president demanded. The prime minister disagreed. The queen was delighted. And you will never find out unless you listen to Blue Danube Radio.
VO: Blue Danube Radio. Sounds great!

MONROE.
PRESENTER: Sooner or later we will get you. Listen how!(*singing to a Marilyn Monroe track*) "I wanna be loved by you, just you, nobody else but you..."
VO: Blue Danube Radio. Sounds great!

Campaign

ART DIRECTOR
Antony Redman

COPYWRITERS
Antony Redman, Danny Higgins

CREATIVE DIRECTORS
Jim Aitchison, Norman Alcuri

DIRECTORS
Antony Redman, Ric Curtin

AGENCY
The Ball Partnership Euro RSCG

CLIENT
Yet Con

Campaign

ART DIRECTOR
Gerard Stamp

COPYWRITER
Loz Simpson

PRODUCER
Ronnie Holbrook

DIRECTOR
Graham Rose

AGENCY
BSB Dorland Ltd.

CLIENT
H.J. Heinz & Co., Ltd.

Campaign

ART DIRECTOR
Dianne Eastman

COPYWRITER
Ian Mirlin

PRODUCER
Angela Carroll

DIRECTOR
Rick Levine

AGENCY
Harrod & Mirlin

CLIENT
Levi Strauss & Co., (Canada) Ltd.

FLIRT. RECIPES. WAITER.
SFX: The raucous cacophony of the Yet Con at lunchtime is heard throughout. Great food but deafening ambience.

ROAD DRILL. WASHING MACHINE.
SFX: Natural throughout
VO: Rich, thick, and delicious. There's no ketchup quite like Heinz.

SIGN LANGUAGE. CHRISTMAS. CORNER STORE.
SFX: Music up and under the opening super. Music bed is instrumental only throughout the spot. As the end super appears one line of lyric is sung: "The beat goes on."

Campaign

ART DIRECTOR
Mathias Babst

COPYWRITER/CREATIVE DIRECTOR
Hansjörg Zürcher

PRODUCERS
S. Fraefel, P. Egger

DIRECTOR
Ernst Wirz

AGENCY
Comsult/Advico Young & Rubicam

CLIENT
Migros Genossenschafts-Bund

Campaign

ART DIRECTOR
J.R. D'Elboux

COPYWRITER
Luciana Salles

PRODUCER
Jodaf

DIRECTOR
Rodolfo Vanni

AGENCY
DPZ Propaganda

CLIENT
Mobil

Campaign

ART DIRECTOR
David Kelso

COPYWRITER
Bradley Riddoch

PRODUCER
Nancy Bradley

DIRECTOR
Alan Marr

AGENCY
MacLaren:Lintas Inc.

CLIENT
Thomas J. Lipton

MOBIL OIL DO BRAZIL.
ANNOUNCER: If any of these objects is what you think is the most important thing in your car, please don't buy our oil.
VO: Mobil. New life for your car.
ANNOUNCER: Or, at least don't let anyone find out.

SNACK ONE.
MAN: Hi. So you must be setting in to watch tonight's movie. And as we both know, in the next couple of hours you're going to get hungry. As usual you'll think potato chips, popcorn, cheese and crackers...Not tonight. 'Cause remember that package of Chicken Noodle Lipton Cup-a-Soup that you got in the mail and we told you not to eat. Well, tonight you get to eat it—as a snack. Now I know this is a radical new concept. But don't panic. We'll go through it step by step. See ya' soon.

Campaign

ART DIRECTORS/CREATIVE DIRECTORS
Philip Wilson, Geoff Mander

COPYWRITER
Nick Theobald

PRODUCER
Shinta Lee

AGENCY
BBDO Hong Kong

CLIENT
Federal Express

  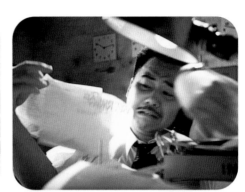

CORPORATE.

VO: You wouldn't believe how much some air express companies want you to think that their vans can do everything. Federal Express is different. We have our own fleet of aircraft, so your packages will really fly. Only Federal Express delivers your packages overnight by 10:30 a.m. to virtually anywhere in the U.S....Guaranteed.

SKATES.

VO: Would you believe that most air express companies are still skating around with passenger airlines to deliver your packages? Federal Express is different. With our own planes, your packages really fly. Only Federal Express delivers your packages overnight by 10:30 a.m. to virtually anywhere in the U.S....Guaranteed.

TRACKING.

VO: Some air express companies want you to believe they've got everything under control. But when it comes to tracking, they only think they know where your package is. At Federal Express, our tracking system tells you where your package is every step of its journey. Only Federal Express delivers your packages overnight by 10:30 a.mm to virtually anywhere in the U.S....Guaranteed.

Campaign

ART DIRECTOR
Rick Kemp

COPYWRITER
Jeff Finkler

PRODUCER
Pat Lyons

DIRECTOR
Jeff Jones

AGENCY
Leo Burnett Co., Ltd.

CLIENT
William Neilson Ltd.

Campaign

ART DIRECTOR
Rick Kemp

COPYWRITER
Jeff Finkler

PRODUCER
Pat Lyons

DIRECTOR
Jeff Jones

AGENCY
Leo Burnett Co., Ltd.

CLIENT
Kellogg Canada Inc.

Campaign

ART DIRECTOR
Michael McLaughlin

COPYWRITER
Stephen Creet

PRODUCER
Sandy Cole

DIRECTOR
Neil Williamson

AGENCY
MacLaren:Lintas Inc.

CLIENT
Lever Brothers

TWINS.
SHORT GUY: Hi, I'm Emilio. This is my twin brother Dave. How ya doing?
VO: Between the ages of twelve and seventeen...
SHORT GUY: Until high school we were the same size.
VO: The average teenager grows about seven inches.
SHORT GUY: Then something happened. I dunno what.
VO: Exactly the size of a Mr. Big.
SHORT GUY: I think some weird gene thing kicked in.
VO: Coincidence? Maybe...maybe not. Can you afford to take that chance?
SFX: Door slam.
VO: When you're this big they call you mister.

DID YOU KNOW?
INTERVIEWER: Did you know that rice has complex carbohydrates?
GUYS: I knew that.
INTERVIEWER: And did you know that rice is part of a wholesome diet?
GUYS: I knew that.
INTERVIEWER: This is Kellogg's Rice Krispies. Most people don't know that each Rice Krispie is made with a real grain of rice.
FIRST GUY: I knew that.
SECOND GUY: I didn't know that. I mean I didn't know that most people didn't know that.
VO: For everyone who didn't know that Kellogg's Rice Krispies is made with real rice, we have one question: What the heck did you think it was made with?
GUYS: I don't know.

PANDA.
SFX: Sounds of train yard, shop, dog barks, radio playing train song.
VO: Sunlight. The grease cutting detergent for dirty dogs. And dirty dishes.

Campaign

ART DIRECTOR
Axel Windhorst

COPYWRITER
Monika Kuffner

CREATIVE DIRECTOR
Hans Fahrnholz

PRODUCER
Viva Film München

STUDIO
Gardena Kress & Partner

CLIENT
Service Plan Werbeagentur

Campaign

ART DIRECTOR
Lara Palmer

COPYWRITER
Dean Hore

PRODUCER
Annie O'Donnell

DIRECTOR
Steve Gordon

AGENCY
McKim Baker Lovick BBDO

CLIENT
Polaroid

Campaign

ART DIRECTOR
E. Vervroegen

COPYWRITER
C. Quadens

PRODUCER
B. Dupont

DIRECTOR
J.C. Wauters

AGENCY
Grey

CLIENT
Chat Noir Coffee

MEDICINE MAN. COWBOYS. SNAKE CHARMER.
VO: Gardena. The rainmakers.

WHY TRUST IT TO MEMORY
MAN: (*deep voice off camera*) Honey, what'd the fireplace in the second house look like again?
SFX: Polaroid camera going off.
VO: Why trust to memory when you can trust it to Polaroid Instant Pictures.

SEE IT YOUR WAY.
WOMAN: (*voice off camera*) Convince me it was in mint condition before it broke.
SFX: Polaroid camera going off.
VO: Get them to see it your way. Prove it with Polaroid Instant Pictures.

SAVE YOUR BREATH.
MAN: (*voice off camera*) So what exactly does this part look like.
SFX: Polaroid camera going off.
VO: Save your breath. Take a Polaroid Instant Picture.

WOOD.
VO: Here, the wood smells like wood, and coffee tastes like coffee.
Chat Noir, the real taste of coffee.

WILD.
VO: Here, what is wild stays wild, and coffee tastes like coffee.
Chat Noir, the real taste of coffee.

FRIEND.
VO: Here, a friend is a friend, and coffee tastes like coffee.
Chat Noir, the real taste of coffee.

Campaign

ART DIRECTOR
J. Luyten

COPYWRITER
Ph. de Ceuster

DIRECTOR
A. Degastines

AGENCY
Grey

CLIENT
Samsonite Bags

Campaign

ART DIRECTOR/CREATIVE DIRECTOR
Hiroshi Sasaki

COPYWRITERS
Hiroshi Sasaki, Masahiko Sato,
Masumi Uchino

DIRECTOR
Shinya Nakajima

AGENCY
Dentsu Inc./Nitten Alti Creatives

CLIENT
Fuji Television Network Inc.

ART DIRECTOR
Silke Handschuch

COPYWRITERS
Harald Hotopp, Matthias Mayer

DIRECTOR
Yves Lafaye

AGENCY
Lintas:Hamburg

CLIENT
VPRT

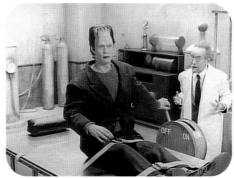

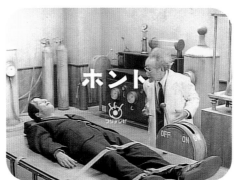

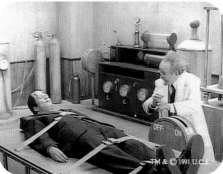

HIS/HER.

VO: His dad, his mum, his neighbor, his cat, his sister, his way-out Sammies by Samsonite.

VO: Her dad, her mum, her neighbor, her grandpa, her teacher, her way-out Sammies by Samsonite.

VO: Truly. Fuji Television.

DOG.

DOG: Well, how do you snap up a bargain? Very simply, I say it's psychology. You've got to wait for the right moment. Look. Wait. Consider. But don't just jump around blindly. Everything comes to those who are patient. My secret: head in at just the right moment. Grab it.

POSTMAN: Good boy, Rufus.

VO: We still know our customers by name—and that's the way it's gonna stay. POST SERVICE. We've taken on a big job.

ART DIRECTOR
Manfred Schmitt
COPYWRITERS
Wolfgang Stiesch, Konrad Wick
CREATIVE DIRECTOR
Bernd Misske
DIRECTOR
Michael v. Schmidt-Pauli
AGENCY
Young & Rubicam GmbH

ART DIRECTOR
José Ricardo Cabaço
COPYWRITER
Edson Athayde
AGENCY
Young & Rubicam Portugal

ART DIRECTOR/CREATIVE DIRECTOR/PRODUCER
Tony Segarra
COPYWRITER/CREATIVE DIRECTOR/PRODUCER
F. Fernandez de Castro
DIRECTOR
Aixala
AGENCY
Delvico Bates Barcelona

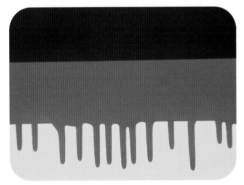

FLAG.
VO: If this goes on, and the majority keeps silent, the Germans too will have to apply for a silent abroad. Stop the Mob!

BEACH.
VO: If you don't mind showing your chest to the whole world every summer, why don't you show it to your doctor every six months?

ART DIRECTOR
Enric Aguilera
COPYWRITER
Toni Segarra
CREATIVE DIRECTORS/PRODUCERS
Toni Segarra, F. Fernandez de Castro
DIRECTOR
Ricardo Albiñana
AGENCY
Delvico Bates Barcelona

ART DIRECTOR
Wolfgang Christ
COPYWRITERS
Harald Hotopp, Mario Vernier
PRODUCER
J. Bauerschmidt
DIRECTOR
Patrick Morgan
AGENCY
Lintas:Hamburg
STUDIO
Petersen/Naumann

ART DIRECTOR/DIRECTOR
Bill Argus
COPYWRITER
Peter Gardiner
CREATIVE DIRECTOR
Gary Prouk
PRODUCER
Frances Smith
AGENCY
Scali, McCabe, Sloves
CLIENT
Canadian Childrens Foundation

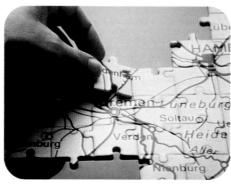

POINT.
VO: This is a cancer. If you give us a little help, we can stop it for a while. If you give us a lot of help, we might have enough time to stop it forever. The Spanish Cancer Association. A million thanks.

PUZZLE.
VO: Hamburg, Dortmund, Frankfurt, Munich, Dresden, and Berlin anyone can find. But, who brings people in Mellingen, Ostheim, Geiselhöring, Wöllstein, and Manfeld their letter and packages? We do. Because on our map there are no blank spaces. POST SERVICE. We've taken on a big job.

KIDS HELP PHONE.
SFX: Music up.
VO: This isn't the most important reason to give money to Kids Help Phone. Neither is this. As hard as it may be to believe, neither is this. Even this isn't the reason. Sadly and terribly, this is the most...
SFX: Busy signal.
VO: ...important reason to give money to Kids Help Phone.

ADVERTISING

ART DIRECTOR
Eddie Bones
COPYWRITER
Neil Williams
PRODUCER
Barbara Simon
DIRECTOR
Kevin Hewitt
AGENCY
DMB&B
CLIENT
COI/Department of Transport

ART DIRECTOR
Atsushi Mizukawa
CREATIVE DIRECTOR
Mamoru Inoue
PRODUCER
Takahiro Kashiwakura
DIRECTOR
Masaya Yamamoto
AGENCY
Dentsu Inc./Taiyo Kikaku Co., Ltd.
CLIENT
Tokyo Metropolitan Government

ART DIRECTOR/CREATIVE DIRECTOR
Mark Denton
COPYWRITER/CREATIVE DIRECTOR
Chris Palmer
PRODUCER
Paul Fenton
DIRECTOR
Bert Sprote
AGENCY
Simons Palmer

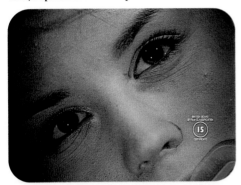

EYES.
POLICEMAN: Have you been drinking, sir?
PARAMEDIC #1: Stand clear.
DRUNK DRIVER: Just a quick one. I thought I'd be okay. (*pause*) Is she gonna be all right?
PARAMEDIC #1: Stand clear.
POLICEMAN: They're doing the best they can, sir.
PARAMEDIC #2: Still no pulse. Still no response. Pupils not reacting.
PARAMEDIC #1: Still nothing. The patient is now asystolic.
DRUNK DRIVER: (*distressed*) I didn't mean it!
SFX: 1/2-second silence. Familiar chaotic sounds from scene of a road accident throughout the spot. Sound of breathing apparatus.
PARAMEDIC #1: One. Two. Three. Four. Five.
DRUNK DRIVER: Is she gonna be all right? Look, make her be all right.
POLICEMAN: Alright, calm down, sir. (*pause*) Were you the driver of the vehicle, sir?
SFX: Sound of breathing apparatus.
PARAMEDIC #1: One. Two. Three. Four. Five.
PARAMEDIC #2: No pulse. No response.
PARAMEDIC #1: Patient still in V.F. Charging up to 360.

TEAM PORTRAIT.
VO: Remember when Britannia ruled the waves...My! What a team we had then!!! Boots Wellington...Chopper Dickens... Dangerous Darwin... Nobbler Nightingale... Bomber Brunel...John Marston...
JUDGE: Who?
CHOIR: Good old John Marston, a great Victorian bloke. He brought us Marston's...the first ale from casks of oak...brewed the Burton Union way up until the present day...and Pedigree's his finest brew in all the land!
CROWD: Hurrah!!!
VO: Thank Heavens some things are what they used to be.

Special Effects

ART DIRECTOR
Tom Notman

COPYWRITER
Alastair Wood

PRODUCER
Paul Rothwell

DIRECTOR
David Garpath

AGENCY
BSB Dorland Ltd.

CLIENT
Tennents

Special Effects

ART DIRECTOR
Tom Notman

COPYWRITER
Alastair Wood

PRODUCER
Barry Stephenson

DIRECTOR
Richard Dean

AGENCY
BSB Dorland Ltd.

CLIENT
Woolworth

Promotional Video

ART DIRECTOR
Pau Bosch

PRODUCER
Rafael Garcia Mediano

DIRECTOR
Juan Cueto

STUDIO
Canal + Spain

CLIENT
Canal + Spain

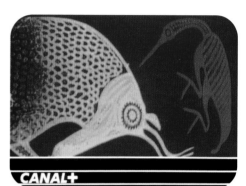

BEACH.
SFX: 1/2-second silence.
NICK: We're looking for the world's smallest off-license.
MAN: Yes, this is it.
MARK: You haven't any Tennent's Pilsner have you?
MAN: Brewed with Czechoslovakian yeast?
NICK: Yes. To taste a bit different.
MAN: Be careful. There are the last two.
NICK: Don't worry. We will keep it under our hats.
MAN: Is someone pulling your Pilsner?

CHAUFFEUR.
SFX: Natural throughout.
VO: Rich, thick and delicious. There's no ketchup quite like Heinz.

Promotional Video

ART DIRECTOR
Martijn v. Sonsbeek

COPYWRITER/CREATIVE DIRECTOR
Ron Walvisch

PRODUCER
Peter Burger

DIRECTOR
Harre Slokkers

AGENCY
N&W/Leo Burnett

CLIENT
Audi

Promotional Video

ART DIRECTOR
Ryo Honda

COPYWRITERS
Ryo Honda, Yutaka Hoshino

PRODUCER
Shuji Kakimoto

DIRECTOR
Daihachi Yoshida

AGENCY
Denstu Inc./TYO Productions, Inc.

CLIENT
Kyodo Oil Co., Ltd.

Promotional Video

ART DIRECTOR
Ryo Honda

COPYWRITER
Makoto Takenaka

PRODUCERS
Jun Hara, Hirotaka Ogata

DIRECTOR
Keizo Kurita

AGENCY
Dentsu Inc./AOI Advertising Promotion Inc.

CLIENT
Toshiba Co.

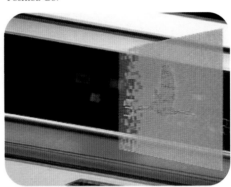

VO: When we decided to sponsor the Dutch Olympic team, we asked ourselves what would our athletes really jump at. A well-cut blazer? Perhaps some anabolic steroids? Ben Johnson's private doctor? Or would they rather have an Audi 80? You've probably guessed. Audi is sponsoring the Dutch Olympic team with 200 Audi 80s.

Promotional Video

ART DIRECTOR
Martijn v. Sonsbeek

COPYWRITER/CREATIVE DIRECTOR
Ron Walvisch

PRODUCER
Peter Burger

DIRECTOR
Harre Slokkers

AGENCY
N&W/Leo Burnett

CLIENT
Audi

Promotional Video

ART DIRECTOR
Ryo Honda

COPYWRITERS
Ryo Honda, Yutaka Hoshino

PRODUCER
Shuji Kakimoto

DIRECTOR
Daihachi Yoshida

AGENCY
Denstu Inc./TYO Productions, Inc.

CLIENT
Kyodo Oil Co., Ltd.

Promotional Video

ART DIRECTOR
Ryo Honda

COPYWRITER
Makoto Takenaka

PRODUCERS
Jun Hara, Hirotaka Ogata

DIRECTOR
Keizo Kurita

AGENCY
Dentsu Inc./AOI Advertising Promotion Inc.

CLIENT
Toshiba Co.

Promotional Video
ART DIRECTORS
Kristina Karlsson, Lewis Hall
DESIGNER
Kristina Karlsson
CREATIVE DIRECTOR
John Ridgeway
STUDIO
TV4 Nordisk Television

Film & TV Art Direction
ART DIRECTOR
Markus Huber
COPYWRITER
Johannes Krammer
PRODUCER
Waltraud Bròz
DIRECTORS
Bady Minck, Stefan Stratil
AGENCY
Demner & Merlicek
CLIENT
Profil Magazine

Film & TV Copywriting
ART DIRECTOR/EXECUTIVE PRODUCER
Klaus Lind
CREATIVE DIRECTOR
Michael Hausberger
PRODUCER
Nicholas Unworth
DIRECTOR
Peter Darrel
AGENCY
BBDO Düsseldorf

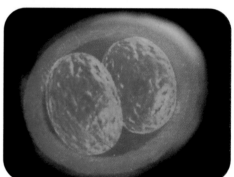

SAD MOOD.
CHANCELLOR: (*singing*) I'm in a sad mood...
VO: Sorry, *Profil* will be out again on Monday.

1/100 SECOND.
VO: In a hundredth of a second this bird beats its wings six times. In a hundredth of a second a cloud can burst. And a great idea can be conceived. All around there are things we can't hear, and things we can't see. In a hundredth of a second life can start. And life can be protected by the Audi safety system Procon-Ten. The safety belts are tightened. The steering wheel is pulled out of the way. In a hundredth of a second! So when it comes to your safety, speed is sometimes essential. Audi.

Newspaper
ART DIRECTOR/DESIGNER
David Sin
COPYWRITER
Dharma Somasundram
CREATIVE DIRECTOR
Rick Lane
AGENCY
Dentsu, Young & Rubicam
CLIENT
The Borneo Bulletin

Newspaper
ART DIRECTOR
Ricardo Colombotto
COPYWRITER
Fabiana Renault
CREATIVE DIRECTORS
Jorge Willegas, Ariel Pari
AGENCY
Graffiti DMB&B

Newspaper
ART DIRECTOR
Edd Baptista
COPYWRITER/CREATIVE DIRECTOR
Peter Holmes
AGENCY
Franklin Dallas Advertising

Newspaper
ART DIRECTOR
Benjamin Vendramin
COPYWRITER
Robert McDougall
CREATIVE DIRECTOR
Larry Anas
AGENCY
Foster Advertising
CLIENT
Revlon

Newspaper

ART DIRECTOR/DESIGNER/COPYWRITER/
CREATIVE DIRECTOR
Manfred Knuth

PHOTOGRAPHER
Charles Liddal

AGENCY
Zender-Fang

Newspaper

ART DIRECTOR
Andy Clarke

COPYWRITER
Jim Aitchison

CREATIVE DIRECTORS
Jim Aitchison, Norman Alcuri

AGENCY
The Ball Partnership Euro ESCG

Newspaper

ART DIRECTOR
Jim Whitney

COPYWRITER
Vaughn Whalen

CREATIVE DIRECTOR
Mark Giacomelli

AGENCY
Robins Sharpe Assoc. Ltd.

CLIENT
American Standard

Newspaper

ART DIRECTOR/COPYWRITER
Antony Redman

CREATIVE DIRECTORS
Jim Aitchison, Norman Alcuri

AGENCY
The Ball Partnership Euro RSCG

Newspaper
ART DIRECTOR/CREATIVE DIRECTOR
Ken Ichihashi
COPYWRITERS
Eiichi Yanagisawa, Masaki Hayashi,
Masahiro Yoshimura, Ken Ichihashi,
Haruo Kubota, Shunichiro Kon,
Koichi Hama, Katsushi Ishikawa
AGENCY
Tokyo Agency, Inc.
CLIENT
Volkswagen

Newspaper
ART DIRECTOR
Andy Clarke
COPYWRITER
Jim Aitchison
CREATIVE DIRECTORS
Jon Aitchison, Norman Alcuri
PHOTOGRAPHER
Alex Kaikeong
AGENCY
The Ball Partnership Euro RSCG

Newspaper
ART DIRECTOR
Annette Quinlivan
COPYWRITER
Jenny Stock
CREATIVE DIRECTOR
Paul Jones
AGENCY
DDB Needham Sydney
CLIENT
Sun Herald

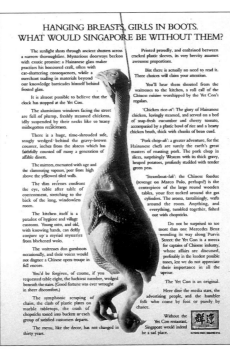

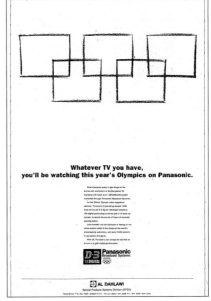

Newspaper
ART DIRECTORS
Keiichi Matsuda, Isshow Matsushiro
COPYWRITERS
Reiko Negishi, Isshow Matsushiro
PHOTOGRAPHER
Kou Chifusa
STUDIO
Ad Brain
AGENCY
Denstu Inc.
CLIENT
The Long-Term Credit Bank
of Japan, Ltd.

Newspaper
ART DIRECTOR
Rafael Ramos
COPYWRITER
Faruk Cassis
AGENCY
JMC/Young & Rubicam
CLIENT
Ceteco

Newspaper
ART DIRECTOR
Don Nicolson
CREATIVE DIRECTOR/COPYWRITER
Edward Jones
ILLUSTRATOR
Bobot Manginsay
AGENCY
Saatchi & Saatchi
CLIENT
Dahlawi/Panasonic

Newspaper
ART DIRECTOR
Antony Redman
CREATIVE DIRECTORS
Jim Aitchison, Norman Alcuri
COPYWRITER
Antony Redman, Jim Aitchison
PHOTOGRAPHER
Alex Kaikeong
AGENCY
The Ball Partnership Euro RSCG

Newspaper
ART DIRECTOR
Gerard Stamp
CREATIVE DIRECTOR
Andrew Cracknell
DESIGNER
Trevor Slabber
COPYWRITER
Loz Simpson
ILLUSTRATOR
Barry Driscoll
AGENCY
BSB Dorland Ltd.

Newspaper
ART DIRECTOR
Gerard Stamp
CREATIVE DIRECTOR
Andrew Cracknell
DESIGNER
Trevor Slabber
COPYWRITER
Loz Simpson
AGENCY
BSB Dorland Ltd.

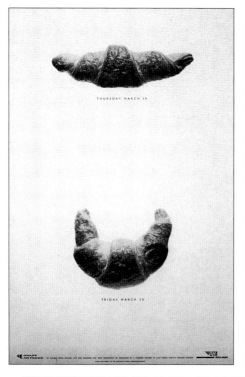

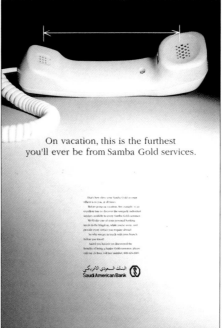

Newspaper
ART DIRECTOR
Martijn V. Sonsbeek
CREATIVE DIRECTOR/COPYWRITER
Ron Walvisch
PHOTOGRAPHER
Jaap Vliegenthart
AGENCY
N&W/Leo Burnett
CLIENT
NCM

Newspaper
ART DIRECTOR
Bobot Manginsay
PHOTOGRAPHER
Geoffrey Adams
AGENCY
Saatchi & Saatchi
CLIENT
Saudi American Bank

Newspaper
ART DIRECTOR
Albert Poon
CREATIVE DIRECTOR/COPYWRITER
Neil Webster
PHOTOGRAPHER
Yenakat Studio
AGENCY
Dentsu, Young & Rubicam
CLIENT
Swedish Motors (BKK)

Newspaper
ART DIRECTOR
Yoichi Komatu
COPYWRITER
Tetsuya Sakota
PHOTOGRAPHER
Y. Uchibori
STUDIO
Asatu Inc.
CLIENT
Toshiba Inc.

Newspaper
ART DIRECTOR
Norman Alcuri
CREATIVE DIRECTORS/COPYWRITERS
Norman Alcuri, Jim Aitchison
PHOTOGRAPHER
Alex Kaikeong
AGENCY
The Ball, Partnership Euro RSCG

Newspaper
ART DIRECTOR
Jörg Birker
CREATIVE DIRECTOR/COPYWRITER
André Benker
PHOTOGRAPHER
Peter Forster
AGENCY
Advico Young & Rubicam
CLIENT
Mazda (Suisse) SA

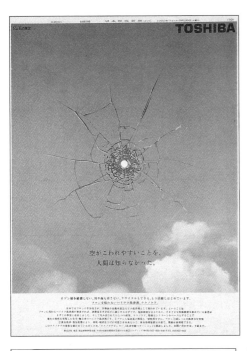

Newspaper
ART DIRECTOR
Jörg Birker
CREATIVE DIRECTOR/COPYWRITER
André Benker
PHOTOGRAPHER
Andi Rosasco
AGENCY
Advico Young & Rubicam
CLIENT
Mazda (Suisse) SA

Newspaper
ART DIRECTOR/CREATIVE DIRECTOR
Les Broude
COPYWRITERS
Les Broude, Jane Clarke
PHOTOGRAPHER
A. Avlonitis
AGENCY
McCann-Erickson
CLIENT
Marketplace

Newspaper
ART DIRECTOR/CREATIVE DIRECTOR
Les Broude
COPYWRITER
Jane Clarke
PHOTOGRAPHER
A. Avlonitis
AGENCY
McCann-Erickson
CLIENT
Marketplace

Newspaper
ART DIRECTOR
Antonie Reinhard
CREATIVE DIRECTOR/COPYWRITER
Stephan Michel
ILLUSTRATOR
Martin Vivian
AGENCY
Seiler DDB Needham, Atelier Jaquet
CLIENT
ZVSM

Newspaper
ART DIRECTOR/CREATIVE DIRECTOR
Hein Botha
COPYWRITER
Hugh Bush
AGENCY
Young & Rubicam
CLIENT
M-Net

Newspaper
ART DIRECTOR/CREATIVE DIRECTOR
Pieter van Velsen
CREATIVE DIRECTOR/COPYWRITER
Wim Ubachs
PHOTOGRAPHER
Malcolm Venville
AGENCY
Saatchi & Saatchi
CLIENT
Pon's Automobliehandel/Audi

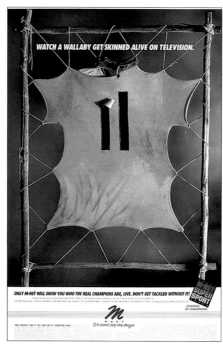

Newspaper
ART DIRECTOR
Michael McLaughlin
COPYWRITER
Stephen Creet
PHOTOGRAPHER
Nigel Dickson
AGENCY
MacLaren:Lintas Inc.
CLIENT
Molson Breweries of Canada

Newspaper
ART DIRECTOR
Shuji Muya
DESIGNERS
Naoki Nakano, Takashi Ohta
PHOTOGRAPHER
Seiji Takihara
AGENCY
Daiko Advertising Inc.
CLIENT
Matsushita Electric Industrial Co., Ltd.

Newspaper
ART DIRECTOR/COPYWRITER
Daniel Pezzi
AGENCY
JMC/Young & Rubicam
CLIENT
Acide

Newspaper/Campaign
ART DIRECTOR
Cathy Heng
CREATIVE DIRECTOR
Jeremey Pemberton
COPYWRITER
Tony Brugnull
PHOTOGRAPHER
Richard Lenney
AGENCY
DMB&B

Newspaper/Campaign
ART DIRECTOR
Alma Carrara
CREATIVE DIRECTORS
Gianfranco Marabelli, Enrico Bonomini
COPYWRITER
Andrea Ballarini
AGENCY
Verba DDB Needham

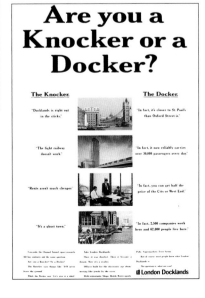

Newspaper/Campaign

ART DIRECTOR
Edith Kilger

CREATIVE DIRECTOR
Norbert Herold

COPYWRITER
Dietmar Dahmen

AGENCY
Heye + Partner

CLIENT
Betten Rid

Newspaper/Campaign

ART DIRECTOR/CREATIVE DIRECTOR/DESIGNER
Julia Koo

COPYWRITER
Brian Daisley

PHOTOGRAPHERS
Scott C. Schulman, J. LaBounty,
Toni Hafkenscheid

AGENCY
Grey Advertising

STUDIO
Ken Koo Creative

Newspaper/Campaign
ART DIRECTOR/CREATIVE DIRECTOR
Ken Ichihashi
DESIGNERS
Masaki Hayashi, Masahiro Yoshimura
COPYWRITER
Eiichi Yanagisawa
AGENCY
DDB Needham Worldwide/
Tokyu Agency, Inc.
CLIENT
Volkswagon Audi Nippon KK

Newspaper/Campaign
ART DIRECTOR/CREATIVE DIRECTOR
Les Broude
COPYWRITERS
Jane Clarke, Les Broude
PHOTOGRAPHER
A. Avlonitis
AGENCY
McCann-Erickson
CLIENT
Marketplace

Newspaper/Campaign
ART DIRECTOR/PHOTOGRAPHER
Andy Clarke
COPYWRITER
Danny Higgins
CREATIVE DIRECTORS
Norman Alcuri, Jim Aitchison
AGENCY
The Ball Partnership Euro RSCG

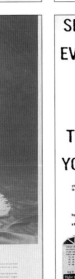

Newspaper/Campaign

ART DIRECTOR/CREATIVE DIRECTOR
Tomek Luczynski

COPYWRITER
Johannes Krammer

DESIGNER
Doris Forsthuber

PHOTOGRAPHER
Thomas Popinger

AGENCY
Demner & Merlicek

Newspaper/Campaign

ART DIRECTOR
Shosha Gurfinkel

CREATIVE DIRECTOR
Arza Anolik

COPYWRITER
Vered Lavi

PHOTOGRAPHER
Menachem Reiss

AGENCY
Bing Linial

CLIENT
Xerox-Isreal

Newspaper/Campaign

ART DIRECTOR
Elisabetta Torossi

CREATIVE DIRECTOR
Franco Moretti

COPYWRITER
Fabrizio Russo

AGENCY
McCann-Erickson Italiana

CLIENT
Coca-Cola Italiana

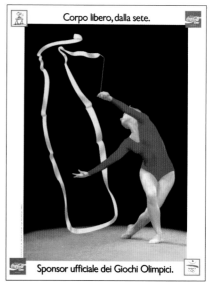

Newspaper/Campaign
ART DIRECTOR
Michael McLaughlin
COPYWRITER
Stephen Creet
PHOTOGRAPHER
Nigel Dickson
AGENCY
MacLaren:Lintas Inc.
CLIENT
Molson Breweries of Canada

Newspaper/Campaign
ART DIRECTOR
Kazuo Okada
DESIGNERS
Masahiro Morinaga, Mizue Harimoto
COPYWRITERS
Kazuo Gemma, Hiroki Haruna,
Tsuneaki Tsummra
AGENCY
Hakuhodo Inc.
CLIENT
Olympus Optical Co., Ltd.

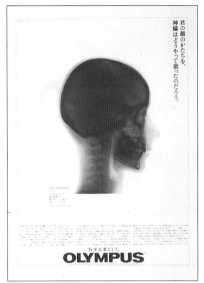

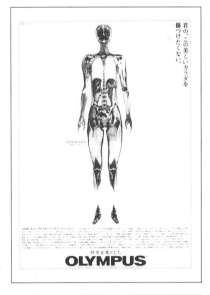

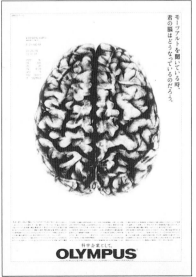

Newspaper/Campaign

ART DIRECTOR
Daniel Meier

CREATIVE DIRECTOR
Markus Gabriel

COPYWRITER
Pascal Schaub

AGENCY
McCann-Erickson

Newspaper/Campaign

ART DIRECTORS
Jim Aitchison, Sue Robertson

CREATIVE DIRECTORS
Jim Aitchison, Norman Alcuri

COPYWRITERS
Stuart D'Rozario, Jim Aitchison

AGENCY
The Ball Partnership Euro RSCG

Public-Service Newspaper

ART DIRECTOR/CREATIVE DIRECTOR
Norman Alcuri

COPYWRITER/CREATIVE DIRECTOR
Jim Aitchison

PHOTOGRAPHER
Alex Kaikeong

AGENCY
The Ball Partnership Euro RSCG

Public-Service Newspaper

ART DIRECTOR/COPYWRITER/CREATIVE DIRECTOR
Peter Holmes

AGENCY
Franklin Dallas Advertising

CLIENT
Metropolitan Toronto Ambulance

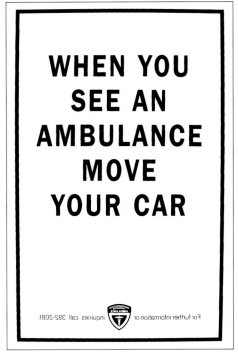

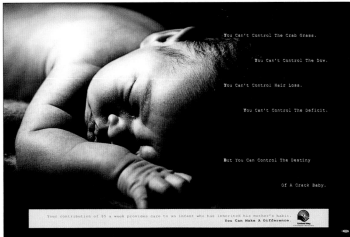

Public-Service Newspaper

ART DIRECTOR
Lynda Chalmers

COPYWRITER
Joe Perry

CREATIVE DIRECTOR
Mike Drazen

PHOTOGRAPHER
Claude Vazquez

AGENCY
Earle Palmer Brown & Spiro

CLIENT
United Way

Public-Service Newspaper

ART DIRECTOR
Lynda Chalmers

COPYWRITER
Joe Perry

CREATIVE DIRECTOR
Mike Drazen

PHOTOGRAPHER
Claude Vazquez

AGENCY
Earle Palmer Brown & Spiro

CLIENT
United Way

Public-Service Newspaper

ART DIRECTOR
Dieter Hofman

COPYWRITER
Hansjörg Zürcher

AGENCY
Advico Young & Rubicam

CLIENT
Badener Tagblatt

Public-Service Newspaper

ART DIRECTOR
Kevin Bratley

COPYWRITER
John Townshend

PHOTOGRAPHER
Barry Lategan

TYPOGRAPHER
Leonie Brierley

AGENCY
DMB&B

CLIENT
Cancer Research

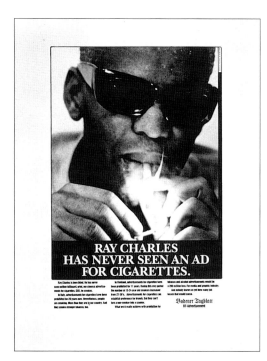

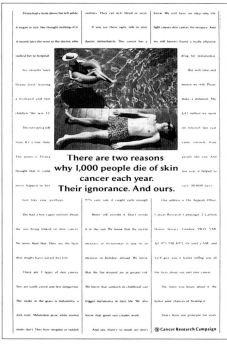

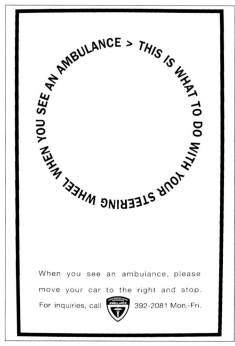

Public-Service Newspaper

ART DIRECTOR
Kevin Bratley

COPYWRITER
John Townshend

PHOTOGRAPHER
Rory Carnegie

TYPOGRAPHERS
Leonie Brierley, Ed Church

AGENCY
DMB&B

CLIENT
Cancer Research

Public-Service Newspaper

ART DIRECTOR/CREATIVE DIRECTOR
Tony Riggs

COPYWRITER/CREATIVE DIRECTOR
Roger Holdsworth

PHOTOGRAPHER
Rory Carnegie

AGENCY
DMB&B

CLIENT
COI/Department of Employment

Public-Service Newspaper

ART DIRECTOR/CREATIVE DIRECTOR
Peter Holmes

COPYWRITERS
Michael O'Reilly, Peter Holmes

AGENCY
Franklin Dallas Advertising

CLIENT
Metropolitan Toronto Ambulance

Public-Service Newspaper/Campaign

ART DIRECTOR
Lynda Chalmers

COPYWRITER
Joe Perry

CREATIVE DIRECTOR
Mike Drazen

PHOTOGRAPHER
Claude Vazquez

AGENCY
Earle Palmer Brown & Spiro

CLIENT
United Way

Public-Service Newspaper/Campaign

ART DIRECTOR
Gary Monaghan

COPYWRITER
Gary Sollof

PHOTOGRAPHER
Rory Carnegie

CREATIVE DIRECTORS
Roger Holdsworth, Tony Riggs

AGENCY
DMB&B

CLIENT
COI/Department of Employment

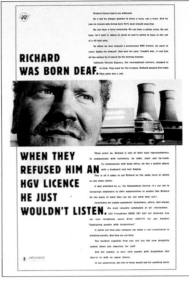

Magazine
AGENCY
The Jupiter Drawing Room

Magazine
ART DIRECTOR
Adam Hunt
COPYWRITER
Ben Nott
CREATIVE DIRECTOR
Paul Jones
AGENCY
DDB Needham Sydney
CLIENT
Adnews

Magazine
ART DIRECTOR
Jim Saunders
COPYWRITER
Edward Richards
CREATIVE DIRECTOR
David Bourne
PHOTOGRAPHER
Peter Luxton
AGENCY
Magnus Nankervis & Curl
CLIENT
Cypress Lakes Golf & Country Club

Magazine
ART DIRECTORS
Don Nicolson, Bobot Manginsay
COPYWRITER/CREATIVE DIRECTOR
Edward Jones
PHOTOGRAPHER
Ian Pearce
AGENCY
Saatchi & Saatchi
CLIENT
Emam/Fuji

Magazine
ART DIRECTORS
Andy Clarke, Jim Aitchison
COPYWRITER
Jim Aitchison
CREATIVE DIRECTORS
Jim Aitchison, Norman Alcuri
AGENCY
The Ball Partnership Euro RSCG
CLIENT
Singapore Stock Exchange

Magazine
ART DIRECTOR
Michael McLaughlin
COPYWRITER
Stephen Creet
CREATIVE DIRECTORS
Michael McLaughlin, Stephen Creet,
Bill Durnan
AGENCY
MacLaren:Lintas, Inc.
CLIENT
Lever Brothers

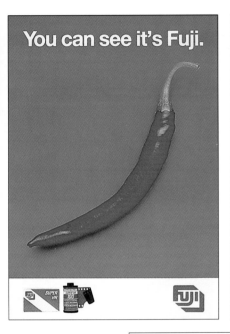

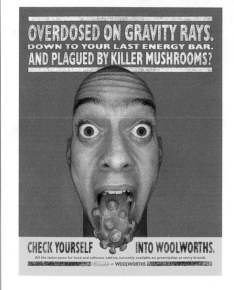

Magazine
ART DIRECTOR
Tom Notman
COPYWRITER
Alistair Wood
DESIGNER
Trevor Slabber
CREATIVE DIRECTOR
Chips Hardy
PHOTOGRAPHER
D. Chalmers
AGENCY
BSB Dorland Ltd.

Magazine
ART DIRECTOR
Bruce McKay
COPYWRITER
Andrew Shaddick
CREATIVE DIRECTOR
Mike Smith
PHOTOGRAPHER
Shin Sugino
AGENCY
Miller Myers Bruce Dallacosta

Magazine
ART DIRECTOR
Michael McLaughlin
COPYWRITER
Stephen Creet
CREATIVE DIRECTORS
Stephen Creet, Michael McLaughlin,
Bill Durnan
AGENCY
MacLaren:Lintas Inc.
CLIENT
Best Foods

Magazine
ART DIRECTORS
Jim Aitchison, Grover Tham
COPYWRITER
Jim Aitchison
CREATIVE DIRECTORS
Jim Aitchison, Norman Alcuri
AGENCY
The Ball Partnership Euro RSCG

Magazine
ART DIRECTOR
Enric Aguilera
COPYWRITER/CREATIVE DIRECTOR
Toni Segarra
PHOTOGRAPHERS
Antonio Gomez, R. Serrano
AGENCY
Delvico Bates Barcelona

Magazine
ART DIRECTORS
Janna Thür, Io Wögenstein
COPYWRITER
Angelo Peer
DESIGNER
Io Wögenstein
PHOTOGRAPHER
Heinz Schmölzer
AGENCY
Demner & Merlicek
CLIENT
Wirtschafts-Trend-Verlag

Magazine

ART DIRECTOR
Enric Aguilera

COPYWRITER
Toni Segarra

CREATIVE DIRECTORS
Toni Segarra, F. Fernandez de Castro

PHOTOGRAPHER
David Levin

AGENCY
Delvico Bates Barcelona

Magazine

ART DIRECTOR
Minoru Inoue

COPYWRITER
Takashi Yaoi

DESIGNER
Kazuto Arai

PHOTOGRAPHER
Junji Yoshida

AGENCY
Daiko Advertising

CLIENT
Matsushita Electric Industrial Co., Ltd.

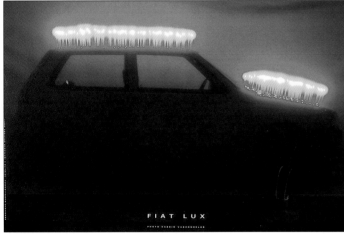
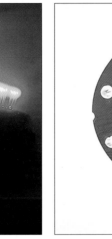

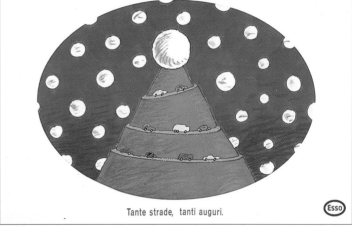

Magazine

ART DIRECTOR/CREATIVE DIRECTOR
Marcello Serpa

AGENCY
DM9 Publicidade

CLIENT
Fiat

Magazine

ART DIRECTOR/ILLUSTRATOR
Tonino Risuleo

COPYWRITER
Oscar Molinari

CREATIVE DIRECTORS
Antonio Maccario, Oscar Molina

AGENCY
McCann Erickson Rome

CLIENT
Esso

Magazine

ART DIRECTOR
Andy Clarke

COPYWRITER
Antony Redman

CREATIVE DIRECTORS
Jim Aitchison, Norman Alcuri

PHOTOGRAPHER
Alex Kaikeong

AGENCY
The Ball Partnership Euro RSCG

Magazine

ART DIRECTOR
Michael Kirkland

COPYWRITER
Zak Mroueh

CREATIVE DIRECTOR
Michael Paul

PHOTOGRAPHER
George Simhoni

AGENCY
SMW Advertising Ltd.

CLIENT
Merrell Dow Pharmeceuticals

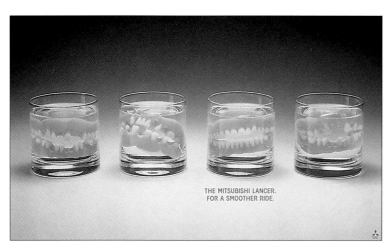

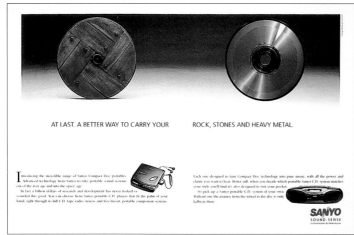

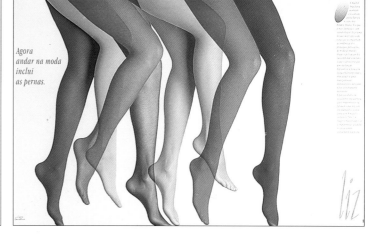

Magazine

ART DIRECTOR/CREATIVE DIRECTOR
Hein Botha

COPYWRITER
Hugh Bush

AGENCY
Young & Rubicam Transvaal

CLIENT
Teltron

Magazine

ART DIRECTOR
Marcello Serpa

COPYWRITER
Alexandre Gama

CREATIVE DIRECTOR
Nizan Guanaes

AGENCY
DM9 Publicidade

CLIENT
Grupo Rosset

Magazine
ART DIRECTOR
Marcello Serpa
COPYWRITER
Alexandre Gama
CREATIVE DIRECTOR
Nizan Guanaes
AGENCY
DM9 Publicidade
CLIENT
Grupo Rosset

Magazine
ART DIRECTOR
Marcello Serpa
COPYWRITER
Alexandre Gama
CREATIVE DIRECTOR
Nizan Guanaes
AGENCY
DM9 Publicidade
CLIENT
Grupo Rosset

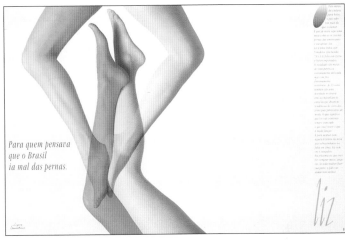

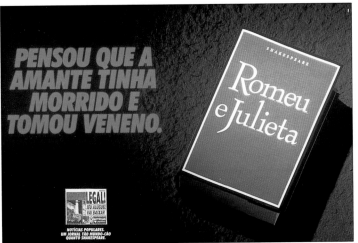

Magazine
ART DIRECTOR
Clark Prosperi
CREATIVE DIRECTOR
Luiz Toledo
COPYWRITER
Eugenio Mohallem
AGENCY
DM9 Publicidade
CLIENT
Noticias Populares Newspaper

Magazine
ART DIRECTOR
Clark Prosperi
CREATIVE DIRECTOR
Luiz Toledo
COPYWRITER
Eugenio Mohallem
AGENCY
DM9 Publicidade
CLIENT
Noticias Populares Newspaper

Magazine
ART DIRECTOR
Luciano Zuffo
COPYWRITERS
Murilo Felisberto, Rondon Fernandes
CREATIVE DIRECTORS
Roberto Duailibi, Murilo Felisberto
AGENCY
DPZ Propaganda SA
CLIENT
LBV

Magazine
ART DIRECTOR/COPYWRITER
Antony Redman
CREATIVE DIRECTORS
Jim Aitchison, Norman Alcuri
AGENCY
The Ball Partnership Euro RSCG

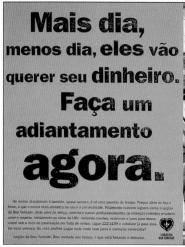

Magazine
ART DIRECTOR
Jim Saunders
COPYWRITER
Edward Richards
CREATIVE DIRECTOR
David Bourne
PHOTOGRAPHER
James Wood
AGENCY
Magnus Nankervis & Curl
CLIENT
Thai Airways International

Magazine
ART DIRECTOR
Nick Simons
CREATIVE DIRECTOR
R. Williams
DESIGNER
Trevor Slabber
COPYWRITER
David Prideaux
PHOTOGRAPHER
D. Stewart
AGENCY
BSB Dorland Ltd.

Magazine
ART DIRECTOR
David Wong
COPYWRITER
Ed Tettemer
CREATIVE DIRECTOR
Mike Drazen
PHOTOGRAPHER
Craig Cutler
AGENCY
Earle Palmer Brown & Spiro
CLIENT
General Accident

Magazine
ART DIRECTOR
Marcello Serpa
COPYWRITER
Alexandre Gama
CREATIVE DIRECTOR
Nizan Guanaes
AGENCY
DM9 Publicidade
CLIENT
Petybon

Magazine
ART DIRECTOR
Shotaro Sakaguchi
COPYWRITER
Takashi Yamamoto
CREATIVE DIRECTOR
Kazuo Hatakeyama
PHOTOGRAPHER
Hatsuhiko Okada
AGENCY
Denstu Inc.
CLIENT
Osaka Cable Radio Station

Magazine
ART DIRECTOR
Martin Hermans
COPYWRITER
Mark Bell
CREATIVE DIRECTOR
Michael Fitzpatrick
PHOTOGRAPHERS
Andris Apse, Dennis Hitchcock
AGENCY
Backer Spielvogel Bates
CLIENT
Arnotts Biscuits Ltd.

Magazine

ART DIRECTOR
Ed McGrady

COPYWRITER
Ed Tettemer

CREATIVE DIRECTOR
Mike Drazen

PHOTOGRAPHER
Steve Hone

AGENCY
Earle Palmer Brown & Spiro

CLIENT
Turner

Magazine

ART DIRECTOR
Roberto Cipolla

COPYWRITER/CREATIVE DIRECTOR
Luiz Toledo

AGENCY
DM9 Publicidade

CLIENT
CIA. Maritima

Magazine

ART DIRECTOR
Marcello Serpa

COPYWRITER
Alexandre Gama

CREATIVE DIRECTOR
Nizan Guanaes

AGENCY
DM9 Publicidade

CLIENT
Petybon

Magazine

ART DIRECTOR
Marcello Serpa

COPYWRITER
Alexandre Gama

CREATIVE DIRECTOR
Nizan Guanaes

AGENCY
DM9 Publicidade

CLIENT
Sharp

Magazine

ART DIRECTOR/CREATIVE DIRECTOR
Rodger Williams

COPYWRITER/CREATIVE DIRECTOR
Chips Hardy

PHOTOGRAPHER
David Stewart

TYPOGRAPHER
Trevor Slabber

AGENCY
BSB Dorland Ltd.

Magazine

ART DIRECTOR
Nick Simons

COPYWRITER
David Prideaux

CREATIVE DIRECTORS
Chips Hardy, Rodgers Williams

PHOTOGRAPHER
David Stewart

TYPOGRAPHER
Trevor Slabber

AGENCY
BSB Dorland Ltd.

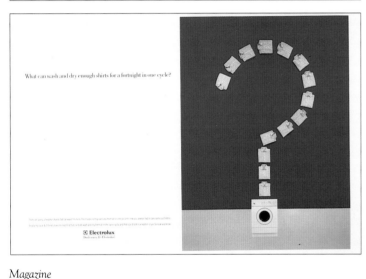

Magazine

ART DIRECTOR/CREATIVE DIRECTOR
Rodger Williams

COPYWRITER/CREATIVE DIRECTOR
Chips Hardy

PHOTOGRAPHER
David Stewart

TYPOGRAPHER
Trevor Slabber

AGENCY
BSB Dorland Ltd.

Magazine

ART DIRECTOR
Stuart Wilson

COPYWRITER
David McKenzie

CREATIVE DIRECTORS
Loz Simpson, Gerard Stamp

PHOTOGRAPHER
B. Barbey

TYPOGRAPHER
Trevor Slabber

AGENCY
BSB Dorland Ltd.

Magazine

ART DIRECTOR
Stuart Wilson

COPYWRITER
David McKenzie

CREATIVE DIRECTORS
Loz Simpson, Gerard Stamp

PHOTOGRAPHER
D. McCullin

TYPOGRAPHER
Trevor Slabber

AGENCY
BSB Dorland Ltd.

Magazine/Campaign

ART DIRECTOR
Stuart Wilson

CREATIVE DIRECTORS
L. Simpson, G. Stamp

COPYWRITER
David McKenzie

PHOTOGRAPHER
B. Barbey

AGENCY
BSB Dorland Ltd.

Magazine

ART DIRECTOR
Martin Hermans

COPYWRITER
Mark Bell

CREATIVE DIRECTOR
Michael Fitzpatrick

PHOTOGRAPHERS
Andris Apse, Dennis Hitchcock

AGENCY
Backer Spielvogel Bates

CLIENT
Arnotts Biscuits Ltd.

Magazine/Campaign

ART DIRECTOR
Pascal Midavaine

COPYWRITER
Pascale Chadenat

ILLUSTRATOR
James Dignan

PHOTOGRAPHER
Tierney Gearon

AGENCY
BDDP

CLIENT
3 Suisses

Magazine/Campaign

ART DIRECTOR
Tiana Lapper

CREATIVE DIRECTOR
Rita Haque

COPYWRITER
Khalid Chaudhari

PHOTOGRAPHER
Charles Liddall

AGENCY
DMB&B/Tokyu

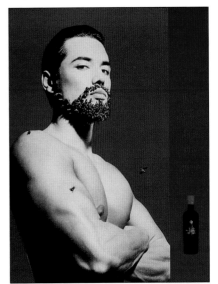

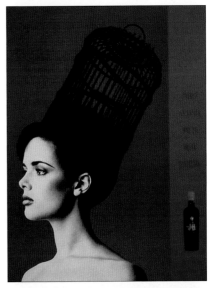

Magazine/Campaign

ART DIRECTOR
Andy Clarke

CREATIVE DIRECTORS
Jim Aitchison, Norman Alcuri

COPYWRITER
Danny Higgins

PHOTOGRAPHER
Charles Liddall

AGENCY
The Ball Partnership Euro RSCG

Magazine/Campaign

ART DIRECTOR
Hervé Lopez

CREATIVE DIRECTORS
Rémi Babinet, Philippe Pollet Villard

COPYWRITER
Jaques Strang

PHOTOGRAPHER
Chrisophe Rillet

AGENCY
BDDP

CLIENT
Virgin Megastore

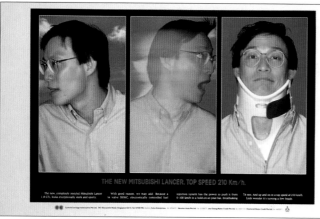

If you want to poison your wife on a Sunday, you can poison her. But if you'd rather go out and buy a good thriller, too bad for your wife.

In 1992 selling books and records on Sundays is still prohibited.

In the case of a sudden urge for poetry on a Sunday, kindly wait till Monday.

Magazine/Campaign

ART DIRECTOR
Rodger Williams

CREATIVE DIRECTORS
Rodger Williams, Chips Hardy

DESIGNER
Trevor Slabber

COPYWRITER
Chips Hardy

PHOTOGRAPHER
D. Stewart

AGENCY
BSB Dorland Ltd.

Magazine/Campaign

ART DIRECTOR
Jim Saunders

CREATIVE DIRECTOR
David Bourne

COPYWRITER
Edward Richards

AGENCY
Magnus Nankervis & Curl

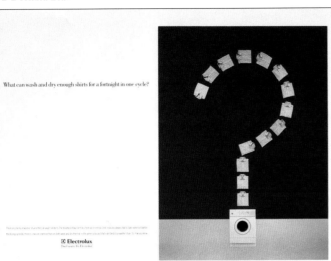

Magazine/Campaign

ART DIRECTOR
Fabio Ferri

CREATIVE DIRECTORS
Guido Cornara, Luca Albanes

COPYWRITER
Stefano Maria Palombi

PHOTOGRAPHER
Ferdinand Scianna

AGENCY
Saatchi & Saatchi

Magazine/Campaign

ART DIRECTOR/CREATIVE DIRECTOR
Ted Curl

COPYWRITER
Gail Shaw

ILLUSTRATOR
Nigel Buchanan

PHOTOGRAPHER
Peter Luxton

AGENCY
Magnus Nankervis & Curl

Magazine/Campaign

ART DIRECTOR/CREATIVE DIRECTOR
Ted Curl

COPYWRITERS
John Nankervis, Gail Shaw

ILLUSTRATOR
Susan Boyle

PHOTOGRAPHER
Jacquie Stevenson

AGENCY
Magnus Nankervis & Curl

Magazine/Campaign

ART DIRECTOR
Masaaki Hiromura

DESIGNER
Takafumi Kusagaya

PHOTOGRAPHER
Robert Tardio

STUDIO
Hiromura Design Office

CLIENT
On Limits Inc.

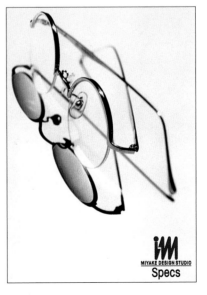

Magazine/Campaign

ART DIRECTOR/DESIGNER
Junichiro Morita

COPYWRITER
Eisaku Sekihashi

AGENCY
JWT Japan Ltd.

CLIENT
Kodak Japan Ltd.

Magazine/Campaign

ART DIRECTOR
Uli Weber

CREATIVE DIRECTORS
Uli Weber, Brigitte Fussnegger

COPYWRITER
Brigitte Fussnegger

PHOTOGRAPHER
Hans Hansen

AGENCY
Leonhardt & Kern Werbung GmbH

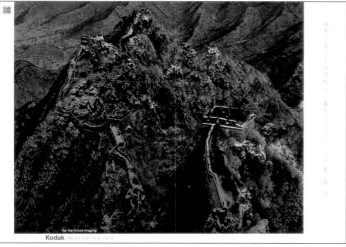

Magazine/Campaign

ART DIRECTOR/CREATIVE DIRECTOR
Ted Curl

COPYWRITER
Gail Shaw

ILLUSTRATOR
Robert Giusti

PHOTOGRAPHER
Phillip Quirk

AGENCY
Magnus Nankervis & Curl

Magazine/Campaign

ART DIRECTOR/DESIGNER
Takashi Nomura

CREATIVE DIRECTOR/COPYWRITER
Eisaku Sekihashi

PHOTOGRAPHER
Yasuhiro Miyahara

AGENCY
JWT Japan Ltd.

CLIENT
Häagen-Dazs Japan Ltd.

Magazine/Campaign

ART DIRECTORS
Takashi Kitamura, Nobuyuki Nakanishi

CREATIVE DIRECTOR
Kazuhide Kimoto

COPYWRITER
David Dach

PHOTOGRAPHER
Michio Kuroda

AGENCY
Hakuhudo Inc.

Magazine/Campaign

ART DIRECTORS/DESIGNERS
Osamu Fukushima, Atsushi Sakurada

COPYWRITER
Tetsuya Sakota

ILLUSTRATOR
Osamu Fukushima

PHOTOGRAPHER
Junko Yamada

AGENCY
Asatsu Inc.

CLIENT
Campbell Japan Inc.

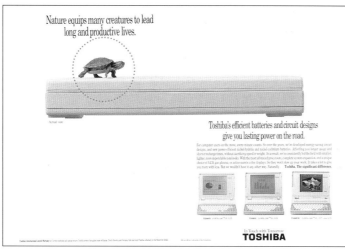

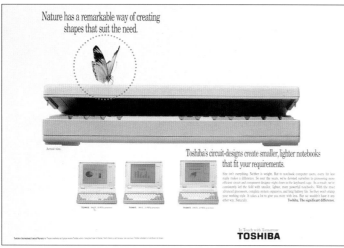

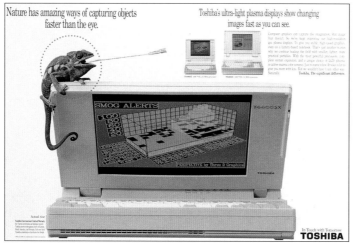

Magazine/Campaign

ART DIRECTOR/CREATIVE DIRECTOR
Fritz Tschirren

COPYWRITER
Marco Ferri

PHOTOGRAPHER
Jean-Pierre Maure

AGENCY
STZ

Magazine/Campaign

ART DIRECTOR
Tomek Luczynski

COPYWRITER
Stefan Pott

GRAPHICS
Petra Engeljehringer

PHOTOGRAPHER
Bernhard Angerer

AGENCY
Demner & Merlicek

CLIENT
Mazda

Il tappeto Sisal rende la casa più bella e accogliente.

Il tappeto Sisal rende la casa più bella e accogliente.

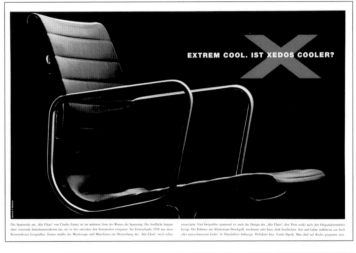

Il tappeto Sisal rende la casa più bella e accogliente.

Magazine/Campaign
ART DIRECTOR
Markus Huber
COPYWRITER
Sabine Gruber
GRAPHICS
Angela Mani, Josef Perndl, Karin Stelzer
PHOTOGRAPHER
Elfie Semotan
AGENCY
Demner & Merlicek
CLIENT
Silhouette

Magazine/Campaign
ART DIRECTORS
Ursula Kerkar, Dhun Cordo
PHOTOGRAPHER
Hemant Shirodkar
PHOTOGRAPHER
Suresh Cordo
AGENCY
Graphitecture
CLIENT
Cox & Kings Travel Ltd.

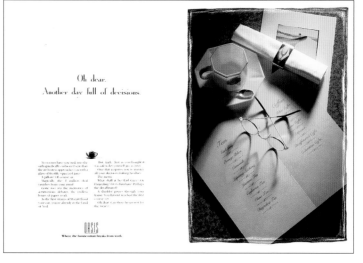

Magazine/Campaign

ART DIRECTOR
Enric Aguilera
COPYWRITER
Toni Segarra
CREATIVE DIRECTORS
Toni Segarra, F. Fernandez de Castro
PHOTOGRAPHER
Ricardo Miras
AGENCY
Delvico Bates Barcelona

Magazine/Campaign

ART DIRECTOR
Enric Aguilera
COPYWRITER
Toni Segarra
CREATIVE DIRECTORS
Toni Segarra, F. Fernandez de Castro
PHOTOGRAPHER
Ricardo Miras
AGENCY
Delvico Bates Barcelona

Magazine/Campaign

ART DIRECTOR
Enric Aguilera
COPYWRITER
Toni Segarra
CREATIVE DIRECTORS
Toni Segarra, F. Fernandez de Castro
PHOTOGRAPHER
Maria Espeus
AGENCY
Delvico Bates Barcelona

Magazine/Campaign

ART DIRECTOR
Agostino Toscana

COPYWRITER/CREATIVE DIRECTOR
Pasquale Barbella

PHOTOGRAPHERS
Arcangelo Argento, Antonio Capa

AGENCY
Barbella Gagliardi Saffrio

CLIENT
Barbella Gagliardi Saffrio

Magazine/Campaign

ART DIRECTOR/CREATIVE DIRECTOR
Hein Botha

COPYWRITER
Hugh Bush

AGENCY
Young & Rubicam Transvaal

CLIENT
Teltron

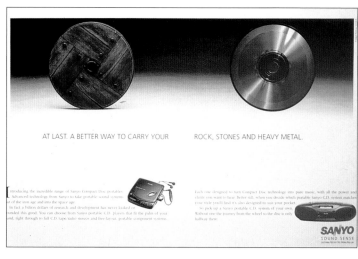

AT LAST. A BETTER WAY TO CARRY YOUR ROCK, STONES AND HEAVY METAL.

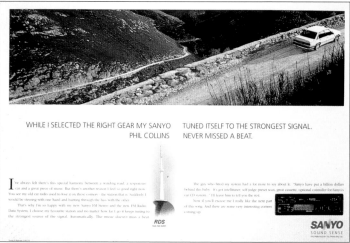

WHILE I SELECTED THE RIGHT GEAR MY SANYO PHIL COLLINS TUNED ITSELF TO THE STRONGEST SIGNAL. NEVER MISSED A BEAT.

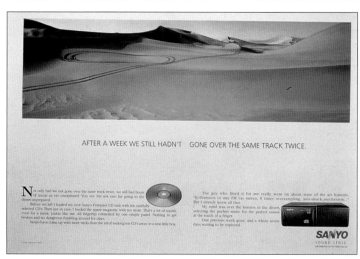

AFTER A WEEK WE STILL HADN'T GONE OVER THE SAME TRACK TWICE.

Magazine/Campaign

ART DIRECTOR
David Snider

COPYWRITER
David Wallen

CREATIVE DIRECTOR
Bill Durnan

PHOTOGRAPHER
Phillip Rostrin

AGENCY
MacLaren:Lintas Inc.

CLIENT
McNeil Consumer Products

Magazine/Campaign

ART DIRECTOR
Larry Gordon

COPYWRITER
David Innis

CREATIVE DIRECTOR
Bill Durnan

PHOTOGRAPHER
George Simhoni

AGENCY
MacLaren:Lintas Inc.

CLIENT
Nestle-Carnation

Magazine/Campaign

ART DIRECTOR
D. Logan

COPYWRITER
D.H. Hoines, G.V.Warsop, S.
Andrew

CREATIVE DIRECTORS
G.V. Warsop, D. Logan, D.H. Hines

AGENCY
The Jupiter Drawing Room

Magazine/Campaign

ART DIRECTOR
Kornelius Wilkens

COPYWRITER
Frank Neyenhuys

CREATIVE DIRECTOR
Klaus Fehsenfeld

AGENCY
W.A.F. Werbegesellschaft

CLIENT
Sender Freies Berlin

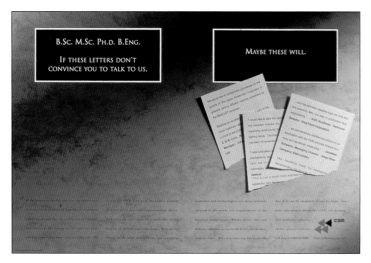

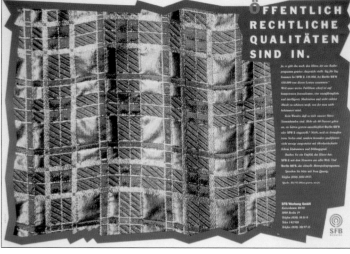

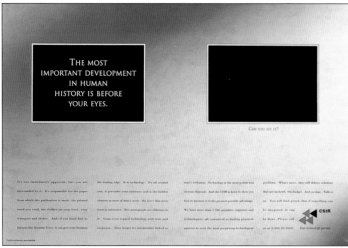

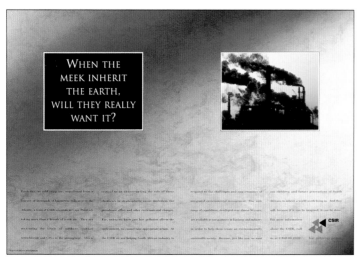

Public-Service Magazine

ART DIRECTOR
Nelson Sinem

COPYWRITER
Jorge Teixeira

AGENCY
Young & Rubicam Portugal

Public-Service Magazine

ART DIRECTOR
Stefano Lidström

COPYWRITER
Håkan Olofsson

AGENCY
Lads Production

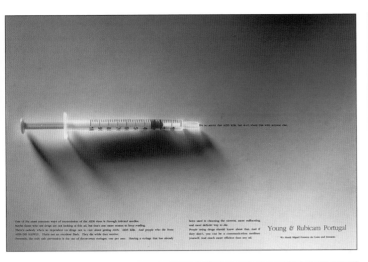

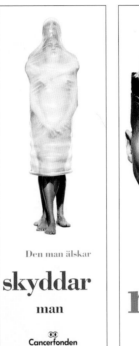

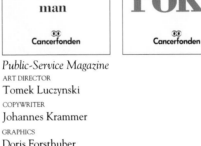

Public-Service Magazine

ART DIRECTOR
Tomek Luczynski

COPYWRITER
Johannes Krammer

GRAPHICS
Doris Forsthuber

AGENCY
Demner & Merlicek

Public-Service Magazine

ART DIRECTOR
Risto Hankaniemi

COPYWRITER
Reijo Taajaranta

AGENCY
Aapiset Oy

CLIENT
HeKu Oy

Public-Service Magazine

ART DIRECTOR
José Ricardo Cabaio

COPYWRITER
Edson Athayde

AGENCY
Young & Rubicam Portugal

Newspaper
ART DIRECTOR
Armin Jochum, Gregor Huhle
CREATIVE DIRECTOR
Thomas Elser, Fritz Reuter
COPYWRITER
Kai Kittelberger
PHOTOGRAPHER
Thomas Kettner
AGENCY
Wensauer DDB Needham

Magazine
ART DIRECTOR/CREATIVE DIRECTOR
Sigi Mayer
COPYWRITER/PHOTOGRAPHER
Horst Stasny
STUDIO
Fotostudio H. Stasny
CLIENT
Mahringer Verlag

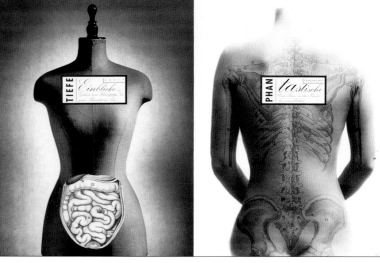

Magazine
ART DIRECTOR
Hans-Georg Pospischil
DESIGNERS
Peter Breul, Bernadette Gotthardt
COPYWRITERS/PHOTOGRAPHERS
Erasmus Schröter, Bernd Hiepe
PUBLICATION
Frankfurter Allgemeine Magazin

Magazine/Series

ART DIRECTOR

Hans-Georg Pospischil

DESIGNERS

Peter Breul, Bernadette Gotthardt

COPYWRITER/PHOTOGRAPHER

Wilfried Bauer

PUBLICATION

Frankfurter Allgemeine Magazin

Magazine/Series

ART DIRECTOR

Hans-Georg Pospischil

DESIGNERS

Peter Breul, Bernadette Gotthardt

COPYWRITER/PHOTOGRAPHER

Bastienne Schmidt

PUBLICATION

Frankfurter Allgemeine Magazin

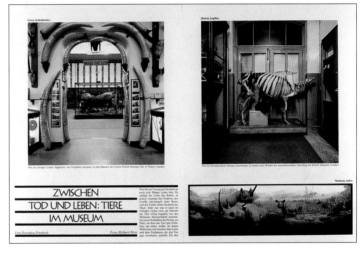

Magazine/Series

ART DIRECTOR

Hans-Georg Pospischil

DESIGNERS

Peter Breul, Bernadette Gotthardt

COPYWRITER/PHOTOGRAPHER

Karl De Keyer

PUBLICATION

Frankfurter Allgemeine Magazin

Magazine/Series

ART DIRECTOR

Hans-Georg Pospischil

DESIGNERS

Peter Breul, Bernadette Gotthardt

COPYWRITER/PHOTOGRAPHER

Richard Ross

PUBLICATION

Frankfurter Allgemeine Magazin

Magazine/Series

ART DIRECTOR
Hans-Georg Pospischil

DESIGNERS
Peter Breul, Bernadette Gotthardt

COPYWRITER/ILLUSTRATOR
Heinz Edelmann

PUBLICATION
Frankfurter Allgemeine Magazin

Book Design

ART DIRECTOR/DESIGNER
Ikko Tanaka

PHOTOGRAPHER
Irving Penn

STUDIO
Ikko Tanaka Design

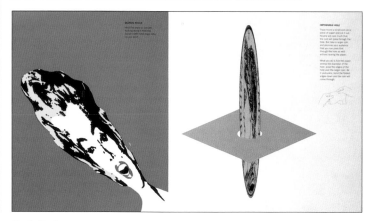

Book Design

ART DIRECTOR/CREATIVE DIRECTOR/
DESIGNER/COPYWRITER
Koeweiden/Postma

PHOTOGRAPHER
Yani

STUDIO
Koeweiden/Postma

Book Design

ART DIRECTOR
David Hillman

DESIGNER/ILLUSTRATOR
Akio Morishima

COPYWRITER
David Gibbs

STUDIO
Pentagram Design

PUBLICATION
Edbury Press

Book Design
ART DIRECTOR
Antonie Reinhard
DESIGNER
Sandra Gaiser
COPYWRITERS
Vrone Malzacher, Martin Volkart
PHOTOGRAPHERS /ILLUSTRATORS
Adrian Fritschi, Christine Stöckli
AGENCY
Seiler DDB Needham, Atelier Jaquet
CLIENT
Schweizer Wirteverband/SHV

Book Design
ART DIRECTOR/DESIGNER/COPYWRITER
Michael Mirfin

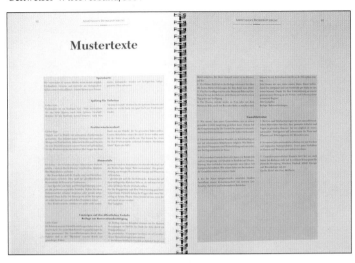

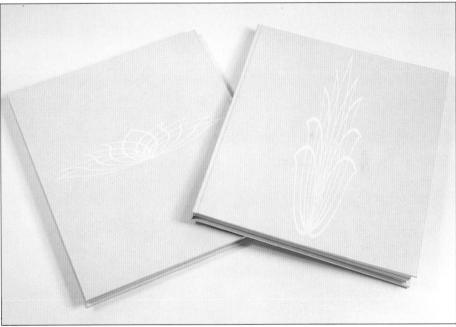

Book Design
ART DIRECTOR
Koichi Hara
CREATIVE DIRECTOR
Shigeo Goto
DESIGNERS
Takash Igarashi, Eiichi Shimaz
PHOTOGRAPHER
Katsuo Hanzawa
PUBLISHER
Kodansha Publisher

Book Design
ART DIRECTOR/CREATIVE DIRECTOR
Ken Miki
DESIGNERS
Ken Miki, Junji Osaki
ILLUSTRATOR
Nob Fukuda
ARTISTS
Kosho Shimizu, Kazumi Shimizu,
Ayami Shimizu
STUDIO
Ken Miki & Assoc.
CLIENT
Leggy Inc.

Book Design

ART DIRECTOR/CREATIVE DIRECTOR/COPYWRITER
Michael Baviera

DESIGNER
Hans-Georg Köhl

ILLUSTRATOR
Siegrun Nuber

PHOTOGRAPHER
Edi Hueber

STUDIO
BBV

PUBLISHER
City of Zurich

Book Design

ART DIRECTOR/DESIGNER
Kan Akita

PHOTOGRAPHER
Yutaka Saito

STUDIO
Akita Design Kan Inc.

PUBLISHER
TOTO Shuppan

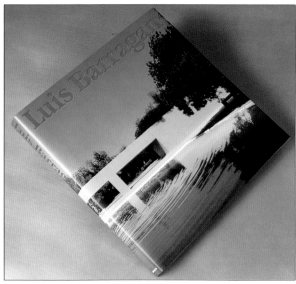

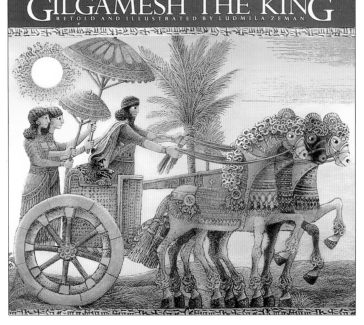

Book Design

ART DIRECTOR/AUTHOR
May Cutler

DESIGNER
Dan O'Leary

ILLUSTRATOR
L. Zeman

PUBLISHER
Tundra Books, Inc.

Book Design

ART DIRECTOR/ILLUSTRATOR
Thomas Sassenbach

COPYWRITER
Jan Schmodde

AGENCY
Sassenbach & Schmodde

Book Design

ART DIRECTOR/DESIGNER
Pieter Brattinga

COPYWRITER
Johannes van der Wolk

Book Design

ART DIRECTOR/AUTHOR
May Cutler

DESIGNER
Dan O'Leary

ILLUSTRATOR
Y. Moore

PUBLISHER
Tundra Books, Inc.

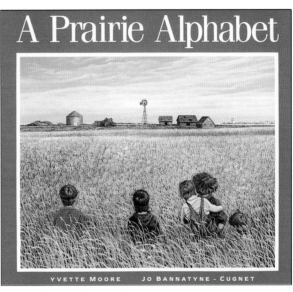

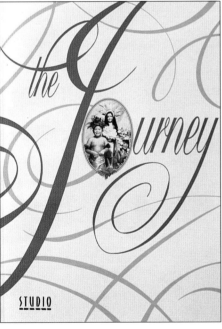

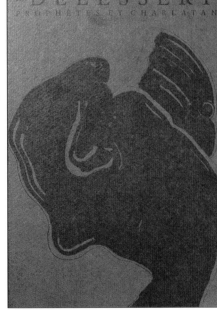

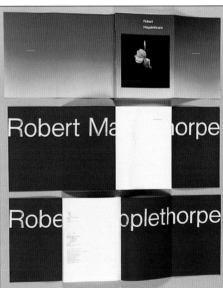

Book Design

ART DIRECTORS
John Lee, Ian Yap

DESIGNER
Abdul Samad Jaffar

COPYWRITER
Tan Kheng Hua

PHOTOGRAPHER
Suzanne Read

STUDIO
Equinox Art & Design

PUBLISHER
Studio Tangs

Book Design

ART DIRECTOR
Rita Marshall

COPYWRITERS
Bertil Galland, Francois Nourissier

ILLUSTRATOR
Etienne Delessert

STUDIO
Delessert & Marshall

PUBLISHER
Musee Jenisch

Book Design

ART DIRECTOR/DESIGNER
Kijuro Yahagi

STUDIO
Kijuro Yahagi, Inc.

PUBLISHER
Art Tower Mito

Book Design
ART DIRECTOR/DESIGNER
Kijuro Yahagi
STUDIO
Kijuro Yahagi, Inc.
PUBLISHER
The Museum of Modern Art, Saitama

Book Design
ART DIRECTOR
Carolyn Stuckey
CREATIVE DIRECTOR
Toman Rom
ILLUSTRATOR
Kafri
PHOTOGRAPHERS
Herinde Koelbl, Joyce Tennson
STUDIO
Werkstudio

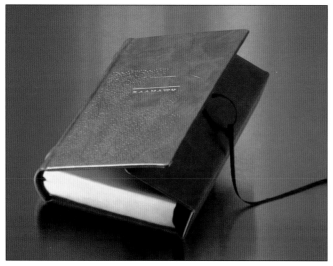

Book Design
ART DIRECTOR
Marjaana Virta
PUBLISHER
WSOY

Book Design
ART DIRECTOR
Max Rindlisbacher
COPYWRITER
Erich Grasdorf
PHOTOGRAPHER
Michael Wissing
PUBLISHER
ASGS Editorial

Book Design
ART DIRECTOR/DESIGNER/ILLUSTRATOR/PHOTOGRAPHER
Yasutake Miyagi
STUDIO
Miyagi Design Studio
PUBLISHER
Nippon Geijutsu Shuppansha

Book Design
ART DIRECTOR
Yasuhiko Naito
AUTHOR/ILLUSTRATOR
Ryo Honda
EDITOR
Hideshi Aida
AGENCY
H Associates, Inc.
PUBLISHER
Gakken

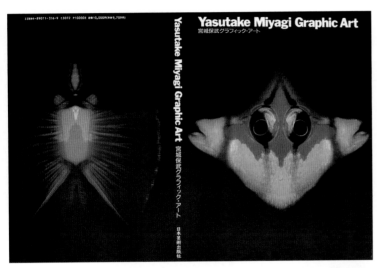

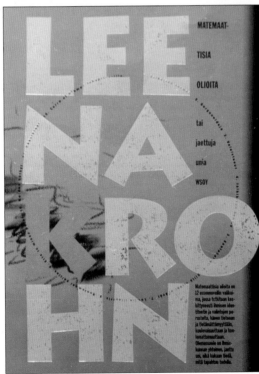

Book Design
ART DIRECTOR
Marjaana Virta
COPYWRITER
Leena Krohn
PUBLISHER
WSOY

Poster
ART DIRECTOR
Setsue Shimizu
COPYWRITER
Daisuke Yazawa
DESIGNER
Koji Toda
PHOTOGRAPHER
Hidemichi Ohmori
STUDIOS
C' Co., Ltd., Nambokusha Inc.
CLIENT
Toyota Motor Corp.

Poster
ART DIRECTOR/DESIGNER/ILLUSTRATOR
Tadashi Hara
STUDIO
Tadashi Hara Design Office
CLIENT
International Design Center

Poster
ART DIRECTOR/DESIGNER
Koichi Sato
PHOTOGRAPHER
Yoh Nagata
CLIENT
Sabie

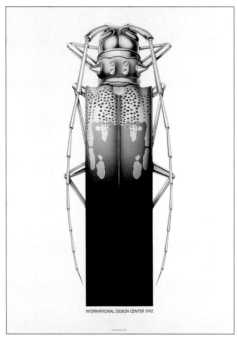

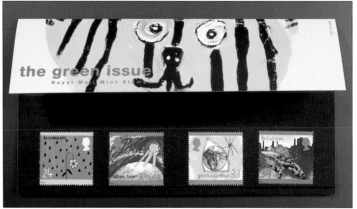

Annual Report
ART DIRECTORS
Lynn Trickett, Brian Webb
DESIGNER
Andrew Thomas
COPYWRITER
Neil Mattingley
STUDIO
Trickett & Webb Ltd.
CLIENT
Royal Mail

Annual Report/Series
ART DIRECTOR/CREATIVE DIRECTOR/
DESIGNER/COPYWRITER
Mary Lewis
ILLUSTRATOR
Geoffrey Appleton
AGENCY
Lewis Moberly
CLIENT
Sogrape Vinhos de Portugal

Annual Report
ART DIRECTOR
Peter Saville
DESIGNER
Stephen Wolstenholme
PHOTOGRAPHER
Nina Short
CLIENT
Yohji Yamamoto

Annual Report/Series

ART DIRECTOR
Tamako Uno

CREATIVE DIRECTOR
Osamuo Ogawa

DESIGNER
Hiroyuki Yamashina

ILLUSTRATOR
Junichi Ichimura

STUDIO
Ogawa Design Office Co., Ltd.

CLIENT
Victor Musical Industries Inc.

Annual Report

ART DIRECTOR/DESIGNER
Judy Hungerford

COPYWRITER
NSW Treasury Corporation

ILLUSTRATOR
Tony Pyrzakowski

PHOTOGRAPHER
Paul Henderson-Kelly

STUDIO
Julie Henniker Graphic Productions

CLIENT
New South Wales Treasury Corp.

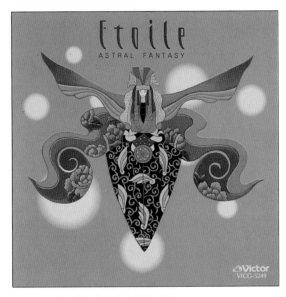

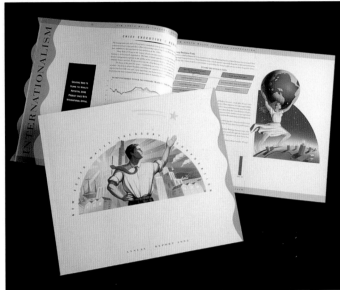

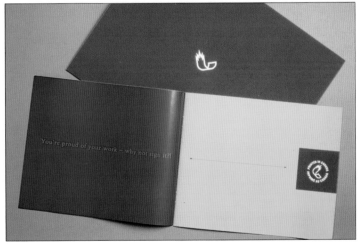

Annual Report/Series

ART DIRECTORS
John Pylypczak, Diti Katona

DESIGNER
John Pylypczak, Susan McIntee

STUDIO
Concrete Design

CLIENT
Canadian Printing Industries Assoc.

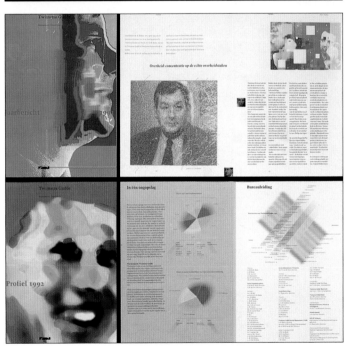

Annual Report

ART DIRECTOR
Edo Smitshuyzew

DESIGNER
Marc Goslinga

COPYWRITER
Twijnstra Gudde

ILLUSTRATOR
Edo Smitshuyzew

STUDIO
BRS Premseza Vonk

Annual Report/Series

ART DIRECTOR
Nakagawa Kenzo

COPYWRITER
Tanaka Azusa

ILLUSTRATOR
Taki Ono

PHOTOGRAPHERS
Hiro, Satch, Hiroyuki, Norika

STUDIO
NDC Graphics

CLIENT
Hokuetsu Paper

Annual Report

ART DIRECTOR
John McConnell

DESIGNER
Jason Godfrey

PHOTOGRAPHER
Steve Rees

STUDIO
Pentagram Design

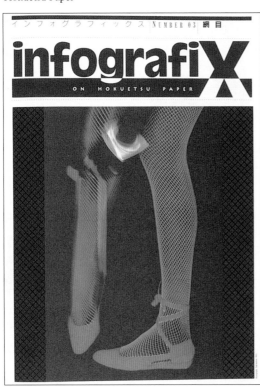

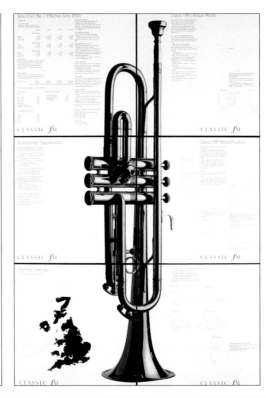

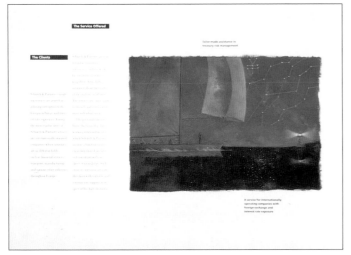

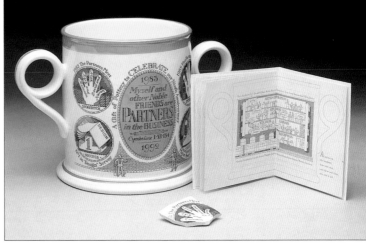

Annual Report/Series

ART DIRECTOR
Enrico Sempi

DESIGNER
Antonella Trevisan

COPYWRITER
Hargitay

ILLUSTRATOR
Guido Pigni

AGENCY
Tangram Strategic Design

Annual Report

ART DIRECTOR
David Stuart

DESIGNERS
Peter Carrow, Glen Stone

COPYWRITER
Beryl McAlhone

ILLUSTRATOR
George Hardie

STUDIO
The Partners

Annual Report
STUDIO
Pentagram Design

Poster
ART DIRECTORS
Lynn Trickett, Brian Webb
DESIGNER
Andrew Thomas
COPYWRITER
Neil Mattingley
STUDIO
Trickett & Webb
CLIENT
Royal Mail

Annual Report
ART DIRECTOR/CREATIVE DIRECTOR/DESIGNER
Ashted Dastor
STUDIO
Ashted Dastor Assoc.

Annual Report
ART DIRECTORS
James Beveridge, Jim Sutherland
DESIGNER
Jim Sutherland
ILLUSTRATORS
Malcolm English, Line & Line
PHOTOGRAPHER
John Edwards
STUDIO
The Partners
CLIENT
Centrum 100

Annual Report
ART DIRECTOR/CREATIVE DIRECTOR
Byron Jacobs
DESIGNERS
Byron Jacobs, Chris Chan
PHOTOGRAPHER
Ka-Sing Lee
ILLUSTRATORS
Percy Chung, Robin Whyler
STUDIO
PPA Design Ltd.
CLIENT
Sing Cheong

Annual Report
ART DIRECTOR/DESIGNER
Alan Herron
PHOTOGRAPHER
Michael Banks
STUDIO
Giant Ltd.
CLIENT
Britannia Life

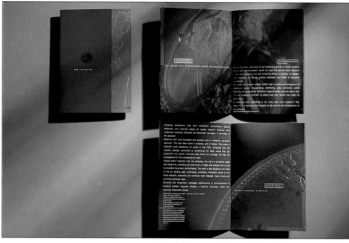

Annual Report
ART DIRECTOR
Steve Mykolyn
COPYWRITER
Steve Mykolyn, Russell Monk
PHOTOGRAPHER
Russell Monk
STUDIO
MBI
AGENCY
MBI/Russell Monk

Annual Report

ART DIRECTOR
Gerhard Plakolm

COPYWRITER
Paul Rosenthal

CREATIVE DIRECTORS
Gerhard Plakolm, Udo Titz

PHOTOGRAPHER
Bernhard Angerer

STUDIO
Czerny, Celand, Plakolm

CLIENT
Ludwig Reiter

Annual Report

ART DIRECTOR
Stephen Gibbons

COPYWRITER
Maurice Smelt

DESIGNER
David Kimpton

PHOTOGRAPHER
Mark Tilly

STUDIO
The Partners

CLIENT
Åke Larson Ltd.

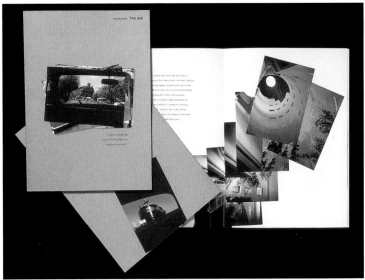

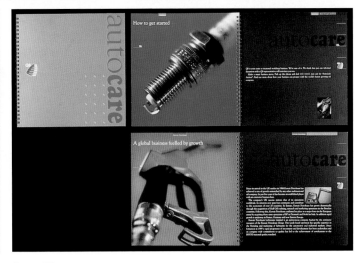

Annual Report

ART DIRECTOR
Isabelle Paquin

DESIGNER
Jean-François Couvignou

PHOTOGRAPHER
Longpré

ILLUSTRATOR
Pol Turgeon

STUDIO
Sun Communications-Design

CLIENT
Dottmar Specialty Fine Papers

Annual Report

ART DIRECTOR/DESIGNER
Neil Smith

PHOTOGRAPHER
Michael Banks

STUDIO
Giant Ltd.

CLIENT
Kuwait Petroleum Lubricants

Annual Report
ART DIRECTOR/CREATIVE DIRECTOR
Isabelle Paquin
DESIGNERS
Isabella Paquin, Luc Lepage
ILLUSTRATORS
Couture Gagnon Illustrations,
Alain Reno
STUDIO
Sun Communications-Design
CLIENT
Dottmar Specialty Fine Papers

Annual Report
ART DIRECTOR
Byron Jacobs
DESIGNERS
Byron Jacobs, Chris Chan
PHOTOGRAPHER
Neil Farrin
ILLUSTRATOR
Liliane Tsui
STUDIO
PPA Design Ltd.
CLIENT
Cathay Pacific

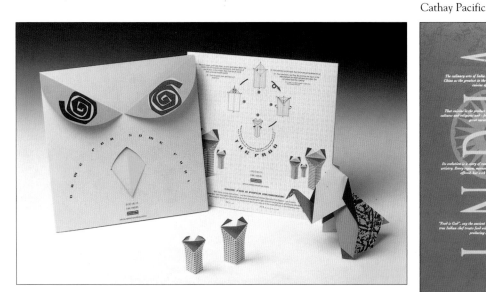

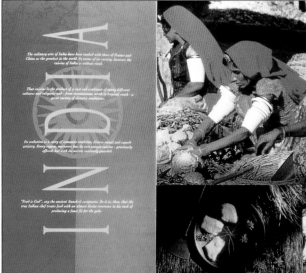

Annual Report
ART DIRECTOR
Sean Lee
CREATIVE DIRECTOR
G. V. Warsop
AGENCY
The Jupiter Drawing Room

Annual Report
ART DIRECTOR
David Pocknell
DESIGNER
Kathryn Wong
STUDIO
Pentagram Design
CLIENT
London Transport

Annual Report/Series
ART DIRECTOR/CREATIVE DIRECTOR
Keizo Matsui
DESIGNER
Yuko Araki
STUDIO
Keizo Matsui & Assoc.
CLIENT
Okamura Printing Industry

Annual Report/Series
ART DIRECTOR
Markus Huber
CREATIVE DIRECTOR
Mariusz Jan Demner
COPYWRITER
Ingeborg Frauendorfer
DESIGNER
Angela Mani
PHOTOGRAPHER
Mario Katzmayr
AGENCY
Demner & Merlicek

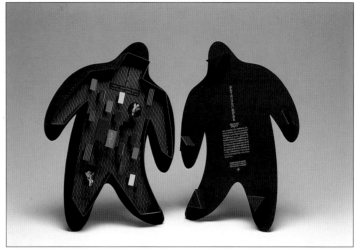

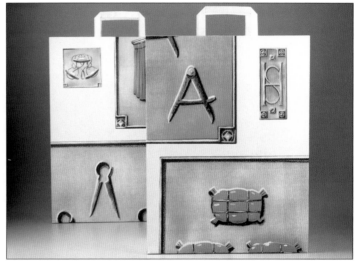

Annual Report/Series
ART DIRECTOR
Adelaide Acerbi
COPYWRITER
Fullio Crace
PHOTOGRAPHER
Emilio Tremolada
STUDIO
Lambda

Packaging
ART DIRECTOR/DESIGNER/CREATIVE DIRECTOR
Mary Lewis
PHOTOGRAPHER
Geoffrye Appleton
STUDIO
Lewis Moberly
CLIENT
Heal's

Packaging

ART DIRECTOR
Mary Lewis

DESIGNERS
Margaret Nolan, Peter Kay,
Mary Lewis, Robin Broadbent

STUDIO
Lewis Moberly

CLIENT
Parfums Icardi Egan

Packaging

ART DIRECTOR/CREATIVE DIRECTOR
Mary Lewis

COPYWRITERS
Mary Lewis, Christine Lalumia

DESIGNERS
Jimmy Yang, Mary Lewis

ILLUSTRATOR
Jimmy Yang

STUDIO
Lewis Moberly

CLIENT
Geffrye Museum

Calendar

ART DIRECTORS
Lynn Trickett, Brian Webb

DESIGNER
Steve Edwards

COPYWRITER
Neil Mattingley

ILLUSTRATORS
Various

STUDIO
Trickett & Webb, Ltd.

CLIENT
Augustus Martin/
Trickett & Webb, Ltd.

Calendar

ART DIRECTORS
Mike Meiré, Wolfgang Heuwinkel

CREATIVE DIRECTOR
Wolfgang Heuwinkel

DESIGNER
Mike Meiré

COPYWRITER
M. Baccar, Dr. Ch. Machat

AGENCY
mieré & mieré

Calendar
ART DIRECTOR/CREATIVE DIRECTOR/DESIGNER
Koeweiden/Postma

Calendar
ART DIRECTOR
Franz Merlicek
GRAPHICS
Judith Modl
PHOTOGRAPHER/ILLUSTRATOR
Christine de Grancy, Jörg Gaisbauer
AGENCY
Demner & Merlicek
CLIENT
Agrana Foodstuffs Industry

Calendar
ART DIRECTOR
Koji Mizutani
DESIGNERS
Masashi Yamashita, Hiroshi Ohmizo
ARTIST
Ken Matsubara
STUDIO
Mizutani Studio
CLIENT
Nishiki Printing Co. Ltd.

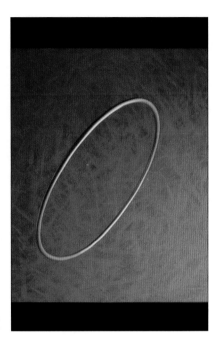

Calendar
ART DIRECTOR/DESIGNER
Ikko Tanaka
STUDIO
Ikko Tanaka Design Studio

Calendar
ART DIRECTOR
Akio Okumura
DESIGNER
Shuichi Nogami
STUDIO
Packaging Create Inc.
CLIENT
Inoue Yoshiten Co., Ltd.

Packaging

ART DIRECTOR
Barbara Poxleitner

CREATIVE DIRECTOR
Thomas Heuter

COPYWRITER
Werner Busam

PHOTOGRAPHER
Achim Straub

AGENCY
Grey Düsseldorf

CLIENT
B.A.T.

Packaging

ART DIRECTOR
Osamu Furumura

CREATIVE DIRECTOR
Michiko Koshino

DESIGNER
Shinji Yamaguchi

PHOTOGRAPHER
Manabu Yamanaka

STUDIO
See Saw Inc.

CLIENT
Michiko Japan Inc.

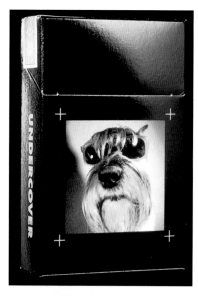

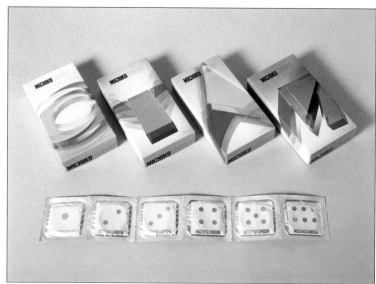

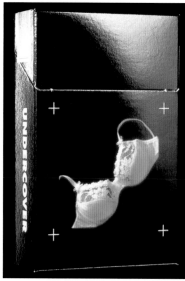

Packaging

ART DIRECTOR
John Rushworth

DESIGNER
Vince Frost

PHOTOGRAPHER
Steve Rees

STUDIO
Pentagram Design

CLIENT
Farmers Dairy Co.

Packaging

ART DIRECTORS
Toru Ando, Michiharu Takahashi

CREATIVE DIRECTOR
Toru Ando

DESIGNERS
Toshimi Yagi, Chika Nakajima

STUDIO
Mitsukoshi Ltd.

CLIENT
Mitsukoshi Ltd.

Packaging

ART DIRECTOR
Jorg Willich

DESIGNERS
Jorg Willich, Wayne James

COPYWRITER
Martin Franklin

ILLUSTRATORS
Carl Stevenson, Jorg Willich

CLIENT
SDV-Tontraeger

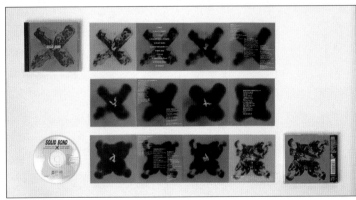

Packaging

ART DIRECTOR/CREATIVEDIRECTOR/ PHOTOGRAPHER
Yoichirou Fujii

DESIGNERS
Yoichirou Fujii, Sayoko Ueno

ILLUSTRATOR
Keiko Maekawa, Yoichirou Fujii

AGENCY
Sony Music Comm.

CLIENT
CS Artists

Packaging

ART DIRECTOR/CREATIVE DIRECTOR
Isao Suzuki

DESIGNERS
Yoshimasa Hayashi, Atsushi Urata

COPYWRITER
Tsuyoshi Fujimoto

PHOTOGRAPHER
Seiichi Inoue

AGENCY
Asatsu Inc.

CLIENT
Sony Records

Packaging

ART DIRECTOR/DESIGNER
Atsushi Ebina

CREATIVE DIRECTOR/COPYWRITER
Hideaki Matsuoka

PHOTOGRAPHER
Atsushi Ueda

STUDIO
Verve Inc.

CLIENT
Epic/Sony Records

Packaging

ART DIRECTOR/CREATIVE DIRECTOR
Byron Jacobs

DESIGNERS
Byron Jacobs, Tracy Hoi

COPYWRITER
Joanne W. Jones

PHOTOGRAPHER
Ka-Sing Lee

STUDIO
PPA Design Ltd.

CLIENT
Cathay Pacific

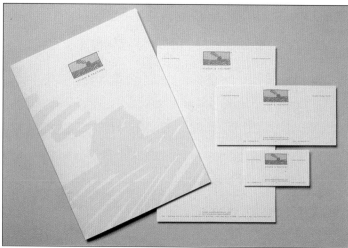

Letterhead, Business Card & Envelope

ART DIRECTOR/COPYWRITER/ILLUSTRATOR
Hugo Puttaert

Letterhead, Business Card & Envelope

ART DIRECTORS
John Pylypczak, Diti Katona

DESIGNER
Susan McIntee

ILLUSTRATOR
Jeff Jackson

STUDIO
Concrete Design Comm.

CLIENT
Four Seasons Aviation

Letterhead, Business Card & Envelope

ART DIRECTOR
John Pylypczak, Diti Katona

DESIGNER
John Pylypczak

STUDIO
Concrete Design Comm.

CLIENT
Contor Industries

Corporate Identity

ART DIRECTOR/CREATIVE DIRECTOR/DESIGNER
Mary Lewis

STUDIO
Lewis Moberly

CLIENT
Heal's

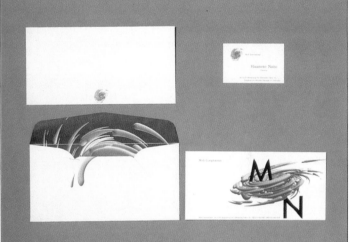

Letterhead, Business Card & Envelope

ART DIRECTOR/DESIGNER
Norihito Shinmura

COPYWRITER
Kazutaka Shinmura

AGENCY
I&S Corporation

CLIENT
Shinmura Suisan

Letterhead, Business Card & Envelope

ART DIRECTOR
Hisamoto Naito

DESIGNERS
Masao Kimura, Takafumi Yamanishi

ILLUSTRATOR
T. Kimura

AGENCY
Dentsu Cotec Inc.

Corporate Identity
ART DIRECTORS/DESIGNERS
John Pylypczak, Diti Katona
STUDIO
Concrete Design Comm.
CLIENT
Design Exchange

Corporate Identity
ART DIRECTORS
John Plylypczak, Diti Katona
DESIGNER
John Pylypczak
STUDIO
Concrete Design

Corporate Identity
ART DIRECTOR
Adelaide Acerbi
COPYWRITER
Cristina Brigidini
STUDIO
Lambda

Poster

ART DIRECTOR
Hiroshi Kojitani

DESIGNER
Kensuke Irie

PHOTOGRAPHER
Nob Fukuda

STUDIO
Kojitani & Irie Design

CLIENT
Tokyo Designers Space

Poster

ART DIRECTORS
Rico Lins, Jaire De Souza

COPYWRITER/DESIGNER/ILLUSTRATOR
Rico Lins

STUDIO
Rico Lins Studio

CLIENT
Saque Sagaz

Poster

ART DIRECTOR
Susan Griak

COPYWRITER
Luke Sullivan

AGENCY
Fallon McElligott

CLIENT
J.D. Hoyt's

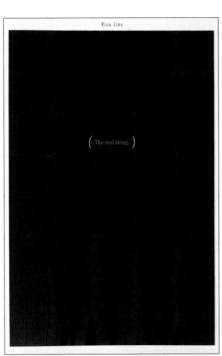

Poster

ART DIRECTOR
Mark Denton

CREATIVE DIRECTORS
Chris Palmer, Mark Denton

COPYWRITER
Sean Doyle

PHOTOGRAPHER
Malcolm Venville

STUDIO
Simons Palmer

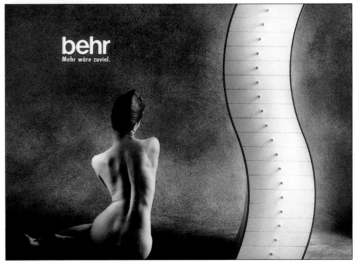

Poster

ART DIRECTOR
Karina Geideck

COPYWRITER
Michael Sochiera

PHOTOGRAPHER
Horst Wackerbarth

AGENCY
BF&P

Poster

ART DIRECTOR
Rita Marshall

DESIGNERS
Rita Marshall, Etienne Delessert

STUDIO
Delessert & Marshall

CLIENT
UQAM Graphic Center, Montreal

Poster

ART DIRECTOR
Hiroaki Nagai

CREATIVE DIRECTOR/COPYWRITER
Hiroshi Mitsui

DESIGNERS
Hiroaki Nagai, Makoto Yamamoto

PHOTOGRAPHER
Tamotsu Fujii

AGENCY
Commons Co., Ltd.

CLIENT
The Yokohama Rubber Co., Ltd.

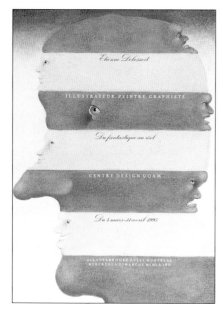

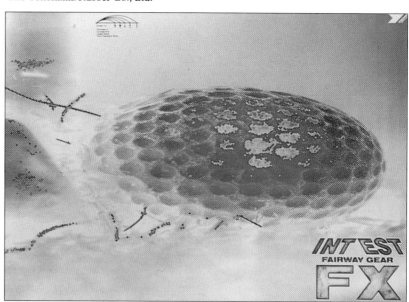

Poster

ART DIRECTOR
Kenzo Izutani

DESIGNERS
Kenzo Izutani, Aki Hirai

COPYWRITER
Hinako Maruyama

PHOTOGRAPHERS
Masayuki Tsutsui, Tomio Watanabe

STUDIO
Kenzo Izutani Office Corp.

CLIENT
Tokyo Broadcasting System

Poster

ART DIRECTOR
Aziz Cami

DESIGNERS
Greg Quinton, Gillian Thomas

STUDIO
The Partners

CLIENT
Association of Photographers

Poster

ART DIRECTOR
Minoru Inoue

COPYWRITER
Shuhei Sakae

DESIGNER
Manabu Okamoto

CREATIVE DIRECTOR
Masaharu Higashizawa

AGENCY
Daiko Advertising Inc.

CLIENT
Matsushita Electric Industrial Co., Ltd.

Poster

ART DIRECTOR
Michael McLaughlin

COPYWRITER
Stephen Creet

CREATIVE DIRECTORS
Stephen Creet, Michael McLaughlin,
Bill Durnan

AGENCY
MacLaren:Lintas Inc.

CLIENT
Molson Breweries of Canda

Poster

ART DIRECTOR/DESIGNER
Vince Frost

STUDIO
Pentagram Design

CLIENT
Eddie & The Hot Rods

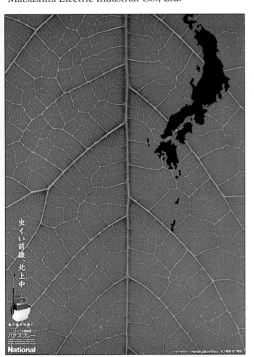

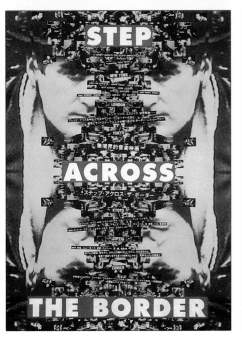

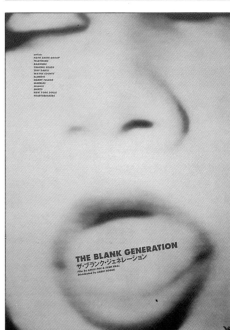

Poster

ART DIRECTOR/DESIGNER
Atsushi Ebina

STUDIO
Verve Inc.

CLIENT
Cable Hogue

Poster

ART DIRECTOR/COPYWRITER
Uwe Loesch

DESIGNERS
Michael Gais, Iris Utikal

STUDIO
Arbeitsgemeinschaft für Visuelle
und Verbale Kommunikation

CLIENT
Second United Nations Conference
of Environment and Development in Rio

Poster

ART DIRECTOR/DESIGNER
Atsushi Ebina

CREATIVE DIRECTOR
Natsuki Haryu

STUDIO
Verve Inc.

CLIENT
Cable Hogue/Parco Co., Ltd.

Poster
ART DIRECTOR/COPYWRITER/PHOTOGRAPHER
Yumiko Nakayama
STUDIO
Val Design Group Co., Ltd.

Poster
ART DIRECTOR/DESIGNER
Vince Frost
PHOTOGRAPHER
The Douglas Brothers
STUDIO
Pentagram Design
CLIENT
Royal Shakespeare Co.

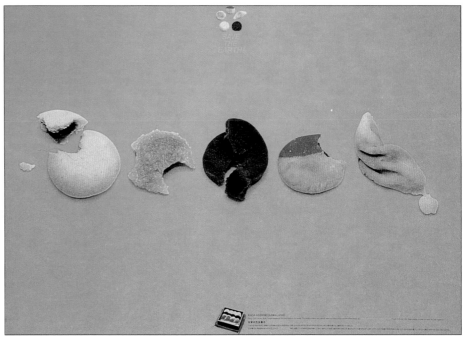

Poster
ART DIRECTOR
Masaaki Hiromura
DESIGNER
Takafumi Kusagaya
PHOTOGRAPHER
Ryuichi Okano
STUDIO
Hiromura Design Office
PUBLISHER
Rikuyosha Publishing, Inc.

Poster
ART DIRECTOR/DESIGNER/COPYWRITER
Mabito Yoshida
PHOTOGRAPHER
Wakihiko Noca
STUDIO
Val Design Group Co., Ltd.

Poster
ART DIRECTOR/CREATIVE DIRECTOR/DESIGNER/
COPYWRITER/CALLIGRAPHER
Tamako Uno
STUDIO
Ogawa Design Office Co., Ltd.
CLIENT
Tamako Uno

Poster
ART DIRECTOR/DESIGNER/COPYWRITER
Yoshimi Ohba
AGENCY
Val Design Group Co., Ltd.

Poster
ART DIRECTOR/DESIGNER
Takeshi Yamamoto
PHOTOGRAPHER
Yoshihiko Ueda
AGENCY
JIC
CLIENT
Energy Plaza '93

Poster
ART DIRECTOR/DESIGNER
Shin Fukui
CREATIVE DIRECTOR
Masaaki Izumiya
COPYWRITER
Kazuya Koshimo
PHOTOGRAPHER
Yoshihiko Ueda
AGENCY
Hakuhodo Inc.
CLIENT
Recruit Co., Ltd.

Poster

ART DIRECTORS
Takuya Onuki, Naoya Okada

DESIGNER
Yuji Masuda

COPYWRITER
Koji Ando

PHOTOGRAPHER
Takeshi

AGENCY
Hakuhodo Inc.

CLIENT
Toshimae

Poster/Series

ART DIRECTOR/CREATIVE DIRECTOR
Daisuke Nakatsuka

DESIGNER
Yasuhiko Matsumoto

COPYWRITER
Hideo Okano

PHOTOGRAPHER
Toru Kogure

AGENCY
Nakatsuka Daisuke Inc.

CLIENT
Rengo Co., Ltd.

Poster/Series

ART DIRECTOR
Charly Frei

COPYWRITER
Andreas Schalko

CREATIVE DIRECTOR
Chrigel Ott

PHOTOGRAPHER
Dr. Koschnitzke

AGENCY
Young & Rubicam Vienna

CLIENT
Kodak GesmbH

Poster/Series

ART DIRECTOR/DESIGNER
Atsushi Ebina

CREATIVE DIRECTOR
Okihiko Okubo

COPYWRITER
Takao Fujino

AGENCY
I & S

CLIENT
Parker Pen Japan

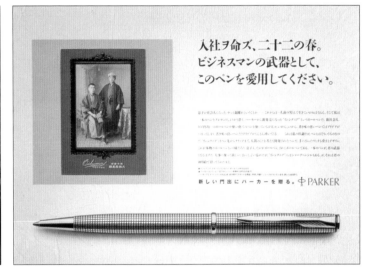

Poster/Series

ART DIRECTOR
Michael McLaughlin

CREATIVE DIRECTORS
Stephen Creet, Michael McLaughlin,
Bill Duman

COPYWRITER
Stephen Creet

PHOTOGRAPHER
Nigel Dickson

AGENCY
MacLaren:Lintas Inc.

CLIENT
Molson Breweries of Canada

Poster/Series

DESIGNER
Shu Kataoka

Poster/Series

ART DIRECTOR
Masaaki Hiromura

DESIGNER
Takafumi Kusagaya

PHOTOGRAPHER
Ryuichi Okano

AGENCY
Hiromura Design Office

CLIENT
K. E. Academy Inc.

Poster/Series
ART DIRECTOR/CREATIVE DIRECTOR
Koji Mizutani
DESIGNER
Hiroshi Ohmizo
PHOTOGRAPHER
Sachiko Kuru
STUDIO
Mizutani Studio
CLIENT
Hiroko Koshino Design Office

Poster/Series
ART DIRECTORS/DESIGNERS
Osamu Fukushima, Atsushi Sakurada
CREATIVE DIRECTOR
Yasuo Fukuda
COPYWRITER
Tetsuya Sakota
PHOTOGRAPHERS
Osamu Fukushima, Junko Yamada
AGENCY
Asatsu Inc.
CLIENT
Campbell Japan Inc.

Poster/Series
ART DIRECTOR/DESIGNER/ARTIST
Makoto Saito
PHOTOGRAPHER
Kouichi Nakazawa
AGENCY
Makoto Saito Design Office Inc.
CLIENT
Taiyo Printing Co., Ltd.

Poster/Series
ART DIRECTOR/COPYWRITER
Uwe Loesch
DESIGNERS
Michael Gais, Iris Utikal
STUDIO
Arbeitsgemeinschaft für Visuelle
und Verbale Kommunikation
CLIENT
Political Club Cologne

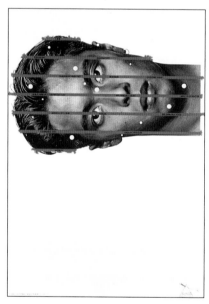

Poster/Series
ART DIRECTOR/COPYWRITER
Katsumi Asaba
DESIGNER
Keiko Mineishi
PHOTOGRAPHER
Kazumi Kurigami
CLIENT
Process Center Co., Ltd

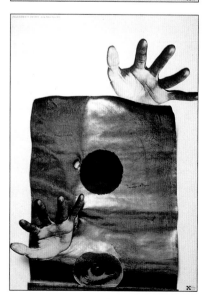

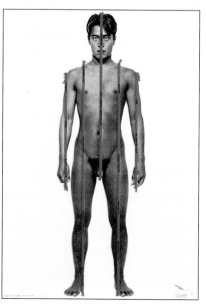

Poster/Series
ART DIRECTOR
Katsumi Asaba
DESIGNERS
Keiko Mineishi, Teruo Kataoka
PHOTOGRAPHER
Eiichiro Sakata
CLIENT
G8 Gallery

Poster/Series
ART DIRECTOR/DESIGNER/PHOTOGRAPHER
Susumu Endo

Poster/Series
ART DIRECTOR/DESIGNER/ILLUSTRATOR
Masakazu Tanabe
AGENCY
Media Co., Ltd.
CLIENT
Media Co., Ltd.

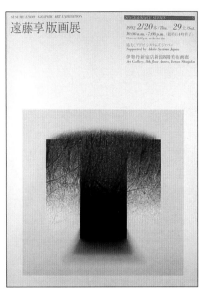

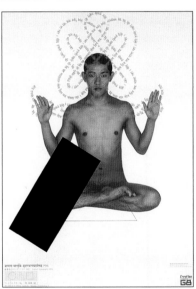
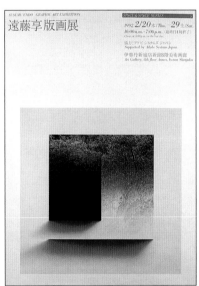
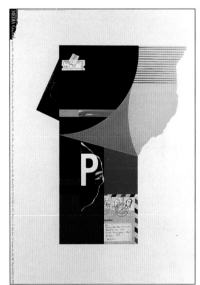

Poster/Series

ART DIRECTOR/COPYWRITER/DESIGNER/
CREATIVE DIRECTOR/PHOTOGRAPHER/ILLUSTRATOR
Matthies

STUDIO
Matthies, Holger

CLIENT
Niedersachsiche Staatstheater

Poster/Series

ART DIRECTOR/DESIGNER/ARTIST
Makoto Saito

CREATIVE DIRECTOR
Ryozo Shibata

AGENCY
Makoto Saito Design Office Inc.

CLIENT
Alpha Cubic Co., Ltd.

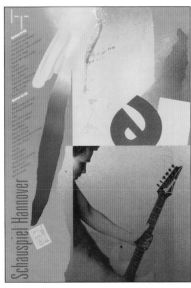

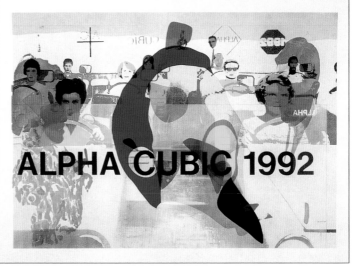

Poster/Series

ART DIRECTOR
Michael McLaughlin

CREATIVE DIRECTORS
Stephen Creet, Michael, Bill Duman

COPYWRITER
Stephen Creet

PHOTOGRAPHER
Nigel Dickson

AGENCY
MacLaren:Lintas Inc.

CLIENT
Molson Breweries of Canada

Poster/Series

ART DIRECTOR/DESIGNER/ARTIST
Makoto Saito

CREATIVE DIRECTOR
Kenichi Aki

PHOTOGRAPHER
Herb Ritts

AGENCY
Yomiko Advertising Inc.

CLIENT
Edwin Co., Ltd.

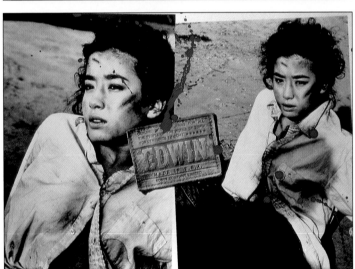

Poster/Series

ART DIRECTOR/DESIGNER/ARTIST
Makoto Saito

AGENCY
Makoto Saito Design Office Inc.

CLIENT
Kind Wear Corp.

Poster/Series

ART DIRECTOR/DESIGNER
Koji Toda

CREATIVE DIRECTOR
Kozo Koshimizu

COPYWRITER
Daisuke Yazawa

PHOTOGRAPHER
Hiroshi Harada

AGENCY
C'(C-dash) Co., Ltd

CLIENT
Honda Clio Kanagawa

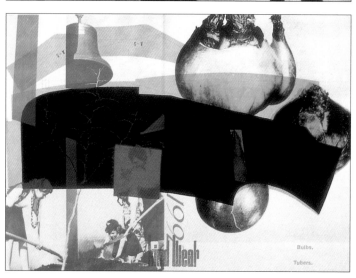

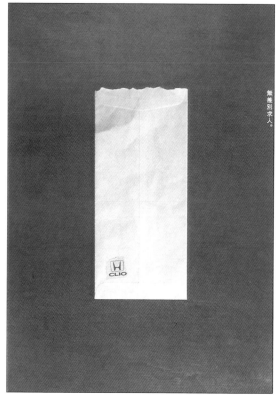

Poster/Series

ART DIRECTOR
Takuya Onuki

DESIGNER
Yuichi Shimabayashi

PHOTOGRAPHER
Yoshiko Ueda

STUDIO
Hakuhodo Inc.

CLIENT
Laforet Harajuku

Public-Service Poster

ART DIRECTOR/COPYWRITER/DESIGNER/
CREATIVE DIRECTOR
Jiro Kanahara

PHOTOGRAPHER
Kan Takahama

AGENCY
Asatsu Inc.

CLIENT
Press House Inc.

Public-Service Poster

ART DIRECTOR/DESIGNER/PHOTOGRAPHER
Susumu Endo

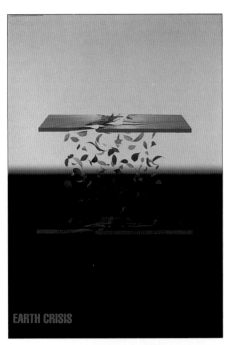

Public-Service Poster

ART DIRECTOR/COPYWRITER/DESIGNER/ILLUSTRATOR
Takashi Akiyama

STUDIO
Takashi Akiyama Studio

Public-Service Poster

ART DIRECTOR/DESIGNER
Minoru Araya

COPYWRITER
Toshifumi Sakakura

STUDIO
Luke Co., Ltd.

Public-Service Poster
ART DIRECTOR/ILLUSTRATOR
Shunyo Yamauchi
COPYWRITER
Maki Sano
STUDIO
Shunyo Yamauchi Design Office
PUBLICATION
Nabe Studio Inc.

Public-Service Poster
ART DIRECTOR/DESIGNER/CREATIVE DIRECTOR
Yoshiko Watanabe
COPYWRITER
Nobuo Uchiyama
PHOTOGRAPHER
Eisho Watanabe
STUDIO
Recruit Co., Ltd.
CLIENT
Jagda

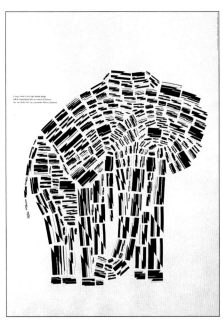

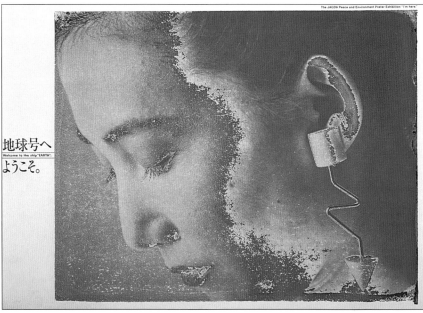

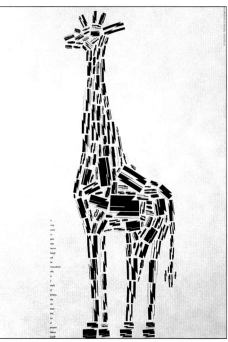

Public-Service Poster
ART DIRECTOR/DESIGNER/PHOTOGRAPHER
Yasutake Miyagi
STUDIO
Miyagi Design Studio
CLIENT
Nikko Process Co. Ltd.

Public-Service Poster
ART DIRECTOR/ILLUSTRATOR
Shunyo Yamauchi
COPYWRITER
Maki Sano
STUDIO
Shunyo Yamauchi Design Office
PUBLICATION
Nabe Studio Inc.

Public-Service Poster
ART DIRECTOR/COPYWRITER/DESIGNER
Toshio Iwata
ILLUSTRATOR
Eiji Komatsu
PHOTOGRAPHER
Tetsuya Abe
STUDIO
Popcorn Inc.

Public-Service Poster/Campaign
ART DIRECTOR/DESIGNER
Hirokatsu Hijikata
CLIENT
Hibiya Green Salon

Public-Service Poster/Campaign
ART DIRECTOR/COPYWRITER/DESIGNER/ILLUSTRATOR
Takaharu Matsumoto
CREATIVE DIRECTORS
Takaharu Matsumoto,
Masanori Saji
STUDIO
MR.88 Co., Ltd.

Public-Service Poster/Campaign
ART DIRECTOR/DESIGNER
Shunichi Nakajima
STUDIO
Jima Co., Ltd.
CLIENT
Jima Co., Ltd.

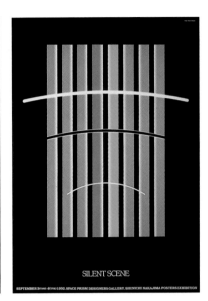

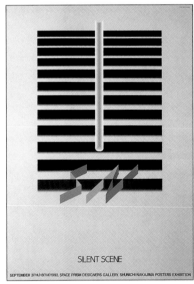

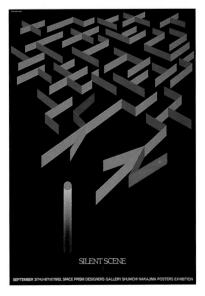

Public-Service Poster/Campaign
ART DIRECTOR
Takaharu Matsumoto
COPYWRITER
Yoshio Nozaki
DESIGNER
Osamu Yanomoto
CREATIVE DIRECTORS
Takaharu Matsumoto, Masanori Saji
STUDIO
MR. 88 Co., Ltd.

Public-Service Poster/Campaign
ART DIRECTOR/ILLUSTRATOR
Shunto Yamauchi
COPYWRITER
Maki Sano

Public-Service Poster/Campaign
ART DIRECTOR/COPYWRITER/DESIGNER/ILLUSTRATOR
Takashi Akiyama
STUDIO
Takashi Akiyama Studio

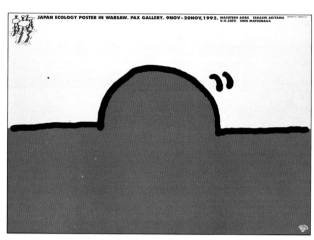

Public-Service Poster/Campaign
ART DIRECTOR/ILLUSTRATOR
Shunto Yamauchi
COPYWRITER
Maki Sano

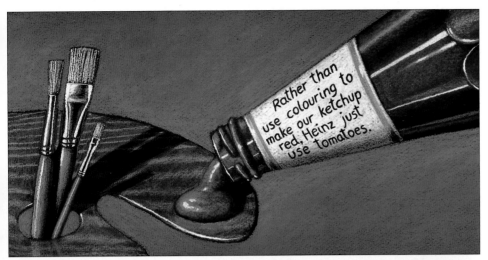

Poster

ART DIRECTOR
Gerard Stamp

COPYWRITER
Loz Simpson

CREATIVE DIRECTOR
Andrew Cracknell

ILLUSTRATOR
Robin Heighway-Bury

AGENCY
BSB Dorland Ltd.

Advertising & Promotion Illustration

ART DIRECTOR
Gerard Stamp

CREATIVE DIRECTOR
Andrew Cracknell

COPYWRITER
Loz Simpson

ILLUSTRATOR
Robin Heighway-Bury

AGENCY
BSB Dorland Ltd.

Advertising & Promotion Illustration

ART DIRECTOR
Gerard Stamp

CREATIVE DIRECTOR
Andrew Cracknell

COPYWRITER
Loz Simpson

ILLUSTRATOR
Robin Heighway-Bury

AGENCY
BSB Dorland Ltd.

Advertising & Promotion Illustration

ART DIRECTOR
Gerard Stamp

COPYWRITER
Loz Simpson

ILUSTRATOR
Robin Heighway-Bury

CREATIVE DIRECTOR
Andrew Cracknall

AGENCY
BSB Dorland

Advertising & Promotion Illustration
ART DIRECTOR
Gerard Stamp
CREATIVE DIRECTOR
Andrew Cracknell
COPYWRITER
Loz Simpson
ILLUSTRATOR
Robin Heighway-Bury
AGENCY
BSB Dorland Ltd.

Advertising & Promotion Illustration
ART DIRECTOR
Gerard Stamp
CREATIVE DIRECTOR
Andrew Cracknell
COPYWRITER
Loz Simpson
TYPOGRAPHER
Trevor Slabber
ILLUSTRATOR
Barry Driscoll
AGENCY
BSB Dorland Ltd.

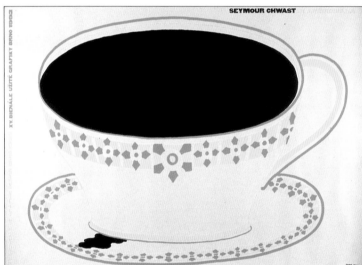

Advertising & Promotion Illustration
ART DIRECTOR/ILLUSTRATOR
Seymour Chwast
AGENCY
The Pushpin Group
CLIENT
Biennale of Graphic Design 1992

Advertising & Promotion Illustration
ART DIRECTORS
Mark Denton, Andy McKay
CREATIVE DIRECTORS
Chris Palmer, Mark Denton
COPYWRITER
Chris Palmer
ILLUSTRATOR
C. F. Payne
AGENCY
Simons Palmer

ART DIRECTOR

Hans-Georg Pospischil

ILLUSTRATOR

Seymour Chwast

AGENCY

The Pushpin Group

PUBLICATION

Frankfurter Allgemeine Magazin

ART DIRECTOR

Hans-Georg Pospischil

ILLUSTRATOR

Seymour Chwast

AGENCY

The Pushpin Group

PUBLICATION

Frankfurter Allgemeine Magazin

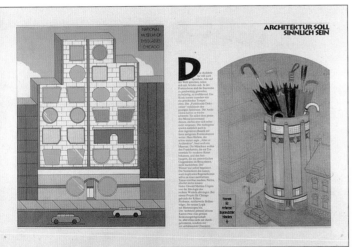

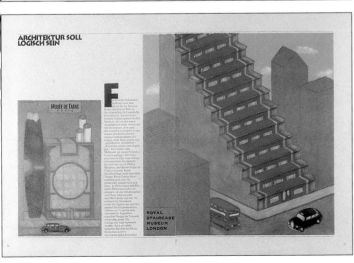

ART DIRECTOR

Hans-Georg Pospischil

ILLUSTRATOR

Seymour Chwast

AGENCY

The Pushpin Group

PUBLICATION

Frankfurter Allgemeine Magazin

THE
72ND
ART DIRECTORS
ANNUAL
AND
7TH
INTERNATIONAL
EXHIBITION

I THANK YOU all for the privilege of having served as your President these past two years.

I thank a Board of Directors whose support and dedication has been unwavering. And especially our Treasurer, Martin Solomon, without whose watchful eye our club could not subsist through rough economic times.

I thank you all for bearing me as I tried to search out new avenues for our club to venture into. Some succeeded. Others, I hope will bear fruit in the near future. And some just fell flat.

I thank all those chairmen and their committees for all their commitment to making the club one of involvement and camaraderie.

I thank all of you who have written me suggestion letters as well as bitch letters. It means you give a damn about the club and that's what counts.

And last but not least, I thank Rhoda Marshall and her staff for their unswerving devotion to our club. They have kept the faith no matter how difficult the times have been.

The most potent fact that I've observed in my tenure as President of the ADC is that our business is alive and thriving as never before. The films we're creating are more creative and innovative than ever. The printed page is being used in more imaginative ways than one could have ever have imagined. The age of electronics is continuing to give us the opportunity to create graphic milestones that were thought to be unreachable just a few years ago.

As I leaf through this our seventy-second Annual I can proudly say "we're better then we've ever been in every area if the creative process."

Again, thank you all for having given me the privilege of serving you again.

KURT HAIMAN

PRESIDENT, ART DIRECTORS CLUB

I WAS ONE of those art students who would pick up the *Art Directors Annual* and go through it for inspiration (who didn't?). It showed me what great work was and I tried to learn from that book. But maybe most importantly it made me excited and proud about being an art director.

This annual has always been a testament to our profession; our commitment to excellence and craftsmanship. But in an industry that is in transformation or evolution (you can substitute your own word) it becomes even more important that the Art Directors Club continue to stand for creative excellence and creative integrity in the era of the bottom line.

Over its seventy year existence, the Art Directors Club through its award annuals, has provided a history of the advertising and design business that is unique. This book continues that tradition with the best work of 1992.

You can be certain some student is at this moment turning these pages, enthralled by the quality of work he or she is seeing. It could be your son or daughter.

There are gold medals waiting for them.

ALLAN BEAVER

PRESIDENT, ART DIRECTORS CLUB

IN THIS 72ND YEAR of the Art Directors Club, we're reminded once again that within our charter is the mandate to help young and promising art students begin their careers in our profession.

The Visual Communicator's Education Fund was established during my presidential administration, and has fortunately continued to grow over the years. This year, we awarded over $14,000 to deserving young art students from various colleges and schools in the New York area.

Over the years, the members of this Fund worked hard to find fund-raising avenues for, and contributors to, this worthy endeavor.

The Annual Art Auctions, to which members and friends of the Club contribute drawings, paintings, photographs, books, and posters, is a major fund-raising event and our special thanks go to Bob Cato and his committee for all of their fine efforts.

Also, one dollar from every entry sent to our Annual Exhibition is donated to the scholarship fund. We hope that personal and corporate donations will help us as well, to finally reach our goal of a permanent endowment so that we can continue to help young and promising art students in perpetuity.

This year, the Scholarship awards gala was held on Thursday evening, April 29th. Student Scholarship recipients, donors, college deans, instructors, families, and friends joined us at the Club for the presentation of the awards and the best evening imaginable, heartwarming, encouraging, and rewarding!

Our heartiest congratulations go to the deserving young recipients of the 1993 Art Director's Club VCEF Scholarships. May all past, present, and future recipients find continued success in this illustrious profession.

VCEF BOARD

Eileen Hedy Schultz, *President*

William Brockmeier

William Buckley

Meg Crane

Kurt Haiman

Walter Kaprielian

Bob Smith

WINNERS

COOPER UNION
Fernando Megallanes, Beverly Joel, Megan Rovitto

FIT
Daniel McElwee, Yulia Dudnik, Michael Brothers, Gabrielle Pelerin, Raymond Rualo, Shamina Rao, Kerry Higgins, Jessica Bach, Jennifer Hoehn

NEW YORK TECHNICAL COLLEGE
Frank Babich, Ramon Pereyra, Howard Sun, Margaret Tsui

PARSONS
Kory Kennedy, Junghorn-Daniel Pak, Julia Wargaski, Adie Lee, Miao Moy, Jennifer Lee, Aenee Sheen, Eun Son Jin, Jinah Han, Patricia Choi, Takuyo Takahashi, Duvan Hoffman, Stephanie Zelman, Ming-Yen Tung, Eun Kyoung (Veronica) Ahn

PRATT INSTITUTE
Rodrigo Galvan, Brian Merril, Nancy Rivera

PRATT MANHATTAN
David Damman, Edward Pusz

SCHOOL OF VISUAL ARTS
Gerardo Blumenkrantz, Peggy Ferrand, Sharoz Makarechi, Wai-Man Yau

THE ART DIRECTOR'S ANNUAL is a visual accounting of the best work created in 1992 by art directors, creative directors, designers, photographers, illustrators, animators, computer artists, and copywriters worldwide. By annually publishing this book we provide a continuous record of the best ideas produced—putting it up to the reader as a subject for study, inspiration, and conclusions about the state of the art.

What's the use in publishing an annual? Cynics say that it's just a big public portfolio for reaching potential clients or that it's creatives patting their own backs in print. But the denotation of the word "book" provides a retort to these claims: a book is any set of ideas or rules regarded as authoritative. The exhibition entries were judged by industry professionals who are recognized for their own talent. This is an authoritative representation of the new design axioms and trends that are shaping present-day and future communication vernacular.

This is a time when the creative industries are experiencing radical transitions in their economic expectations, sociol responsibilities, and technological capabilities as well as their position in the world at large. Creatives have become more aware of the need for larger-scale communications systems: "globalization", "universality", "multi-linguistic" have become part of the creative concern along with budget, deadline, and quality. Research has always been necessary before the invention of new vehicles for creative expression. More than ever there is the need for creatives to study the visual record of both their past and present. Annuals provide a substantial portion of this much needed research material in a viable format.

Many thanks to the wonderful work of RotoVision, S.A. and Watson-Guptill in spreading this information to a wide audience. A round of applause to the creatives who have contributed to this year's annual: Seymour Chwast for his painted steel sculptures which appear on the cover, part title and chapter opening illustrations; Sara Giovanitti for her elegant design of the cover, opening pages, and text pages; and Ryuichi Minakawa for the complex job of page layout of the medalist and finalist pages. Thanks also goes to the book construction team that included the copyediting and production work by Jared M. Brown and Barbara B. Renard; William Lee, assisting Sara Giovanitti. Finally, thanks to the staff at the Art Directors Club Rhoda Marshall and Verese Weatherspoon; and the ADC exhibition staff: Carol LaPlante and Tracey Thomas.

ANISTATIA R. MILLER

PRESIDENT, ADC PUBLICATIONS

CARL FISCHER, the designer of the 1992 National Call for Entries, is a photographer and consulting art director who graduated from The Cooper Union and studied in Europe as a Fulbright scholar before beginning his career as an advertising agency art director.

His work has won numerous awards, including the Art Director's Club of New York's gold and silver medals. His early portraits of Southern segregationist leaders were exhibited in The Museum of Modern Art's "The Photo Essay" show. Some of his later portraits have appeared at The International Center of Photography and in the permanent collections of several museums including The Metropolitan Museum of Modern art in New York. He regularly contributes covers and editorial work to American and European magazines. Frequent articles about his work have appeared both here and abroad.

He is a principal in Ken & Carl Fischer Photography, a studio that specializes in computer-manipulation, as well as design and photography.

PER ARNOLDI, the designer of the 1992 ADC International Call for Entries is a self-taught artist, painter, graphic designer, television host and reconteur of global renown.

His works are represented in the permanent collections of the Museum of Modern Art in New York, the Victoria and Albert Museum in London, and the Neues Museum für Angewanote Kunst in Munich, just to name a few. He has appeared internationally as a guest lecturer in such places as Art Center, Europe, the World Economic Forum, Tama University, and The Art Directors Club. Arnoldi has also designed posters for The Guggenheim Museum, Carnegie Hall, British Rail, The Royal Theatre, Copenhagen, and DuPont.

Many articles about his work have appeared in design industry publications, and he has received numerous international awards.

SARA GIOVANITTI, the designer of the 72nd Annual, is a publication designer and consultant.

Having majored in Fine Arts at Hunter College, she began her career as assistant to *Mademoiselle* magazine's Bradbury Thompson, followed by a number of years as *Mademoiselle*'s Promotions Art Director.

While raising her children, Giovanitti continued to design and redesign a variety of publications. This led to an offer to be one of the first newspaper art directors in the country—for the *Des Moines Register*, followed by five years as the first Design Director of the *Boston Globe*.

Returning to New York in 1983 to open her own design office, Giovanitti became a member of the Parsons Faculty until 1991—when she joined the School of Visual Arts.

One of the founders of The Society of Newspaper Design, Giovanitti is active in the Art Directors Club and has served on its Executive Committee. She has received numerous awards and was featured in *IDEA* magazine's "Women Designers of America."

A

Robert Abriola
Rea Ackerman
Donald Adamec
Tina Adamek
Gaylord Adams
Steven Adams
Patricia Addiss
Peter Adler
Charles S. Adorney
Dennis Ahlgrin
Betty Alfenito
Olivia Altschuler
Carlo Ammirati
Kevin R. Amter
Joseph Anderson
Susan Andreason
Gennaro Andreozzi
Laurie Angel-Sadis
Rick Angeloni
Al Anthony
Phyllis Aragaki
Frank S. Arcuri
Arnold Arlow
David Armario
Lawrence A. Armour
Dennis Arnold
Stephanie Arnold
Herman Aronson
Rochelle L. Arthur
Tadashi Asano
Marvin Asch
Seymour Augenbraun
Joel Azerrad

B

Jeff Babitz
Robert O. Bach
Ronald Bacsa
Arati S. Badrinath
Priscilla Baer
Ronald Ballister
Ray Barber
Floyd Barker
Christine Barrett
Don Barron
Robert Barthelmes
Gladys Barton
Wendy Bass
Mary K. Baumann
Allan Beaver
Lois Bender
Ephram Benguiat
Edward J. Bennet
Laurence Key Benson
Jerome Berard
Bill Berenter
John Berg
Jeanie Bergin

Pamela J. Berman
Walter L. Bernard
Loren Bernstein
Neale Berthen
Peter Bertolami
Frank Bertulis
Robert Best
Barbara Binzen
Janet Blank
Peter J. Blank
Robert Blattner
Robert H. Blend
Anthony Bloch
Bruce Bloch
David S. Block
Arnold Blumberg
Edward Boches
Robert Bode
Sharon Bodenschatz
George Warren Booth
Robert Bothell
Jean Bourges
Harold A. Bowman
Carolyn Bowyer
Doug Boyd
Douglas C. Boyd
Jean L. Brady
Simeon Braguin
Jean Brandt
Fred J. Brauer
Al Braverman
Barry Braverman
Lynn Dreese Breslin
William Brewer
William P. Brockmeier
Ed Brodsky
Ruth Brody
Sam Brody
John Brooke
Adrienne Brooks
Alan Brooks
Joe Brooks
Leslie Brooks
Annette S. Browdy
Steve Brower
Robert Bruce
Bruno E. Brugnatelli
Alice Bryce
Lee Buchar
Susanne Buckler
William Buckley
Ron Burkhardt
Laurie Burns

C

Bill Cadge
Albert J. Calzetta
Arline Campbell
Bryan G. Caniff
Andrew Cantor

James Caporimo
Elise M. Caputo
James Cardillo
Thomas Carnase
David E. Carter
Ralph Casado
Emmett Cassell
Angelo Castelli
Diana Catherines
Bob Cato
John R. Centanni
Carol F. Ceramicoli
C. Edward Cerullo
Mitchel Chalek
Jean Chambers
Margaret Ann
   Champion
Scott Walker Chaney
Andrew Chang
Anthony Chaplinsky Jr.
Pang B. Chen
Vivian Chen
John Cherry
Roberta Chiarella
Younghee Choi
Shui-Fong Chong
Alan Christie
Hoi Ling Chu
Stanley Church
Seymour Chwast
Robert Ciano
Jon Cisler
Herbert H. Clark
Thomas F. Clemente
Raymond Clifford
Mahlon Cline
Victor Closi
Joel Cohen
Peter Cohen
Michael Coll
Elaine Crawford
   Conner
Catherine Connors
Lee Corey
Eva Costabel
Sheldon Cotler
Susan Cotler-Block
Ron Couture
Jac Coverdale
Stacie Cowan
Phyllis R. Cox
Robert Cox
Thomas Craddock
James Edward Craig
Meg Crane
Brian A. Cranner
Constance Craven
Gregory Crossley
Bob Crozier
Louis F. Cruz
Leslie Cullen

Jerry Cummins
Christine Curry
Charles Cutler
Ethel R. Cutler
Gregory F. Cutshaw

D

Russel J. D'Anna
Deborah Dalton
Derek Dalton
Andrew Damon
David Davidian
Kathryn Davidian
Steven Davidson
David R. Davis
Joseph Davis
Paul B. Davis
Philip Davis
Victor de Castri
William de Corso
Perri L. de Fino
Tony de Gregorio
Diane de Pasque
Jan Dechabert
Lynda Decker
Robert Defrin
Joe del Sorbo
Erick Demartino
Jerry Demoney
Thomas A. Derderian
David Deutsch
Frank M. Devino
Frank Devito
Peter J. Deweerdt
Charles Dickinson
Charles Dicomo
Carolyn Diehl
Edward P. Diehl
John Digham
Dennis Divincenzo
Charles Dixon
Charles P. Doherty
Jody Dole
Louis Donato
Chel Dong
Shelley Doppelt
Louis Dorfsman
Marc Dorian
Andra Douglas
Kay Elizabeth Douglas
Matthew Drance
Nick Driver
Rina Drucker
Faye Ellen Druiz
Ann Dubiel
Donald H. Duffy
Laura Duggan
Rosalyn C. Dunham
Patrice Dunn

E

Stephen T. Eames
Heidi K. Eckman
Bernard Eckstein
Peter Edgar
Michael Edwards
Don Egensteiner
Jac Ehn
Antonie Eichenberg
Zenith Eidel
Nina Eisenman
Stanley Eisenman
Robert Eisner
Judith Ellis
Elaine Ellman
Jack Endewelt
David Epstein
Lee Epstein
Shirley Ericson
Suren Ermoyan
Robert H. Essel

F

Joseph Fama
Rose Farber
Gene Fedele
Gene Federico
Judy Fendelman
John Ferrell
Roger Ferritter
Guy A. Fery
Michael Fidanzato
Len Fink
William F. Finn
Lou Fiorentino
Blanche Fiorenza
Gonzalo Firpo
Carl Fischer
Anne Marie Fitzmeyer
John Flanagan
Morton Fleischer
Gilbert D. Fletcher
Patricia Fletcher
Donald P. Flock
I.L. Fraiman
John Fraioli
Stephen O. Frankfurt
Richard Franklin
Bill Freeland
Ruby Miye Friedland
Beverly Friedman
Michael K. Frith
Oren Frost
Neil Fujita
Leonard W. Fury

G

Mark A. Gable
Harvey Gabor
Raymond Gaeta
Robert Gage
Rosemarie Galioto
Danielle Gallo
Gene Garlanda
Joel Garrick
David Gatti
Joseph T. Gauss
Alberto Gavasci
Mari Gaydos
Steff Geissbuhler
Charles Gennarelli
Robert J. George
Vida Geranmayeh
Michael Germarkian
Linda Gersh
John Geryak
Carl Gessman
Victor Gialleonardo
Joann Giannobile
Edward Gibbs
Kurt Gibson
Carol Bonnie Gildar
Donald Gill
Peter Gilleran
Frank C. Ginsberg
Sara Giovanitti
Hal Glantz
Milton Glaser
Maureen R. Gleason
Eric Gluckman
Marc Gobe
Bill Gold
Irwin Goldberg
Les Goldberg
Benjamin Goldfarb
Roz Goldfarb
Eli W. Goldowsky
Gary Goldsmith
Jo Ann Goldsmith
Andres Gonzalez
Rod Gonzalez
Joanne Goodfellow
Laura Goodman
Rhonda Gotthainer
Jean Govoni
Roy Grace
Diana Graham
Nathan Grau
Albert Greenberg
Allan Greenburg
Adam Greiss
Richard Grider
Jack Griffin
Jeffrey Griffith
Erika Groeschel
Glen P. Groglio

Phillip Growick
Susan Grube
Ira Alan Grunther
Nelson Gruppo
Kimberly Guerre
Rollins S. Guild

H

Steven Haas
Jane Haber
Hank Hachman
Robert Hack
Dean Hacohen
Kurt Haiman
Bruce W. Hall
Everett Halvorsen
Shoichiro Hama
Edward Hamilton
Frances Hamilton
David F. Haney
Cabell Harris
George Hartman
Alan Hartwell
Barry Hassel
Dorothy Hayes
Saul Heff
William G. Heinrich
Amy Heit
Steven Heller
William Hemp
William Hendricks
Randall Hensley
Robert S. Herald
James J. Hermann
Louis F. Hernandez
Susan Herr
Jannike Hess
Chris Hill
Peter Hirsch
Thomas Hitchcock
Jitsuo Hoashi
Gordon Hochhalter
Ronald Hodes
Marilyn Hoffner
Robert Holden
Steve Horn
William David Houser
Paul Howard
Debra Morton Hoyt
Julie Hubner
Thomas M. Hughes
Wayne Hulse
Jud Hurd
Brian Hutter
Steff Hynek

I

Tom J. Ide
Ana J. Inoa

Henry Isdith
Skip K. Ishii

J

Harry Jacobs
Melissa A. Jacoby
Holly Jaffe
Lee Ann Jaffee
Jack E. Jamison
John Jay
Bill Jensen
Patricia Jerina
Paul Jervis
Barbara John
Shaun Johnston
Bob Jones
Len Jossel
Joanne Jubert

K

Nicki Kalish
Kiyoshi Kanai
Walter Kaprielian
Jerry Karpf
Judy Katz
Paul Kaufman
Brian M. Kelly
Ward Kelvin
Alice Kenny
Nancy Kent
Myron W. Kenzer
Ellen Sue Kier
Bokyoung Kim
Hyeson Kim
Ran Hee Kim
Soon Kim
Sam Kintzer
Hedy Klein
Judith Klein
Leslie Alfin Klein
Hilda Stanger Klyde
Andrew Kner
Henry O. Knoepfler
Ray Komai
Robert Kopelman
Arthur Korant
Kati Korpijaakko
Oscar Krauss
Helmut Krone
Thaddeus B. Kubis
Bill Kuchler
Anna Kurz

L

Howard La Marca
Anthony La Petri
Christine Lane Lafferty
James E. Laird

Abril Lamarque
Edward Lamport
David R. Lance
Joseph O. Landi
Hope Langson
David W. Langston
Michael Lanotte
Lisa A. Larochelle
Lawrence Larstanna
Pearl Lau
Kenneth H. Lavey
Marie Christine
Lawrence
Sal Lazzarotti
Lee Le Van
Shawn Le Vesque
Steven W. Lebeck
Daniel Lee
Edwin Lee
Elizabeth Diane
Lemondies
John Lenaas
Marcia Lerner
Robert C. Leung
Richard Levenson
Joanne Levey
Peter Levine
Rick Levine
Alexander Liberman
Henriette E. Lienke
Paul Livornese
Susan Llewellyn
George Lois
Benedetta Lombardi
Henry R. Loomis
George Lott
Robert Louey
Jacques Lowe
Alfred Lowry
Ruth Lubell
John Lucci
Richard Luden
Thomas R. Lunde
Lisa Lurie
Larry Lurin
Robert W. Lyon, Jr.
Michael J. Lyons

M

Charles MacDonald
Richard Macfarlane
David H. MacInnes
Frank Macri
Samuel Magdoff
Lou Magnani
Carol A. Maisto
Nancy L. Makris
Anthony Mancino
Mitchell Mandell
Pamela G. Manser

Jean Marcellino
Eric Marcus
Diane Margolin
David R. Margolis
Jack Mariucci
Andrea Marquez
Hector W. Marrero
Jorge Martell
Joel Mason
Guy Mastrion
Michael Mastros
Theodore Matyas
Andrea Fruend Mauro
Marce Mayhew
Victor John
Mazurkiewicz
Joan Mazzeo
Michael Mazzeo
Sheila McCaffery
William McCaffery
Eileen McClash
Brian P. McDermott
Mark S. McDowell
Colleen McKay
Philip McKenna
Scott A. Mednick
William Meehan
Nancy A. Meher
Barney Melsky
Scott Menchin
Mario Messina
Alice Messinger
Lyle Metzdorf
Jackie Merri Meyer
Thomas A. Miano
Emil Micha
Francis Middendorf
Eugene Milbauer
Anistatia R. Miller
Lawrence Miller
John Milligan
Isaac Millman
Ryuichi Minakawa
Wendell Minor
Michael Miranda
Mark Mitchell
Leonard Mizerek
Allan Mogel
Clement Mok
Joseph Montebello
Ken Montone
Diane Moore
Richard Moore
Rafael Morales
Claudia Moran
Paul Moran
Viorel Moraru
Katherine Moreno-
Sanchez
Jeffrey Moriber
Minoru Morita

Mami Morooka
Leonard Morris
William R. Morrison
Amy Morton
Thomas Morton
Roger Paul Mosconi
Louie Moses
Roselee Moskowitz
Geoffrey Moss
Tobias Moss
Dale Moyer
Robert Mueller
Robbi G. Muir
Virginia Murphy-
  Hamill
Timothy J. Musios
Ralph J. Mutter

N

Daniel Nelson
Barbara Nessim
John Newcomb
Susan Newman
Catherine Newmark
Stuart Nezin
Mary Ann Nichols
Raymond Nichols
Joseph Nissen
Michael Nix
Evelyn C. Noether
George Noszagh
David November

O

Frank O'Blak
Lisa O'Donnell
Craig O'Keefe
John O'Neil
Hugh O'Neill
Kevin James O'Neill
Bill Oberlander
Sharon Occhipinti
Jack Odette
James Offenhartz
John Okladek
Charles S. Olton
Susan Alexis Orlie
Jose Ortiz
Nina Ovryn
Bernard S. Owett

P

Onofrio Paccione
Zlata W. Paces
Robert Paganucci
Jack Palancio
Jane Palecek
Tony Palladino

Brad Pallas
Roxanne Panero
Jacques Parker
Paul E. Parker, Jr.
Grant Parrish
Kathleen Pascoe
Antonia Pascual
Charles W. Pates
Arthur Paul
Dee Paul
Dianne M. Pavacic
Leonard Pearl
Alan Peckolick
B. Martin Pedersen
Partrick Peduto
Carol Peligian
Adriane Pender
Meryl Penner
Pierre Pepin
Paul Perlow
Bea Perron
David Perry
Harold A. Perry
Roberta Perry
Victoria I. Peslak
John Peter
Christos Peterson
Robert Petrocelli
Chris Petrone
Theodore Pettus
Allan Philiba
Daryl Phillips
James Phillips
Alma Phipps
George Pierson
Michael Pilla
Ernest Pioppo
Peter Pioppo
Robert Pliskin
Raymond Podeszwa
George Polk
Kathi Porter
Richard Portner
Louis Portuesi
Frances Posen
Anthony Pozsonyi
Byron Preiss
Harry Prichett
Robert Procida
Rory James Pszenitzki

Q

Michael Quackenbush
Charles W. Queener
Elissa Querze
Anny Queyroy
Kathleen Quinn Fable
Mike Quon

R

Judith Radice
Robert Raines
Paul Rand
Elaine Raphael
Samuel Reed
Sheldon Reed
Patrick Reeves
Wendy Talve Reingold
Herbert Reinke
Harris Reitman
Joseph Leslie Renaud
Anne Marie Renzi
David Rhodes
Ruthann Richert
Edward E. Ricotta
Julian Lee Riedler
Barbara Rietschel
Roxy Rifkin
Arthur Ritter
Valerie Ritter
Barbara B. Roberts
Judy Roberts
Kenneth Roberts
Bennet Robinson
Lenox I. Robinson
Harry Rocker
Harlow Rockwell
Randy Rodriguez
Margaret T. Rogers
Peter Rogers
Andy Romano
Lee Rosenberg
Bobbi Rosenthal
Charles Rosner
Andrew Ross
Mark Ross
Richard Ross
Richard J. Ross
Arnold Roston
Tom Roth
Cynthia Rothbard
Alan Rowe
Randee Rubin
Julie Ruddy
Thomas P. Ruis
Robert Miles Runyan
Tom-Nicholas Rupich
Henry N. Russell
Albert Russo
Don Ruther
Thomas Ruzicka

S

Stewart Sacklow
Moriyoshi Saito
Robert Saks
Peter Saladino
Tracey Salaway

Richard M. Salcer
Ludvic Saleh
Robert Salpeter
James Salser
Karen Salsgiver
Ina Saltz
George Samerjan
Jim Sant'Andrea
Anthony Santore
Betty Saronson
Audrey Satterwhite
Xavier Saucedo
Hans Sauer
John Sayles
David J. Saylor
Mike Saz
Sam Scali
Peter Scannell
Ernie Scarfone
Roland Schenk
Paula Scher
Glen Scheuer
Ava Schlesinger
Klaus F. Schmidt
Joyce Schnaufer
Beverly Schrager
Sharon Schuerman
Carol Schulter
Eileen Hedy Schultz
Nancy K. Schulz
Adiane Schwartz
Martin Schwartz
Victor Scocozza
Elizabeth F. Scott
Ruth Scott-Brody
Julie Scwartzman
Alexis Seabrook
William Seabrook, III
J.J. Sedelmaier
Jacquelin Segal
Leslie Segal
Sheldon Seidler
Tod Seisser
Amy Seissler
John L. Sellers
Kaede Seville
Alexander Shear
Minoru Shiakawa
Jonathan S. Schlafer
Jerry Siano
Louis Silverstein
Robert Simmons
Alice Simpson
Milt Simpson
Leslie Singer
Meera Singh
Leonard Sirowitz
Lucy Sisman
Jack Skolnik
Paul Slutsky
Carol Lynn Smith

Dwayne Smith
George Smith
Jay J. Smith
Paul Smith
Robert S. Smith
Edward Sobel
Andrew Sokol
Darryl Solomon
Martin Solomon
Mark Solsburg
Elaine Sorel
Harold Sosnow
Carmen Soubriet
Michelle Spellman
Ared Spendjian
Lisa Speroni
Victor E. Spindler
Paige Elizabeth St. John
Martin St. Martin
Isaac Stackell
David L. Stahlberg
Shelly Laroche
  Stansfield
Mindy Phelps Stanton
Karsten Stapelfeldt
Lynn Steck
Irena Steckiv
Emily Stedman
Douglas Steinbauer
Karl Eric Steinbrenner
Vera Steiner
Diane Steinmetz
Barrie Stern
Gerald Stewart
Linda Stillman
Bernard Stone
Otto Storch
Lizabeth Storrs
Ilene Strizver
William Strosahl
Shunsaku Sugiura
Brenda Suler
Pamela Sullivan
Sharon Sullivan
Pat Suth
Ken Sweeny
Leslie Sweet
Robin Sweet
Janice Sztabnik

T

Barbara Taff
Daniel L. Tagbo
Norman Tanen
Jo Ann Tansman
Melissa K. Tardiff
Vincent Taschetti
Melcon Tashian
William Taubin
Jack Tauss

Mark Tekushan
George Tenne
Ciro Tesoro
Nell Thalasinos
Margery Theroux
Richard Thomas
Bradbury Thompson
Paula Thomson
Geraldine Thordsen
  Hughs
Maureen Tobin
Robert S. Todd
Harold Toledo
Shinchiro Tora
Victor Trasoff
Joanne Trovato
Susan B. Trowbridge
Joseph P. Tully
Anne Twomey

U

Clare Ultimo
Frank Urrutia

V

Michael Valli
George Vasquez
Pamela Vassil
Barbara Vaughn-Davis
Haydee N. Verdia
Jeanne Viggiano
Amy Vischio
Frank A. Vitale
Michael Vitiello
Thomas Vogel
David L. Vogler
Louis Volpini
Constance
  von Collande
Barbara von Schreiber
Jordana von Spiro
Cal Vornberger
Thuy Vuong

W

Dorothy Wachtenheim
Allan R. Wahler
Jurek Wajdowicz
Joseph O. Wallace
Michael Wallin
John W. Warner
Ann Watt
Laurence Waxberg
Meri Wayne
Jessica Weber
Peter Weber
Art Weithas
Karl M. Wessel

Gail Wiggin
Richard Wilde
Rodney C. Williams
Jack Williamson
Anna Willis
Lauren Winarsky
David Wiseltier
Rupert Witalis
Ross Wittenberg
Henry Wolf
Jay Wolf
Laura E. Woods
Elizabeth G. Woodson
Orest Woronewych
Homer Wright

Y

Ronny Yakov
Ira Yoffe
Zen Yonkovig

Z

Bruce Zahor
Carmile S. Zaino
Gary Zamchick
Ulla Zang
Paul Zasada
Lisa Zaslow
Elaine Zeitsoff
Maxim Zhukov
Mikael T. Zielinski
Bernie Zlotnick
Perry Zompa
Anthony Zurro
Alan Zwiebel

INTERNATIONAL

ARGENTINA
Daniel Verdino

AUSTRALIA
Ron Kambourian

AUSTRIA
Mariusz Jan Demner
Helmut Klein
Franz Merlicek

BELGIUM
Julien Behaeghel

BRAZIL
Oswaldo Miranda
Adeir Rampazzo

FRANCE
Jean Feldman

GERMANY
Olaf Leu
Hans-Georg Pospischil

HOLLAND
Pieter Branttiga

HONG KONG
Elman Chan

INDIA
Brendan Pereira
Rohana
  Wickramanayake

ISRAEL
Asher Kalderon
Dan Reisinger

ITALY
Titti Fabiani

JAPAN
Masuteru Aoba
Hiroyuki Aotani
Katsumi Asaba
Yuji Baba
Peter Brenoe
Satoru Fujii
Terunobu Fukushima
Osamu Furumura
Akio Hirai
Mitsutoshi Hosaka
Ken Ichihashi
Yasuyuki Ito
Tetsuro A. Itoh
Michio Iwaki
Toshio Iwata
Masaaki Izumiya
Takahisha Kamijyo
Hideyuki Kaneko
Pete Kobayashi
Ryohei Kojima
Yoshikatsu Kosakai
Mitsuhiko Kotani
Pepie Krakower
Kazuki Maeda
Keizo Matsui
Takaharu Matsumoto
Takao Matsumoto
Shin Matsunaga
Iwao Matsuura
Keisuke Nagatomo
Michio Nakahara
Yasuhara Nakahara
Makoto Nakamura
Toshiyuki Ohasi
Takeshi Ohtaka
Shigeo Okamoto
Motoaki Okuizumi
Akio Okumura
Shigeshi Omori
Susumu Sakane
Takayuki Shirasu
Seiji Sugii
Yasua Suzuki
Yutaka Takahama
Masakazu Tanabe
Teruo Tanabe
Ikko Tanaka
Soji George Tanaka

Ben Tomita
Yusaku Tomoeda
Norio Uejo
Michihiro Usami
Masato Watanabe
Yoshiko Watanabe
Akihiro H. Yamamato
Yoji Yamamoto
Takeo Yao

MEXICO
Felix Beltran
Diana Garcia de Tolone
Luis Efren Ramirez
  Flores

PHILIPPINES
Emily A. Abrera

SINGAPORE
Kellie Chang
Chiet-Hsuen Eng

SWITZERLAND
Bilal Dallenbach
Moritz Jaggi
Dominque Schuetz
Philipp Welti

UNITED KINGDOM
Barry L. Day
Keith Murgatroyd
Celia Stothard
Len Sugarman

WEST MALAYSIA
Peter Wong

ZIMBABWE
Chaz Maviyane-Davies

AFFILIATES

THE COLAD GROUP
Nancy Hammett
CREATIVE BLACK BOOK
Lee Le Van
JCH GROUP, LTD.
Harris Reitman

NEW YORK CITY
TECHNICAL COLLEGE
Joel Mason
PARSONS SCHOOL OF DESIGN
Albert Greenberg
PETER ROGERS ASSOCIATES
Dee Paul

PRATT INSTITUTE
Ray Barber
SCHOOL OF VISUAL ARTS
Leslie Brooks
TOPPAN PRINTING
Ryuichi Minakawa
UNION CAMP CORPORATION
Stewart J. Phelps

WE WOULD LIKE TO THANK the following sponsors for their kind support for the publication of this year's ADC Annual. It is with their help that we at the Art Directors Club are able to present you with the best work in the visual communications industries.

SPONSORS

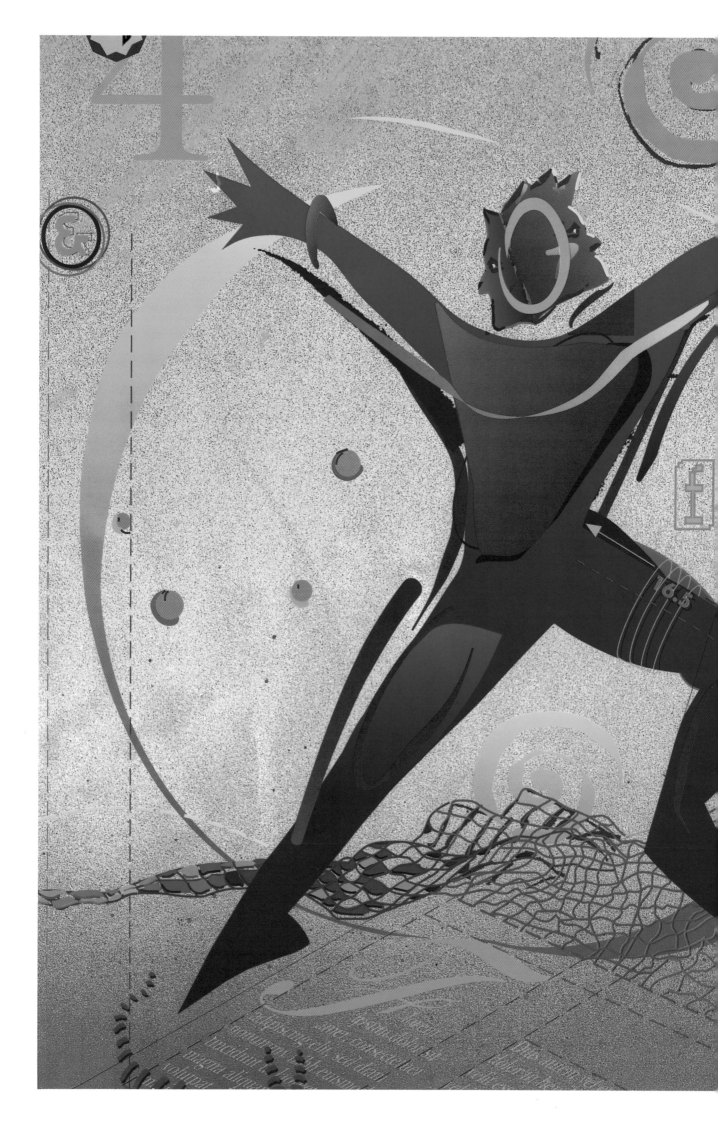

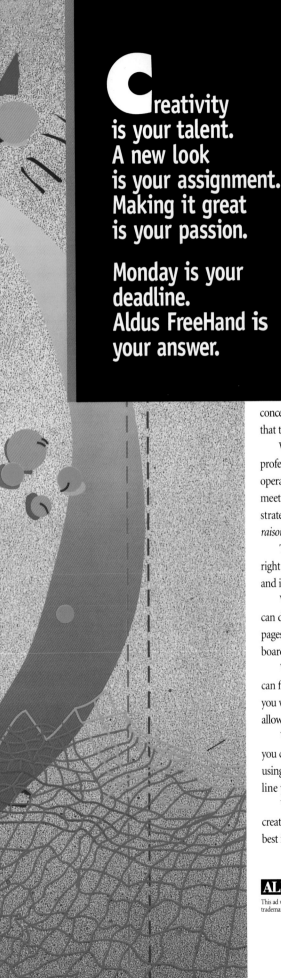

Creativity is your talent. A new look is your assignment. Making it great is your passion.

Monday is your deadline. Aldus FreeHand is your answer.

Most people don't know how you do what you do. Maybe you don't even know yourself.

But you do it. And that's all that matters. Magic happens.

And to help you make that magic—and make it easier, faster, freer, and more forgivingly than ever before—there's the new Aldus FreeHand® 4.0.

Finally, you can design and illustrate from concept to reality—naturally. And you can take that to the bank.

Which is the whole point. As a creative professional, you're in a visual business. And the operative word is *business*. Your creativity has to meet business objectives, respond to business strategies, and deliver to that ultimate business *raison d'etre*: the bottom line.

That's why Aldus FreeHand 4.0 is the right tool for you. It's the right creative tool— and it's the right business tool.

With its powerful page-design tools, you can design, illustrate, and produce multiple pages in multiple sizes on a large "live" paste-board then output them from a single file.

With its superior typographic control, you can fit any copy to any shape, creating anything you want rather than only what the program allows you.

With its extensive graphics capabilities, you can create new objects quickly and easily using path-editing shortcuts that help stream-line your creative process and save you time.

With its eleven floating palettes, you can create the on-screen environment that works best for you. You can manage and control page design, text, colors, tints, layers, and more. You can drag and drop colors from palettes right into your design, just as you might with paint to a canvas. And you can "lock" layers to protect them from accidental edits or deletions.

And it smoothly integrates with Aldus® PageMaker.® Using hotlinks, you can edit Aldus FreeHand files seamlessly from within PageMaker 4.2 or 5.0. And since they share many conventions, such as keyboard shortcuts, color libraries, and hyphenation dictionaries, you can work smarter instead of harder.

Create and consolidate complex projects in a single file.

Aldus FreeHand 4.0 gives you the freedom to be more creative—and the power to be more productive.

So if the bottom line is making it work, but the top line is making it great, you need the new Aldus FreeHand 4.0 for Macintosh.

Call us and we'll send you more information and a self-running demo disk so you can see for yourself how Aldus FreeHand can help you make a difference.

Call toll-free (800) 685-3608.

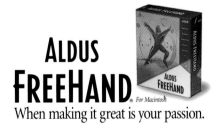

ALDUS FREEHAND ® *For Macintosh*
When making it great is your passion.

need an umbrella?

buy the book

You can find these umbrellas and more, plus 250 other categories in the finest resource for creative brainstorming– the *Bettmann Portable Archive.* This new and updated edition of the communications professionals' classic contains 336 pages filled with over 6,000 color and black-and-white images. The definitive visual reference tool from the world's leading source of historical and news pictures. Sixty-five dollars. Order now. For Visa or Master Card orders, call 1-800-897-3377. To order by mail, send check or money order (include three dollars shipping and handling) to: Bettmann, Dept. G, 902 Broadway, New York, NY 10010. NY and MD residents, please add applicable sales tax.

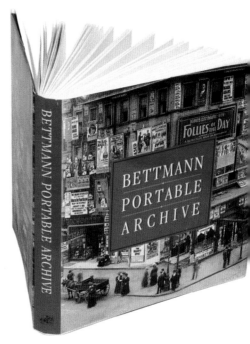

BETTMANN

THE BETTMANN ARCHIVE · BETTMANN NEWSPHOTOS · REUTERS AND UPI PHOTO LIBRARIES

JOAN JEDELL
Represents
Some of the Best
Photographers
In the Country

Jedell Productions

212 / 861-7861

The Best Ideas are Part Paper™

All It Takes Is Imagination.

Yours and Mine.

If you have any questions,

or would like additional

samples, please call.

Thank you.

David Lesh

317.253.3141

FAX 317.255.8462

Sia Aryai Photography 837 traction ave. la ca, 90013 fax: 213 617 9740 tel: 213 617 9001

TODD HAIMAN

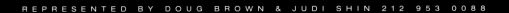

WHERE DO YOU FIND GREAT ART DIRECTORS THESE DAYS?

You'll find them reading Graphis. You'll find them in Graphis, along with great photographers, great architects and all the other great talent doing great work these days. And now's a great time to get this great magazine at a great price.*

Just call: 1-800-351-0006. Outside USA call: +1-212-532-9387.

*ONE YEAR (SIX ISSUES) $79.00. LOCAL PRICES APPLY TO NON-USA ORDERS. ADVERTISEMENT BY ONOFRIO PACCIONE, A GREAT ART DIRECTOR.

National/Television
ART DIRECTOR
Gill Witt
COPYWRITER
George Logothetis
PRODUCER
Amy Saunders
DIRECTOR
Jeff Gorman
AGENCY
Chiat/Day/Mojo
CLIENT
Reebok

National/Television
ART DIRECTORS/COPYWRITERS
Dick Sittig, Lee Clow
PRODUCER
Amy Saunders
AGENCY
Chiat/Day/Mojo
CLIENT
Reebok

National/Television
ART DIRECTOR
Dawn Prestom
COPYWRITER
Rob Slosberg
PRODUCERS
Peter Cline, Diane Rowell
DIRECTOR
Gary Johns
AGENCY
Chiat/Day/Mojo
CLIENT
Reebok

National/Television
ART DIRECTOR
Bill Schwab
COPYWRITER
Dick Sittig
PRODUCERS
Peter Cline, Diane Rowell
DIRECTOR
Gary Johns
AGENCY
Chiat/Day/Mojo
CLIENT
Reebok

National/Television
ART DIRECTOR
Jac Coverdale
COPYWRITER
Josh Denberg
DIRECTOR
Greg Winter
AGENCY
Clarity Coverdale Rueff
CLIENT
United Recovery Center

National/Television
ART DIRECTOR
Chuck Finkle
COPYWRITER
Dean Hacohen
DIRECTOR
Henry Sandbank
AGENCY
Goldsmith/Jeffrey
CLIENT
NYNEX Business-to-Business Diretcory

National/Television
ART DIRECTOR
Bill Nosan, Mitch Boyd
COPYWRITER
Tom Woodward
AGENCY
Cramer Krasselt Orlando

National/Print Advertising
ART DIRECTOR
Peggy Redfern
COPYWRITER
C. Strickland
AGENCY
CHD
CLIENT
The Spy Factory

National/Print Advertising
ART DIRECTOR
Jimmy Olsen
COPYWRITER
Pete Kellen
PHOTOGRAPHER
Scott Lanza
AGENCY
Cramer-Krasselt
CLIENT
Coin Appliances Inc.

National/Print Advertising

ART DIRECTOR/ COPYWRITER
Brett Stiles

CREATIVE DIRECTOR
Tim Fisher

COPYWRITER
Tom Kane

PHOTOGRAPHER
Robert Peak

AGENCY
Anson-Stoner Inc.

CLIENT
Pizza Hut, Inc.

National/Print Advertising

ART DIRECTOR
Bob Meagher

COPYWRITER
Joe Alexander

PHOTOGRAPHER
Cathy Groth, Dean Hawthrone

AGENCY
The Martin Agency

National/Print Advertising

ART DIRECTOR
John Vitro

COPYWRITER
John Robertson

PHOTOGRAPHER
Art Wolfe

AGENCY
Franklin Stoorza

CLIENT
Taylor Guitar

National/Campaign/Print Advertising

ART DIRECTOR
Margaret McGovern

COPYWRITER
Paul Silverman

PRODUCTION
John Holt Studio

AGENCY
Mullen

CLIENT
The Timberland Co.

National/Print Advertising

ART DIRECTOR
Dean Hanson

COPYWRITER
Doug de Grood

ILLUSTRATOR
Mary Northrup

AGENCY
Fallon McElligott

CLIENT
Communities Caring For Children

National/Editorial Design

ART DIRECTOR
Patricia Bradbury

DESIGNER
Peter Comitini

PUBLICATION
Newsweek

National/Editorial Design

ART DIRECTOR
Patricia Bradbury

DESIGNER
Peter Comitini

PUBLICATION
Newsweek

National/Editorial Design

ART DIRECTOR
Patricia Bradbury

DESIGNER
Peter Comitini

ILLUSTRATOR
Barbara Kruger

PUBLICATION
Newsweek

National/Editorial Design

ART DIRECTOR
Patricia Bradbury

DESIGNER
Ron Meyerson

ILLUSTRATOR
Rafael Olbinsky

PUBLICATION
Newsweek

National/Editorial Design
ART DIRECTOR
Janet Froelich
DESIGNER
Kandy Littrell
PHOTOGRAPHER
Sally
PUBLICATION
The New York Times Magazine

National/Editorial Design
ART DIRECTOR
Janet Froelich
PHOTOGRAPHER
Michael O'Brien
PUBLICATION
The New York Times Magazine

National/Editorial Design
ART DIRECTOR
David Armario
PUBLICATION
Stanford Medicine
ILLUSTRATOR
Terry Allen

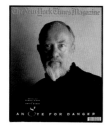

National/Editorial Design
ART DIRECTOR
David Armario
ILLUSTRATOR
Gary Baseman
PUBLICATION
Stanford Medicine

National/Editorial Design
ART DIRECTOR
David Armario
ILLUSTRATOR
Terry Allen
PUBLICATION
Stanford Medicine

National/Editorial Design
ART DIRECTOR
David Armario, James Lambertus
PHOTOGRAPHER
Todd Gray
PUBLICATION
Discover Magazine

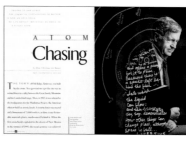

National/Editorial Design
ART DIRECTOR
Joan Ferrell
ILLUSTRATOR
Wiktor Sadowski
STUDIO
Lang Communications
PUBLICATION
Working Mother Magazine

National/Editorial Design
ART DIRECTOR
Don Morris
DESIGNERS
Susan Foster, Dorothy O'Connor, Kayo Der Sarkissian
PHOTOGRAPHER
Mark Seliger
PUBLICATION
Metropolitan Home

National/Editorial Design
ART DIRECTORS
Carl Lehmann-Haupt, Nancy Cohen
WRITER
Naomi R. Pollock
PHOTOGRAPHER
David Stetson
PUBLICATION
Metropolis Magazine

National/Editorial Design
ART DIRECTOR
Patrick Mitchell
PHOTOGRAPHER
Deborah Samuel
STUDIO
Patrick Mitchell
PUBLICATION
Garbage, Dovetail Publishers

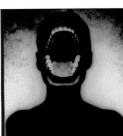

National/Editorial Design
ART DIRECTOR
Jennifer Wavereck
WRITER
Sarah Medford
PHOTOGRAPHER
Bruce Wolf
PUBLICATION
Martha Stewart Living

National/Editorial Design
DESIGN DIRECTOR
Marilu Lopez
DESIGNER
Penny Blatt
PHOTOGRAPHER
Tom Schenk
PUBLICATION
McCall's Magazine

National/Editorial Design
ART DIRECTOR
Marcia Jennings
ILLUSTRATOR
Lane Smith
STUDIO
Lang Communications
PUBLICATION
Working Mother Magazine

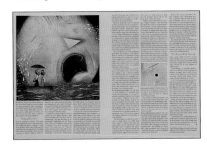

National/Distinctive Merit/Editorial Design
ART DIRECTOR
Matthew Drace, Gaemer Gutierrez
PUBLICATION
Men's Journal

National/Editorial Design
ART DIRECTOR
Walter Bernard, Milton Glaser
DESIGNER
Frank Baseman
STUDIO
WBMG, Inc.
CLIENT
U&lc/International Typeface Corp.

Natiol/Campaign/Editorial Design
ART DIRECTOR
B. Martin Pedersen
WRITER
Jurgen Kesting
PHOTOGRAPHER
Gunther Raupp
STUDIO
Pedersen Design Inc.
PUBLICATION
Graphis

National/Editorial Design
ART DIRECTOR
B. Martin Pedersen
WRITER
Peter Ujlaki
STUDIO
Pedersen Design Inc.
PUBLICATION
Graphis

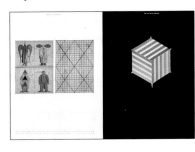

National/Editorial Design
ART DIRECTOR
Linda Hinrichs
ILLUSTRATOR
Mark Selfe
STUDIO
Powell Street Studio
CLIENT
SF Museum of Modern Art

National/Editorial Design
DESIGN DIRECTOR
Jeffrey Keyton
ART DIRECTORS
Stacy Drummond, Steve Bryam
WRITERS
Sharon Glassman, Cheryl Family
CLIENT
MTV Networks

National/Editorial Design
ART DIRECTORS
John Muller, Sal Costello
STUDIO
Muller & Co.
CLIENT
Kansas City Art Institute

National/Editorial Design
ART DIRECTOR
Celia Fuller
AUTHOR
Dexter Cirillo
PHOTOGRAPHERS
Michel Monteaux, Stephan Northup
PUBLISHER
Abbeville Press

National/Editorial Design
ART DIRECTOR
Alex Castro
AUTHOR
Randolph Carter
PUBLISHER
Abbeville Press

National/Editorial Design
ART DIRECTOR
B. Martin Pedersen
PHOTOGRAPHER
Greg Gorfkle
STUDIO
Pedersen Design Inc.
CLIENT
Graphis

National/Editorial Design
ART DIRECTOR
David High, Fiona Scrymgour
PHOTOGRAPHERS
FPG international, Doris Kloster
STUDIO
iT Design, Inc.
CLIENT
Grove Press

National/Editorial Design
ART DIRECTOR
David High, Fiona Scrymgour
STUDIO
iT Design, Inc.
CLIENT
Plume

National/Editorial Design
ART DIRECTOR
Henry Sene Yee
AUTHOR
Cal Morgan
PUBLISHER
St. Martins Press

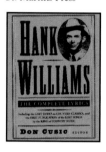

National/Editorial Design
ART DIRECTOR
Michael Accordino
PUBLISHER
St. Martins Press

570

National/Editorial Design
ART DIRECTORS
Nat Estes, Mike Accordino
AUTHORS
Jim Fitzgerald, Alex Kucznski
PUBLISHER
St. Martins Press

National/Editorial Design
ART DIRECTOR
Michael Accordino
ILLUSTRATOR
Eric Dinyer
PUBLISHER
St. Martins Press

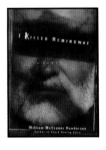

National/Editorial Design
ART DIRECTOR
Henry Sene Yee
PHOTOGRAPHER
TETSU/Photonica
PUBLISHER
St. Martins Press, A Thomas Dunne Book

National/Editorial Design
ART DIRECTOR
Henry Sene Yee
AUTHOR
Regan Arthur
ILLUSTRATOR
Maureen Meehan
PUBLISHER
St. Martins Press, A Thomas Dunne Book

National/Editorial Design
ART DIRECTOR
Jackie Merri Meyer
ILLUSTRATOR
Phil Huling
PUBLISHER
Warner Books

National/Editorial Design
ART DIRECTOR
Jackie Merri Meyer
DESIGNER
Louise Fili
ILLUSTRATOR
Phil Huling
PUBLISHER
Warner Books

National/Distinctive Merit/Editorial Design
ART DIRECTOR
Susan Mitchell
DESIGNERS
Craig Warner, Keith Sheridan
PHOTOGRAPHER
Gary Issacs
STUDIO
Keith Sheridan Assoc. Inc.

National/Silver/Graphic Design
ART DIRECTOR
Loid Der
CREATIVE DIRECTOR
Scott Mednick
DIRECTOR
Greg Gold
AGENCY
The Mednick Group

National/Graphic Design
COPYWRITER
Mary Anne Costello
PHOTOGRAPHER
Tom Wood
STUDIO
Wood Design
CLIENT
Louis Dreyfus Property Group

National/Graphic Design
ART DIRECTOR
Paul Marciano
DESIGNER
Samantha Gibson
PHOTOGRAPHER
Ellen Von Unwerth
CLIENT
Guess?, Inc.

National/Graphic Design
ART DIRECTOR
Mark Oldach
COPYWRITER
Linda Chryle
PHOTOGRAPHER
Kechele, Oldach
STUDIO
Mark Oldach Design

National/Distinctive Merit/Graphic Design
ART DIRECTOR
David Sterling, Jane Kosstein, Monica Halpert
DESIGNER
Klaus Kempenaars, Eric Spillman
COPYWRITER
Danny Altman
STUDIO
DoubleSpace
CLIENT
Marvel Entertainment Group

National/Graphic Design
ART DIRECTOR
Mitchell Mauk
STUDIO
Mauk Design
CLIENT
MacUser Magazine

National/Photography & Illustration
ART DIRECTOR
Janet Froelich
DESIGNER
Kathi Rota
PHOTOGRAPHER
Michele Clement
PUBLICATION
The New York Times Magazine

National/Photography & Illustration
ART DIRECTOR
Jack Frakes, Braldt Bralds.
AGENCY
ALFA Romeo USA
ILLUSTRATOR
Braldt Bralds

National/Photography & Illustration
ART DIRECTOR/ILLUSTRATOR
Don Weller
COPYWRITER
Gary Kimball
STUDIO
The Weller Institue for the Cure of Design
PUBLICATION
Park City Lodestar Magazine

National/Television Advertising
ART DIRECTOR
Craig Miller
COPYWRITER
Norm Weill
PRODUCER
Steve Freidman
DIRECTORS
Leslie Dektor, Rye Dahlman
AGENCY
Saatchi & Saatchi
CLIENT
Paine Webber

National/Television Advertising
ART DIRECTOR
Vince Engel
COPYWRITER
Jerry Cronin
PRODUCER
Ben Grylewicz
DIRECTOR
Brant Thomas
AGENCY
Wieden & Kennedy
CLIENT
Subaru of America

National/Print Advertising

ART DIRECTOR
Craig Tanimoto

COPYWRITER
Glen Wachowiak

AGENCY
Ad Hut

CLIENT
Classy Chassis

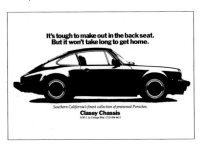

National/Print Advertising

ART DIRECTOR
Craig Tanimoto

COPYWRITER
Glen Wachowiak

AGENCY
Ad Hut

CLIENT
Classy Chassis

National/Print Advertising

ART DIRECTOR
Dabni Harvey

COPYWRITER
Steve Price

AGENCY
Saatchi & Saatchi

CLIENT
Salomon North America

National/Print Advertising

ART DIRECTOR
Bob Barrie

COPYWRITER
Mike Gibbs

PHOTOGRAPHER
Bettman Archive

AGENCY
Fallon McElligott

CLIENT
Continental Bank

National/Print Advertising

ART DIRECTOR
Bob Barrie

COPYWRITER
Mike Gibbs

PHOTOGRAPHER
Bettman Archive

AGENCY
Fallon McElligott

CLIENT
Continental Bank

National/Print Advertising

ART DIRECTOR
Dave Hoffman

COPYWRITER
Mike Bednarski

PHOTOGRAPHER
Scott Lanza

ELECTRONIC IMAGING
Risser Digital Imaging

AGENCY
Cramer-Krasselt/Milwaukee

CLIENT
East Towne Jewelers

National/Distinctive Merit/Print Advertising

ART DIRECTOR
Jelly Helm

COPYWRITER
Joe Alexander

PHOTOGRAPHER
Dublin Productions

AGENCY
The Martin Agency

CLIENT
Health-tex

National/Distinctive Merit/Print Advertising

ART DIRECTOR
Jelly Helm

COPYWRITER
Joe Alexander

PHOTOGRAPHER
Dublin Productions

AGENCY
The Martin Agency

CLIENT
Health-tex

National/Print Advertising

ART DIRECTOR
Brian Doyle

COPYWRITER
Don Koeberle

PHOTOGRAPHER
Dan Arsenault

AGENCY
Della Femina, McNamee

CLIENT
Toshiba

National/Graphic Design

ART DIRECTOR
Kent Hunter

DESIGNER
Steven Fabrizio

ILLUSTRATOR
Ann Field

PHOTOGRAPHER
John Ashworth

AGENCY
Frankfurt Gips Balkind

CLIENT
Tambrands Inc.

National/Graphic Design

ART DIRECTOR
Kerry Leimer

ILLUSTRATOR
Carla Siboldi

PHOTOGRAPHER
Jeff Corwin

STUDIO
Leimer Cross Design

CLIENT
Expeditors International

National/Graphic Design

ART DIRECTOR
Linda Warren

DESIGNER/CALLIGRAPHER
Kimberly Hillman

ILLUSTRATOR
Kevin Burke

PHOTOGRAPHER
Becky Heavner

STUDIO
The Warren Group, Venice USA

CLIENT
Harvard-Westlake School

National/Graphic Design

ART DIRECTOR/DESIGNER
Steve Ditko

COPYWRITER
Jill Spear

PHOTOGRAPHER
Rick Rusing

STUDIO
Campbell Fisher Ditko Design

CLIENT
Uh Oh Clothing

National/Graphic Design

ART DIRECTOR
Mike Campbell

COPYWRITER
Virginia Senior

PHOTOGRAPHER
Scott Baxter

STUDIO
Campbell Fisher Ditko Design

CLIENT
Oest Metalworks

National/Silver/Graphc Design

ART DIRECTOR
Paula Scher

DESIGNER
Ron Lowe

STUDIO
Pentagram Design

CLIENT
Bard College

National/Editorial Design

ART DIRECTOR
Tina Adamek

ILLUSTRATOR
Dale Gottlieb

PUBLICATION
Postgraduate Medicine, McGraw Hill, Inc.

National/Editorial Design

ART DIRECTOR
Tina Adamek

ILLUSTRATOR
Mary Grandpré

PUBLICATION
Postgraduate Medicine, McGraw Hill, Inc.

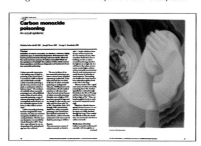

National/Editorial Design

ART DIRECTOR
Tina Adamek

ILLUSTRATOR
Jane Hurd

PUBLICATION
Postgraduate Medicine, McGraw Hill, Inc.

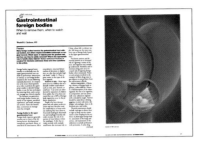

National/Editorial Design

ART DIRECTORS
Walter Bernard, Milton Glaser

DESIGNERS
Frank Baseman, Sharon Okamoto

ILLUSTRATOR
Mirko Ilic

STUDIO
WBMG, Inc.

CLIENT
International Typeface Corp./U&lc

National/Graphic Design

ART DIRECTOR
Bill Cahan

DESIGNERS
David Gilmour, Stuart Flake

COPYWRITER
Theresa Brown

PHOTOGRAPHERS
David Peterson, Bradley Burns, Steve Crouch

STUDIO
Cahan & Associates

CLIENT
America First Financial Corp.

National/Graphic Design

ART DIRECTOR
Frank Oswald

DESIGNER
David Dunkelberger

COPYWRITER
Frank Oswald

PHOTOGRAPHER
Ann Spurling, Tom Collicott

STUDIO
WYD Design, Inc.

CLIENT
Zurich International (Bermuda) Ltd.

National/Graphic Design

ART DIRECTOR
Lana Rigsby

DESIGNER
Troy S. Ford

COPYWRITER
JoAnne Stone

ILLUSTRATOR
Andy Dearwater

PHOTOGRAPHERS
C. Shinn, J. Sims, J. Baraban

STUDIO
Rigsby Design, Inc.

CLIENT
Serv-Tech, Inc.

National/Graphic Design

VP CREATIVE
Thomas Tercek

PRODUCER
Graham McCulum

AGENCY
Mmalum Kennedy D'Auria

CLIENT
MTV Networks

National/Graphic Design

ART DIRECTORS
Scott Bremner, Mike Mazza

DESIGNER
Tom Saputo

CREATIVE DIRECTOR
Tom Cordner

COPYWRITER
Steve Silver

PHOTOGRAPHER
Michael Ruppert

AGENCY
Team One Advertising

National/Graphic Design

ART DIRECTOR
Rex Peteet

COPYWRITER
Mary Keck

STUDIO
Sibley/Peteet Design

CLIENT
James River Corp.

National/Graphic Design
ART DIRECTOR
Jeffrey Morris
PHOTOGRAPHER
Jayme Phillips
STUDIO
Studio Morris
CLIENT
Hot Sox

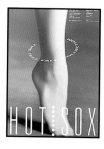

National/Graphic Design
ART DIRECTOR
Bob Mould
PHOTOGRAPHERS
Mark C., Kevin O'Neill
CONCEPT
Conrad Warre
CLIENT
Ryko Disc

National/Graphic Design
ART DIRECTOR
Ron Sullivan
DESIGNER
Art Garcia
COPYWRITERS
Mark Perkins, Priscilla Siegel
ILLUSTRATORS
Jon Flaming, Art Garcia
STUDIO
Sullivan Perkins
CLIENT
Donahue Schriber, Glendale Galleria

National/Graphic Design
ART DIRECTOR
Peter Windett
DESIGNER
Penelope P
ILLUSTRATOR
Karen Murray
STUDIO
Peter Windett & Assoc.
CLIENT
Crabtree & Evelyn

National/Graphic Design
ART DIRECTOR/ILLUSTRATOR
Thomas Au
STUDIO
Poung Au Design

National/Graphic Design
ART DIRECTOR
Carolyn M. Kiely
COPYWRITER
Elaine Goodale Eastman
STUDIO
Kiely & Co.
CLIENT
Lisa & John Fixx

National/Graphic Design
ART DIRECTOR
David Ring
DESIGNER
Bryan Burlison
COPYWRITERS
David Ring, Bryan Burlison
PHOTOGRAPHER
Phillip Esparza
STUDIO
The Richards Group
CLIENT
Mike & Terri Wodka

National/Graphic Design
ART DIRECTOR
Bonnie Smelts
STUDIO
Bonnie Smelts Design
CLIENT
The Nature Company

National/Graphic Design

ART DIRECTOR
Jeffrey McKay

CREATIVE DIRECTOR
Ward Pennebaker

STUDIO
Pennebaker Design

CLIENT
Grady Gators Middle School

National/Graphic Design

ART DIRECTOR
Kitty Strozier

AGENCY
Longwater Advertising

CLIENT
United Arab Agencies, Inc.

National/Photography & Illustration

ART DIRECTOR/COPYWRITER/ILLUSTRATOR
Debra Thompson

AGENCY
Welch + Nehlan Advertising

CLIENT
Welch + Nehlan Advertising

National/Photography & Illustration

ART DIRECTOR/COPYWRITER
David Angelo

PHOTOGRAPHER
Joe Baraban

AGENCY
DDB Needham Worldwide

CLIENT
New York Lottery

National/Photography & Illustration

ART DIRECTOR
Janet Froelich

DESIGNER
Kathi Rota

PHOTOGRAPHER
Michele Clement

PUBLICATION
The New York Times Magazine

National/Photography & Illustration

ART DIRECTOR
David Orr

PHOTOGRAPHER
The photo booth at Little Ricky's

STUDIO
Doubling Comm.

CLIENT
The Knitting Factory

National/Photography & Illustration

ART DIRECTOR/ILLUSTRATOR
Brad Holland

DESIGNER
Jim McCune

CLIENT
AIGA Wichita

National/Editorial Design
ART DIRECTOR
Patricia Fabricant
AUTHOR
Sarah Key
ILLUSTRATOR
Deyne Design
PUBLISHER
Abbeville Press

National/Graphic Design
ART DIRECTOR
Brenda Kilmer, Richard Kilmer
COPYWRITER
David Jones
PHOTOGRAPHER
Michael Barley
ILLUSTRATOR
Richard Kilmer
CLIENT
Diagonstek, Inc.

National/Editorial Design
ART DIRECTOR
Molly Shields
AUTHOR
Abbeville Press & Ediciones Lariviere
PUBLISHER
Abbeville Press

National/Editorial Design
DESIGNER
Takaaki Matsumoto
STUDIO
M Plus M Incorporated
PHOTOGRAPHER
Hiroshi Sugimoto
CLIENT
Kyoto Shoin Publishing

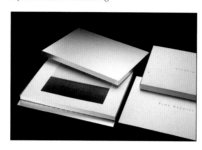

National/Editorial Design
ART DIRECTOR
Jacki Gallagher
WRITERS
Jeff Levin, Jane Slate Siena
PUBLICATION
Conservation, The GCI Newsletter

National/Print Advertising
ART DIRECTOR
Jac Coverdale
COPYWRITER
Jerry Fury
PHOTOGRAPHER
Shawn Michenzi
AGENCY
Clarity Coverdale Rueff
CLIENT
Northwestern National Life

International/Graphic Design
ART DIRECTOR
Andreas Netthoevel
COPYWRITER
Any Persons
DESIGNERS
Martin Gaberthuel, Andreas Netthoevel
STUDIO
Andreas Netthoevel
CLIENT
Raum-Design

International/Graphic Design
ART DIRECTOR/DESIGNER
Mitsuo Katsui
PHOTOGRAPHER
Keiichi Tahara
STUDIO
Mitsuo Katsui
CLIENT
Pentax

International/Graphic Design
ART DIRECTOR/DESIGNER
Brett Wickins
COPYWRITER
Baseline/Bob Campbell
ILLUSTRATOR
Nick Turner
STUDIO
Pentagram Design Ltd.
CLIENT
Baseline Magazine

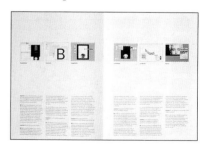

International/Graphic Design

ART DIRECTORS/DESIGNERS
Christof Gassner, Fabian Nicola

WRITER
Dirk Maxeiner

PUBLICATION
Natur Magazine

International/Print Advertising

ART DIRECTOR
Jams Jung

CREATIVE DIRECTOR
Brian Harrod

COPYWRITER
Bill Daniel

PHOTOGRAPHER
Bert Bell

AGENCY
Harrod & Mirlin

CLIENT
Levi Strauss & Co. (Canada)

International/Print Advertising

ART DIRECTOR
Haydn Morris

CREATIVE DIRECTORS
Antonio Maccario, Oscar Molinari

COPYWRITER
Antonio Maccario

PHOTOGRAPHER
Daniele Fiore

AGENCY
McCann Erikson Rome

CLIENT
Rai

International/Print Advertising

ART DIRECTOR
Bob Goulart

COPYWRITER
Grahame Arnould

PHOTOGRAPHER
Vince Noguc

AGENCY
Harrod & Mirlin

CLIENT
Moosehead Breweries Ltd.

International/Print Advertising

ART DIRECTOR
Kazumi Murata

CREATIVE DIRECTOR
Akira Odagiri

COPYWRITER
Makoto Tsunoda

DESIGNER
Shikoh Kimura

PHOTOGRAPHER
Takayuki

AGENCY
Dentsu Inc.

CLIENT
All Japan Radio & Television Company

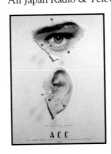

International/Print Advertising

ART DIRECTOR/DESIGNER/ILLUSTRATOR
Edi Berk

STUDIO
KROG

CLIENT
MGL

International/Print Advertising

ART DIRECTOR
Katsumi Asaba

DESIGNERS
Keiko Mineishi, Teruo Kataoka

PHOTOGRAPHER
Naruyasu Nabeshima

STUDIO
Asaba Design Co. Ltd.

CLIENT
G8 Gallery

International/Print Advertising

ART DIRECTOR
Jürgen Däuwel

CREATIVE DIRECTOR
Bernd Misske

COPYWRITER
Hartmut Bauer

PHOTOGRAPHER
Archiv-slide-NASA

AGENCY
Young & Rubicam GmbH

CLIENT
Hessicher Rundfunk

International/Print Advertising

ART DIRECTOR/DESIGNER
Ikko Tanaka

STUDIO
Ikko Tanaka Design Studio

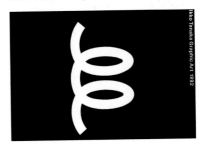

International/Print Advertising
ART DIRECTOR/DESIGNER
Kyoji Kotani
STUDIO
Kyoji Kotani Design Office

International/Print Advertising
ART DIRECTOR/CREATIVE DIRECTOR/DESIGNER
Bruno Oldani
COPYWRITER
Michael Brady
STUDIO
Bruno Oldani
CLIENT
AGI

International/Print Advertising
ART DIRECTOR
Andy Clarke
CREATIVE DIRECTOR
Jim Aitchinson, Norman Alcuri
COPYWRITER
Antony Redman
AGENCY
The Ball Partnership Euro RSCG

International/Print Advertising
ART DIRECTOR/CREATIVE DIRECTOR/DESIGNER/ILLUSTRATOR
Péter Pócs
PHOTOGRAPHER
P. Walter
STUDIO
Póster V Ltd.

International/Print Advertising
ART DIRECTOR/DESIGNER/ILLUSTRATOR
Kari Piippo
STUDIO
Kari Piippo Oy
CLIENT
Trama Visual

International/Print Advertising
ART DIRECTOR/CREATIVE DIRECTOR/DESIGNER/ILLUSTRATOR
Péter Pócs
PHOTOGRAPHER
P. Walter
STUDIO
Póster V Ltd.

International/Print Advertising
ART DIRECTOR/CREATIVE DIRECTOR
Joseph Pölzelbauer
DESIGNERS
Joseph Pölzelbauer, K. Karlitzky
STUDIO
Joseph Pölzelbauer
CLIENT
Congress Centrum

International/Print Advertising
ART DIRECTOR/DESIGNER/COPYWRITER
Santiago Pol
ILLUSTRATOR
Flora Gonzalez
STUDIO
Polster Publicity
CLIENT
Cinemateca Nacoinal

International/Print Advertising
ART DIRECTOR/DESIGNER/ILLUSTRATOR
Kari Piippo
STUDIO
Kari Piippo Oy
CLIENT
Mikkelin Teatteri

International/Print Advertising
ART DIRECTOR/DESIGNER
Mitsuo Katsui
ILLUSTRATOR
Masahiko Fujii
CG OPERATION
Kohichiro Nakayama
STUDIO
Katsui Design Office Inc.
CLIENT
Toppan Printing Co. Ltd.

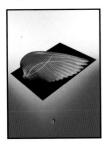

International/Print Advertising
ART DIRECTOR/DESIGNER
Taihei Ohkura
COPYWRITER
Hideyuki Kuroiwa
ILLUSTRATOR
Chihiro Okayasu
PHOTOGRAPHER
Manabu Oda
AGENCY
Dentsu Inc.
CLIENT
Ajinomoto K.K.

International/Print Advertising
ART DIRECTOR
Alexander Bartel
CREATIVE DIRECTOR
Norbert Herold
COPYWRITERS
Achim Szymanski, Helmut Dietl
AGENCY
Heye + Partner
CLIENT
Classic Media

International/Print Advertising
ART DIRECTOR
Hirokazu Ariji
CREATIVE DIRECTOR/COPYWRITER
Takao Fujino
DESIGNER
Masao Imanaga
PHOTOGRAPHER
Robert Maplethorpe
AGENCY
I&S Corporation
CLIENT
Ishioka Shokai

International/Print Advertising
ART DIRECTORS
Masamachi Yoshino, Tetsu Gotoh
COPYWRITERS
Hidenori Fukuoka, Yoshio Okado
ILLUSTRATOR
John Lennon
AGENCY
Dentsu Inc.
CLIENT
Asahi National Broadcast

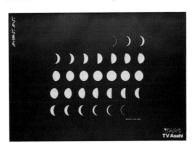

International/Print Advertising
ART DIRECTOR/DESIGNER
Taihei Ohkura
COPYWRITER
Aki Tanaka
PHOTOGRAPHER
Yasuhiro Iizuka
AGENCY
Dentsu Inc.
CLIENT
Ajinomoto K.K.

International/Print Advertising
ART DIRECTOR
G.P. Vinti, L. Maroni
COPYWRITER
Fabrizio Russo
AGENCY
McCann-Erikson Italiana
CLIENT
Coca-Cola Italiana

International/Print Advertising
ART DIRECTOR/COPYWRITER/DESIGNER/CREATIVE DIRECTOR
Kazuyuki Mori
PHOTOGRAPHER
Yoshida
STUDIO
Luke Co. Ltd.

International/Print Advertising
ART DIRECTOR/DESIGNER/ILLUSTRATOR
Fumihiko Enokido
PHOTOGRAPHER
Toiu Kinoshita
STUDIO
Fusion International

International/Print Advertising
ART DIRECTOR/DESIGNER/ILLUSTRATOR
Fumihiko Enokido
PHOTOGRAPHER
Toiu Kinoshita
STUDIO
Fusion International
CLIENT
Workshop Fund M

International/Print Advertising
ART DIRECTOR/CREATIVE DIRECTOR/DESIGNER/ILLUSTRATOR
Bruno Oldani
COPYWRITER
Rolf Karlstrom
STUDIO
Bruno Oldani
CLIENT
Håg

International/Print Advertising
ART DIRECTORS
Emiko Ibishi, Shotaro Sakaguchi, Kenichi Hatano
CREATIVE DIRECTOR
Katsumi Yutani
COPYWRITER
Taketo Suzuki
DESIGNER
Yukio Sato
PHOTOGRAPHER
Kazunari Koya
AGENCY
Dentsu Inc.
CLIENT
Dentsu Inc.

International/Print Advertising
ART DIRECTOR
Katsuo Mizuguchi
CREATIVE DIRECTOR/COPYWRITER
Hiroshi Sasaki
DESIGNER
Takaya Shibasaki
PHOTOGRAPHERS
Eiichiro Sakata, Takashi Seo
AGENCY
Dentsu Inc.
CLIENT
Fuji Television Network Inc.

International/Print Advertising
ART DIRECTOR
Masuteru Aoba
DESIGNER
Isao Fujii
PHOTOGRAPHER
Masaaki Kawaguchi
STUDIO
A&A
CLIENT
Kosé Co. Ltd.

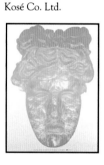

International/Print Advertising
ART DIRECTOR/DESIGNER
Mitsuru Ueda
AGENCY
Art Inter-Relations Inc.
CLIENT
Inoue Public Relations

International/Print Advertising
ART DIRECTOR/DESIGNER
Taisei Yamada
CREATIVE DIRECTOR/COPYWRITER
Yuichi Watanabe
PHOTOGRAPHER
Gisen Katahira
AGENCY
JIC
CLIENT
JR Group

International/Print Advertising
ART DIRECTOR
Hajime Morimoto
COPYWRITER
Yoshimitsu Sawamoto
DESIGNERS
Toshiya Watanabe, Michiaki Uemura
PHOTOGRAPHER
Hatsuhiko Okada
AGENCY
Dentsu Inc.
CLIENT
Magazine House Ltd.

International/Print Advertising
ART DIRECTOR
Hiroshi Yonemura
COPYWRITER
Koichi Yahata
DESIGNER
Naoki Baba
PHOTOGRAPHER
Masanobu Seike
AGENCY
Hakuhodo Inc.
CLIENT
Parco Co., Ltd.

International/Print Advertising
ART DIRECTOR
Hirokazu Ariji
COPYWRITER
Kazutaka Sato
DESIGNER
Masao Imanaga
PHOTOGRAPHER
Eugine Oneil
AGENCY
I&S Corp.
CLIENT
Kinki Nippon

International/Television Advertising
ART DIRECTOR
Eric Muller
COPYWRITER
Stefanie Kölz
DIRECTOR
Caspar Hogerzeil
AGENCY
Wensauer DDB Needham
CLIENT
Volkswagen

International/Television Advertising
ART DIRECTOR
Carlos Baccetti
COPYWRITER
Ramiro Agulla
DIRECTOR
Martin Lobo
AGENCY
Young & Rubicam

International/Television Advertising
ART DIRECTOR
Annarita Colombo
COPYWRITER
Aldo Guidi
PRODUCER
Lorella Stortini
DIRECTOR
Carlo Sigon
AGENCY
Universal Advertising
CLIENT
RCS Rizzoli Periodici

International/Television Advertising
CREATIVE DIRECTOR
Takashi Kitazawa
COPYWRITER
Yoshinobu Yokoo, Mayuko Kamo
PRODUCER
Hiroyuki Taniguchi
DIRECTOR
Kikuhide Sekiguchi
PHOTOGRAPHER
Eiichiro Sakata
AGENCY
Dentsu Inc., Tohokushinsha Film Corp.
CLIENT
Sanyo Electric Co., Ltd.

International/Television Advertising
ART DIRECTOR
Seiichiro Terao
COPYWRITER
Taku Nakamura, Takuya Isojima
PRODUCER
Masaaki Sugano
DIRECTOR
Tadakazu Takahashi
PHOTOGRAPHER
Masayoshi Sukita
AGENCY
Dentsu Inc., Boys Inc.
CLIENT
International Digital Communication Inc.

International/Television Advertising

ART DIRECTOR
Mark Lees
COPYWRITER
Peter Barry
PRODUCER
Claire Seffrin
DIRECTOR
Rowan Dean
AGENCY
Foote Cone & Belding

International/Television Advertising

ART DIRECTOR
Kunihiko Tainaka
COPYWRITER
Tatsuya Ishii
PRODUCER
Norio Kiyokawa
DIRECTOR
Jun Ichikawa
AGENCY
Dentsu Inc., Koei Kikaku Inc.
CLIENT
Duskin Inc.

International/Television Advertising

ART DIRECTOR
Annette Quinlivan
COPYWRITER
Jenny Stock
PRODUCER
Sean Ascroft
DIRECTOR
Terry Bunton
AGENCY
DDB Needham

International/Television Advertising

ART DIRECTOR
Gunter Bauregger
COPYWRITERS
Christian Franke, Julia Stackmann
PRODUCER
Juan Bayona
DIRECTOR
Volker Schlegel
AGENCY
Lintas:Hamburg

International/Television Advertising

ART DIRECTOR
Paul Bennell
COPYWRITER
Ben Nott
PRODUCER
Karen Andersen
DIRECTOR
Nick Donkin
AGENCY
DDB NEedham Sydney

International/Television Advertising

ART DIRECTOR
Jeff Champtaloup
COPYWRITER
Nick Bleasel
PRODUCER
Monique Pardavi
DIRECTOR
Paul Martin
AGENCY
DDB Needham Sydney

International/Television Advertising

ART DIRECTOR
Annette Quinlivan
COPYWRITER
Jenny Stock
PRODUCER
Sean Ascroft
DIRECTOR
Terry Bunton
AGENCY
DDB Needham Sydney

International/Television Advertising

ART DIRECTOR
Masahiro Sumino, Masashi Deguchi
COPYWRITER
Masahiro Sumino
PRODUCER
Masanori Katakura
DIRECTOR
Ryoji Shimizu
PHOTOGRAPHER
Shigeru Furuhata
AGENCY
Dentsu Inc., The Nine Co., Ltd.
CLIENT
Salomon & Taylormade

International/Television Advertising

ART DIRECTOR/CREATIVE DIRECTOR
Mauro Mortaroli

DESIGNER
Claudio Antonaci

DIRECTOR
Alessandro D'Altari

AGENCY
Armando Testa S.p.A.

CLIENT
ACRAP/Verolax

International/Television Advertising

ART DIRECTOR
Gary Monaghan

COPYWRITER
Gary Sollof

PRODUCER
Colin Hickson

DIRECTOR
Les Blair

AGENCY
DMB&B

CLIENT
Philips

International/Television Advertising

ART DIRECTOR
Antonio Gomez

COPYWRITERS/CREATIVE DIRECTORS
Segarra, Fernandez de Castro

PRODUCER
Antonio Gomez

DIRECTOR
Aixala

AGENCY
Delvico Bates Barcelona

International/Television Advertising

ART DIRECTOR
Carlo Jové

COPYWRITER
Christoph Bohn

DIRECTOR
Reto Salimbeni

PRODUCTION COMPANY
G.L.A.S.S.

AGENCY
Guye Marketing

CLIENT
SSR Travel

International/Television Advertising

ART DIRECTOR/CREATIVE DIRECTOR
Gerard Stamp

COPYWRITER/CREATIVE DIRECTOR
Loz Simpson

PRODUCER
Ronnie Holbrook

DIRECTOR
Graham Rose

AGENCY
BSB Dorland Ltd.

CLIENT
H.J. Heinz & Co., Ltd.

International/Television Advertising

ART DIRECTOR/CREATIVE DIRECTOR
Peter Holmes

COPYWRITER
Steve Denvir

PRODUCER
Marion Bern

AGENCY
Franklin Dallas Advertising Inc.

International/Television Advertising

ART DIRECTOR
Jürgen Däuwel

COPYWRITER
Hartmut Bauer

PRODUCER
Dieter Losch

DIRECTOR
Paula Walker

AGENCY
Young & Rubicam GmbH

CLIENT
Kodak AG

International/Television Advertising

ART DIRECTOR/CREATIVE DIRECTOR
Gerard Stamp

COPYWRITER/CREATIVE DIRECTOR
Loz Simpson

PRODUCER
Ronnie Holbrook

DIRECTOR
Graham Rose

AGENCY
BSB Dorland Ltd.

CLIENT
H.J. Heinz & Co., Ltd.

International/Television Advertising
ART DIRECTOR
Ryo Honda
COPYWRITERS
Ryo Honda, Chitose Okita
PRODUCERS
Shigeichiro Suzuki, Hiroshi Nakagawa
DIRECTOR
Nobuaki Shibuya
PHOTOGRAPHER
Katsumi Inomata
AGENCY
Dentsu Inc., H Associates
CLIENT
Fuji Xerox Co., Ltd.

International/Television Advertising
ART DIRECTORS
Grahame Arnould, Michael Mills
PRODUCER
Angela Carroll
PRODUCTION COMPANY
Michael Mills Production Ltd.
AGENCY
Harrod & Mirlin
CLIENT
Evian Source de France

International/Television Advertising
ART DIRECTOR
Peter Holmes
COPYWRITER
Steve Denvir
PRODUCER
Marion Bern
DIRECTOR
Doug Moshoian
AGENCY
Franklin Dallas Advertising Inc.

International/Television Advertising
ART DIRECTOR
Tony Wong Hee
COPYWRITER/CREATIVE DIRECTOR
Paul Jones
PRODUCER
Sean Ascroft
DIRECTOR
Peter Cherry
AGENCY
DDB Needham Sydney

International/Television Advertising
ART DIRECTOR
François de Villiers
COPYWRITER
Howard Fisher
AGENCY
Young & Rubicam Transvaal
CLIENT
Cadbury

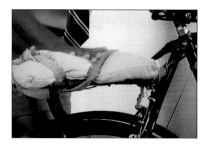

International/Television Advertising
ART DIRECTOR
Tom Notman
COPYWRITER
Alastair Wood
PRODUCER
Barry Stephenson
DIRECTOR
Richard Dean
AGENCY
BSB Dorland Ltd.
CLIENT
Woolworths

International/Television Advertising
ART DIRECTOR
Ed Morris
COPYWRITER
James Sinclair
PRODUCER
Tracy Stokes
DIRECTOR
Adrian Moat
AGENCY
BDDP
CLIENT
Polaroid

International/Television Advertising

ART DIRECTOR
Andy Ward
COPYWRITER
James von Leyden
PRODUCER
Sarah Bradshaw
DIRECTOR
John Lloyd
AGENCY
BSB Dorland Ltd.
CLIENT
H.J. Heinz & Co., Ltd.

International/Television Advertising

ART DIRECTOR
Steven Ang
COPYWRITER
S.P. Lee
PRODUCER
Florence Yeoh
DIRECTOR
Barney Lee
AGENCY
Dentsu, Young & Rubicam
CLIENT
Toyota Land Cruiser

International/Television Advertising

ART DIRECTOR
Onno Kraft van Ermel
COPYWRITER
Henk Druppers
PRODUCER
Linda Peryer
DIRECTOR
Bill Marshall
AGENCY
DMB&B Advertising B.V.
CLIENT
Philips DAP

International/Television Advertising

ART DIRECTOR
Osamu Saotome
COPYWRITER
Yoshihisa Ogata
PRODUCER
Koichi Ito
DIRECTOR
Masatake Saomi
PHOTOGRAPHER
Yoshio Uesugi
AGENCY
I&S Corp.
CLIENT
Lion Corp.

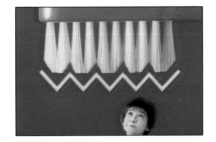

International/Television Advertising

ART DIRECTOR
Rolf Gnauck
COPYWRITER
Gerriet Danz
PRODUCER
Klaus Lind
DIRECTOR
Ian Gabriel
AGENCY
BBDO Düsseldorf

International/Television Advertising

ART DIRECTOR
Peiter van Velsen
COPYWRITER
Wim Ubachs
PRODUCER
Daantje van de Polder
DIRECTOR
Richard Goleszowski
AGENCY
Saatchi & Saatchi Advertising
CLIENT
Rabobank Nederland

International/Television Advertising

ART DIRECTOR
Paul Rietveld
COPYWRITER
Maarten van der Spoel
PRODUCER
Abeline van ber Bijl
AGENCY
Saatchi & Saatchi Advertising
CLIENT
Rabobank Nederland

International/Television Advertising

ART DIRECTOR
Jean-Michel Vigier

COPYWRITER
Thomas Stern

PRODUCER
Benoit Renaud

AGENCY
Publicis Conseil

International/Graphic Design

ART DIRECTOR
Gerald Stamp

COPYWRITER
Loz Simpson

ILLUSTRATOR
Robin Heighway-Bury

AGENCY
BSB Dorland Ltd.

International/Graphic Design

ART DIRECTOR
Mark Denton

PHOTOGRAPHER
Malcolm Venville

AGENCY
Simons Palmer

International/Graphic Design

ART DIRECTOR
Carolyn Stuckey

ILLUSTRATOR
Kafri

PHOTOGRAPHERS
Herinde Koelbl, Joyce tenneson

STUDIO
Werkstudio

International/Graphic Design

ART DIRECTOR/DESIGNER
Motomitsu Takagi

COPYWRITER
Tohru Baba

ILLUSTRATOR
Hitoshi Miura

PHOTOGRAPHER
Kazuki Futazuka

AGENCY
Muira Creation

International/Graphic Design

ART DIRECTOR/ DESIGNER/ILLUSTRATOR
Masakazu Tanabe

AGENCY
Media Co., Ltd.

International/Television Advertising

ART DIRECTOR
Ian Davidson

COPYWRITER
Achim Link

CREATIVE DIRECTOR
Renate Gunther-Greene

PRODUCER
Dietmar Bengisch

DIRECTOR
Derek Coutts

AGENCY
Grey Dusseldorf

CLIENT
Visa International

International/Graphic Design

ART DIRECTOR
Jacqueline Parisier

CLIENT
Cindy B

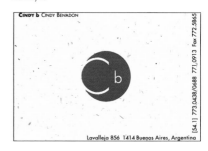

International/Television Advertising

ART DIRECTOR
Jeff Eamer

COPYWRITER
Michael O'Reilly

CREATIVE DIRECTOR
Peter Holmes

DIRECTOR
Richard D'Alessio

AGENCY
Franklin Dallas Inc. Advertising

CLIENT
Fisions Consumer Health

International/Print Advertising

ART DIRECTOR
Gerard Stamp

COPYWRITER
Loz Simpson

ILLUSTRATOR
Andrew Cracknell

AGENCY
BSB Dorland Ltd.

International/Distinctive Merit/Editorial Design

ART DIRECTOR/CREATIVE DIRECTOR
Lai Mayer

COPYWRITER/PHOTOGRAPHER
Horst Stasny

STUDIO
Fotostudio H. Stasny

CLIENT
Mahringer Verlag

International/Television Advertising

ART DIRECTOR
Lara Palmer

COPYWRITER
Dean Hore

CREATIVE DIRECTOR
Boris Damast

PRODUCER
Annie O'Donnell

DIRECTOR
Steve Gordon

AGENCY
McKim Baker Lovick BBDO

CLIENT
Polaroid

International/Television Advertising

ART DIRECTOR
Allun Turner

COPYWRITER
Annelize Haxton

CREATIVE DIRECTOR
Gerrit Rautenbach

PRODUCER
Judi can Eerden

DIRECTOR
André Liebenburg

AGENCY
Lintas:Hamburg

International/Graphic Design

ART DIRECTOR/DESIGNER/ILLUSTRATOR
Michel Bouvet

CLIENT
Museé ATP

International/Television Advertising

ART DIRECTOR
Mark Shap

COPYWRITER
Mike Macina

PRODUCER
Marlene Bartos

DIRECTOR
Jim Sonzero

AGENCY
Young & Rubicam New York

CLIENT
Bausch & Lomb, Ray Ban

International/Graphic Design

ART DIRECTOR/DESIGNER
Heloisa Farla

STUDIO
A3

National/Editorial Design

ART DIRECTOR
Deborah Withey

ILLUSTRATOR
Terry Widener

PUBLICATION
Detroit Free Press

National/Print Advertising

ART DIRECTOR
John Vitro

COPYWRITER
John Robertson

PHOTOGRAPHER
Art Wolfe

AGENCY
Franklin Stoorza

CLIENT
Taylor Guitar

National/Graphic Design

ART DIRECTOR
Loid Der

CREATIVE DIRECTORS
Scott Mednick, Cheryl Rudich

PHOTOGRAPHERS
Chris Wimpsey, Susan Werner

ILLUSTRATOR
Mark Lehrman, Loid Der

AGENCY
The Mednick Group

CLIENT
Bell Sports Inc.

National/Graphic Design

ART DIRECTOR
Kent Hunter

DESIGNERS
David Suh, Jeff Jordan

AGENCY
Frankfurt Gips Balkind

CLIENT
Harcourt Brace Jovanovich

National/Print Advertising

ART DIRECTOR
Mark Ware

COPYWRITER
Tim Mamis

CREATIVE DIRECTOR
Denise Sulivan

AGENCY
John Dough Advertising

CLIENT
Dunkin' Donuts

National/Editorial Design

ART DIRECTOR
Mark Geer

DESIGNER
Morgan Bomar

WRITER
Karen Kephart

PHOTOGRAPHER
Michael Hallaway

ILLUSTRATORS
Rob Day, Morgan Bomar, Mike Fisher, Thom Sevalrud, Lane Smith, Eric Dinyer

STUDIO
Geer Design, Inc.

PUBLICATION
Caring

National/Editorial Design

ART DIRECTORS
Mark Geer, Heidi Flynn Allen

DESIGNER
Morgan Bomar

WRITER
Allyson K. Edwards

PHOTOGRAPHERS/ILLUSTRATOR
Terry Asker, Mark Baudin, John Craig

STUDIO
Geer Design

PUBLICATION
Coastal World

National/Graphic Design

ART DIRECTOR/DESIGNER
Jack Anderson

DESIGNERS
Julie Tanagi-Lock, Mary Hermes, Lian Ng

ILLUSTRATOR
Julia LaPine

STUDIO
Hornall Anderson Design Works

CLIENT
Starbucks Coffee Company

National/Print Advertising

ART DIRECTOR
Craig Tanimoto

COPYWRITER
Hillary Jordan

PHOTOGRAPHER
Jim Arndt, Lamb & Hallistock

AGENCY
Chiat/Day/Mojo

CLIENT
Mitsubishi

National/Graphic Design

ART DIRECTORS/DESIGNER
Jeff Larsen, Scott Johnson

COPYWRITER
Keith Christianson

STUDIO
Larson Design Associates

CLIENT
Champion International

National/Graphic Design

ART DIRECTOR
Lois Harrington

COPYWRITER
Tony Wells

DESIGNERS
Lois Harrington, William Olmstead

PHOTOGRAPHER
Marshall Harrington

STUDIO
Lois Harrington Design

CLIENT
Nissan North America

National/Graphic Design

ART DIRECTOR
Toni Bowerman

COPYWRITER
Lee Nash

ILLUSTRATOR
Jean-Christian Knaff

STUDIO
Cipriani Kremer Design

CLIENT
Wang Laboratories Inc.

National/Editorial Design

ART DIRECTOR
Carol Layton

PHOTOGRAPHER
William Coupon

PUBLICATION
Worth Magazine

National/Graphic Design

ART DIRECTOR/ILLUSTRATOR
Jon Anders Bjornson

STUDIO
Studio B Ltd.

CLIENT
Myers Constructs

National/Editorial Design

DESIGN DIRECTOR
Diana LaGuardia

ART DIRECTOR
Audrey Razgaitis

ILLUSTRATOR
Jana Brennings

PUBLICATION
Condé Nast Traveler

National/Editorial Design

ART DIRECTOR
Laurie Haycock Makela

PHOTOGRAPHER
Don Williamson

CLIENT
The Getty Center

National/Editorial Design

ART DIRECTORS
Richard Wilde, Judith Wilde

WRITER
Judith Wilde

ILLUSTRATORS
Students of the School of Visual Arts

STUDIO
Wilde Design

PUBLISHER
Watson-Guptill

National/Editorial Design

ART DIRECTOR
Edward Chiquitucto

PUBLISHER
The School of Visual Arts

National/Editorial Design
ART DIRECTOR
Donna M. Bonavita
WRITER
Diane Raines Ward
TITLE TREATMENT
Margo Chase, Nancy Ogami
STUDIO
KPMG Peat Marwick Communications
PUBLICATION
World

National/Print Advertising
ART DIRECTOR/COPYWRITER
Dino Santilli
PHOTOGRAPHER
Doug Burrows
STUDIO
Mendelsohn/Zien
CLIENT
Wok East Partners

National/Graphic Design
ART DIRECTOR
Carter Weitz
COPYWRITERS
Maureen Waldron, Doug Cook
PHOTOGRAPHER
Jim Krantz
AGENCY
Bailey Lauerman & Associates
CLIENT
Metropolitan Utilities District

National/Graphic Design
ART DIRECTOR
Alane Gahagan, Lori Littlehale
COPYWRITER
Allan Oshan
PHOTOGRAPHER
Lee Friedman
STUDIO
Ziff Marketing
CLIENT
Tisch Center for the Arts

National/Graphic Design
ART DIRECTOR/DESIGNER/ILLUSTRATOR
Loid Der
CREATIVE DIRECTORS
Scott Mednick, Cheryl Rudich
PHOTOGRAPHERS
Vanessa Adams, Susan Werner, John Huet,
Mark Hanauer, Loid Der
AGENCY
The Mednick Group
CLIENT
Reebok International, Ltd.

National/Editorial Design
ART DIRECTOR
Fred Norgaard
PHOTOGRAPHER
Al Tielmans, Duomo
PUBLICATION
The New York Times

National/Photography & Illustration
ART DIRECTOR
Tom Roth
COPYWRITER
Mark Ledermann
PHOTOGRAPHER
Fred Vanderpoel
AGENCY
Anderson & Lembke, Inc.
CLIENT
Fred Vanderpoel

National/Print Advertising
ART DIRECTOR/DESIGNER
Harvey Marco
COPYWRITER
David Smith
AGENCY
Ammirati & Puris, Inc.
CLIENT
Nikon, Inc.

National/Editorial Design
STUDIO
Drenttel Doyle Partners
PUBLISHER
The Museum of Modern Art, New York